THE CROSS AND THE CROWN

MARY BAKER EDDY

THE CROSS
AND
THE CROWN

The History of Christian Science
by NORMAN BEASLEY

Duell, Sloan and Pearce · *New York*
Little, Brown and Company · *Boston*

LIBRARY OF CONGRESS CATALOG CARD NO. 52–9086

Published October 1952
Reprinted November 1952
Reprinted November 1953

DUELL, SLOAN AND PEARCE–LITTLE, BROWN
BOOKS ARE PUBLISHED BY
LITTLE, BROWN AND COMPANY
IN ASSOCIATION WITH
DUELL, SLOAN & PEARCE, INC.

Published simultaneously
in Canada by McClelland and Stewart Limited

PRINTED IN THE UNITED STATES OF AMERICA

Introduction

In 1875, seldom more than twenty persons gathered for Sunday services in a small, rented hall in Lynn, Massachusetts; twenty-five years afterwards, a new church edifice was being built every four days; now, wherever Christianity is preached, there are teachings of Christian Science.

Coming in the humblest, most unobtrusive guise — the healing of a sick woman — it is a movement without parallel in modern history.

As the Discoverer and Founder of Christian Science, Mary Baker Eddy made the decision to measure the strength of her Church by the depth of the understanding (and not by the numbers) of its members. It was this decision which permitted her to require of her followers that, as she said in her 1901 *Message to The Mother Church,* they follow "their Leader only so far as she follows Christ."

By its very wording, this was a call that included obedience to the instructions, "Heal the sick, cleanse the lepers, raise the dead, cast out devils" — and a summons to return to the full teachings of the Master by restoring to Christianity the practice of healing.

It was a denial of a belief in miracles, and a reminder to doubters that in so far as they yield to the argument that "healing was an act of Jesus, denied to us," they turn against the words, "Verily, verily, I say unto you, He that believeth on me, the works that I do shall he do also; and greater *works* than these shall he do; because I go unto my Father."

As a watcher on the ramparts of the kingdom of God, Mary Baker Eddy had an inextinguishable faith that the words and the works of Jesus would be triumphantly justified.

Because of that faith, she has become one of the most controversial figures in all religious history.

Note on the Frontispiece

THE portrait of Mary Baker Eddy, which is reproduced as a frontispiece, was painted by Howard Chandler Christy out of gratitude. The artist told of his experience in 1937, in the October 2 issue of the *Christian Science Sentinel:*

"It is fitting that I should give testimony of my healing in Christian Science on this Easter morning, as it was twenty-eight years ago at Easter time when first my health was returned to me. Previous to this time I had been partially blind, and numb from the knees down. I had tried all kinds of cures, but no help. I tried to forget through drink. The doctors said I could live but a few months.

"One day my relative, a Christian Science practitioner, called to see me. I managed to hobble into the front room where she was sitting and during the conversation she asked me if I would like her to give me a treatment. Right then something told me from within that I would regain all my strength; so I answered: 'Yes, go ahead.' While she was talking everything in the room began to clear. I could even see the color of her eyes, which were blue. It was as if a fog had lifted. I stood up and wanted to walk out in the clear air, and did for a three-mile walk — bought tickets for the theatre that night, and actually saw the actors clearly for the first time in many months.

"That night I read three pages of the Christian Science textbook, 'Science and Health with Key to the Scriptures' by Mary Baker Eddy, and had no trouble reading the fine print. The next day I went to work and have worked ever since. In a few minutes' time my life was changed from discouragement to joy, and light, and happiness, and gratitude is mine and will always be so long as I live."

Contents

	Introduction	v
	Note on the Frontispiece	vii
1	A Woman Starts Alone, on a Great Search	3
2	"That Woman of Lynn"	14
3	The First Edition of *Science and Health*	31
4	They Felt the Threat of Her Presence	52
5	Pursuing a Lie with Eagerness	72
6	She Held Her Ground by Advancing	94
7	Not with Trumpets	107
8	Keeper of the Gate	130
9	Preparation for Leadership	152
10	Rebellion	174
11	A Decision of Great Importance	194
12	A Story of Prayer	216
13	"Who Owns God's Temple?"	234
14	According to the Promise	263
15	Pleasant View	298
16	"Acknowledged as Law by Law"	321

17 An Unexplained Call 344

18 Christian Science Abroad 370

19 "And What Singing It Was!" 393

20 "Gross Deception at Pleasant View" 416

21 A Conspiracy Collapses 437

22 The Peace of Her Years 471

23 The Things That Bound Them 496

24 The Woman the Clergy Derided 539

APPENDICES

(1) "Christ My Refuge" by Mary Baker Eddy 565

(2) Article by Mrs. Eddy in the Lynn _Transcript,_ February 3, 1872 569

(3) "Principle and Practice" by Mary Baker Eddy 573

(4) Mrs. Eddy's Reply to Bishop Fallows 575

(5) First Church of Christ, Scientist, Oconto, Wisconsin 580

(6) Building Plans Announced in the _Christian Science Journal,_ March 1892 583

(7) Deed of Trust Executed by Mrs. Eddy, September 1, 1892 586

(8) Dedication Services, January 6, 1895 591

(9) Mrs. Eddy's Address to the World's Parliament of Religions, 1893 611

(10) Deed of Trust Executed by Mrs. Eddy, March 6, 1907   618

(11) "Youth and Young Manhood" by Mrs. Eddy   624

(12) Brief History of the Early Christian Church   627

     Index   645

THE CROSS AND THE CROWN

CHAPTER ONE

A Woman Starts Alone, on a Great Search

IT WAS in the early evening of a winter day in 1866 in Lynn, Massachusetts, that a woman fell on an icy sidewalk, was rendered unconscious, was picked up by friendly hands, and carried into the nearest house. A doctor was summoned. He examined the patient, said her injuries were internal, and cautioned against moving her. But the following day she insisted on being taken to her home. They took her there.

On Saturday, February 3, 1866, the *Lynn Reporter* published this paragraph: "Mrs. Mary Patterson of Swampscott fell upon the ice near the corner of Market and Oxford streets on Thursday evening and was severely injured. She was taken up in an insensible condition and carried into the residence of S. M. Bubier, Esq., nearby, where she was kindly cared for during the night. Dr. Cushing,[1] who was called, found her injuries to be internal and of a severe nature, inducing spasms and intense suffering. She was removed to her home in Swampscott yesterday afternoon,[2] though in a very critical condition."

On Sunday morning, fearful she was dying, a member of

---

[1] Dr. Alvin M. Cushing.
[2] The newspaper was in error. The woman was removed to her home on Friday morning.

her household sent for a minister. Awaiting the clergyman's arrival, a neighbor was anxiously watching at the bedside when the woman asked that she be left alone with her Bible.

Opening the Book at the ninth chapter of St. Matthew, she began to read:

> And, behold, they brought to him a man sick of the palsy, lying on a bed; and Jesus seeing their faith said unto the sick of the palsy; Son, be of good cheer: thy sins be forgiven thee.
>
> And, behold, certain of the scribes said within themselves, This *man* blasphemeth.
>
> And Jesus knowing their thoughts said, Wherefore think ye evil in your hearts?
>
> For whether is easier to say, *Thy* sins be forgiven thee; or to say, Arise, and walk?
>
> But that ye may know that the Son of man hath power on earth to forgive sins, (then saith he to the sick of the palsy,) Arise, take up thy bed, and go unto thine house.
>
> And he arose, and departed to his house.

The woman's eyes returned to "they brought to him a man sick of the palsy," went back to the words, "Arise, take up thy bed, and go unto thine house." For years, in her search for God, she had studied the Bible, had asked doctors about life, and had questioned preachers about death, and had listened to explanations that always made one a part of the other.

Now, in the words, "Arise, take up thy bed, and go unto thine house," she heard not an explanation, but an answer. For the first time she heard, and she heard clearly, unmistakably, that Life is not breath, not a heartbeat, not matter, and not form — that Life is eternal; that Life is God; that, as she later wrote, "there is but one God, or Life, one cause and one effect"; [3] and as she also wrote, "God never decreed disease." [4]

Coming in the most unobtrusive guise, this moment marked the end of any belief she might have had that God created man into two parts — a body that rots, and a soul that lives.

Thereafter doubt never reached her.

She realized God as Spirit, and man as His image.

Instantly healed, the woman rose from her bed, dressed, and left her sickroom.

Immeasurably grateful for this small glimpse of perfection, she began the quest for the cause of her healing. Seizing on the single proposition that all life is in and comes from God, she searched her Bible to find there the teachings the world now knows by what she called them, Christian Science.

In this way, on the outskirts of Lynn, in a village so small that the United States Census Bureau made no record of its population, began a movement without parallel in history. Not only have great numbers of people been healed of sickness and disease through the teachings, but the presence of these teachings has leavened the doctrine of the Christian Church generally, and affected the practice of medicine itself. . . .

A sickroom, and a woman critically injured reading her Bible — that was all there was on February 4, 1866, to in-

[3] *Miscellaneous Writings,* p. 25.
[4] *Science and Health,* p. 221.

dicate a time when churches and societies and reading rooms would speak of Christian Science wherever there are people free to practice their belief in God.

The world now knows this woman by the name Mary Baker Eddy.[5]

Although born in New England, with its heritage of religious persecution, its witchcraft and its memories of Salem executions, Mary Baker Eddy had within her the freedom of generations of forebears who sturdily disagreed among themselves in matters of religion, but just as sturdily believed God gave them their minds for one purpose — to use them — and to decide, each for himself, what to believe, what not to believe.

Forty-five years old at the time of her accident in Lynn, Mrs. Eddy had been an invalid much of her life. In an effort to find a healing she had visited doctors often, had studied medical books, and had subjected herself to periods of fasting. In 1862, she became a patient at the Granite State Water Cure, operated by Dr. W. T. Vail, in Hill, New Hampshire. While she was there another patient, Julius A. Dresser, was pronounced incurable and abandoned the water treatments. Going to Portland, Maine, he placed him-

[5] Mary Baker Eddy, daughter of Abigail and Mark Baker, was born in Bow, N. H., on July 16, 1821. In 1843 she married George Washington Glover, who died in 1844. After his death, a son was born. She named him after his father. Unable to care for the child because of her own invalidism, and upon the insistence of her sister with whom she was living, Mrs. Glover permitted adoption of the infant by a nurse who had become attached to him. In 1853 Mary Glover married Dr. Daniel Patterson, a dentist. In 1873 she divorced him, charging abandonment in 1866, in preference to the charge of adultery. In 1877 she married Asa Gilbert Eddy, who was a great helper in the formative years of Christian Science. Asa Gilbert Eddy died in 1882.

self under the care of Phineas P. Quimby, a "magnetic healer," as he called himself.

Soon afterwards Dresser, much improved physically, returned to Hill and visited the hydropathic hospital. After seeing him, a number of patients, including Mrs. Eddy, went to Portland.

Quimby's method of treatment was mainly one of manipulation, principally of the head, his expressed theory being that such manipulation generated electricity, thereby benefiting the patient. An earnest seeker of knowledge, Quimby often talked with Mrs. Eddy about the Bible and her growing belief — not fixed, but growing since 1844 — that back of all healing was "the science of mind, which had nothing to do with matter, electricity, or physics." [6]

This point of view greatly interested Quimby, and he made many notes of their conversations. After receiving some relief from Quimby's treatments, Mrs. Eddy suffered a relapse. She left his care, convinced, as she told him, that if she were to find a healing it would have to be in the Bible.

She was convinced because, as she told Irving C. Tomlinson, "In the absence of Dr. Quimby from Portland, a man was brought to the hotel where I was staying, who was in a pitiable condition. He had sometime previous met with an accident and he was well-nigh broken to pieces. His knees and ankles were out of place and he was suffering untold agonies. The proprietor of the hotel came to me and besought me to do something for the poor sufferer. At first I thought I could not. Then I said, 'God can do it.' I went to his bedside and lifted my thought silently to God. At the conclusion of my prayer I said, 'Now you can arise and open the door for me.' The man arose, and with the iron clamps

[6] *Miscellany*, p. 307.

he wore rattling as he walked, went and opened the door." [7]

It was this experience, and others, that brought into her thought that Christianity is more than a repetition of words of apostolic origin; more than canon law and expedient resolution; something a great deal more than practices and prejudices whose authenticity can be gravely challenged.

She knew there is but one God, and she was beginning to perceive that the fundamental of all religion is law — law which eternally is silent, invincible, changeless, just; law which says: As it was in the beginning, so is it now and ever shall be, as it was in the beginning; law which permits no man to be free without giving him a glimpse of the Divine Presence.

In her moment of healing Mrs. Eddy saw this law. Having seen it as clearly as she did, she believed what happened was an inevitable consequence. She was healed. She believed the healing to be God's law in operation. Law which says, Life being eternal, only the spiritual is without blemish. Law which decrees that Life is eternal, and not something on loan for years, for days, or for moments. . . .

As shown in her writings, Mary Baker Eddy accepted eternal Life as indistinguishable from spiritual Truth.

She knew that Jesus never once spoke of Life as being anything but continuous. Knowing this, she regarded the argument of a life divided into two parts (a here, and a hereafter) as a fraud created by those who sought authority not in His name, but in their own.

So it was on the day of her healing that she began searching long-familiar verses for the single purpose of learning the way to do what the Master Christian commanded His

[7] *Twelve Years with Mary Baker Eddy;* copyright, 1945, The Christian Science Board of Directors; published by The Christian Science Publishing Society.

disciples to do: "Heal the sick, cleanse the lepers, raise the dead, cast out devils."

How were these healings done?

How could they be done again?

Naturally, she did not find the way all at once. Unlike material knowledge, what she was seeking could not be found in books and could not be taught, but could be known, and could be proved.

It was known by Jesus, and proved by Him. It was known by all the great teachers, and proved by them. It was known by the early Christians, and proved by them.

Gibbon wrote about the healings of the early Christians in *The Decline and Fall of the Roman Empire:* ". . . The miraculous cure of diseases of the most inveterate or even preternatural kind can no longer occasion any surprise, when we recollect that in the days of Irenaeus, about the end of the second century, the resurrection of the dead was very far from being esteemed an uncommon event; that the miracle was frequently performed on necessary occasions, by great fasting and joint supplication of the church of the place, and that the persons thus restored . . . lived afterwards among them many years. At such a period, when faith could boast of so many wonderful victories over death, it seems difficult to account for the skepticism of those philosophers who still rejected and derided the doctrine of the resurrection. . . ."

Mary Baker Eddy was aware that what she sought could not be found in books and could not be taught, but could be known and could be proved. This awareness was shown in her writings: "Who would stand before a blackboard, and pray the principle of mathematics to solve the problem?

The rule is already established, and it is our task to work out the solution." [8]

In her first meditations upon "How were these healings done?" and "How could they be done again?" it seemed to Mrs. Eddy that "centuries of spiritual growth" [9] would be needed. Healing, an integral part of the early Christian teachings, was a part of truth long lost — lost in the change that came over Christianity when coming under the protection of Constantine, in Rome, in 313 A.D.

No longer able to heal, those who preferred authority solved their problem by introducing into Christianity that most powerful force of all savage religions — fear of death — and they made it the most powerful force in Christian theology.

Thus, with Christianity becoming tolerated by political decree, the center of theological thought became death and not life, fear and not love, form and not God.

A counterfeit of God's promise of eternal life was the cleric's emphasis on death — to the obedient, assurance of an afterlife of everlasting bliss; to the disobedient, damnation in a hereafter of everlasting torment in hell.

Through the centuries fear darkened the portals of Christian churches until the Christian religion became a terrifying thing, and sermons preached by Jonathan Edwards in the middle seventeen-hundreds set the mark at which nearly all clergymen aimed: ". . . The God that holds you over the pit of hell, much as one holds a spider, or some loathesome insect, over the fire, abhors you, and is dreadfully provoked; His wrath toward you burns like fire; He looks upon you as worthy of nothing else, but to cast into the fire; He is

[8] *Science and Health*, p. 3.
[9] *Miscellaneous Writings*, p. 380.

of purer eyes than to bear to have you in His sight; you are ten thousand times so abominable in His eyes as the most hateful and venomous serpent is in ours. . . ."

In his *Letters and Social Aims*, Emerson wrote of those times, and of his own: ". . . The books read, the sermons and prayers heard, the habits of thought of religious persons were all directed on death. All were under the shadow of Calvinism, and of the Roman Catholic purgatory, and death was dreadful. The emphasis of all the good books to the young people was on death. We were all taught that we were born to die; and over that, all the terrors that theology could gather from the savage nations was added to the gloom."

It was in this climate — when "the books read, the sermons and prayers heard, the habits of thought of religious persons were all directed on death" — that Mary Baker Eddy began her search.

She knew that throughout the Bible appeared the message that God is the healer; and she was sure Jesus would not have commanded His disciples to "heal the sick, raise the dead, cleanse the leper, cast out devils" had such a command not been in accordance with His mission. She read, and reread many times, such statements as "Of myself I can do nothing" . . . "My Father doeth the work" . . . "My Father worketh within me" — and the Scriptural abjuration, "He came to do the will of God . . . came to fulfill the law."

What law?

Could disease be a law of God?

She believed it could not be, else the Galilean would not have healed it. To have done so would have been in disobedience to the will of God. She perceived that what the great Teacher acknowledged when He said "the Father that dwelleth in me, he doeth the works," was "the Spirit of life" which, as Paul wrote to the Romans, "made me free from the law of sin and death."

Believing with Paul that "the Spirit of life made me [man] free from the law of sin and death," Mrs. Eddy knew she would have to repudiate any teaching that included disease and death as a law of God; and she came to realize that, to be able to heal, the center of her thought had to be Life and not death, Love and not fear, God and not form.

She did not hesitate, even though what she believed required that she break with the theology long entrenched in the convenient notion that God is a personal agent who can be beguiled into granting personal favors.

Jesus said:

"God is a Spirit; and they that worship him must worship him in spirit and in truth."

Accepting that, Mary Baker Eddy saw, as accessible and available, the immutable law of God.

Jesus also said:

"No man can serve two masters; for either he will hate the one, and love the other: or else he will hold to the one, and despise the other. Ye cannot serve God and mammon."

Accepting the accessibility and availability of spiritual law, Mrs. Eddy saw that if the words "Ye cannot serve God and mammon" meant anything, they meant that whatever is material is not of God.

More than three years had passed since her healing.

They were years of comparative seclusion, years in which her thought was on the deep meanings in the Bible, just as her search was for "the rule already established."

She found what she believed to be that rule.

She found it in her momentous realization that whatever is material does not represent — but *misrepresents* — God.

And, if misrepresenting Him, misrepresents man as created by Him, in His own image.

Out of that momentous realization, the realization that God, or Spirit, is All, and beyond God is nothing, came her discovery.

She healed many persons of many diseases and put her inspired thoughts on paper, first writing only for herself but, in so doing, writing for everyone.

She began teaching Christian Science [10] to the few who listened, and to the very few who believed.

But, although few listened and very few believed, she did teach and she did write. Feebly, as she said afterwards, but in challenge. Daring to tell the world it was wrong. Ordering it to empty its ears of all it had heard about the power of evil. Instructing it on the unreality of evil. Proclaiming the power of good.

Defiantly declaring we are born to live, and not to die.

[10] The words "Christian Science" were not original with Mary Baker Eddy, but she was the first to give them wide circulation. In 1840, Abraham Coles used the words in verse, as also did Sara Josepha Hale, in 1848. In 1850 William Adams published a series of addresses on Moral Philosophy and called his work *Christian Science*. Doubtless, before 1840, there were others who used the words. However, Mrs. Eddy's use of them was not poetical, but in their widest meaning — the widest meaning she could span — and in their widest application.

CHAPTER TWO

"That Woman of Lynn"

AFTER her healing, Mary Baker Eddy continued her residence in Swampscott until March 1866, when she moved to Lynn. Here she boarded with two different families; she returned to Swampscott in the late summer and then went back to Lynn in the early autumn where, in the home of George D. Clark, she found among the boarders her first student. His name was Hiram S. Crafts, and he was an employee of a local shoe factory.

Around the turn of the year the Crafts family moved to a cottage they owned on Pond Street in East Stoughton (now Avon, Massachusetts) and invited Mrs. Eddy to come with them. In April 1867, they moved again, this time to Taunton, where, under his teacher's guidance (in an apartment on the second floor of a building at 8086 Main Street), Crafts became the first Christian Science practitioner. Despite success as a practitioner, Crafts yielded to his wife's disapproval — she being a spiritualist — and abandoned his work.

Meanwhile, Mrs. Eddy left Taunton to visit her brother in Tilton; from there, late in 1867, she went to Amesbury, where she rented a room in the home of Mrs. Mary Webster, 5 Mechanic Street. The following summer she resided in the home of a student, Mrs. Sarah Bagley, 277 Main Street, also in Amesbury, where she began writing *The Science of Soul,* later called *The Science of Man by Which the Sick are*

Healed (now known as *The Science of Man*) , which she copyrighted in 1870. This essay is now called "Recapitulation," in *Science and Health with Key to the Scriptures.*

In the autumn of 1868 she moved to Stoughton, where she lived with Mrs. Sally Wentworth on Center Street and completed her manuscript. A bronze tablet has been erected there which reads: "Mary Baker Eddy, the Discoverer and Founder of Christian Science, resided in this house from the autumn of 1868 to the spring of 1870." Another tablet tells that it was here she finished writing *The Science of Man,* which was the first contribution to Christian Science literature.

Of these and the years which immediately followed, Mary Baker Eddy wrote that they were "sweet, calm and buoyant with hope, not selfish, nor depressing." [1] To her illumined thought doubtless they were such years; but, also, they were years of poverty, of scorn, of suspicion and betrayal.

Most of the places where she lived were boardinghouses. Cost of living in them was low, which was why she chose them. Her income was two hundred dollars a year. Fortunately, she was frugal.[2] She was handy with a needle, making and repairing her own clothes. For the most part she spent the daytime hours in her room, studying the Bible and putting on paper such thoughts as came to her. Usually the evenings were given over to discussions with other boarders around the supper table and, after supper, in the parlor.

[1] *Science and Health,* p. 109.

[2] It was a winter evening chore for the children in the Baker home in Bow to shell corn as feed for the chickens. One night a grain of corn fell from Mary's lap and she used her foot to push it toward the fireplace.

"Mary, get down and pick up that corn," ordered her mother.

"Oh, Mother, it is only a grain of corn," protested the child.

"Never mind, it will help to make a meal for a hungry chick."

Mary Baker Eddy never forgot that admonition, and often told the story.

After a little while of listening to views that were so at variance with popular beliefs, proprietors of a number of the boardinghouses requested of Mrs. Eddy that she gather up her belongings and leave.

Those were times when spiritualism was a lively competitor for the interest of the people. Nightly séances were held in thousands of homes in New England, and C. C. Helberg's *A Book of Spirit Writings* was a familiar volume on parlor tables. It was said that the assassinated Lincoln was a believer and the rumor gave tone to darkened rooms and to the tinkling bells that usually announced the arrival of spooks.

Mrs. Eddy's flat disagreement with spiritualism and her dissatisfaction with what was being taught in Christian churches made her a woman who was pointed at, and gossiped about, in the villages and towns of Massachusetts.

Although people wanted to believe in a less harsh religion, and the Unitarian voices of Emerson, Channing, and Parker were denying the depravity of man, the denunciations of Jonathan Edwards still echoed from the pulpits in Lynn, Taunton, Tilton, Amesbury, and Boston.

"God still holds us over the pit of hell" . . . "Sinners are thrown into everlasting fires, there to suffer through all eternity" . . . "Temptation is God's test for righteousness" . . . "God inflicts sickness and death in punishment of sin" . . . "As Jesus bore a cross, so is it ordained that all should bear crosses" — These were the words of the pulpit; and to say, as Mrs. Eddy was saying, that "Sickness, sin and death, being inharmonious, do not originate with God, nor belong to His government," [3] was bold and reckless to an unheard-of degree.

Mrs. Eddy was a woman who was not living with her hus-

[3] *Science and Health,* p. 472.

band. They made much of that. Clergymen came to see her. She explained to them that all she was trying to do was to understand the teachings of Jesus so she might do as He demanded of His followers.

She was advised to abandon such ambitions, lest she be sent to a mental institution; and, in one city (Worcester, Massachusetts) where she was visiting, the superintendent of an institution for the feeble-minded did call on her for the purpose of locking her up. He apologized, as he left her, saying he had learned much that would be of benefit to him in the treatment of his patients.

Her brother and her two sisters disowned her, although while visiting them she healed one sister's daughter of what the doctors called "a dangerous ulcerous condition." Wherever she went she healed, and her first healing was in the home of Thomas Phillips, in Lynn. A son, Dorr Phillips, was suffering from a felon on his finger. It disappeared. Hearing of this cure, Charles Winslow, also of Lynn, said to Mrs. Eddy: "If you will make Abbie walk, I will not only believe your theory, but I will reward you liberally. I think I would give a thousand dollars to see her walk."

Winslow was referring to his wife, who was an invalid and who had not walked for sixteen years. This offer of money was declined but, soon afterwards, the invalid not only walked but took long walks, unaided. Unhappily, after several months of freedom from her invalidism, she rejected the teachings and returned to her bed. She did not believe, as Mrs. Eddy told her: "God will do the work, if you will let Him."

Nor did townspeople and country people believe. They said Mrs. Eddy was a witch, and accused her of practicing witchcraft. She was called "a child of Satan," and prayers were offered in the churches that she "might realize, before it is too late, the terrible meaning in the Scriptural warning, 'Vengeance is mine, saith the Lord.' "

The accusations against her were many. They said she did not believe in God, in the Bible, in Christ, in prayer; that she should be in jail instead of being permitted to delude people into believing, as afterwards she wrote in *Unity of Good*, that "by knowing the unreality of disease, sin and death, you demonstrate the allness of God."

These things, of course, were in keeping with the dark fact that the history of Christianity is not a story of brotherhood, as Jesus intended, but a story of violence.[4]

But such hostility did not keep students away. In her presence the sick were healed. For the most part those who sought her teaching in the early years were people from the factories and the mills. She healed and she taught, knowing as she did both that they were "feeble attempts to state the Principle and practice of Christian healing."[5]

In teaching, she met her students singly. Using the Bible as her only authority, she wrote her notes of instruction, asking her pupils to study them carefully and to return them to her for explanation if, after study, there were points not

---

[4] Compared with the slaughter of Protestants in Europe during the Reformation, Christians have suffered but little from non-Christian hands. In a single province (The Netherlands) during a single reign (Charles V) more than a hundred thousand Protestants were executed by Roman Catholics. It is very doubtful if in the first two hundred years of Christian history more than two thousand Christians were martyred in the entire Roman Empire, which, during that time, was under the rule of pagan emperors.

Nor have Protestants been without intolerance. Colonial penalties for dissenters, which included boring holes in the tongue, slitting the nostrils, cutting off ears, whipping, branding with hot irons, chopping off hands, hanging, imprisonment, and banishment, do not furnish items for the better chapters of Protestantism.

[5] *Science and Health*, p. ix.

understood. She made it clear to each that the papers were for study only and, when not in use, must be returned to her. The basis for this practice was her own increasing understanding: she believed it wiser to restrict her teachings than to allow these first writings to be circulated at a time when recastings might better illustrate what her constant studies were revealing.[6]

In addition to her desire to better instruct her students, Mrs. Eddy was aware of the ridicule her teachings were encountering; and she was aware of the defection of some students who used her writings to further this ridicule.

Her own progress in what she then was calling "Moral Science" is illustrated by her instructions to Hiram S. Crafts in 1867. Compare these writings with her chapter on "Prayer" in *Science and Health with Key to the Scriptures,* or with any of her later writings.

Here is how she instructed her first student:

Written in 1867

By Mary Baker G. Eddy in the presence of
her first student, Hiram S. Crafts.

VERSES	CHAP.	BOOK
		Matthew
2	14	Argument against the spiritual phenomena
2	14	Argument in favor of the spiritual sense only of the scriptures.
22	"	The principle going before the shadows —

[6] In the *Christian Science Sentinel* (July 4, 1908) Mrs. Eddy said: "What I wrote on Christian Science some twenty-five years ago I do not consider a precedent for a present student of this Science. The best mathematician has not attained the full understanding of the principle thereof in his earliest studies or discoveries. Hence, it were wise to accept only my teachings that I know to be correct and adapted to the present demand."

VERSES	CHAP.	BOOK
5	14	A call for matter to feed on, and the reply of truth.
26, 27	"	Guide in a chemical.
28, 29	"	Truth calling upon Error, and the fear of error causing it to lose sight of Truth.
2, 3	15	An enquiry of Error why Truth hath left the tradition of the elders, in that it takes no matter form in healing the sick. Wisdom answers, why do ye transgress the commandments of God by your traditions?
4	"	You should honor the Father which is your principle. The error which curseth this Wisdom let him die the death of error.
5, 6	"	
" "	"	But whosoever says, I have given the gift of healing, dishonors his Father, Wisdom.
7, 8	"	Ye Hypocrites which draweth near to Wisdom with the lips, while the heart is far from it; ie. the understanding is not in Truth while they claim to know it.
9	"	Such as teach . . . the beliefs of man, need not claim to worship wisdom, for Truth says it is in vain.
11	"	It is not that which produces only a sensation, which defiles a man, or idea, but when the reason accepts it as a belief then it cometh out of the mouth, and is that which defileth.
12	"	Truth, or its disciples, said to wisdom this saying hath offended Error!

VERSES	CHAP.	BOOK
13	15	Truth replied, every root or belief which wisdom hath not planted shall be rooted up.
14	"	Error is the blind leading the blind and both shall fall into the ditch.
15, 16	"	A disciple of truth asks for the explanation . . . Truth replies, Are you *yet* without understanding this?
17	"	Truth explains, by saying, that which is received through the personal senses goes into a waste place, for it is not yet really believed, hence it is cast out into the draught.
18	"	But those things which cometh out of the mouth ie, which can be talked — have been received into the understanding, and therefore believed, if they came from the heart; and those are they which produce the results of error in sickness, immorality, and death, thus defiling the whole idea man.
19, 20	"	Enumerating the errors which defile an idea, or man, but not a mere ceremony neglected can defile a man; such as washing the hands, or . . . making appearances good.
21	"	Truth enters the atmosphere of another idea and an error calls for it, being convicted of its own worthlessness to heal the sick and asks that it will restore one of its own offspring from error to truth, i.e., heal her own daughter.
22	"	

In 1870,[7] Mrs. Eddy was back in Lynn and with her was a young student. His name was Richard Kennedy. In Amesbury, Kennedy was a pupil with Sarah Bagley and became so interested in the teachings that he pleaded with Mrs. Eddy for permission to accompany her to Lynn that he might continue his studies and, at the same time, take up the practice of healing.

She consented, and they rented the second floor of a three-story building at South Common and Shepard Streets. Kennedy proposed that they share equally in any income he might receive from his practice, in return for which he was to be given help with patients, and, also, was to receive continued instruction. Mrs. Eddy agreed to this proposition. It permitted her to spend time on a book that was beginning to take shape in her mind.

Testing had proved to her that her teachings could be demonstrated by others, and she had reached the conclusion that the time was approaching when "a work on the subject could be profitably studied." [8]

A personable young man, Kennedy was successful in his practice, and a number of his patients began seeking out Mrs. Eddy for instruction in this "new Science which healed them." Among the students was a sailor named George Tuttle, whose sister was healed of tuberculosis. For a short time Tuttle was a regular attendant at Mrs. Eddy's classes. For only a short time. While still attending class, he healed a friend of dropsy; and he became so frightened he never returned.

But Tuttle's brother-in-law, Charles S. Stanley, a shoe

[7] In February 1868 the *Lynn Reporter* published some of the original verses of one of Mrs. Eddy's best-known hymns, "Christ My Refuge." See Appendix 1.

[8] *Science and Health,* p. ix.

worker, and husband of the woman who had been healed of tuberculosis, was not frightened. He was argumentative, and argued so combatively that the teachings were not in keeping with Christianity that he disrupted the class and Mrs. Eddy was forced to dismiss him. Wallace M. Wright, a bank clerk and son of a local Universalist minister, was another in this same group of students who had difficulty with the teachings.

Wright went to Knoxville, Tennessee, to practice Christian Science healing but soon began, as he wrote in the *Lynn Transcript* on January 13, 1872, "to question the propriety of calling this treatment 'moral science' instead of mesmerism. Away from the influence of argument which the teacher of this so-called science knows how to bring to bear upon students with such force as to outweigh any attempts that they may make at the time to oppose it, I commenced to think more and more independently, and to argue with myself as to the truth of the positions we were called upon to take. The result of this course was to convince me that I had studied the science of mesmerism. . . ."

There began, at once, a controversy in Lynn newspapers between five students and Wright, with the latter ignoring them and firing at his former teacher. On February 3, 1872, the *Lynn Transcript* published what is believed to be the first public statement by Mrs. Eddy about her teachings.[9]

In this statement, Mrs. Eddy announced she was writing a book and, in part, said in the newspaper article:

> . . . "Moral Science belongs to God, and is the expression or revelation of love, wisdom and truth. It reaches the understanding, first, through inspiration, and secondly, through explanation.

[9] See Appendix 2 for complete statement.

Those who receive it must obey its requirements
if they would understand it. . . .

. . . All that is good, God has made, but all that
is not good, man has sought out through many inventions. Moral Science enables us to determine
good from evil, and to destroy the latter. . . .

. . . To be able to control our bodies by the
soul, i.e. through God, is to be able not to let our
bodies control us through the senses. Moral Science teaches this soul-control, and just in the proportion to the greater or lesser extent that this
truth is understood, will be the success . . . of its
students. . . ." [10]

Wright challenged Mrs. Eddy to support her "soul-control" theory by "walking on the water." When his challenge
was ignored he announced he was closing the controversy —
which had attracted attention throughout Massachusetts —
by flatly stating, on February 27, 1872, that Mrs. Eddy "and
her Science were practically dead and buried."

Less than three months later, or on May 11, 1872, the
partnership between Mrs. Eddy and Richard Kennedy was
dissolved.[11] Up to this time Mrs. Eddy had permitted her
students to manipulate the head while treating patients. She
now insisted that this practice be stopped. Kennedy protested, then refused. The dissolution of the partnership followed, immediately.

[10] Capitalization may have been the newspaper's.

[11] In May, 1907, Kennedy wrote in *McClure's Magazine:* "I went to
Lynn to practice with Mrs. Eddy. Our partnership was only in the practice,
not in her teaching. The mode was operating upon the head by giving
vigorous rubbing. This was a part of her system that I had learned. The
special thing she was to teach me was the science of healing by soul power.
She gave me a great deal of instruction in the so-called principle, but I
have not been able to understand it."

Kennedy moved out and Mrs. Eddy continued, for a time, in the South Common Street location. Although her years of poverty were over, she still had to watch her funds. Her share of the income from the two years of the partnership with Kennedy was about four thousand dollars, some of which she had saved. Also, she saved from her fees for teaching.

With her mind on the book she proposed writing, she gave up practically all teaching. Feeling unable to continue to support, financially, the South Common Street quarters, she moved out and returned to the protection of the George G. Clarks, and the boardinghouse where she first stayed after leaving Swampscott.

Here she secluded herself and began writing her book.

Despite the slander, the taunting to prove herself by "walking on the water," and the alien faces that met her almost everywhere, there was an earnestness about "that woman of Lynn," as she was being called throughout the countryside, that would not be stopped.

Her purpose was to share what she was receiving from her Bible studies. At the time she was not thinking of a church separate from the denominational Christian bodies. She was a regular attendant, and pew holder, in the Lynn Christian Church and her expectation was that her findings, after verification, would be welcomed by all Christian denominations, and would be practiced by them.

But there was scoffing then, as afterwards, to the effect that Mrs. Eddy was not learned in the vast history of Christianity.

If this charge meant that she was not entangled in the emotional grandeur of intellectual accomplishment, it is true. However, scholarship and intellectual accomplishment are not the gates to understanding. Lao-tse, the greatest of all Chinese teachers and one of the great teachers in all history, lived in a surrounding of books but remained untouched by the thoughts of other men. His understanding was within himself.

Mary Baker Eddy's concern was not scholasticism.

Her concern was in summoning mankind to free itself from its belief in matter, in exhorting Christian churches to free themselves from doctrines of limitation — to learn, as Paul taught the Corinthians, "where the Spirit of the Lord is, there is liberty."

Not being caught up in a net of emotional grandeur, she saw, as did Paul, that liberty is indistinguishable from God and that man is a prisoner only when he is a captive of his human beliefs.

These were years when Mrs. Eddy was passing through the first part of her prophetic career. Still clinging to her were a few customs of her Congregational upbringing and impressions of her long talks with Phineas P. Quimby. That some such things should cling to her was natural in the process of her growth. A few more years and they were gone. She was beginning to express her innermost thoughts with clearness. True, most people did not understand, but that was not the fault of her words. Some of these words were strangers in the language of Christian theology.

Exactly where the rumor began that she was rewriting the Bible, or who started the rumor, is not known. Probably it first became currency among the gossips of Lynn, although it just as easily could have been put into circulation in any one of the dozen other communities. To heal the sick, as she was doing, and to differ with the clergy as, also, she was doing, were quite different things from rewriting the Bible.

That was blasphemy!

The belief that every word of the Bible was the Word of God still ruled the pulpits, although truth-seekers found it inadvisable to accept, literally, such things as the shaping of Eve from a rib of Adam, or the six-day creation of the universe.

Mrs. Eddy's interest in the canonical writings was not in their literal meaning.

Having seen that what she believed represented God, she likewise saw the Christian Church as one that should be founded upon the spiritual interpretation of the Bible; and, having seen it this way, she perceived it as a Church having no uneasiness over chemistry, no concern with geology or with discoveries in a world of atoms. On that basis there could never be another inquisition of another Galileo, or any conflict over the part each individual must play in his own progress into the moral code.

Is it coincidence that the time Mrs. Eddy was searching for the things of the Spirit was also the time of man's growing fascination with the material side of his nature? A few more years in history — less than one hundred — and fascination with what is material in his nature brought mankind devastating wars, a world drenched with atheism, and a face-to-face choice between weapons and moral values.

Could hers have been *the* mission to bring religion new meaning, new understanding?

Thinking along spiritual lines had been made impossible for centuries. For centuries Christianity was the worship of a God of miracles, thus a God of chance — for that is what God became when Christianity degenerated into a state religion. For twelve centuries, and until the Reformation, the clergy exercised as dogmatic a dictatorship over men's minds as history has seen; and the Reformation, while freeing men to dwell openly upon the meaning of life, did nothing to extricate them from bondage to a God of intermittent mercy.

In their hurry to get away from clerical despotism, a great many of the Reformists cast aside one particular thing which remained from the early teachings. That one thing pertained to the instruction that God is the healer. Although by now almost inundated with ceremony, this instruction still was strong enough, when the thought was pure, to heal the sick. Peering through veils of incense, the clergy hailed the healings without comprehending, it seemed, that by surrendering to chance, and cloaking chance with mysticism, they actually were distrusting God's universality.

But if the Protestants left behind compulsory and stringent practices that stifled open search into the meaning of life, they brought with them an uncompromising attitude concerning all that was said in Holy Writ.

In the King James version they had their own Bible. They conceived this version as God's truth, and in so conceiving it made God a prisoner within the covers of its literal text. The frequent statement in this text that God is the healer was largely ignored. Instead, God was pictured as being remote from His creation; man, brought sharply into focus, was excoriated as a loathsome creature.

With freedom to explore, men's minds turned from the rigors of religion and into investigations of the world about them. Before long there were a thousand, then ten thousand, Galileos disputing the dogma that the world was flat, that it was but six thousand years old, and other legends the clergy offered as truth and attempted to prove by applying mathematics to the Bible. Soon material scientists were as dogmatic as the clergymen they assailed. Charmed by the new things invention was bringing in, multitudes deserted one formalism for another and promptly found themselves a swarm in a world of materialism presided over by a deity of test tubes and slide rules.

The Christianity Mary Baker Eddy envisioned was one that would make adequate answer to the destructive criticism that was beginning to sweep the world. To her, as has been pointed out, there is no conflict between what is material and what is spiritual, no excuse for confusing Caesar with God.

To her, whatever is spiritual has no relationship with what is material, and whatever is not spiritual has no place in the teachings of the Christian Church.

As she saw it, the great problem of religion is not in rationalizing discoveries in materialism.

The great problem is man, himself.

Not his toys, not his seven-league boots carrying him farther and farther into the witchery of a materialistic world, not his stomach, and not his brain — but his conscience; his spiritual and not his physical stature.

Man himself — in his eternal relationship to God.

To show man how to better understand this relationship was the purpose of her book — a book and, beside it, the Bible; both open for all to read.

At the time Mrs. Eddy was preparing her book, George Clark, son of the owners of the boardinghouse, also was writing. His was a story of the sea. He completed his manuscript in the summer of 1872, and told Mrs. Eddy he was taking it to Boston for consideration by Adams and Company, publishers. She asked if she might accompany him for the purpose of submitting a prospectus of her own book to the same publishers.

They returned to Lynn. Clark was happy. His manuscript had been accepted. Mrs. Eddy's trip was not successful. Her prospectus had been rejected. The publishers told her such a book had no possibilities and advised her to give up all ideas of writing it.

On the way back from Boston, Clark was chatty, planning his future — then their conversation subsided. Mrs. Eddy was in a mood Clark had come to know. In silence and in deep thought, she got off the train; and they were walking home from the station, when Mrs. Eddy suddenly reached out and stopped her companion.

"George!" she exclaimed, pointing to a church — "Someday, I shall have a church of my own."

Apparently the hostility of the clergy, and the poor opinion of the Boston publishers for the prospectus of her book, brought realization that a church of her own was "essential for the propagation, protection and usefulness of her discovery." [12]

She believed the truth was appearing to her, and she saw it as a fortress that had to be garrisoned.

[12] *Historical Sketches,* by Clifford P. Smith; copyright, 1934, 1936, 1941, by The Christian Science Publishing Society.

CHAPTER THREE

The First Edition of *Science and Health*

FOR NEARLY THREE MORE YEARS Mary Baker Eddy studied and wrote, while gossip persisted and resentment grew.

News that her "Bible," as it was being called, had been rejected by the Boston publishers was received with general satisfaction — but now, it was rumored, she was going ahead with it, anyway. In her infrequent daylight appearances on the streets of Lynn, or on her frequent evening walks, people drew aside as she passed.

Stones shattered the window in the room where she secluded herself. Judging her "an offspring of the devil," pulpits warned their congregations that the Bible is the Word of God and declared, then, that inasmuch as when God speaks He speaks the truth, it was their duty as guardians of that truth to keep the devil from contaminating it.

It never seemed to occur to the clergy, and to the congregations, that God has no anxiety over His reputation.

They did not seem to realize that Mrs. Eddy's effort to find new meaning in the Bible was perfectly natural — that it is always natural, as truth-seekers know, for conscience to seek the Revealer within itself; as inescapable as the fact that religion is in the heart and not in the ceremony; as certain as the knowledge that God used a manger and not an altar for His temple.

Mary Baker Eddy's detractors were not deaf to what she was saying. They were as determined to keep the multitudes from hearing as she was determined to be heard.

They knew that long since their churches had departed from the simple teachings that revealed men as brothers, not as priest and supplicant. They knew if they dared look squarely at their authority they would see only authority they had taken to themselves. For nearly two hundred years — the first years of Christianity — congregations reposed in the clergy no authority. As individuals, the early Christians considered themselves full equals with their bishops and their presbyters in spiritual affairs.

Is it to be believed that any pursuit which liberates itself from the material and goes in search of the spiritual is not in the path of truth?

If it is to be believed that such a search is not in the path of truth, then all that is spiritual loses its meaning; if it is to be believed that such a search *is* in the path of truth, then all that is personal is of little moment.

Many books have been written about Mary Baker Eddy. Some are vicious; some are laudatory. Without exception, her critics center on this period of her work, this period from 1866 to approximately 1890. They make much of the Quimby influence; dwell on her inability to get along with many of her students; doubt her authorship of *Science and Health;* emphasize her frugality, calling it greed; scornfully refer to her three marriages; and scoff at any and all claims that she was an inspired woman.

Even if all the things her critics say are true — and how could they be? — the fact remains that what they say is of slight importance.

The only important thing was her search for her spiritual destiny.

After her own healing, she devoted herself constantly to bettering her understanding of her relationship with God. That cannot be denied. What she found enabled her to heal the sick, and to teach others to do the same thing. That cannot be disputed. She instructed her followers to follow her only so far as she followed Christ. No Christian can quarrel with that.

Her work in those things is the history of the movement she founded.

All that really matters is whether she was right, or whether she was wrong.

The Architect of us all has no concern with religion, and has not so constructed His universe as to depend upon it. His universe is as He is, and His law is as He is — Spirit, and Spiritual. Physical scientists are acknowledging that, even though religions seem less ready to do so.

Religions can adapt themselves to increasing their understanding of what is spiritual — ridding themselves of what is material, and obeying His law — or they will be swept aside and the work undertaken by those who will . . . for the desire to understand is in the hearts of men, and will remain there so long as men hope and aspire and reflect upon the meaning of life, and the responsibilities it entails.

In these years of teaching and writing, as in the years immediately following her healing, Mrs. Eddy lived in boardinghouses. In the spring of 1875 she was living at 9 Broad Street, in Lynn. Her manuscript, which she had entitled

Science and Health,[1] was in the hands of W. F. Brown and Company, printers, 50 Bromfield Street, Boston. A contract for printing one thousand copies of a book containing four hundred and thirty pages at a total cost of one thousand dollars had been made and, on February 9, an initial payment of five hundred dollars had been made. In discussing the venture with her students, Mrs. Eddy had been promised financial help, if needed; and all were confident it would be possible to dispose of the entire edition at two dollars a copy.

The proof sheets were beginning to come from the printer. She was making changes and thinking about the difficulties of putting into clearer words the thoughts that crowded the pages when, looking out of a window, her eyes rested on a FOR SALE sign on a house across the way at 8 Broad Street.

A few days later, on March 31, she bought the house, paying $5,650. The building was a frame, two-and-one-half-story structure. For living quarters she took one small bedroom in the attic. This was a room lighted only by a skylight, which could be opened for ventilation. For her classroom she reserved the parlor on the first floor, furnishing it with plain chairs and a table. The remainder of the house she rented to others. Because she had used most of her savings in buying the house, and in making the initial payment of five hundred dollars on the cost of her book, she found it necessary to increase her fee for teaching.

[1] The title came to Mrs. Eddy one night after six weeks of prayer for guidance in naming her book. Six months after *Science and Health* was published, one of her students called her attention to John Wyclif's use of the same words in his translation of the New Testament. This was Mrs. Eddy's first knowledge of their prior use. See *Message to The Mother Church*, 1902, pp. 15–16.

In 1870, when she organized her first class, she charged one hundred dollars for ten lessons. Students who could not afford to pay, and the greater number could not afford to pay, were taught free. With a few she made arrangements to have a 10 per cent participation in their incomes if they took up the practice of healing. With those who paid, she often contracted to return to them what they paid if they were not successful as practitioners. There were such instances. Mrs. Eddy recognized, very early in her work, that there would be some who would not be able to take what she was holding out for them.

Asking pupils to share their incomes was a hard choice for her. She felt it unwise, but she also felt she was entitled to a measure of payment because she was always being asked to help whenever problems were encountered. In the Archives of The Mother Church, Boston, are her notebooks. They show she counted every penny she received, just as she counted every penny of her own spending. Items such as "postage 18 cts; expressage 15 cts" are frequent, particularly items of postage. She carried on an extensive correspondence with her students, watching their development, rebuking and encouraging, as the occasion required.

In the Archives is a message to one of her pupils, informing him: "Now you have a home offered you and no rent to pay for it. So do not be cast down. I thank God more for this than anything that I have a shelter . . . to go to in an hour of want and to welcome those who need a little time to meet the hour." She turned over to this family five of her seven rooms.

Soon after her purchase of the house she changed her fee from one hundred dollars for ten lessons to three hundred dollars for twelve lessons. She now called her teachings "the

Science of Life" and, as before, most of her students could not afford to pay. These, of course, she taught without charge. Participation in income was abandoned. Those who paid but who failed as practitioners were reimbursed. As with the fee of one hundred dollars, the charging of this new fee was a hard decision. In the Archives is a letter she wrote to Mrs. Clara E. Choate in which she spoke of her new class, saying, "I shall teach them as soon as they will study," and explained that "taxes, coal, repairs on the new building, and *book*" had drained her resources.

Her method of instruction was not changed. Students were forbidden to make notes, nor did she teach from notes. She felt, and felt strongly, the student must grasp what was said and not distract others by writing notes, or risk hampering himself by writing incorrectly. Whatever written instructions were needed, she supplied — maintaining "however little be taught, or learned, that little shall be right." [2]

Critics have dealt harshly with Mrs. Eddy for charging students, accusing her of being mercenary. This criticism is hard to understand, considering that professors in theology in universities and in colleges are paid for teaching. However, and wholly aside from such argument, Mrs. Eddy was troubled over being forced to insist on payment. She came to see that it was the proper thing to do.

In addition, people who came to her for help sometimes did not pay, even when rid of the conditions that brought them. Often she urgently needed the money, but she never pressed for payment and always advised her students against such action. In Mrs. Eddy's experience in the early years of teaching and healing is found the reason for a rule that appears in the *Manual of The Mother Church:*

[2] *Retrospection and Introspection,* by Mary Baker Eddy, p. 61.

A member of The Mother Church shall not, under pardonable circumstances, sue his patient for recovery of payment for said member's practice, on penalty of discipline and liability to have his name removed from membership. Also he shall reasonably reduce his price in chronic cases of recovery, and in cases where he has not effected a cure. A Christian Scientist is a humanitarian; he is benevolent, forgiving, long-suffering, and seeks to overcome evil with good.

She held half-day classes, not every day, but when she was not teaching she was in her room, studying and editing. Until work was completed on her manuscript no one, excepting herself, was permitted to enter this room, against one wall of which was a framed inscription: THOU SHALT HAVE NO OTHER GODS BEFORE ME. Covering the floor was a carpet, and the furnishings consisted of a horsehair rocker, a table, a straight-backed chair, a bed, and a bureau. On the table was a Bible, a supply of paper, pencils, and corrected proof sheets.

It was the summer of 1875; on August 14, the printer was paid two hundred dollars on account. Directly after this payment he stopped work on the book and, although Mrs. Eddy often pleaded with him to continue the work, he just as often declined. In *Retrospection and Introspection,* Mrs. Eddy recalled:

After months had passed, I yielded to a constant conviction that I must insert in my last chapter a partial history of what I had already observed of mental malpractice. Accordingly, I set to work, contrary to my inclination, to fulfill this painful

task, and finished my copy for the book. As it afterwards appeared, although I had not thought of
such a result, my printer resumed his work at the
same time, finished printing the copy he had on
hand, and then started for Lynn to see me. The
afternoon that he left Boston for Lynn, I started
for Boston with my finished copy. We met at the
Eastern depot in Lynn, and were both surprised,
— I to learn that he had printed all the copy on
hand, and had come to tell me he wanted more, —
he to find me *en route* for Boston, to give him
the closing chapter of my first edition of Science
and Health. Not a word had passed between us,
audibly or mentally, while this went on. I had
grown disgusted with my printer, and become
silent. He had come to a standstill through motives
and circumstances unknown to me.

On October 30, the book was ready. Bound in a pale-green
cloth cover, it contained four hundred and fifty-six pages,
embracing these subjects: "Natural Science," "Imposition
and Demonstration," "Spirit and Matter," "Creation,"
"Prayer and Atonement," "Marriage," "Physiology," and
"Healing the Sick." There was a "Preface" of approximately
two pages, in which the author wrote:

. . . The time for thinkers has come; and the
time for revolutions, ecclesiastic and social, must
come. Truth, independent of doctrines or time-
honored systems, stands at the threshhold of
history. Contentment with the past, or the cold
conventionality of custom, may no longer shut the
door on science; though empires fall, "He whose

right it is shall reign." Ignorance of God should no longer be the stepping stone to faith; understanding Him "whom to know aright is Life" is the only guaranty of obedience.

. . . The science of man alone can make him harmonious, unfold his utmost possibilities, and establish the perfection of man. To admit God the Principle of all being, and live in accordance with this Principle, is the Science of Life, but to reproduce the harmony of being, errors of personal sense must be destroyed, even as the science of music must correct tones caught from the ear, to give the sweet concord of sound. There are many theories of physic, and theology; and many calls in each of their directions for the right way; but we propose to settle the question of "What is Truth?" on the ground of proof. Let that method of healing the sick and establishing Christianity be adopted that is found to give the most health, and make the best Christians, and you will then give science a fair field; in which case we are assured of its triumph over all opinions and beliefs. Sickness and sin have ever had their doctors, but the question is, have they become less because of them?

. . . We find great difficulties in starting this work right: some shockingly false claims are already made to its practice; mesmerism (its very antipode), is one. Hitherto we have never in a single instance of our discovery or practice found the slightest resemblance between mesmerism and the science of Life. No especial idiosyncrasy is requisite for a learner; although spiritual sense is more adapted to it than even the intellect; and those who would learn this science without a high moral standard will fail to understand it until they go up higher. Owing to our explanations constantly vibrating between the same points an irksome repetition of words must occur; also, the use of capital letters, genders and technicalities peculiar to the science, variety of language, or beauty of diction, must give place to close analysis, and unembellished thought. . . .

In this edition the words "Christian science" make their first appearance in her published works, on page 23, where is this sentence: "The great Teacher of Christian science knew a good tree sendeth not forth evil fruit."

The printing bill was $2,285.35, instead of the original price of one thousand dollars. The many changes in the proofs accounted for the difference. In striving for "unembellished thought," Mrs. Eddy canceled composition and plates on 525 pages; and this was but one item in her corrections. Efforts of students to sell the book were not very successful, and Mrs. Eddy, herself, was far from satisfied with her own effort.

In her notebooks she recorded "490 typographical errors in words besides paragraphs and pages wrong, and punctuation"; and, in a letter to a student (after telling of her plans for a new edition) she continued: "There are grammatical errors in Errata and some in the book doubtless that I have not touched . . . and if you see them and are sure of what is right in the case correct them but *not* otherwise, don't meddle with the punctuation but mark any doubtful cases so you can point them out to me. Our next printer should have a proof reader who is *responsible* for this. . . ."

But allowing for the many typographical and grammatical mistakes, the poor punctuation, and the misplaced paragraphs and pages, much of the book is clumsy in its wording, although the meaning is clear. Mrs. Eddy recognized the difficulty of putting into words thoughts for which there are no words.

As indicated, she made a point of this in her "Preface," and she later referred to the difficulty this way:

> Mozart experienced more than he expressed. The rapture of his grandest symphonies was never heard. He was a musician beyond what the world knew. This was even more strikingly true of Beethoven, who was so long hopelessly deaf. Mental melodies and strains of sweetest music supersede conscious sound.[3]

None the less, and in her own account, Mrs. Eddy probably made a great many mistakes in spelling, in grammar, and in punctuation in her manuscript; and not because she was not aware of how words should be put together. She did much of her writing with a pad of paper resting on her knee, pencil flying across the pages; when a page was completed it was brushed aside and to the floor. Her handwriting clearly discloses the great haste in which she recorded thoughts that hurried her pencil beyond its capacity to keep pace — and not until the high moments of inspiration were ended did she pause to gather and arrange the pages strewn about her.

But, despite the sale of only a few hundred copies of the

[3] *Science and Health*, p. 213.

first edition of *Science and Health,* word that it had been published swept over Massachusetts. Students went from door to door, or walked miles to a remote farmhouse, in search of a sale. Often they were driven from the premises. Newspapers ridiculed the book, and pulpits assailed the author.

Mrs. Eddy was saying there is no death — that man, in his real definition, is never separate from his Maker, and that as his Maker is eternal, so is man. Against this, for more than fifteen centuries, Christian theology had been teaching that death is a penalty inflicted by God in order to pass judgment on His children.

She was saying a proper understanding of the Bible heals the sick. For more than fifteen centuries there had been theological denial of the full flavor of the teachings of Jesus, and the proof of their efficacy.

She was saying there is no such individual as the devil. Fifteen centuries of ecclesiastical authority had elevated the devil to a stature secondary only to God.

She was saying heaven and hell are here-and-now conditions within ourselves. For more than fifteen centuries the clergy had been preaching heaven and hell were death's destination points, where the traveler found his reward — or his penalty.

Radical, too, was her declaration, "There is no life in matter."

Considering what Christian theology had been teaching for centuries, and considering, too, human preoccupation with superstition since earliest times, it is easy to understand why Mrs. Eddy's teachings aroused so much bitterness.

* * *

There is no death.

Mrs. Eddy was talking about man as a spiritual being; and what she was saying had been said by inspired voices everywhere through many, many centuries.

Since the dawn of human intelligence, however, human beings have been beset by superstition and fear. As a result, death became the chosen instrument of pagan priesthood in its sacrificial rites to appease the menace of storm and equinox. The step from use of death as a rite of appeasement to its use as a weapon guaranteeing absolute priestly authority must have been a short one, considering human fear, if it was a step at all.

Its use as an ordeal of sacrifice, and as a weapon, was still common in the time of Jesus, but His words, "Because I live, ye shall live also," destroyed its validity.

For some two hundred years His words were promises Christians chose as their own, but in the third century familiar words from pagan teachings began to replace them. Ambitious for temporal power, the clergy buttressed a Christianity weakened with strife and with loss of healing by bringing into it pagan fears, pagan rites, and pagan authority over tenure of the soul. Useless in eternity but invincible during the moment of temporal authority, fear of death became the most powerful weapon at the command of the priesthood.

God is the healer.

Before Jesus, and after Him, all the great teachers were healers. Moses, Elijah, Elisha, Isaiah, Peter, John, James, all the disciples, the apostle Paul; all were healers. The seventy He sent out returned to Him, crying: "Lord, even the devils are subject unto us through thy name."

For more than one hundred and fifty years after the crucifixion healing was practiced by Christians wherever they
gathered. This was not a new doctrine Mrs. Eddy was proclaiming, merely a neglected and unpopular one — unpopular because early in Christian history there had been clerical
preference for material possessions, and neglected because of
clerical preference for temporal power in place of the things
of the Spirit.

No such person as the devil.

In savage times it was a belief that, as it was possible to
shift the burden of carrying a stone to another savage, so was
it possible to shift the burden of whatever was evil to the
demons that populated the forest. As time went on, the devil
emerges from the demons to become, in the melodrama
that was replacing Christianity, a most convenient villain
and quite as essential as were the demons to savage sorcerers.

It is often said by preachers that the devil took Jesus to a
high mountain, showed Him the kingdoms of the world, and
said He could have them all "if thou wilt fall down and
worship me." Could not the Bible story be interpreted to
mean that Jesus was being tempted by *thoughts* of material
possessions, and by *desires* not of God?

Can it be accepted that God created evil, and the devil?

The Bible states, "God saw every thing that he had made,
and, behold, it was very good"; the Bible also says, "All
things were made by him; and without him was not any
thing made that was made"; and Jesus said, "But if I cast
out devils by the Spirit of God, then the kingdom of God
is come unto you."

*   *   *

Heaven and hell are not places.

If we have to believe in a God and a devil of applied psychology, it is not inconsistent that they should be reduced by the limitations human beings place upon themselves.

The Bible states that "God is a Spirit." If so, how can He become an anthropomorphic being? God being a Spirit eliminates any theory of time and place, and this gives meaning to the words: "The kingdom of God is within you." In those words, Jesus was referring to that — and to only that —- in which we live, and move, and have our being.

As God is pure, so must our thoughts of Him be pure until we find ourselves in the heaven of our own spirituality, with a hell plaguing us only so long as our thoughts are evil, and of the devil.

There is no life in matter.

A great many physicists now agree. Years after Mrs. Eddy said it, physicists re-examined matter and flatly affirmed that a strictly materialistic theory of life was no longer tenable. To this conviction they added the belief that if man would free himself from the despotism of the body, he must develop that which is within himself, and come closer to the perfect ideal of the Christ.[4]

Seventy-five years after Mrs. Eddy said, "There is no life in matter," Dr. Edmund W. Sinnott, Dean of Sheffield Scientific School, of Yale University, was publicly declaring: "Let us face the fact that what the world must have is a fuller cultivation of those qualities which are best termed spiritual . . . for on their strength depends our own survival. The good old days of billiard-ball atoms, Euclidean geometry, and the indestructibility of matter are now gone. . . . Mat-

[4] *Human Destiny* by Lecomte du Noüy (1946).

ter in the old sense has ceased to be. The universe in which our fathers felt so comfortably at home has ceased to be. . . . The idealist who followed the ancient highway of the spirit toward reality has gained a more respectful audience than was his half a century ago. . . . Belief in something constant and unchangeable, call it by whatever name we will, is a necessity not only for religion but equally for science and the arts, and forms a common meeting ground and starting point for men who travel on the highway of the mind and those who use the road of the spirit. . . ."

In his book, *The Universe and Dr. Einstein,* Lincoln Barnett, after referring to "sense-imprisoned man," said: "Physicists have been forced to abandon the ordinary world of our experience, the world of sense perceptions . . . even space and time are forms of intuition, which can no more be divorced from consciousness than can our concepts of color, shape or size. Space has no objective reality except as an order or arrangement of the objects we perceive in it, and time has no independent existence apart from the order of events by which we measure it."

There is no death — God is the healer — no such person as the devil — heaven and hell are not places — there is no life in matter.

In 1875, Mary Baker Eddy was saying these things on paper and in the church services that had been started. Little wonder that when she spoke of Life, and dismissed death, she was assailed from the pulpit and ridiculed in the press.

What she was doing was establishing a religion tributary to the timelessness of the Spirit and the nothingness of matter. After centuries of teaching that we have to die to learn these things, most knew so little of the one that how could they possibly understand the other?

Jealous of rites already ancient when Christianity began, what else could press and pulpit do but clamor against her who saw only the flame of the Resurrection and not the ashes of the crucifixion?

The first Sunday services — which began in 1875 — came as the result of a meeting called, and presided over, by Daniel H. Spofford.

Several years before, when employed in a Lynn shoe factory, although he was a watchmaker by trade, Spofford had copied several of Mrs. Eddy's manuscripts. They had been loaned to him by a student and he had set himself up in Lynn as "a mental healer."

Hearing of his efforts, Mrs. Eddy invited him to join her next class "and receive my instruction in healing the sick without medicine — without money and without price." Spofford accepted, and it was at the conclusion of his class instruction that he called a meeting at which the following resolutions were approved and adopted:

Whereas, in times not long past, the Science of healing, new to the age, and far in advance of all other modes, and introduced into the city of Lynn by its discoverer, a certain lady, Mary Baker Glover.[5]

And, whereas, many friends spread the good tidings throughout the place, and bore aloft the standard of life and truth which had declared freedom to many manacled with the bonds of disease or error,

And, whereas, by the wilful disobedience of an individual, who has no name in Love, Wisdom or Truth, the light was ob-

[5] Mary Baker Eddy.

scured by clouds of misinterpretations and mists of mystery, so that God's work was hidden from the world and derided in the streets,

Now, therefore, we students and advocates of this moral science, called the Science of Life, have arranged with the said Mary Baker Glover to preach to us or direct our meetings on the Sabbath of each week, and hereby covenant with one another, and by these presents do publish and proclaim that we have agreed to do each and all agree to pay weekly, for one year, beginning with the sixth day of June A.D. 1875, to a treasurer chosen by at least seven students the amount set opposite our names, provided, nevertheless, the moneys paid by us shall be expended for no other purpose, or purposes, than the maintenance of said Mary Baker Glover as teacher and instructor, than the renting of a suitable hall and other necessary incidental expenses, and our signatures shall be a full and sufficient guarantee of our faithful performance of this contract.

[*Signed*]

ELIZABETH M. NEWHALL ...	$ 1.50
DAN'L H. SPOFFORD ...	2.00
GEORGE H. ALLEN ...	2.00
DORCAS B. RAWSON ...	1.00
ASA T. N. MACDONALD ...	.50
GEORGE W. BARRY ...	2.00
S. P. BANCROFT ...	.50
MIRANDA R. RICE ...	.50
	$10.00

The place chosen for Sunday services was Good Templars Hall. The services consisted of a sermon by Mrs. Eddy, prayer, and hymns. S. P. Bancroft led the singing and his wife played the melodeon. Seldom were there more than twenty persons in the congregation — but at these services the Church of Christ, Scientist, was born.

* * *

As he was instrumental in organizing the first Sunday services, so was Spofford instrumental in organizing dissension among Mrs. Eddy's students.

Among the students was Asa Gilbert Eddy, who lived in East Boston and acted as an agent for a sewing-machine company. Eddy had suffered a general physical breakdown, and among his friends was one who had been healed of blood poisoning. This friend encouraged Eddy to go to Lynn; Eddy did go, and was healed.

He became so interested in the teachings that he remained for class instruction. Quickly he became one of the better students, and he was the first to open an office and use the words CHRISTIAN SCIENTIST on his practitioner's sign. He was so successful that he soon had the full confidence of his teacher.

Several months having passed, with few sales of *Science and Health,* Mrs. Eddy sent for Spofford in 1876. She told him of her dissatisfaction with the manner in which the book was being handled and asked him to take on the job of disposing of whatever copies were on hand in anticipation of the publication of a second edition.

Spofford hesitated, inquiring about the continuance of his practice. It was suggested he turn it over to Asa Eddy, inasmuch as the latter had proved himself a good worker. Spofford still hesitated, and brought up the name of George W. Barry,[6] who, at the time of the publication of the book,

---

[6] Suffering from tuberculosis, Barry came to Mrs. Eddy for help following her return to Lynn in 1870. Grateful over being healed, he proposed an arrangement under which there would be "an exchange of services without compensation"; he was to receive class instruction and, in turn, was to do whatever chores were necessary. Although he did not live there, he spent much time in his teacher's home before and after his marriage.

had been put in charge of sales. Mrs. Eddy told Spofford that she had talked over the matter with Barry and, while the latter did not seem in agreement, she felt he had not measured up to the assignment, and should be relieved. Spofford remained reluctant, asked for time to think over the proposal, and, after a short time, consented to assume the responsibility. In anger, Barry departed from Mrs. Eddy's teachings.

Spofford's efforts as a salesman were halfhearted, and toward the end of the year he returned to his practice. On New Year's Day, 1877, Asa Gilbert Eddy and his teacher were married. In the spring of 1877, without warning, George W. Barry brought suit against Mrs. Eddy for $2700 which he claimed she owed him for services over a period of about five years, such services as selecting carpets, moving furniture, assistance in buying the house at No. 8 Broad Street, liaison work with the printers of her book, and so on. He itemized everything, including a charge of fifty cents for each scuttleful of coal he brought up from the cellar. An attempt was made by Mrs. Eddy to make a settlement. Barry was unwilling, insisting upon full payment. The court allowed him $350.

Spofford chose this time to dispute the advisability of publishing a second edition of *Science and Health,* saying there was no need for it and that no good purpose would be served. Mrs. Eddy insisted that there was need. She spoke of the many mistakes in editing and in proofreading in the first edition, emphasized her own increasing perception, and made it clear that the book must do the work it was intended to do.

Spofford contended that it was not possible to finance a second edition and stressed the growing discontent of students over their inability to heal the sick. Mrs. Eddy told Spofford that she was well aware of this discontent, and informed him that these students had been properly taught and said, "I believe this hour is to try my students who think they have the cause at heart and see if it be so."

She earnestly solicited Spofford to devote the month (it was now July 1877) to completing the task she had given him to do. Spofford disposed of the several hundred unsold copies for six hundred dollars, and turned over this sum to Elizabeth Newhall and George W. Barry, who had paid the printer's bill (less seven hundred dollars Mrs. Eddy had paid), and then put in a bill for five hundred dollars for his own services.

So went the history of the first edition of *Science and Health* — ridicule, dissension, loss of money (Miss Newhall and Barry were paid in full, later), and loss of students. Moreover, the manuscript for the second edition of *Science and Health* was now in the printer's hands, and Mrs. Eddy was without funds to start the work. There was even talk that Spofford was planning to sue her.

CHAPTER FOUR

They Felt the Threat of Her Presence

M RS. EDDY felt herself in a hostile world; and she was. Not only was her book a failure, but the antagonism toward her was so great that A. Bronson Alcott, founder of the Concord School of Philosophy, came to see her, explaining, "I have come to comfort you." He was not of the opinion of her critics. He urged her to keep studying and to keep writing, assuring her she could not fail.

He did not become a follower, but he did become so interested in her teachings that he invited her, with her husband, to come to Concord and go with him on a visit to Emerson. Accompanied by Alcott, the Eddys spent a quiet evening with the New England philosopher. And, at this point, something may as well be dealt with, although it is out of place chronologically, in a history of the Christian Science movement, because the claim actually was not made until later.

It has been said that Mrs. Eddy was influenced by Emerson. Those who say so point to similarity in some of the writings — to such a statement as "The true meaning of spiritual is real," as compared with Mrs. Eddy's "Spirit is the real and eternal." The partial sentences do sound much alike, but Emerson completed his thought this way, "that law which executes itself, which works without means, and which cannot be conceived as not existing," whereas Mrs. Eddy's sentence ends this way, "matter is the unreal and temporal."

Placing the sentences after each other, they read:

Emerson: "The true meaning of spiritual is real; that law which executes itself, which works without means, and which cannot be conceived as not existing." [1]

Eddy: "Spirit is the real and eternal; matter is the unreal and temporal." [1]

In their completeness the sentences are very different. Nevertheless, similarity in phrasing means little when spirituality is under discussion. The very nature of the subject lends to similarity in expression. Many of Jesus's sayings derived from ancient Hebrew proverbs. He lifted them to spiritual heights. The great distinguisher between the teachings of Emerson and the teachings of Mrs. Eddy is easily discerned.

Emerson was abstract; Mrs. Eddy was practical.

Emerson was satisfied to declare; Mrs. Eddy was determined to prove.

That they should agree on many spiritual truths is not surprising. Truth is always revealing itself; it always has and it always will. It is even possible Emerson foresaw the very church that Mrs. Eddy foresaw, because he wrote: ". . . There will be a new church founded on moral science, at first cold and naked, a babe in a manger again, the algebra and mathematics of ethical law, the church of men to come . . . it will have heaven and earth for its beams and rafters; science for symbol and illustration; it will fast enough gather beauty, music, picture, poetry . . . it shall send man home to his central solitude, shame these social, supplicating man-

[1] Emerson, *Worship.* Eddy, *Science and Health,* p. 468.

ners, and make him know that much of the time he must have himself as his friend. He shall expect no co-operation, he shall walk with no companion. The nameless Thought, the nameless Power, the superpersonal Heart — he shall repose alone on that. . . ." [2]

And, again, there is the great distinguisher. Mrs. Eddy set about to do it, to create what Emerson dreamed about. Each was a truth-seeker. The borrowing was not done by her from him, but by both from the same Source.

Coming as it did, and when it did, the encouragement of Alcott helped greatly. She gave him a copy of *Science and Health,* and he wrote her about it: ". . . The sacred truths which you announce sustained by facts of the Immortal Life, give to your work the seal of inspiration — reaffirm in modern phrase, the Christian revelations. In times like ours so sunk in sensualism, I hail with joy any voice speaking an assured word for God and Immortality. And my joy is heightened the more when I find the blessed words are of woman's divinings."

Alcott recognized better than did most, if not all, that Mrs. Eddy was not declaring opinions, but declaring herself as she acknowledged "the kingdom of God" within her. The conviction was so strong in her that she did not hesitate to say it, any more than did the Scotsman, John Caird:

If [man] were only a creature of transient sensations and impulses, of an ever coming and ever going succession of intuitions, fancies, feelings, then nothing could ever have for him the character of objective truth or reality. But it is the prerogative of man's spiritual nature that he can yield himself up to a thought and will that are infinitely larger than his own. As a

[2] Emerson, *Conduct of Life.*

thinking, self-conscious being, indeed, he may be said, by his very nature, to live in the atmosphere of the Universal Life.

As a thinking being, it is possible for me to suppress and quell in my consciousness every movement of self-assertion, every notion and opinion that is merely mine, every desire that belongs to me as this particular Self, and to become the pure medium of a thought that is universal — in one word, to live no more my own life, and let my consciousness be possessed and suffused by the Infinite and Eternal life of spirit.

And yet it is just in this renunciation of self that I truly find myself, or realize the highest possibilities of my own nature. For whilst in one sense we give up self to live the universal and absolute life of reason, yet that to which we surrender ourselves is in reality our truer self. The life of absolute reason is not a life that is foreign to us.[3]

Had Mary Baker Eddy been content only to declare, probably she would not have encountered the opposition she did. But, in demonstrating and thus sealing her work, she also *acted* in a manner that was dangerous to established religions.

The pulpits felt the threat of her presence.

On the whole, Mrs. Eddy's early students were more harmful than helpful.[4] There was avarice, spite, and jealousy among them. She was severe in her rebukes, and these rebukes often were misunderstood. Few understood that when she rebuked it was to keep them from hindering their own progress. Once she rebuked Spofford and he frankly told her, now that he had disposed of the previously unsold copies of the first edition, that it was his intention to prevent publication of a second edition because "You have

[3] *An Introduction to the Philosophy of Religion*, by John Caird; published in London and New York, 1890.
[4] Of her first one thousand students, only a few remained loyal.

proved yourself incapable as a leader, and I propose to carry on this work myself, and alone." [5]

This purpose he communicated to her students, announcing that he was their leader, and he called upon them to follow him. Some did. Others remained loyal and pleaded with Mrs. Eddy to appeal to the courts for a restraining order to prevent interference with her work. She refused.

In an attempt to get followers, Spofford called on Lucretia Brown, of Ipswich. Miss Brown, a patient of Dorcas Rawson's, charged that Spofford's visit caused her great discomfort. Miss Rawson complained to Mrs. Eddy, and was advised to treat her patient according to what was taught in Christian Science. Instead, Miss Rawson urged Miss Brown to bring suit against Spofford; and suit was instituted, with Miss Brown claiming injuries "of an irreparable nature" and stating an "inability to escape from the control of [Spofford] so exercises . . . and from the aforementioned effects of such control and influence."

The case was tried before the Supreme Judicial Court in Salem in May 1878, with Edward J. Arens, a young student in Christian Science, arguing for the plaintiff. Spofford was acquitted, the Court deeming it had "no power to control the defendant's mind." The trial, which quickly became known as the "Ipswich Witchcraft Case," attracted wide attention, all of it unfavorable to Mrs. Eddy, "whose method," the newspaper accounts related, "produces disease, as well as cures it."

After the trial, Mrs. Eddy strongly rebuked Miss Rawson and Arens and, by so doing, set them to intriguing against her.

[5] *The Life of Mary Baker Eddy,* by Sibyl Wilbur; copyright, 1907–1929, The Christian Science Publishing Society.

Again Alcott came to see her, to repeat his words of assurance. To give emphasis to his words, he brought with him the Reverend J. L. Dudley, and presented him as a friend.

Secretly, a number of Mrs. Eddy's followers began meeting for the purpose of beseeching God to do mental harm to those who opposed their teacher. Hearing of these meetings, Mrs. Eddy ordered them stopped, and reminded her followers as she later wrote: "Animal magnetism has no scientific foundation, for God governs all that is real, harmonious, and eternal, and His power is neither animal nor human." [6]

Altogether, there was a great deal in the newspapers about Mrs. Eddy in the spring and summer of 1878; and, in the autumn, headlines told of the arrest of Asa Gilbert Eddy and Edward J. Arens on suspicion of murder. The victim — so stated the *Boston Herald* of October 29, 1878 — was Daniel H. Spofford, and his body was in the city morgue.

A week or two later Spofford, alive and well, turned up in Boston; but instead of releasing Eddy and Arens, the grand jury, acting on testimony of a man named James I. Sargeant, brought in an indictment charging the two men with "conspiring to kill Daniel Spofford." In December 1878, the case was filed in the Superior Court, in Boston, the indictment reading, in part: ". . . That Edward J. Arens and Asa G. Eddy of Boston, aforesaid, on the 28th day of July, in the year of our Lord one thousand eight hundred and seventy-eight in Boston aforesaid, with force and arms, being persons of evil minds and dispositions, did then and there unlawfully conspire, combine, and agree together feloniously, wilfully, and of their malice aforethought, to procure, hire, incite and solicit one James I. Sargeant, for a certain sum of

[6] *Science and Health,* p. 102.

money, to wit, the sum of five hundred dollars, to be paid to said Sargeant by them, said Arens and Eddy, feloniously, wilfully and of his said Sargeant's malice aforethought, in some way and manner, by some means, instruments and weapons, to said jurors unknown, one Daniel H. Spofford to kill and murder against the law, peace and dignity of said Commonwealth."

On January 27, 1879, the Superior Court in Boston rendered its decision: "This indictment was found and re-turned into Court by the grand jurors at the last December term when the said Arens and Eddy were severally set at the bar, and having the said indictment read to them, they severally said thereof they were not guilty. This indictment was thence continued to the present January term, and now the District Attorney, Oliver Stevens, Esquire, says he will prosecute this indictment no further, on payment of costs, which are thereupon paid. And the said Arens and Eddy are thereupon discharged."

One of the witnesses who appeared in the preliminary hearing was George A. Collier, a friend of Sargeant's. After the hearing, Collier wrote a letter to Eddy and Arens deny-ing his testimony, and on December 17, 1878, he made the following sworn statement:

I, George A. Collier, do on oath depose and say of my own free will, and in order to expose the man who has tried to in-jure Dr. Asa G. Eddy and Edward J. Arens, that Sargeant did induce me by great persuasion to go with him to East Cam-bridge from Boston, on or about the 7th day of November last, the day of the hearing in the municipal court of Boston in the case of Dr. Asa G. Eddy and E. J. Arens for attempting to hire said Sargeant to kill one Daniel Spofford, and that he showed me the place and the cars that he was going to swear to, and told me to say in court, and made me repeat the story until I knew it well, so that I could tell the same story that he would, and there was not one word of truth in it all. I never heard a conversation in East Cambridge between said Eddy and Arens and Sargeant, or saw them pay or offer to pay Sargeant any money.

(Signed) GEORGE A. COLLIER

Other affidavits disclosed that Eddy did not know Sargeant, had never seen him until the day of the arrest, and that even had he known Sargeant, he could not have been with him at the time mentioned because he was engaged in teaching elsewhere. The cars mentioned by Collier in his affidavit were the horse cars that operated between Boston and East Cambridge.

The Commonwealth of Massachusetts dismissed the detective who made the arrests; Sargeant and Collier went to jail on other charges, and the Eddys absolved Spofford of plotting against them — but the story remains as haunting today as it was when it happened, seventy-five years ago.

Missing at the time his body was said to be in the Boston morgue, Spofford disclosed he had been frightened by Sargeant and had, at the latter's order, disappeared. The fear was occasioned by the threat of physical punishment. Spofford was insistent in this explanation, and was believed. Who, then, hired Sargeant?

The perpetrator, or perpetrators, of the plot never came forward. Sargeant never gave up his secret.

Meanwhile, the second edition of *Science and Health* was published. This edition, too, was a failure. It was written to be published in two volumes, but Volume I was destroyed because of its many inaccuracies. Only five hundred copies of Volume II were printed, and even in this single volume it was necessary to include a separate page itemizing proof-reading mistakes.

Asa Gilbert Eddy was the publisher. The printer was Rand, Avery and Company, of Boston, and the book sold for two dollars. The cover is green, with a drawing of Noah's Ark imprinted in gold outline on the cover, thus giving this edition its identification as "the Ark edition." On the spine of the book the author's name is given as Glover, while on the title page the name is given in full as *Mary Baker Glover Eddy, 8 Broad Street, Lynn, Massachusetts.* On the flyleaf is this verse:

> I, I, I, I, itself, I
> The inside and outside, the what and the why,
> The when and the where, the low and the high,
> All I, I, I, I, itself, I.[7]

The book contains 167 pages, with an introduction and five chapters carrying these titles: "Imposition and Demon-

---

[7] The "I" Mrs. Eddy referred to is not herself, and not man, but Principle, God. As Erwin D. Canham, editor of the *Christian Science Monitor,* stated in an address at Northwestern University, Evanston, Illinois, in 1949: "One of the great contributions which Mary Baker Eddy made to contemporary thinking was to emphasis the word Principle as a synonym of God. Many other synonyms of God are to be found in the Bible. Among them are Spirit, Mind, Life, Truth and Love. Each tells us something important and useful about God. Thinking of God in terms of this definition — through these synonyms — God ceases to be a misty assumption and becomes a dynamic reality.

"There is law in the universe; the stars in their courses prove it, and so do you when you add two and two together to apply the principle of mathematics. Any man who recognizes that ours is an orderly universe — and who can deny it? — must also recognize God, for God is order, is Mind, is Principle. To know this is the first step in replacing material counterfeits with spiritual values."

stration," "Physiology," "Mesmerism," "Metaphysics," and "Reply to a Clergyman."

In the chapter "Reply to a Clergyman" is the first indication that Mrs. Eddy was thinking in terms of a newspaper, for she wrote: "We have not a newspaper at our command through which to right the wrongs and answer the untruths, we have not a pulpit from which to explain how Christianity heals the sick, but if we had either of these, the slanderer and the physician would have less to do, and we should have more."

In her second edition Mrs. Eddy again rose to the attack, reiterating and expanding her declaration that sin, sickness, and death are false beliefs; and in her Sunday services in Good Templars Hall, in Lynn, her words never strayed from these convictions:

> . . . Truth destroys error even as light destroys darkness. Sin, sickness and death are error; they are beliefs and this fact found out will at length destroy them. Truth evolves life as a result of itself, for Truth is immortal, and the truth of Life would destroy death. But this understanding comes slowly; even to learn that matter has no sensation is quite a task, although this simple proposition is self-evident.
>
> . . . We may talk to you of metaphysics, its divine Principle, rule and application, once every week, but this gives you little insight, into the Life through which we learned metaphysics, and through [which] you must learn it. This weekly service, however, may point the way like a mile-

stone, — that is all. The apostle says, "How shall they hear without a preacher? and how shall they preach except they be sent?" Paul knew that a theoretical drill, and the grinding of scholastic mills, are not the preparation for a moral teacher. He knew that inspiration cometh from Truth, from the Spirit, and not the letter. A child God-driven is more capable of uttering Truth in its sweet simplicity and the power of Love than a merely manufactured theologian; hence the Scripture, "Out of the mouth of babes . . . thou has perfected praise."

. . . We all shall know when Truth is at work in Science, for it will heal our sicknesses and stop our sins. In the exact proportion that we understand it, Truth will heal us mind and body, and in the proportion that we adopt error will it produce sin, sickness and death. . . .[8]

Students were coming to her from different parts of New England, especially from Boston — where, in addition to giving a series of Sunday afternoon sermons in the Shawmut Baptist Church in the summer of 1878, she delivered thirty-two lectures during the months from November 1878 to July 1879, inclusive.

On April 12, 1879, twenty-six members of the Christian Scientist Association met in the home of Mrs. Margaret Dunshee in Charlestown, Massachusetts, to form, as stated

[8] Copyright by the Trustees under the Will of Mary Baker Eddy.

in the *Manual of the Mother Church,* "a church without creeds, to be called the CHURCH OF CHRIST, SCIENTIST." Among the twenty-six were some who were not favorable to this designation but who did agree to accept it temporarily.

One week later, at Mrs. Eddy's suggestion, they voted, as also stated in the *Church Manual,* "to organize a church designed to commemorate the word and works of our Master, which should reinstate primitive Christianity and its lost element of healing." Mrs. Eddy told her listeners that it was a church that should follow, strictly, the teachings of Christ Jesus; and she also specified that the first Sabbath services of the Church would be held in Salem, Massachusetts, on and after the first Sunday in May 1879.

The very center of Mrs. Eddy's thought was the declaration by Jesus that "The kingdom of God is within you." She knew it was this declaration that brought the vast and everlasting revolution of the world. It was a proclamation that placed God in the hearts of men — and not in the Eucharist or in the burning bush; it was a proclamation that made empty any doctrine claiming Him as the possession of a favored people, or group, anywhere.

God, the universal Father!

That was Jesus's teaching; and because it was, Mary Baker Eddy rejected the dogmatism which seizes God and makes Him a private possession as being defenseless before the generosity of "If a man love me, he will keep my words: and my Father will love him, and we will come unto him, and make our abode with him."

She could not find in these words anything about ritual, about creed — she could find only recognition of people, all people, as all one with God.

If a man love me, he will keep my words: and my Father will love him, and . . . make our abode with him.

Knowing God as the Father, Jesus spoke of Him, and to Him, not as to One outside, but as to One inside. Beyond this recognition that He lived in God, and God in Him, Jesus left no theology.

He left no form of worship, prescribed no ritual — not even the ritual of baptism. In the first hundred years of Christianity baptism was explained, and was taught, according to these words: "The Lord leading us out of disorder, illuminates us by bringing us into light, which is shadowless and is material no longer."

The declaration of His oneness with God, Mrs. Eddy believed to be the fundamental of Jesus's teaching. She was aware of all that had been placed between her and what He taught — aware of a theology that, for fifteen centuries, declined His promise of life being eternal with God, and that offered instead a makeshift doctrine dividing life into separate compartments of here and hereafter, and that, to hide the makeshift, created a dying and reviving God.

Mrs. Eddy often wrote on this subject:

> When speaking of God's children, not the children of men, Jesus said, "The kingdom of God is within you"; that is, Truth and Love reign in the real man, showing that man in God's image is unfallen and eternal. Jesus beheld in Science the perfect man, who appeared to him where sinning mortal man appears to mortals. In this perfect man the Saviour saw God's own likeness, and this correct view of man healed the sick. Thus Jesus taught that the kingdom of God is intact, universal, and

that man is pure and holy. Man is not a material habitation for soul; he is himself spiritual. Soul, being Spirit, is seen in nothing imperfect nor material.[9]

Accepting as highest fact Jesus's revolutionary proclamation that *all* men are children of God, Mrs. Eddy was boldly calling upon people, as did He, to forsake their superstitions and claim their heritage.

She saw Jesus as "the most scientific man that ever trod the globe," [10] and declared: "If Christianity is not scientific, and Science is not of God, then there is no invariable law, and truth becomes an accident." [11] These convictions were behind the naming of her Church — Church of Christ (Scientist) . To her, there could be but one correct religion.

Its common element must be in God, and not in matter, or in any combination of what is spiritual and what is material; therefore, if her Church were to challenge everything that misrepresented God, it would have to be divorced from matter and wedded to spiritual law.

These were her arguments in persuading those who opposed the name she believed proper for her Church. At first she was not able to convince them.

On April 26, 1879, a majority of the members voted to reconsider their action of the previous week and, on May 10, which was the Saturday following the first Sunday church services, they substituted "Church of Christ" unless, as was written in the minutes of the meeting, "there be one [a church] already by that name." At this time they disapproved of the word *Scientist* in the designation of a

[9] *Science and Health,* p. 476–477.
[10] *Science and Health,* p. 313.
[11] *Science and Health,* p. 342.

church; but not long afterwards, and without urging from Mrs. Eddy, they met to give her name unanimous approval. In August 1879 a charter was obtained.[12]

Under the charter the By-Laws provided for a pastor, five directors, a clerk, and a treasurer, and stipulated that the pastor of "this church must be strictly moral, and an earnest and devoted follower of Christ's Truth." The By-Laws contained twenty Articles; and the Tenets of the Church, as written by Mrs. Eddy, were:

> First, — As adherents of Truth, we take the Scriptures for our guide to Life.
>
> Second, — We acknowledge one Father, Son and Holy Ghost — one God, the brotherhood of man, and Divine Science. And the forgiveness of sin, which is the destruction of sin. And the atonement of Christ, which is the efficacy of Truth and Love. And the way of salvation marked out by Jesus healing the sick, casting out devils (evils), and raising the dead — uplifting a dead faith into Life and Love.
>
> Third, — We promise to love one another, and to work, watch and pray; to strive against sin, and to keep the Ten Commandments; to deal justly, love mercy, walk humbly; and inasmuch as we are enabled by Truth, to cast out evil, and heal the sick.

Through the next several months Sunday services were held in the homes of students in Boston and Salem, as well

---

[12] Steps were taken to promote the Church of Christ, Scientist, in April, May and June; formal organization was accomplished and the charter obtained in August 1879 (*Church Manual*, p. 19).

as in Lynn. In late 1879 the Eddys took up temporary residence in Boston and began dividing their time between that city and Lynn. It was becoming apparent that Boston, and not Lynn, would soon be headquarters for the movement.

William James had not yet taken it upon himself to state publicly: "The optimistic ideal of duty forbids us to pay it [Christian Science] the compliment even of explicit attention," and to classify it among the "contemporary vagaries." [13] In connection with this estimate it must be kept in mind that James was a victim of two misconceptions. He did not, as did Alcott, trouble himself personally to investigate Mrs. Eddy's teachings, nor did he take into account the caliber of person he was dismissing as unworthy of his attention.

Had he done either of these things, and particularly the latter, he would have recognized, as did Alcott, a superior person who was constantly alert to what was going on in the field of her choosing, and giving it watchful care and attention. James did agree in his lectures there were "therapeutic triumphs" in mental healing, but he made the mistake of classifying Mrs. Eddy as a teacher of "a faith cure."

At no time did Mrs. Eddy teach Christian Science as "a faith cure"; and, later, she wrote:

> Christian Science is not a faith-cure, and unless human faith be distinguished from scientific healing, Christian Science will again be lost from the practice of religion as it was soon after the period of our great Master's scientific teaching and practice. Preaching without practice of the divine

[13] Gifford Lectures on "Natural Religion," delivered in Edinburgh, 1901–1902.

Principle of man's being has not, in nineteen hundred years, resulted in demonstrating this Principle.[14]

In following Jesus's teachings Mary Baker Eddy's great act of originality was in scientific healing and in demonstrating Principle that was unchanging Law. Her devotion was to God, and her concern was that healing should not "again be lost from the practice of religion." In this devotion and concern is found the strength that missed the attention of William James; and the attention of practically all others, including her own students.

In the minutes of her early church meetings are these items:

August 22, 1879: "The records of previous meetings were read, and approved. Then Mrs. Eddy proceeded to instruct those present as to their duties . . . giving some useful hints as to the mode of conducting the church."

January 2, 1880: Special meeting in Mrs. Eddy's home. "The tone of the meeting before Communion Sabbath was rather sorrowful," and then, at the close of the paragraph, "a feeling of trust in the great Father of Love prevailing over the apparently discouraging outlook. . . ."

January 4, 1880: The Church celebrated its first Communion Sunday as a Church, and "it was a very inspiring season to us all." Two new members were added.

In the March 1880 records of the Christian Scientist Association Mrs. Eddy is quoted as speaking at length on treat-

[14] *Christian Science Sentinel,* September 1, 1917, written by Mrs. Eddy in 1910, and copyrighted by The Christian Science Publishing Society. For complete statement see Appendix 3.

ment and speaking strongly against the touching of patients by practitioners while giving Christian Science treatment.[15] Also, at this same meeting, and at the suggestion of Mrs. Eddy, the Association constitution was amended to read: "None shall be admitted to membership who believe in mediums."

The meetings were not as quiet as the minutes indicate. Dissenting students, often led by Arens, made a practice of attending, assailing Mrs. Eddy with personal questions and, as Spofford had done, threatening her with removal.

On June 2, 1880, the Association expelled Arens, and adopted a resolution warning other students. In this meeting, which was held in Lynn, Mrs. Eddy addressed the Association, pleading with the members to eradicate personal differences, jealousies, and ambitions, and calling upon them to reaffirm the high purposes of the Church they had helped to organize. She reminded them that under the authority of the church charter, unless they did stop bickering among themselves, they would not be permitted to secede, or to resign, but would be expelled from the movement. Her firmness quieted an incipient rebellion.

Having preserved her church organization, Mrs. Eddy turned her attention to the need for protecting her teachings, with their "vital purpose, the establishment of *genuine* Christian Science healing." [16]

Searching the laws of Massachusetts she found an Act, passed in 1874, which permitted her to organize a metaphysical college. She applied for a charter and, in January

[15] Prior to this time it was the practice of some students to reach out and touch the patient while giving treatment.

[16] *Retrospection and Introspection,* p. 48.

1881, her request was granted. It was the first such charter in the United States, and the only one of its nature granted in Massachusetts. Under it, she had powers to confer degrees and issue diplomas, thus holding the right to select those whom she considered qualified to teach.

After the granting of permission to "give instructions in scientific methods of Mental Healing on a purely practical basis, and to impart a thorough understanding of the Divine Mind to restore health, hope and harmony to man." [17] three problems presented themselves. The problems were: subjects to teach, how much to charge, what to name the institution.

With Asa Gilbert Eddy, she decided on these courses: pathology, ontology, therapeutics, moral science, and metaphysics, in their application to the treatment of diseases.

As to the fee, Mrs. Eddy told of her struggle in arriving at a proper sum:

> When God impelled me to set a price on my instruction in Christian Science Mind-healing, I could think of no financial equivalent for an impartation of a knowledge of that divine power which heals; but I was led to name three hundred dollars as the price for each pupil in one course of lessons at my College, — a startling sum for tuition lasting barely three weeks. This amount greatly troubled me. I shrank from asking it, but was finally led, by a strange providence, to accept this fee. God has since shown me, in multitudinous ways, the wisdom of this decision; and I beg disinterested people to ask my loyal students if they

[17] Resolutions of Massachusetts Metaphysical College Corporation, October 29, 1889.

consider three hundred dollars any real equivalent
for my instruction during twelve half-days, or even
in half as many lessons.[18]

In March, 1881, students of her first class, operating
under state charter, were taught at 8 Broad Street, Lynn;
in May, 1881, another class walked up the steps of 569 Columbus Avenue, Boston, and passed under a wooden plate
on which were printed the words MASSACHUSETTS META-
PHYSICAL COLLEGE.

[18] *Retrospection and Introspection,* p. 50. (As with previous classes, Mrs.
Eddy admitted many free students.)

CHAPTER FIVE

Pursuing a Lie with Eagerness

IN A TIME when creeds were still pursuing the ancient practice of taking inventory of God's perfections and im-
perfections, it was certain Mrs. Eddy would have trouble
with her students. All were brought up in these creeds. Few,
very few, wholly accepted her teaching that God is perfect,
unchanging.

They had been taught to worship God; she was requiring
that they establish *worthship* with Him. They were brought
up to think of God as a personage — supreme and omniscient, to be sure, but nevertheless a person listening to argument and distributing His blessings accordingly; she was
teaching that God is impersonal — teaching it is progression
into the sphere of the Infinite that annuls evil, and makes
the individual aware that he does not need to ask for blessings, which are already his.

Throughout childhood and their mature years Mrs.
Eddy's students had been taught to fear God as a punitive
judge sentencing a sinful people (thus making Him as imperfect as human beings) ; they did not see Him as the disciple James did:

> Let no man say when he is tempted, I am
> tempted of God: for God cannot be tempted with
> evil, neither tempteth he any man.
> . . . Every good gift and every perfect gift is
> from above, and cometh down from the Father of

lights, with whom is no variableness, neither shadow of turning.

Mrs. Eddy was as impersonal in her teaching as the law she sought to explain, and as strict. Her concern was to keep her teachings from being diluted, and her effort was to persuade her students to depend on the teachings and not on *any* personality, including her own. It was not long before, among themselves, students were accusing her of being ill-tempered, austere, and dominating.

On October 21, 1881, eight students withdrew their support, and signed their names:

We, the undersigned, while we acknowledge and appreciate the understanding of Truth imparted to us by our teacher, Mrs. Mary B. G. Eddy, led by Divine Intelligence to perceive with sorrow that departure from the straight and narrow road which alone leads to growth in Christlike virtues, which departure is made manifest by frequent ebullitions of temper, love of money, and the appearance of hypocrisy, cannot longer submit to such leadership. Therefore, without aught of hatred, revenge, or petty spite in our hearts, from a sense of duty alone, to her, the cause, and ourselves, do most respectfully withdraw our names from the Christian Science Association and Church of Christ, Scientist.

S. Louise Durant	Jane L. Straw
Margaret J. Dunshee	Anne B. Newman
Dorcas B. Rawson	James C. Howard
Elizabeth G. Stuart	Miranda R. Rice

Disclosure of this action caused dismay within the Association, and caught Mrs. Eddy by surprise. She called a meeting and, on October 31, addressed the Association, beseeching the members to erase from their minds any thoughts of material personality and to hold to the thought that she was seeking only "to expound divine Principle, and not to exalt personality." [1] The Association expelled Howard, Rice, Rawson, and Stuart but withheld action on Durant, Dunshee, Straw, and Newman.

In this same meeting Mrs. Eddy spoke of her anxiety over what several disaffected students were teaching as Christian Science, as well as of the theft of her writings, and told the members of the Association she was closing her home in Lynn and, with her husband, planning to spend the next several months in Washington for the principal purpose of studying laws as affecting copyrights.

On November 16,[2] the Association received a letter from Mrs. Eddy in which she expressed a desire to withdraw her membership. The request was granted, after which the following resolutions were drafted and approved:

1. Resolved, that we the members of the Christian Science Association, do herein express to our beloved teacher and acknowledged leader, Mary Baker Glover Eddy, our sincere and heartfelt thanks and gratitude for her earnest labor in behalf of this Association, by her watchfulness of its interests and persistent efforts to maintain the highest rule of Christian love among its members.

2. Resolved, that while she has had little or no help, except from God, in the introduction to this material age of her book *Science and Health*, and in carrying forward the Christian principles it

[1] *Science and Health*, p. 464.
[2] Accompanied by her husband, Mrs. Eddy went to Washington in February, 1882. It was the inconvenience of traveling back and forth between Boston and Washington that caused her to withdraw her membership.

teaches and explains, she has been unremitting in her faithfulness to her God-appointed work, and we understand her to be the chosen messenger to bear His truth to the nations, and that unless we hear "her voice" we do not hear "His voice."

3. Resolved, that while many and continued attempts are made by the malpractice referred to in *Science and Health* to hinder and stop the advance of Christian Science, it has with her leadership attained a success that calls for the truest gratitude of her students.

4. Resolved, that the charges made against her in a letter signed by J. C. Howard, M. R. Rice and six others, of hypocrisy, ebullitions of temper and love of money, are utterly false, and that the cowardice of the signers in refusing to meet her and sustain or explain such charges be treated with the righteous indignation that it justly deserves. That while we deplore such wickedness and abuse of her who has befriended them in their need, and when wronged met them with honest, open rebuke, we look with admiration and reverence upon her Christlike example of meekness and charity and will, in future, more faithfully follow and obey her divine instructions, knowing that in so doing we offer her the highest testimonial of our appreciation of her Christian leadership.

5. Resolved, that a copy of these resolutions be presented to our teacher and leader, Mary B. Glover Eddy, and a copy be placed on the records of this Christian Science Association.

* * *

In the third edition of *Science and Health,* which was published in 1881, attention was given to the distortions of Mrs. Eddy's teachings, and to the theft of her writings.

Preceding the "Preface," which was written by Mrs. Eddy, are several pages addressed "To The Public," written and signed by Dr. Asa G. Eddy. In these pages, Eddy dwells on the subject of plagiarism and, after presenting a number of illustrations, caustically concludes that "copyrighting books is a farce," but observes, "this (plagiarism) may be convenient for an ignoramus or a villian but a real expounder of 'The Understanding of Christianity or God' would scarcely be caught at it."

Following Eddy's protest is another protest, also addressed "To The Public," and signed by thirty-one students:

The undersigned, in justice to ourselves, hereby publicly state that we believe the abuses denominated mesmerism and malpractice are carried on by some claiming to be metaphysicians; but while our knowledge of metaphysics enables us to defend ourselves and others from their attacks, we are by no means committing their crimes, for our power lies not in mesmerism, but Truth; it is not animal magnetism, but moral and spiritual strength.

And we are fully convinced that no one can reach the height in metaphysics that our teacher, the author of "Science and Health," has reached, and progress as she is progressing, and be a moral or mental malpractitioner.

If the malpractitioner is causing others to believe that we are venturing on his forbidden ground, it is only to screen himself, and to hide the results of his wrong-doing, that take away his ability to heal.

It ought to suffice duplicity, envy, and malice, that Mrs. Eddy has not stopped the plagiarists hitherto from appropriating the results of her labors, and gaining the little they have of the public confidence, through claiming her practice, and publishing her writings under their own signature.

The third edition, in two volumes as was the second, contains 484 pages — 270 pages in the first volume, and 214 pages in the second — and is between purple bindings with the author's name, Mrs. Glover Eddy, on the spine of each book, while inside she is identified as Mary B. Glover Eddy, 8 Broad Street, Lynn, Massachusetts. Dr. Asa G. Eddy is named as publisher.

On the flyleaf are the words "God is Love," the Shakespearean quotation "There is nothing either good or bad, but thinking makes it so," and the verse pertaining to Principle which first appeared in the second edition.

The printers were the University Press, John Wilson & Son, Cambridge, Massachusetts. Unlike the previous printings, this edition was immediately successful.

In many ways, this third edition is one of the most important of all the printings of *Science and Health*. The present book, which has been in use since 1910, began to take shape in the third edition. In this edition and in their consecutive chapter headings, the subjects are:

"Science of Being," "Footsteps of Truth," "Physiology," "Recapitulation," "Healing the Sick," "Demonology," "Imposition and Demonstration," "Creation," "Marriage," "Prayer and Atonement," "Platform of Christian Scientists," and "Reply to a Clergyman."

For the first time, and this is of great importance to Christian Scientists, appear the Cross and the Crown which identify, and will continue to identify — and protect — Mrs. Eddy's writings when copyrights are able to guard them no longer.[3] Symbolically, the following passage gives the meaning of the Cross and the Crown, in its first use and as explained by Ira Oscar Knapp:

[3] Some copyrights have run out, and all expire in 1963.

I think our cross is giving up all for God; putting resolutely aside these things that keep us from, or hinder our growth in Truth. All the petty cares and vexations that come to us each day must be nailed to the cross. Jesus tells us if we take up our cross and follow him, we are indeed his disciples; that is, we must take up this great claim of a "mind of our own," bear it patiently, and be constantly overcoming it by the power of Truth. The material crown, being a symbol of the highest earthly honor, is typical of what we may win — perfect spiritual rest and peace — by giving up all for Truth.[4]

The Cross and the Crown, with the Crown circling the Cross but with the Crown free, are imprinted in gold in the inner of two circles on the cover of the third edition. The background of the inner circle is gold, while within the first circle, as now, are the familiar words: "Heal the sick, raise the dead, cleanse the leper, cast out devils."

Also, in the third edition, there appears for the first time, and in its original form, the "Scientific Statement of Being," so well known to Christian Scientists:

There is no Life, substance, or intelligence in matter; all is Mind. There is no matter. Spirit is immortal Truth; matter is mortal error. Spirit is the real and eternal, matter is the unreal and temporal. Spirit is God, and man is His image and likeness; hence, man is spiritual and not material.

In its final form, the "Scientific Statement of Being" reads:

[4] *Christian Science Journal*, Vol. VIII, p. 497.

There is no life, truth, intelligence, nor substance in matter. All is infinite Mind and its infinite manifestation, for God is All-in-all. Spirit is
immortal Truth; matter is mortal error. Spirit is
the real and eternal; matter is the unreal and temporal. Spirit is God, and man is His image and likeness. Therefore, man is not material; he is spiritual.[5]

In the third edition, in the footnote to her "Preface,"
Mrs. Eddy announced: "The author takes no patients, but
takes students in the treatment of disease through mind."

Her reason for making this announcement was because
many were drawn to her by the healings, instead of coming
to learn, as she hoped they would, that Christian Science is
all, and not a part of Christianity — with healing being, as
she taught, the manifestation of the Christ-consciousness
which encompasses itself in all that is real.

Markedly, there is clarification in the presentation of her
teachings in the third over the first or second edition. The
distinctive character of her writing is more in evidence, with
its emphasis on the poetry of life and its preoccupation with
the need for greater understanding, and greater liberty, and
more love. More and more she was presenting in absolute
terms the consistency of healing as a part of Christianity.

And with this third edition began a publishing arrangement that has continued through many years.

Discouraged by the poor proofreading in the second edition, Asa Eddy went to John Wilson, of the University
Press, for advice. The company was a lineal descendant of
the Stephen Daye Press which, as the first printing firm in

[5] *Science and Health*, p. 468.

the American Colonies, brought out the *Bay Psalm Book* in 1640 and the first Eliot Indian Bible in 1663, as well as being, in later years, the establishment which printed the works of Whittier, Emerson, Longfellow, Hawthorne, Holmes, Lowell, and others.

Wishing to help, Wilson went over the second edition, estimated that approximately one hundred and seven pages could be rescued, and on April 3, 1880, wrote to Eddy:

"Before giving you an estimate we would like to know exactly what is required. How many *new* pages are to be set up; how many pages are already set up and stereotyped; what quality of paper do you wish, — paper having advanced in price. . . . Science and Health makes now, we think, some 130 pages. If so, your intention is, if we understand your note, to add some 270 pages to this book. . . . When you let us know, we shall be most happy to give you [our] figures. We should require one-half of the amount before commencing the work."

After recalling this incident in *Mary Baker Eddy and Her Books*,[6] William Dana Orcutt, who succeeded Wilson as the directing head of the University Press, wrote: "Nothing came of this correspondence, undoubtedly because Mrs. Eddy was unable to advance one-half the cost of the proposed new edition. At all events, she evidently decided to present the case in person, and this explained her presence at the University Press that January afternoon in 1881. . . ."

After spending much of the afternoon going over the problem, Mrs. Eddy and Wilson reached a point where "it was necessary" — as Orcutt also wrote — "for Mrs. Eddy to explain the financial plight in which she found herself, which was worse, even, than when her husband wrote. . . ."

[6] Copyright, 1950, The Christian Science Publishing Society.

"Mrs. Eddy admitted frankly that while she could pay perhaps a few hundred dollars, on account, she could not possibly advance half the cost, as Mr. Wilson had insisted in his letter to her husband.

"Her only income was from her teaching and from the tenants to whom she rented a part of her house at 8 Broad Street, in Lynn, Massachusetts. If this third edition were produced as she believed Mr. Wilson would produce it, she was confident she could sell enough copies to meet the cost but she could not pay in full on delivery.

"Mr. Wilson never explained, even to himself, his reaction to Mrs. Eddy's appeal. From a business standpoint there was every reason to decline the whole proposition. 'Yet,' he would say, after frankly admitting the situation, 'there wasn't a moment's hesitation in my acceptance of that order. I *knew* that the bill would be paid, and I found myself actually eager to undertake the manufacture.'

"He inquired when the manuscript would be ready. Mrs. Eddy reached into her handbag and produced it, completely finished, ready for the printer.

"'You brought this on the chance of my accepting it?' John Wilson asked, surprised.

"Mrs. Eddy smiled. 'No,' she replied. 'Not on a chance. I never doubted.'"

It should be explained, however, that while Mrs. Eddy had ceased taking patients, she did continue to demonstrate healing. In *Twelve Years with Mary Baker Eddy* Irving C. Tomlinson told of a number of healings:

On a certain occasion, Mrs. Eddy, accompanied by a student, went to a furniture store to select some chairs, where they were waited on by a man who was wearing a bandage over one eye. As they were being shown the chairs, Mrs. Eddy became so absorbed that she paid little attention to them, replying to a question with the words, "Any that we can sit on."

Later when the student reproached Mrs. Eddy with her lack of attention to the business in hand, she replied, "Could I think of chairs when the man was suffering?"

When the student returned next day to order the chairs, the salesman asked: "Who was that lady with you yesterday? I had an abscess on my eye and when she went out, I took the bandage off, and there was not a sign of it."

Tomlinson recalled the healing of a clergyman when the Eddys were exploring copyright laws in Washington. With her husband, Mrs. Eddy attended services at a church formerly attended by President Garfield and, as she related to Tomlinson, they were introduced to the clergyman "who spent the afternoon listening to our explanation of the Bible and Christian Science. . . ."

"He asked the privilege of remaining to the six o'clock dinner, explaining he enjoyed the sociability of the occasion although he could not partake of the repast, saying that for years he had been troubled with a stomach difficulty the physicians declared had developed into cancer of the stomach. He avoided all hearty food and confined himself exclusively to a fluid diet.

"All this he told us while we were preparing to go to the dining room. I said to him briefly, that this was an excellent opportunity to put to a test our talk of the afternoon. He replied by saying he hardly could consent to test the doctrine for the sake of killing himself. However, I voiced the truth and asserted his ability to eat in comfort.

"He went with us to the table and soon forgot himself and his false fears and partook heartily of the salad, meat and pastry. At the conclusion of the dinner he said, 'What have I done? Will I ever survive?'

"We assured him there was no danger. He felt no harm and never again was troubled."

Tomlinson explained these healings, and others, by quoting from one of Mrs. Eddy's letters to a student:

> May the light of Divine Love so illumine your mind that you behold yourself in His likeness, even as you are, — the image of perfect Mind. Thus you will find all power, wisdom, and peace in goodness, and demonstrate the grace of Spirit as ever sufficient to help you in every time of need.[7]

After their stay in Washington, the Eddys took up residence at 569 Columbus Avenue, Boston, where Mrs. Eddy devoted herself to teaching in her college, lecturing on Thursday evenings, and to preaching on Sunday afternoons, while her husband assisted in the management of her affairs.

This arrangement continued until June 3, 1882, when, after a brief illness, Asa Gilbert Eddy died. His death left a great vacancy in the movement. From the moment of his healing, he had been content to serve as a worker in the cause. An unassuming man, he acknowledged his wife as his Leader and sought only to protect her and relieve her of detail that she might have more time for her studies, her writing, and her teaching.

His passing gave her the immediate problem of reorganizing her work, and the personal problem of rising from the depths of her own grief.

On June 21, Mrs. Eddy called a meeting of the Association and requested the return of her name to the records.

[7] Copyright, 1936. Trustees under the Will of Mary Baker Eddy.

This was done, and with it the formality of electing her President. In this meeting it was proposed, as a protective measure, that an oath be required of those seeking church membership. Mrs. Eddy objected, saying she did not consider such a proposal as being "good government."

After the proposal was defeated, Mrs. Eddy advised that the proper way to bring the Church, Association, and college closer together was by having a publication; and she declared her intention of having it: "If I have to give up other work, I will have a paper."

She told the members of her plan to close her college for the summer, and to spend this time in Barton, Vermont. Before leaving she delegated the responsibilities of her household to Miss Julia Bartlett and Mrs. Abbie Whiting. In Barton, she spent the summer planning the reopening of the Massachusetts Metaphysical College, the organization of her household along co-operative lines, and the founding of a publication she decided to call the *Journal of Christian Science*.[8]

In the early autumn Mrs. Eddy returned to Boston, bringing with her Calvin A. Frye. A member of one of her classes in Lynn in 1881, Frye was practicing in Lawrence, Massachusetts, when he received a telegram asking him to meet a train at Plymouth, N. H., and ride with Mrs. Eddy to Boston. On the way she questioned him as to his willingness to live in her household and his ability to assume responsibility: and thus did Calvin A. Frye become the co-ordinator of much of her household, and much of her work.[9]

*   *   *

[8] Now the *Christian Science Journal*.

[9] Several months before his passing, Asa Gilbert Eddy recommended the employment of Frye "if a reliable person is ever needed."

It was upon her return from Vermont that Mary Baker Eddy made one of her many important decisions.

In Lynn and other Massachusetts communities nearly all Christian Scientists were factory workers and their wives, or farmers and their wives; in Boston Mrs. Eddy's teachings gained a following among the fashionable of society. In the spring of 1882 she was "presented" at such a gathering brought together by one of her students, and she later informed her followers that Christian Science could not go forward by such methods.

But the same group of students continued to importune, and urged upon her the advantages of furnishing her home with "carpets the feet would sink into, draperies of rich lace and velvet, and paintings." [10] To their chagrin, she put oil-cloth on the floor of the classroom, furnished the room with straight-backed chairs, and, in one corner of the room, on a slightly raised platform, installed for herself a small, plain table and a chair, straight-backed like the others.

Her choice of simple surroundings was important because in the early years of Christianity many Christians fell into the trap of social ambition and, falling, lost their power to heal. Now, eighteen centuries later, temptation was repeating itself. The proposal was dismissed immediately and, in the dismissal, the movement gained and the Church went forward.

Out of the many recollections of her students emerges a clear picture of how Mrs. Eddy managed her household and taught in her college. She was orderly about everything,

[10] *The Life of Mary Baker Eddy*, by Sibyl Wilbur; copyright, 1907–1929, The Christian Science Publishing Society.

permitted no procrastination, was plain in her tastes, did the work that required her personal attention, and kept her household busy executing the duties laid out for it. She took constant note of the thinking of her pupils and was sensitive to mental disturbances of any nature, detecting them at once.

One day she sent for a procrastinating student and asked him if he was clearing a particular problem from his mind.

"I am trying to do it," he answered.

She repeated her question.

Again he attempted to explain, but she stopped him. "I asked you if you were doing what I gave you to do. You replied, 'I am trying to do it.' Now you are either doing a thing, or you are not doing it. Were you doing it?"

"No, I was not."

"When are you going to do it?"

"Now."

"Let me see you do it now."

The student returned to his room and wasted no time, as he recalled, "doing the mental work required." As he completed it, his bell rang and again he went to Mrs. Eddy's study. She was smiling. She made no reference to the conversation of a few minutes previously, and assigned him to the task she had for him.

Slight, of medium height, erect, and with a light, quick step, Mrs. Eddy in her method of teaching gave enlightenment and not dictation. At the opening of each class there always were those whom she had not met. One by one she called their names, asking them to stand, and gave to each the fullest attention of her deep-set, gray-blue eyes. Whatever the subject, her talk was spontaneous, her choice of words arresting, her speech incisive, and whether explaining the Decalogue or the Sermon on the Mount she always returned to her fundamental theme, divine love.

One day a pupil inquired, "Do you mean love of person?" Her reply was prompt. "No. I mean love of God."

"But how shall I know whether love is personal, or impersonal?"

"When your love requires an object to call it forth, you will know it is personal; when it flows freely to all, you will know it is impersonal."

Here, again, she disagreed with popular theology.

Accustomed to hear and to believe that faith was the greatest virtue of a Christian, new students were startled to hear her say such teaching, and such believing, was wrong. Faith was not the greatest virtue of a Christian. Love was, and without hesitation she always led her students to the Authority:

"A new commandment I give unto you, That ye love one another; as I have loved you, that ye also love one another." He gave emphasis to what He was saying by directing, "By this shall all men know that ye are my disciples, if ye have love one to another."

Mrs. Eddy was in full agreement with Henry Drummond's thought that "It [love] is the rule for fulfilling all rules, the new commandment for keeping the old commandments, Christ's one secret of a Christian life"; and in her teachings, Love is interpreted as the law of Spirit — Law, and its consummation.

Often, in classes, she illustrated her points with stories, intentionally selecting amusing incidents because, as she said, "I always like to hear my students laugh," explaining that laughter often broke the mesmerism of personality and brought pupils closer to Truth. Invariably, there was a period when students were closely questioned. She accepted no answers that were memory tests of her writings. She wanted what she had written understood and she detected, quickly, the degree of a student's understanding. According to the need, she explained.

In one class she called for an explanation of the Trinity. The answers did not satisfy her. She gave her own explanation and, a short time afterwards, did an unusual thing. She sent to each student a copy of her explanation:

THE TRINITY

FATHER, is man's divine Principle, Love.

SON, is God's man — His image, or spiritual idea.

HOLY GHOST, is Divine Science, the Messiah or Comforter.

Jesus in the flesh was the prophet or wayshower to Life, Truth, Love, and out of the flesh Jesus was the Christ, the spiritual idea or image and likeness of God.

MARY BAKER EDDY

The first issue of the *Christian Science Journal* was published on April 14, 1883.

Complete in eight pages of three columns each, its stated purpose was to be "an independent Family paper to promote Health and Morals," under the motto: "For the weapons of our warfare are not carnal, but mighty through God, to the pulling down of strongholds." [11] On page three, under

[11] 2 Corinthians x. IV, v. This message of Paul's remains the motto of the *Christian Science Journal*.

the heading, "A Timely Issue," Mrs. Eddy declared: "**An organ from the Christian Scientists has become a necessity** [because] after looking over the newspapers of today, very naturally comes the reflection that it is dangerous to live, so loaded seems the very air with disease. These descriptions carry fears to many minds, to be depicted in some future time on the body. This error we shall be able in great measure to counteract, for at the price we issue our paper we shall be able to reach many homes. . . ."

The subscription price was one dollar yearly, single copies were seventeen cents, and the publication was listed as a bimonthly, with the date of issue being "the first Saturday of each alternate month." Advertisements were solicited at the following rates: "One square, first time, $1; subsequently, each time, 25¢; one square, yearly basis, $2; reading notices, per line, 15¢." Each square was one column wide, and slightly less than one inch in depth. The advertising was confined to the professional cards of the Massachusetts Metaphysical College, and those of a dozen practitioners with offices in Boston, Lawrence, Lowell, Manchester, East Cambridge, and West Medford.

The effort was modest in prose and verse, the subject matter being in keeping with the purpose of counteracting the emphasis on disease which then, as now, found prominence in the editorial and advertising columns of the press. On page six, after more or less general comments on the subject of "Slander," Mrs. Eddy closed her remarks by saying: ". . . But heaven defend us from the spurious imitation (virtuous people) such as make a parade of vanities to be seen of men, going about doing good — and evil, too — and with pious accent and devotion's visage get through lying about a friend in time to say their prayers."

It can be suspected that Mrs. Eddy's sharp words were intended, particularly, for the eyes of former students, especially Arens, who were using her writings as their own. The time had come, she was satisfied, when this thievery had to be stopped.

In May 1883, she brought suit to restrain Arens; and on September 24, 1883, a decision was rendered:

CIRCUIT COURT OF THE UNITED STATES
DISTRICT OF MASSACHUSETTS

DECREE FOR PERPETUAL INJUNCTION:

Sept. 24, 1883: It is ordered, adjudged and decreed as follows; That the copyright heretofore obtained for the complainant under the name of Mary Baker Glover upon the book entitled "The Science of Man," etc., and the copyright upon the book "Science and Health," Vol. 2, by Mary Baker Glover Eddy, whereby there was secured good and valid copyrights, that the said complainant had infringed the said copyrights and upon the exclusive rights of the defendant under the same, by publication, sale and distribution of the works "The Understanding of God, etc.," by E. J. Arens.

And it is further ordered, adjudged and decreed that a perpetual injunction be issued against the defendant according to the prayer of the bill.

And it is further ordered, etc., that the complainant recover cost of suit taxed at ($113.09) one hundred, thirteen dollars and 9–100 cents.

BY THE COURT
ALEX H. TROWBRIDGE,
Deputy Clerk.

Following this decision, an injunction was served upon Arens:

UNITED STATES OF AMERICA

Massachusetts District, *ss:*

THE PRESIDENT OF THE UNITED STATES OF AMERICA

to

EDWARD J. ARENS, OF BOSTON, IN THE
STATE OF MASSACHUSETTS

YOUR AGENTS AND SERVANTS SEND
GREETING

Whereas

Mary B. G. Eddy, of said Boston, has exhibited her Bill of Complaint before the Justices of our Circuit Court of the United States for the First District, begun and holden in Boston, within and for the District of Massachusetts, on the Fifteenth Day of May, A.D., 1883, against you, the said

EDWARD J. ARENS

praying to be relieved touching the matter herein complained of; and whereas, by an order from the said Court, made on the Twenty-fourth day of September, A.D., 1883, it was ordered that a Writ of Injunction issue, under the seal of said Court, to restrain you, and each and every one of you, from doing all the matters and things, from the doing of which you are prayed to be restrained in said Bill, according in full with the prayer of said Bill.

We, therefore, in consideration thereof, enjoin and command you, each and every one of you, that from, and immediately after the receipt and notice of this, one Writ, by you, or any of you, you shall not, directly or indirectly print, publish, sell, give away, distribute, or in any way of manner dispose of a certain work or book entitled "The Understanding of Christianity or God, etc"., by E. J. Arens; or a certain work, or book, entitled "Christianity, or the Understanding of God, etc"., by E. J. Arens, which said books are copies from, and infringements of the copyrighted works of the complainant, as set forth in the Bill of Complaint in this case.

Whereof you are not to fail, on pain of ten thousand dollars to be levied on you and each of your goods, chattels, lands and tenements, to our use.

Witness:

The Honorable Morrison R. Watts, at Boston, this twenty-seventh day of September, in the year of our Lord, one thousand eight hundred and eighty three.

ALEX H. TROWBRIDGE,
Deputy Clerk.

UNITED STATES OF AMERICA

Massachusetts District, *ss:*

Boston, October 4, 1883.

I hereby acknowledge personal service of the within injunction.

EDWARD J. ARENS

This was the only lawsuit Mrs. Eddy ever instigated, and the perpetual injunction granted her by the Federal Court should be sufficient answer to the oftrepeated charge that Phineas P. Quimby was the author of *Science and Health,* as Arens claimed, although, when asked to testify in support of his charge, he refused to support his claim.

Quimby was already dead. He never made such a claim. But, with Arens restrained, others picked up the lie and pursued it with such eagerness that they duped even Samuel L. Clemens. The purpose of the lie was to separate Mary Baker Eddy and her writings — and thus destroy her.

In this decision to take into court and establish, in perpetuity, her authorship of *Science and Health,* Mrs. Eddy made what, possibly, was her most important decision. That she did not want to resort to legal measures is evident by her forgiveness of piracy of her writings over more than a dozen years. But, having taken the position — "In the year 1866, I discovered the Christ Science or divine laws of Life, Truth, and Love, and named my discovery Christian Science," [12] — she had to maintain that position, and take the consequences.

Note that sentence:

"In the year 1866, I discovered the Christ Science or divine laws of Life, Truth, and Love, and named my discovery Christian Science."

It is clear she considered her leadership inseparable from her authority as Discoverer, as Founder, and as Revelator. It is plain she expected her followers to acknowledge her as their Leader. It is manifest she expected them to be alert to her leadership — as it is apparent she knew there would be others after Arens who by theft, by trick, by subterfuge, or by flattery would deny her authority; or, if not openly saying it, would seek to interpret what she taught to suit themselves for the purpose of driving her teachings from the face of the earth.

By taking her stand as Discoverer and Founder of Christian Science, and declaring herself as its Leader, Mary Baker Eddy promulgated the rule that prevents the plundering of her Church.

[12] *Science and Health*, p. 107.

CHAPTER SIX

She Held Her Ground by Advancing

TWO HUNDRED YEARS before, in New England, Mary Baker Eddy probably would have been burned at the stake, or hanged; and, likely enough, her executioners would have said: "Is it not better that one should die than a people be led astray?"

No Protestant was more devout than Increase Mather, yet he voiced no protest over the hanging of Anne Hibbens; no Roman Catholic was more devout than Philip of Spain, but he was tormented on his deathbed, wondering if the reverses that had come to him were not sent by God because he had not burned enough heretics; no Jew was more devout than Annas, the high priest who demanded the crucifixion, but was not he the keeper of the law?

Every misrepresentation and libel her enemies could invent were used against this woman whose only offense was trying to help humanity.

Her enemies, and they were many, were weary of her words; her very name was an offense to them — offended them so much that there were those who accused her, and not always by innuendo, of being a landlady who took in boarders not only to help her in prostituting Bible teachings, but to indulge in prostitution itself.

Practitioners' signs were torn away or defaced under cover

of night, and darkness concealed the chalking of obscene scrawlings on the homes of Christian Scientists, or on sidewalks in front of their homes. Often, practitioners refrained from calling on the sick until after nightfall and, to further protect their patients from neighborhood hostility, went down side streets and entered the homes of the sick through back doors.

The attacks were in keeping with sectarian strife which, in the name of God, has committed every foul and ugly deed that could be committed to disfigure humanity. In Spain, the Holy Inquisition; in the United States and in Europe, the fires and scaffolds of witchcraft; in Jerusalem, the nails, the hammer, and the cross.

Bigotry, hate, cruelty, fanaticism, revenge, a thousand and more wars, treachery, starvation, mutilation, assassination — all in sectarian observance of the teaching, "This is my commandment, That ye love one another, as I have loved you."

Whatever might have been Mrs. Eddy's hope ten years previously, she entertained no thought, now that she was living in Boston, that her teachings would be adopted by other Christian Churches. In the Massachusetts Metaphysical College Mrs. Eddy interpreted the Bible to the exclusion of Spinoza or Kant; she neither disputed about God nor gave attention to ways for formalizing Him.

For this approach to religion theologians called her an ignorant woman; and, of course, she did lack the scholastic traditionalism which, as Ernest Renan said, "draws a profound distinction, in respect to personal worth, between those who have received and those who have been deprived of it."

This is not to say she was unlettered. In her bookcase, and

well thumbed, were writings of Berkeley, Browning, Byron, Drummond, Dickens, Milton, Shakespeare, Ruskin, Tolstoy, Pope, Plato (Jowett's translation), Carlyle, and others; she was on good terms with Longfellow, Whittier, Tennyson, Burns, and Keats, but Boehme, Nietzsche, Seneca, Schopenhauer, and Montesquieu were strangers. Matthew, Mark, John, Paul, Isaiah, Daniel, David, Micah, and all the writers of the Old and New Testaments were friends. She knew them best; and she knew them well.

It was this homemade education, with its lack of traditionalism, that removed her from the vagaries of pedantry and gave her teachings the originality that distinguishes them. The study of God was all she thought worthy of effort, and in that view she was not far from the ancient rabbi who, when asked for the proper time to teach Greek, replied: "At the time when it is neither day nor night; since it is written in the Law, Thou shalt study it day and night."

Hers was a high affirmation of God, and to evaluate her teachings it is necessary to remember that the One she followed permitted no theological doubts to impede His words; it is necessary also to put aside familiarity with ritualism, and important to be aware of the deep-rooted lack of religion in the nineteenth century, or, for that matter, in the twentieth century. With the new belief in physics and with modern skepticism demanding that God show Himself in person, humanity was accepting, more and more, the despotism in material law.

But, as humanity freed itself from tyranny in religion by separating Church and State, so Mrs. Eddy believed the time would come when humanity would free itself from the tyranny of materialism.

She was aware that centuries were needed for humanity to

accustom itself to the thought of defying the rack of the
Church and the sword of the State, but she hoped other
centuries would not be needed for humanity to accustom
itself to the thought that it does not need to be afraid of
sickness, disease, and death.

To her, the teachings of Jesus were the free spirit of religion, and because they were free they were limitless. They
meant, she believed, that humanity does not have to ask in
vain for freedom from tyranny of any kind. They meant,
she was sure, it was the birthright of all to occupy, without
molestation, the kingdom of God.

Counseling His disciples against possessions other than
spiritual, Jesus said:

"For all these things do the nations of the world seek after;
and your Father knoweth that ye have need of these things.
But rather seek ye the kingdom of God; and all these things
shall be added unto you."

Mary Baker Eddy accepted those words.

In his *Life of Jesus*, Ernest Renan brought out that "this
name of 'kingdom of God' was a favorite term of Jesus to
express the revolution which he brought into the world.
. . . 'The kingdom of God is within you,' said he to those
who sought with subtlety for external signs. . . . Jesus did
not speak against Mosaic law, but it is clear that he saw its
insufficiency, and allowed it to be seen that he did. He repeated unceasingly that more must be done than the ancient
sages had commanded."

Continuing, Renan wrote that what Jesus taught was "a
pure worship, a religion without priests and external observances, resting entirely on the feelings of the heart, on
the imitation of God, on the direct relation of the conscience

with the heavenly Father. Jesus never shrank from this bold conclusion, which made him a thorough revolutionist in the very center of Judaism. Why should there be mediators between man and his Father? As God sees only the heart, of what good are these purifications, these observances relating only to the body?"

As Renan enraged the clergy by saying what he did, so did Mrs. Eddy live in the midst of calumny for accepting the full meaning of Jesus's words — for believing, and teaching, and writing:

> . . . Man is tributary to God, Spirit, and to nothing else. God's being is infinity, freedom, harmony, and boundless bliss. "Where the Spirit of the Lord is, there is liberty." [1]

And as Jesus was "a thorough revolutionist in the very center of Judaism," so was Mary Baker Eddy a thorough revolutionist in the midst of the ecclesiasticism that had long been impatient with the Man of Galilee.

It was her conviction that Christian Science was the instrument that would rid humanity of its fears, but only if it remained a religion based wholly on spiritual growth and understanding. As she wrote to a student: "*Demonstration* is the whole of Christian Science, nothing else proves it, nothing else will save it, and continue it with us." [2]

Aware of the resistance to her teachings, she watched and made sure there was no deviation from them. She believed Truth was being revealed to her, and to those among her students who had students of their own, she said: "*Truth alone* must be taught, if in small amounts that is of not so

---

[1] *Science and Health*, p. 481.
[2] Copyright 1936, Trustees under the Will of Mary Baker Eddy.

much importance because if your students come to me, I can give them the fullness. But if a student is taught wrong then I have to go all over it and it takes them *much longer* to get it right." [3]

That was her purpose in organizing the Massachusetts Metaphysical College — to make sure, in so far as she was able to make sure, that what she taught was understood in a manner that permitted students to be teachers.

In teaching, as Tomlinson wrote in his book, Mrs. Eddy would open the Bible, would read and explain:

> "Say not ye, There are yet four months, and then cometh harvest? behold, I say unto you, Lift up your eyes, and look on the fields; for they are white already to harvest.
>
> "And he that reapeth receiveth wages, and gathereth fruit unto life eternal; that both he that soweth and he that reapeth may rejoice together."
>
> " 'Say not ye, There are yet four months, and then cometh harvest? behold, I say unto you, Lift up your eyes, and look on the fields; for they are white already to harvest.' Observe that harvest is already here if we will but see it. It is but our blindness that delays the reaping. See this, and 'look on the fields; for they are white already to harvest.'
>
> "If you have a case that seems protracted, lift up your eyes and realize the eternal presence of peace and harmony. Know that the harvest time of health and life is even now with you. Then 'he that reapeth receiveth wages, and gathereth fruit unto

[3] From original letter in Archives of The Mother Church.

life eternal.' The fruit you gather is not for the moment, it is for eternity. And furthermore, these blessings are ours now, 'that both he that soweth and he that reapeth may rejoice together.'

" 'Judge not according to the appearance, but judge righteous judgment.

" 'Then said some of them of Jerusalem, Is this not he, whom they seek to kill?

" 'But, lo, he speaketh boldly, and they say nothing unto him. Do the rulers know indeed that this is the very Christ?'

"The very Christ is the true idea of God. This idea is ever as much present as is God. Light always has its reflections. Where there is no reflection, then there is no light. When one does not express the reflection then he is not expressing love."

Continuing, Tomlinson recalled:

"Then she questioned us all. 'What do you lack most, faith, hope or love?' We answered 'love.' 'Yes,' said Mrs. Eddy, 'having an understanding of love, you establish health and peace.

" 'What was it that made Jesus the Messiah? The answer given was 'His spiritual understanding.' 'I will give you this answer,' she replied, 'the true answer in the language of the Bible; he 'loved righteousness and hated iniquity.' Then she proceeded to explain that the true Christian not only loves the right, but he hates iniquity and is willing to uncover the evil in himself and in others. She made it clear that he was not a true disciple who

closed his eyes to wrong-doing and took no steps to
unmask the wrong-doer and bring to an end the
evil doing. . . ."

" 'My vineyard, which is mine, is before me;
thou O Solomon, *must have* a thousand and those
that keep the fruit thereof two hundred.

" 'Thou that dwellest in the gardens, the companions hearken to thy voice; cause me to hear it.

" 'Make haste, my beloved, and be thou like a
roe or to a young hart upon the mountains of
spices.'

"Material existence is a dream and unreal, while
the spiritual fact of Life is eternal. This spiritual
fact is not attained by death, but by conscious
union with God, who is Life, Truth and Love.
Now is the day to attain this realization. Now is the
time to prove our faith by our works. 'Now is the
accepted time,' therefore now is the moment to improve every opportunity."

Interpretations such as these were what Mrs. Eddy believed to be true Christianity.

The clergy did not agree; but whether she was right or
wrong, she did not believe in religious militancy.

She counseled her followers

. . . to be charitable and kind, not only towards
differing forms of religion and medicine, but to
those who hold these differing opinions. Let us be
faithful in pointing the way through Christ, as we
understand it, but let us also be careful to "judge
righteous judgment," and never to condemn

rashly. . . . If ecclesiastical sects or medical schools
turn a deaf ear to the teachings of Christian Science, then part from these opponents as did Abraham when he parted from Lot, and say in thy
heart: "Let there be no strife, I pray thee, between
me and thee, and between my herdmen and thy
herdmen; for we be brethren." [4]

This should not be taken to mean that she was timid.
Timidity would not have stood before the world in challenge. She retracted not a single word. To the end she stood
where all the world could see her, serenely confident that
her only recourse from all the vilification was to a way of
life, a way of daily living, a way of daily progress that would
justify her, and justify her teachings, before God, and before the world.

Hers was not a faith that came in moments. In her was
no weakness of doubt. She held her ground by advancing,
and rediscovered her faith in new understanding. She wrote:

. . . The weapons of bigotry, ignorance, envy,
fall before an honest heart. Adulterating Christian
Science, makes it void. Falsity has no foundation.
"The hireling fleeth, because he is an hireling, and
careth not for the sheep." Neither dishonesty nor
ignorance ever founded, nor can they overthrow a
scientific system of ethics. [5]

She saw, as did du Noüy years afterwards, "the necessity
of revivifying religion by a return to its source, to the fundamental principles of Christianity and of fighting against the
superstitions which creep into the doctrines and menace its

[4] *Science and Health,* p. 444.
[5] *Science and Health,* p. 464.

future." She knew, as du Noüy came to know, "that the additions to the Christian religion, and the human interpretations which started in the third century, together with disregard for scientific truths, supplied the strongest arguments to the materialists and atheists in their fight against religion." [6]

She believed Christianity to be a search requiring advancement in spiritual capacity; she taught Christian Science as a religion that searches the Scriptures for only one thing — understanding of God; and she explained Christian Science as a daily procedure — respectful of His law.

Her enemies believed sickness and war and pestilence were punishments inflicted by God on people for their sins, and they taught that the way to amelioration or nullification was through concession to ritual. She believed sickness and war and pestilence were but experiences in human thinking, and her teaching revealed that "For right reasoning there should be but one fact before the thought, namely, spiritual existence. In reality there is no other existence, since Life cannot be united with its unlikeness, mortality." [7]

These were two very different points of view.

These different points of view were in conflict then. They are still in conflict.

One of Mrs. Eddy's great struggles was the effort to persuade her students to depend upon her teachings, and not upon her personality. On one occasion a student said to her:

"I feel much better if I can see you every day."

The rebuke was immediate:

[6] *Human Destiny*, Lecomte du Noüy; copyright, 1947.
[7] *Science and Health*, p. 492.

"If you feel that way, don't come to see me. Turn your thought entirely away from me. You will find me in my writings, not in the flesh."

Time after time after time she stressed the obligation of separating her personality from her teaching. She knew, although some among her students did not seem to know, that reliance upon personality is not Christian Science, but a denial of it — and efforts to deify self a blasphemy. She taught:

> . . . The true understanding of Christian Science Mind-healing never originated in pride, rivalry, or the deification of self. The Discoverer of this Science could tell you of timidity, of self-distrust, of friendlessness, toil, agonies, and victories under which she needed miraculous vision to sustain her, when taking the first footsteps in this Science.
>
> The ways of Christianity have not changed. Meekness, selflessness, and love are the paths of His testimony and the footsteps of His flock.[8]

Despite these reprimands and the teachings, the personal adulation persisted. The Christian Scientist Association, consisting in 1884 of sixty-one members, was the real directing power of the movement; it was through this organization that Mrs. Eddy supervised the activities of her church, the *Christian Science Journal,* and the Massachusetts Metaphysical College.

In the spring of 1884, there came from Chicago an urgent plea for the presence of a teacher.

Mrs. Eddy selected Mrs. Clara E. Choate for the assign-

[8] *Rudimental Divine Science,* p. 17.

ment, but was met with excuses that were equivalent to a
refusal. Questioning disclosed disaffection within the Association. Seeking counsel, Mrs. Eddy called together her
household and stipulated it as a "private meeting." [9] Hearing about it the rebellious student accused her teacher of
seeking to destroy her — and several days later, when a
second private meeting of the household was held, criticism
was in the open.

After an investigation, Mrs. Eddy announced the expulsion of Mrs. Choate and informed members of the Association that for an indefinite period the members would have
to get along without Mrs. Eddy herself because she would be
absent from Boston. Suspending her Thursday night lectures, and her class instruction, she arranged for the filling
of her pulpit at Sunday afternoon services, turned over
direct management of the *Journal* to a student, and she herself went to Chicago.

Here she spent a month, teaching and organizing the
work of expanding the movement of the Western States.
She succeeded beyond her expectations and returned to Boston to learn that, in her absence, the Thursday night meetings frequently had been broken up by former students
under the leadership of Arens — and that Boston clergymen
were inquiring into her rental of Hawthorne Hall for Sun-

---

[9] In Christian Science history these were the famous P. M.'s (Private
Meetings). In *Miscellaneous Writings* (p. 350) Mrs. Eddy referred to the
incident: ". . . The P. M. (Private Meeting) Society met only twice. The
first subject given out for consideration was this: 'There is no Animal
Magnetism.' There was no advice given, no mental work, and there were
no transactions at those meetings which I would hesitate to have known.
On the contrary, our deliberations were, as usual, Christian, and like my
public instructions. The second P. M. convened in about a week from the
first. The subject given out at that meeting was, in substance, 'God is All;
there is none beside Him.' This proved to be our last meeting. . . .'"

day services, in addition to making an investigation into her purchase of the property for her college, and had penetrated the college itself.

The clergy found no irregularities in the purchase of the property, or in the renting of Hawthorne Hall, but among the members of her new class they did find some who were willing to take issue with the teachings.

One such student came to Mrs. Eddy expressing a wish to enter a medical school while continuing his studies in Christian Science. He was told his wishes were inconsistent with teachings that depended upon God, and not matter, for healing. He argued, to be met with a statement which, in essence, was this:

I do not agree with your request, but I do agree you should follow your own desires. Do as you wish. If you wish to study medicine, do so, but do not quarrel with me, or with yourself, about it.

The student left her class, taking with him seven or eight other students. Rumors swept over Boston that the Massachusetts Metaphysical College and Christian Science were in a state of collapse.

CHAPTER SEVEN

Not with Trumpets

A SMALL ROOM in Good Templars Hall in Lynn was large enough in 1875 for the first Sunday services of Christian Scientists. Now, in 1885, in Boston, Sunday congregations were overflowing Hawthorne Hall.

Located at 2 Park Street, Hawthorne Hall faced the Common, while in back, across the street, was the Old Granary Burying Ground. A single dwelling separated the hall from the Park Street Congregational Church with its high steeple dominating the neighborhood. The main floor of the building at 2 Park Street was occupied by Doll & Richards, art dealers, and the hall, designed for lectures and recitals, ran the length of the second floor.

There were four large windows overlooking the Common and, across the rear, six windows, one on either side of the platform and four behind it, each covered with wooden blinds. A middle aisle ran between eighteen rows of seven seats each; there was a cross-aisle, part way down from the platform; also, there was an elevator, and a cloakroom. The seating capacity was 236. The rental for services was eight dollars.

Sunday services were held at three o'clock. Few carriages drew up to the entrance and when there was such a vehicle it usually contained someone crippled or ill. Except for these, the congregation walked, or came in horse cars. Women far outnumbered the men, and few were fashionably dressed. But the hall was always filled before three o'clock and, at three o'clock, the downstairs entrance and the stairs leading to the auditorium were generally crowded with people standing, listening, and singing with the others.

A description of Hawthorne Hall is found in a Boston newspaper account of Mrs. Eddy's last Easter sermon in the hall: "The Church of Christ (Scientist) had their meeting Easter Sunday at Hawthorne Hall, which was crowded one hour before service commenced, and half an hour before the arrival of the pastor, Rev. Mary B. G. Eddy, the tide of men and women was turned from the doors with the information, 'No more standing room.' On each side of the pulpit were beautiful plants and flowers while a table in front of the speaker was laden with an immense cross composed of roses, calla lilies, etc., towering very nearly to the top of the pulpit. It was with difficulty that the speaker, with the assistance of the genial but muscular usher, Mr. Palmer, could force her way through the crowd, blocking the hallway and the aisles, but it was accomplished after a good-natured struggle.

As reported in the May 1885 *Journal,* the speaker took her text from Mark xvi, 3:

WHO SHALL ROLL US AWAY THE STONE FROM THE SEPULCHRE?

"She said: 'This stone, in a spiritual sense, is the human view entertained of the power, resistance, and substance of matter as opposed to the might and supremacy of Spirit; Jesus met this question and settled it on the side of God's love and omnipotence, showing their triumph on all occasions. The resurrection was a momentous truth divinely attested; by it the vague abstractions of metaphysics is animated with immortal proof, the vitalizing power of all truth.

The sacred precincts of the tomb gave Jesus refuge from the heart-sickening brutality of his foes long enough to solve the great problem of being at every microscopic point.

" 'His three days' work in the sepulchre set the seal of eternity on time; it proved life deathless, and love the master of human hate. It met *materia medica,* surgery and hygiene with the power of Mind over matter, and mastered them on this basis.

" 'He neither required drugs to allay inflammation, pure air and nourishment to resuscitate the wasted energies, the skill of a surgeon to support or reinstate his parted palms that he might use those hands to remove the napkins and winding sheet, nor to bind up his wounded side and lacerated feet. Was this supernatural, since the God of nature established it in proof of a man's delegated power? It was not supernatural, but rendered divinely natural, when divinity brought to humanity the understanding of His power.

" 'Oh, the gloom and glory of that hour! His disciples believed him dead; himself was testing the power of Spirit to destroy all human sense of matter — the closed coffin-lid, the earth-bound walls and iron door of his tomb, yea, the power of death — that great stone which must be rolled away to let the human understanding rise to a sense of divine life and power. Jesus met every material condition and law of matter and mastered them when he stepped forth from his loathsome resting-place, wrapped in the glory of a sublime success, an everlasting victory. He hath rolled away the stone of sin and sense from every human mind and body, if this mind will accept his proof for its example, and receive this full salvation.' "

*　　*　　*

Not having music and a hymnal of their own, Christian Scientists used the *Social Hymn and Tune Book* published by the American Unitarian Society in 1880. Often, after services, the crippled and the sick who had used the elevator to reach the second floor walked out and down the stairs; and it happened so often that Boston newspapers referred to it as the "miracle elevator."

Practitioners' signs were appearing in New York, Chicago, Philadelphia, and other cities; students were locating in California and inquiring letters were coming from England; the circulation of the *Journal* was nearly four thousand; [1] *Science and Health* was in its sixth printing, and on its cover were six new words.

They were, *with a Key to the Scriptures;* thus making the full title, *Science and Health with a Key to the Scriptures.*

Published in 1883, the work is in two volumes, in several bindings. The Cross and the Crown are on each cover, and on each spine is the name MRS. GLOVER EDDY. Inside, the author identifies herself as Mary Baker G. Eddy, President of the Massachusetts Metaphysical College, and, also, as publisher.

As with the previous edition, the frontispiece is a reproduction of the healing of Jairus's daughter. The first volume contains 270 pages, and includes these chapters: "Science of Being," "Footsteps of Truth," "Physiology," "Recapitulation," and "Healing the Sick." The second volume contains

---

[1] On March 18, 1884, the Christian Scientist Association agreed that "Every member would subscribe for the *Journal of Christian Science,* and obtain annually not less than six (6) subscribers, . . . or forfeit their membership." It also was agreed that "all members who are practicing healing pay twenty-five cents on every $5.00 they receive from their practice toward supporting the public worship of the Church of Christ, Scientist."

206 pages, and these chapters: "Imposition and Demonstration," "Creation," "Marriage," "Prayer and Atonement," "Platform of Christian Scientists," "Reply to a Clergyman," "Demonology," and "With A Key to the Scriptures."

In the "Preface," Mrs. Eddy again gave attention to the theft of her writings,[2] mentioned the court decision protecting them, and said:

> . . . Not one of our printed works was ever copied or abstracted from the published or from the unpublished writings of anyone. Throughout our publications of metaphysical healing and Christian Science, when writing or dictating them, we have given ourselves to contemplating wholly apart from the observation of the material senses; to look upon a copy would have distracted our thoughts from the subject before us. We were seldom able to copy our own compositions, and have employed an amanuensis for the last six years. Every work that we have published has been extemporaneously written; and out of fifty lectures and sermons that we have delivered the past year, forty-four have been extemporaneous. We have distributed many of our unpublished manuscripts; loaned to one of our youngest students, R. K———y, between three and four hundred pages, of which we were the sole author — giving him liberty to copy but not to publish them. . . .

To help in understanding the Bible, Mrs. Eddy included in the Key many words and interpreted them in what she

[2] Despite the court injunction, a number of groups in Boston were taking extracts from her writings, and using them as their own.

believed to be their spiritual meaning.[3] Interpretations such as these:

ANGELS. God's thoughts passing to man. Spiritual intuitions pure and perfect. The inspiration of good, purity, and immortality, giving the lie to evil, sensuality, and mortality.

BAPTISM. Man purified by Spirit, submerged in Truth. "To be absent from the body and to be present with the Lord." (II Cor. V. 8)

CHURCH. The superstructure of Truth and Love. Whatever rests upon and proceeds from divine Principle. That which affords proof of its utility, is found elevating the race, rousing the dormant understanding from material beliefs to the apprehension of spiritual ideas, and the demonstration of divine science, casting out devils, error, and healing the sick.

FATHER. The great forever, eternal Mind; divine Principle, named God.

MORNING. Light; symbol of Truth, revelation and progression.

MORTAL MIND. All that is erring and mortal; mythology, for Mind is immortal. Belief, creating beliefs and naming them matter. A supposition of material sense, alias the belief that sensation is in matter which is sensationless. A belief that Life, substance and Intelligence are in and of matter. The opposite of Spirit hence the opposite of good, God. The belief that Life has a beginning; therefore an ending; that man is the offspring of

---

[3] Revisions in these, and in other words of the Key, were made in later editions of *Science and Health*.

mortals; that there is more than one Creator. Idolatry. Only that which appears to the so-called senses of matter, but neither exists in science nor to spiritual sense. Belief, sin, sickness and death.

MOTHER. Divine and eternal Principle, — Life, Truth and Love.

SERPENT. *Ophis,* in Greek; *Nacash* in Hebrew. Sublety, a lie; the opposite of Truth, named error. The first statement of mythology and idolatry, the belief in more than one God. Mesmerism, animal magnetism. The first lie of limits, finity; the first claim to an opposite of Spirit, good, termed matter and evil; the first authority that these exist as facts, instead of fable. The first claim to sin, sickness, and death being the realities of Life; the first that said God is not Omnipotent, and there is another power, named evil, that is as real and eternal as good, God.

TIME. Mortal measurements; limits, in which is summed up all human acts, thoughts, beliefs, opinions, knowledge. Matter, error. That which continues after what is termed death, until the erring and mortal disappears, and spiritual perfection appears.

Clergymen did not like such interpretations — Angels: "God's thoughts passing to man" — Baptism: ". . . purified by Spirit" — Church: ". . . superstructure of Truth and Love" — God . . . Father . . . Mother — Morning: "Revelation and progression" — Serpent: "The first statement of mythology and idolatry" — Mortal Mind: "All that is erring and mortal" — Time: "Mortal measurements" —

interpretations such as these were not taught in theological schools and, consequently, Mrs. Eddy and Christian Science were subjects of frequent discussion in the regular meetings of Boston clergymen.

Calling his remarks "Boston Craze and Mrs. Eddy," the Reverend L. T. Townsend, of Boston University, addressed a Boston Methodist Preachers' meeting, saying in part: ". . . This woman claims to be the originator of a new system of philosophy and healing. Were there consistency enough in her teachings to constitute a philosophy it would be called a crude attempt to resuscitate the defunct idealism of the nihilistic type which appeared in the middle ages. Her views upon metaphysical matters — we speak very mildly — are a self-contradicting hotchpotch."

In *Zion's Herald,* in December 1884, Townsend published a challenge proposing: "If Mrs. Eddy or her entire college of doctors will put in place a real case of hip or ankle dislocation without touching it, I will give you [Mrs. Eddy] one thousand dollars. Or, if you, or your entire college, will give sight to one of the inmates of South Boston Asylum for the Blind, that sightless person having been born blind, I will give you two thousand dollars."

Townsend kept up his bombardment, in newspapers, in church papers, and from the pulpit until, in the June issue of the *Journal,* Mrs. Eddy informed him that she considered his challenge "a heathen combat for a religious stake of three thousand dollars," and invited his attention to the refusal by Jesus of the tempter's "bids" and added that she, as His follower, could not consent to prayer-gauge tests.

Mindful that the Master Christian refused "a sign from heaven" when His enemies sought miracles, and that He commanded those He healed to "see thou say nothing to any man," she looked upon the challenges as extravagances. Accepting the healing as the work, not of herself, but of God, she considered it was "a sign" not to be made into a spectacle.

She taught that God reveals Himself not with trumpets, but in silence.

Another Boston clergyman, the Reverend Stacy Fowler, wrote in the *Homiletic Review:* ". . . While 'healers are multiplying' it is evident that the science is waning. Mrs. Eddy . . . may teach the principles of the science in twelve lessons, but she cannot impart her power, her personalism, in twelve, not in twelve hundred lessons. . . . The *ictus* is her personalism. Her pupils are but feeble imitations of their teacher. Hence the spell is losing its charm. The movement is losing its momentum. In its present form it is an epidemic, and as an epidemic it will pass away, as did the Blue Glass mania.[4] It is as transcendental as was Brook Farm,[5] and like that experiment it may be useful in demonstrating that sentiment, fancy and fitful impulses are not the solid facts of science, nor the panacea for human ills."

Mrs. Eddy replied to Fowler by offering free courses in the Massachusetts Metaphysical College to all clergymen who cared to come, explaining the purpose of the offer was "to facilitate an honest investigation of Christian Science."

Instead of accepting, Boston pulpits assailed her in a barrage of sermons, charging her with teaching "free love," with being "a spiritualist and teaching spiritualism," with "denying the efficacy of prayer," with teaching "there is no

[4] A few years previously it was popularly believed that sitting under blue glass was a certain way to health.

[5] Brook Farm was the site of the unsuccessful communistic experiment at West Roxbury, Massachusetts, in 1841–1847.

punishment for sin, so sin to your heart's content," with "disclaiming God by denying a personal Christ."

Using her six-page, issued-every-other-month *Journal,* Mrs. Eddy answered as best she could the attacks in the well-established denominational publications such as *Zion's Herald,* the *Watchman,* and the *Congregationalist,* all of which were published in Boston. The clerical crusade against Christian Science continued until, on February 26, 1885, more than twenty-five hundred persons from all over New England crowded into Tremont Temple to listen to a particularly vitriolic attack by the Reverend A. J. Gordon, a Boston clergyman.[6]

A number of Mrs. Eddy's students requested that their Teacher be given an opportunity to reply. The committee of the "Monday Morning Lectureship," as it was called, refused, and then acceded, agreeing, as stated in the *Congregationalist,* that "the best way of meeting the evil was to let it show itself."[7] The date selected was March 16. Mrs. Eddy was allotted ten minutes for her reply.

It was a cold — and critical — audience that watched as Mrs. Eddy walked down the aisle, up the steps, and onto the platform in Tremont Temple on Monday morning, March 16 — and continued to watch as "in a manner that showed exceeding disrelish," the Reverend Joseph Cook acknowledged her presence and introduced her by simply saying, "It becomes my interesting duty to introduce to this audience, Mrs. Eddy."

---

[6] Indignant over the attack, a committee of students pleaded with Mrs. Eddy to bring suit for slander against Gordon. She quieted them by writing the essay entitled "Love," included in *Miscellaneous Writings* (pp. 249–250). The essay first appeared in the *Christian Science Journal* in May 1885.

[7] The *Congregationalist,* March 19, 1885.

Her small figure standing against the background of the towering organ pipes, Mrs. Eddy looked out upon the clergy and the laity crowding the auditorium and balconies. Without notes, she made her reply, as reported in the *Journal* in May 1885:

> As the time so kindly allotted me is insufficient for even a synopsis of Christian Science, I shall confine myself to questions and answers.
>
> "Am I a spiritualist?"
>
> I am not, and never was. I understand the impossibility of inter-communion with the so-called dead. There have always attended my life phenomena of an uncommon order, which spiritualists have miscalled mediumships; but I clearly understand that no human agencies were employed. That the divine Mind reveals itself to humanity through spiritual law, and to such as are waiting for the adoption, to wit: the redemption of the body. Christian Science reveals man's salvation from sickness and death, as wrought out by Jesus, who robbed the grave of victory, and death of its sting. I understand that God is an ever-present help in all times of trouble, have found Him so, and would have no other gods, no remedies in drugs, no material medicine.
>
> "Do I believe in a personal God?"
>
> I believe in God as the Supreme Being. I know not what the person of Omnipotence and Omnipresence is, or what the Infinite includes; therefore, I worship that of which I can conceive, first, as a loving Father; and as thought ascends the scale of being to diviner consciousness, he becomes to

me what the Apostle declared — "God is Love — divine Principle" — which I worship, and "after the manner of my fathers so worship I him."

"Do I believe in the atonement of Christ?"

I do; and this atonement becomes more to me since it includes man's redemption from sickness as well as sin. I reverence and adore Christ as never before. It belongs to my sense, and the sense of all who entertain this understanding of the science of God, a *whole* salvation.

"How is the healing done in Christian Science?"

This answer includes too much to give you any conclusive idea in a brief explanation. I can name some things by which it is not done.

It is not one mind acting upon another mind; it is not the transference of human images of thought to other minds; it is not supported by the evidence before the personal sense — science contradicts this evidence; it is not of the flesh, but of the Spirit. It is Christ come to destroy the power of the flesh; it is Truth over error; that understood, gives men ability to rise above the evidence of the senses and take hold of the eternal evidences of Truth, and destroy mortal discord with immortal harmony, the grand verities of being. It is not one mortal thought transmitted to another's thought, from the human mind that holds within itself all evil.

Our Master said of one of his students, "he is a devil," and repudiated the idea of casting out devils through Beelzebub. Erring human mind is by no means a desirable or efficacious healer: such

healing I deprecate, it is in no way allied to divine
power. All human control is animal magnetism,
more fatal than all other methods of treating disease.

It is not a remedy of faith alone, but combines
faith with understanding, through which it touches
the hem of His garment, and we know the Omnipotent has all power: "If the Lord be God, there
is none beside Him."

"Is there a personal man?"

The Scriptures inform us that man was made in
the image and likeness of God. I like the Icelandic
translation: "He created man in the image and
likeness of Mind, in the image and likeness of
Mind created He him." To my sense we have not
seen all of man; he is more than personal sense can
recognize, who is the image and likeness of the Infinite. I have not seen a perfect man in mind or
body, and such must be the personality of him who
is the true likeness.

The lost image is not this personality, and personal man is this lost image; hence, it doth not
appear what is the real personality of man. The
only cause for making this question of personality
a point, or of any importance, is that man's perfect
model should be held in mind, whereby to improve his present condition; and his contemplation
of himself should turn away from inharmony,
sickness and sin, to man the image of his Maker.

As Mrs. Eddy left the platform there was bunched applause from the gallery, into which a few of her students had

crowded; other than that, there was no recognition that she had spoken. As she went from the platform, down the aisle, and from the building, the *Congregationalist* told of how "Mr. Cook, with a warmth and cordiality the exact opposite of that shown Mrs. Eddy, introduced the next speaker."

The attacks continued, and spread. The Right Reverend Samuel Fallows, of Chicago, assailed her use of the word "metaphysics" by writing in the magazine, *Mind in Nature:* ". . . I put the word Metaphysics at the head of this article in quotation marks because, as my readers will discover, it is used in a most peculiar sense. After having a meaning pretty clearly defined for thousands of years, it has been re- served for a woman to find out it can mean something the philosophers and savants never dreamed it contained. She had applied it to a professed system of bodily healing by the entering of 'Trust' from the mind of the operator into the mind of the patient, where it destroys 'error,' the false belief of 'mortal mind.' The expulsion of error effects the cure. This system is called Metaphysics, and the treatment, Meta- physical Treatment. . . . The theory which is advanced by the one claiming to be the founder of the system is not worth the snap of a finger, and never cured a single case. The eminent investigators of Telepathy, under which all cases of Metaphysical must be grouped, are very careful to say that they have no theory yet to explain the action of mind upon mind, although they may have a working hypothesis. No theory of electricity causes the electric current to act. A theory that there is no personal God, no personal Devil, and no personal man, that matter is not real, that disease is only a belief of mortal mind, with all the rest of the peculiar notions grouped under Metaphysics, has no more to do with the recovery of the sick than Tenferden Steeple with the formation of the Goodwin Sands.

"The one thing for which Mrs. Eddy deserves credit, is hitting upon a novel plan to cause a *concentration* of one mind upon another for the well being of the body. That is, precisely, in my judgment the *all* of Metaphysics. . . ."

Bishop Fallows returned to the attack the following month, calling his article Fact vs Theory, and stating:

. . . I called attention in my article on "Metaphysics" in the March number to the position that the peculiar *theory* of the reputed founder of the "metaphysical system" had nothing to do with the alleged cures which were performed by professed practitioners of this method. Several communications, which I have since received on the subject, and a thorough re-reading of Mrs. Eddy's books, have only served to convince me of the truth of my statements.

I did not deny at all, as some seem to think, the cures were performed by persons going through the *modus operandi* of metaphysics. But admitting that within a certain limit, there have been bodily cures effected, it by no means follows that the notions of Mrs. Eddy on God, man, soul and mortal mind, materia medica, science, metaphysics, the Holy Scriptures, etc., etc., have the slightest connection with the recovery of the sick. Numbers of the "metaphysicians" have looked into Mrs. Eddy's works and gone straightway into the healing business. They claim to have done as wonderful things as those who think they understand the system.

I repeat, with greater emphasis than before, that the *religious theory* which Mrs. Eddy places at the bottom of her system, a theory which I claim to be utterly *un*-Christian, never cured a case of sickness. It is simply the telepathic power of one mind over another, in harmony, of course, with the Divine law of restoration, which she and her followers are using. . . .

Two months later, in the same publication (*Mind in Nature*), Mrs. Eddy made reply under the title, CHRISTIAN SCIENCE:

. . . I have waited for Bishop Fallows to resign his task of misstating my views, in each of your issues. If his design was to call out my fire, I can assure him I hold no masked battery to open upon my enemies, and shall offer no plea or apology for doing good.

Is the above gentleman quite sure that my statement of "God, man, soul, mortal mind, materia medica, science, metaphysics, the Holy Scriptures, etc., has not the slightest connection with the recovery of the sick?" Also, that "hitting upon a novel plan to cause a concentration of one mind upon another, for the well-being of the body, is *all* of metaphysics?" Then he has gained this knowledge through his ignorance of Christian Science. He tried to support his lame logic by this — that "numbers have read my books and gone into the healing business," and some who are healing by mind-cure repudiate the Science. Here we ask, Does simply "going into the business" prove or disprove one's fitness to heal? And if one becomes a successful healer merely from reading my books, does it not prove that my statement of Christian Science *has* "connection with the recovery of the sick"? And "out of the mouth of babes thou hast perfected praise."

The exorcists of old healed in the name of Christ, and their method might have accorded with

Bishop Fallows' views, but not mine. The chief priests of that period said of Jesus' method of healing, that Christian Science would represent, "He casteth out devils by Beelzebub." If my religious system (as he is pleased to term it) exemplifies the teachings and demonstration of our Lord, it should be known by its fruits; and that system or its adherent, that designates this system unchristian, is at fault. Neither by his writings nor by healing, has the aforesaid gentleman furnished the first evidence, on the basis of my scientific statement, that he understands my works, principle or practice. . . .[8]

Inspired by her enemies, rumors began appearing in New England newspapers that she was suffering from all manner of disease — other rumors said students, made up to resemble her, were taking her place in the lecture room, and in the pulpit — and in the *St. Louis* (Missouri) *Democrat* there appeared a story to the effect that Mary Baker Eddy had killed herself by swallowing poison, and had "bequeathed all her property to Susan B. Anthony, the suffragist."

In sermons, and in religious publications, clergymen insisted that her teachings were pantheistic until, finally, she answered them: "I am anti-pantheist for I see that God, Spirit, is not in His reflection any more than the sun is in the light that comes to the earth through reflection. Can you understand this? No: and no one can fully until I educate the spiritual sense to see the *substance* of Spirit, and the *substanceless* of matter."

[8] For full text, see Appendix 4.

Clergymen objected to the use of the identifying letters C.S., which practitioners used after their names, claiming that Mrs. Eddy's teachings "were not for educational purposes, but for a medical purpose," and gave wide publication to the charge that by conferring "degrees on the graduates of the Massachusetts Metaphysical College she is using her college to get fraudulent medical diplomas from the State."

But, whatever the faultfinding, there were some among the clergy who stood between Mrs. Eddy and her accusers.

One was Andrew Preston Peabody, for twenty-seven years Professor of Christian Morals at Harvard University. At one time President of the university, Peabody was a man of Christian stature, and while he never became her student, he did accept her invitation to preach at five Sunday services in Hawthorne Hall. Pastor Emeritus of Harvard at the time, his first service in Hawthorne Hall was March 9, 1884, and his last, February 1, 1885.

Another was Cyrus D. Bartol. Expressing his dissatisfaction with scholasticism, "which teaches man has no hand in his own salvation," Bartol sought out Mrs. Eddy, listened to her explanation of her teachings, said, "I have preached the living God for forty years, but never felt His presence and power as you do," and from his pulpit in West Church on Cambridge Street, Boston, defended her and preached two sermons commending her teachings.

Edward Everett Hale protected and defended her, writing of her, "She has told me more truth in twenty minutes than I have learned in twenty years"; Orrin P. Gifford, one of the younger clergymen of Boston, took up her battle from the pulpit of the Warren Avenue Baptist Church before going to her and, with his wife, completing one of her classes, although not becoming a Christian Scientist.[9]

Then, too, there was a woman in Connecticut who soon was to disagree with any clerical verdict that Christian Science has "no more to do with the recovery of the sick than Tenferden Steeple with the formation of the Goodwin Sands."

Julia S. Bartlett, an invalid, was given no encouragement by medical men. In 1880, in her home in Connecticut, she received a letter from a friend in Boston, and included with the letter was a circular telling of the founding, in the previous year, of a new church called Church of Christ, Scientist. Of particular interest to the invalid were words written by Mrs. Eddy in the circular:

> This church is designed to perpetuate the teachings of Jesus, to re-instate primitive Christianity, and to restore its lost element of healing.

This message, later incorporated in the *Church Manual*, appealed to Miss Bartlett. She requested her friend in Boston to send her a copy of *Science and Health* and, also, to ask Mrs. Eddy to recommend a practitioner. Mrs. Eddy did so, "recommending," as Clifford P. Smith wrote in *Historical Sketches*, "her husband, Asa G. Eddy, to Miss Bartlett, and the result of his work for her was a quick healing."

A few months after receiving the circular, Miss Bartlett applied for and was given class instruction by Mrs. Eddy.

[9] In 1900, thirty-eight clergymen were represented in a collection of articles published in a book called *Theology of the Dawn of the Twentieth Century*. Gifford, then pastor of the Delaware Avenue Baptist church, in Buffalo, New York, contributed a comprehensive study titled "Exposition of Christian Science."

The class, consisting of three pupils, was held in Lynn and it was while there that Miss Bartlett first attended Christian Science Sunday services. In her memoirs written for The Mother Church, Miss Bartlett, after relating how the services were held in the parlor of Mrs. Eddy's home, said:

"There were about twenty people present. Mrs. Eddy preached the sermon, which healed a young woman sitting near me of an old chronic trouble which physicians were unable to heal. Her husband, who was present with her, went to Mrs. Eddy the next day to thank her for what had been done for his wife."

Returning to her home in Connecticut, Miss Bartlett received a letter from Mrs. Eddy saying, in part:

> . . . Do not forget to be strong in the clear consciousness that you are able to heal and no counter mind can make you weak for a moment through fear or lack of confidence in your power or rather understanding. Remember God, Truth, is the *healer,* the balm in Gilead, and our only Physician, and can never be insufficient for all things.

In 1881, Mrs. Eddy called Miss Bartlett to help with the work in Boston. In August 1884,[10] Miss Bartlett was a member of the first class taught by Mrs. Eddy in the Massachusetts Metaphysical College and, after graduation, she became one of the first of Mrs. Eddy's pupils to become a teacher of Christian Science; but she was one of the very few who understood Mrs. Eddy's instruction that no one need travel beyond himself to find the kingdom of God — and if the

[10] Until August 1884, Mary Baker Eddy was the only authorized teacher of Christian Science.

time ever came when all men would see that the simple
words of the Son still live, the moment would be here when
all would understand ". . . The kingdom of God cometh
not with observation . . . the kingdom of God is within
you." [11] Would believe, as Mrs. Eddy believed, that *all* He
said was true:

> . . . And it was at Jerusalem the feast of the
> dedication, and it was winter. And Jesus walked
> in the temple in Solomon's porch. Then came the
> Jews round about him, and said unto him, How
> long dost thou make us to doubt? If thou be the
> Christ, tell us plainly. Jesus answered them, I told
> you, and ye believed not: the works that I do in
> my Father's name, they bear witness of me.
>
> But ye believe not, because ye are not of my
> sheep, as I said unto you. My sheep hear my voice,
> and I know them, and they follow me: And I give
> unto them eternal life; and they shall never perish,
> neither shall any *man* pluck them out of my hand.
> My Father, which gave *them* me, is greater than
> all; and no *man* is able to pluck *them* out of my
> Father's hand.
>
> I and *my* Father are one.[12]

. . . Would hold, as did Mrs. Eddy, that, as **Paul** said,
spiritual development is an individual responsibility "till
we all come in the unity of the faith, and of the knowledge
of the Son of God, unto a perfect man, unto the measure
of the stature of the fulness of Christ." [13]

. . . Would recognize, as did Mrs. Eddy, that it is a Man-

[11] Luke xvii. 20, 21.
[12] John x. 22–30.
[13] Ephesians iv. 13.

ger and not a crowded inn that is remembered; the Resurrection and not the immolation that is momentous.

Mrs. Eddy's preoccupation with man and His relationship was troublesome for many. They came to hear her teachings, but did not stay.

But, whatever the disputation, she denied it all, seeking only to bring to people the realization that God eternally is managing in their behalf, eternally is just, eternally is right, eternally is good — and pleaded with them to understand that without righteousness there is no progress, and in righteousness there is greater good than is ever dreamed.

To her, the precept in Jesus's teachings is found only in their spiritual interpretation — and the precept is everything. In Boston, more people were accepting that.

On Wednesday, February 4, 1885, at a meeting of the Christian Scientist Association,[14] Mrs. Eddy proposed that, because of the inadequacy of Hawthorne Hall, communion services, scheduled for the following Sunday, be held in Oddfellows' Hall, located at Tremont and Berkeley Streets. Her suggestion was accepted. About eight hundred persons attended; fourteen new members were admitted.

Encouraged by this showing, members of the Association at their meeting the following week decided to engage Chickering Hall, on Tremont Street near West, for Sunday services upon expiration of the lease on Hawthorne Hall.

Rental of Chickering Hall was twenty dollars for each Sunday afternoon, and on a lease basis this was a substantial sum for a congregation composed mostly of women with little money of their own. But they did it, and on October

---

[14] In records of the older Association, the title reads Christian Scientists Association, not Scientist.

25, the first services were held in the new location. The seating capacity was 500, and the hall was filled.

In the November issue of the *Journal* the announcement was made: "Chickering Hall has been engaged for the season; and when this proves too small we will get a larger one."

CHAPTER EIGHT

Keeper of the Gate

S HE DID NOT USE THE WORDS, but Mary Baker Eddy understood that scholarship weakens, and frequently destroys,
the simple faith that sees the fret and fever of the moment
as but the measure of a disbelief in the eternity of now.

One of her students, who became one of her greatest
helpers, also came to understand it.

His name was Edward A. Kimball. A businessman in Chicago, Kimball traveled the medical offices and the hospitals
of the United States and Europe seeking a physician who
would give him hope. One evening, in 1908, in Edinburgh,
Scotland, he told an audience: "Twenty-one years ago, I was
in this city of Edinburgh. I had been sent over here by my
physicians, who could not cure me, in the hope that I might
find some physician in Europe who could. I went around
from place to place, and in the course of time I came to a
halt here in Edinburgh, disconsolate, wretched and in agony.
This was my last place before my return. I had given up all
hope in Europe when I turned from Edinburgh one day to
Liverpool and then on to a steamer to go home to die." [1]

Kimball, a man of extraordinary capabilities and learning, was not quickly healed. Returning to Chicago, he decided, as a last resort, to try Christian Science. He sought out
a practitioner and received treatment, but the sickness persisted. In pain he went back to his doctor, but received no

[1] *Lectures and Articles on Christian Science,* by Edward A. Kimball;
copyright, 1948, by Edna Kimball Wait.

medical encouragement. Instead, the physician advised him his only chance to be healed was in Christian Science.

The healing finally came, but only, as Kimball said, after he had cleared his own thinking of its "philosophy of despair" and his mind was in that state of innocence which brought its own healing. And, too, only after he recognized that Mrs. Eddy was not teaching one new fact. Nor, as he also perceived, did Jesus.

> Verily, verily, I say unto you, He that believeth on me, the works that I do shall he do also; and greater *works* than these shall he do; because I go unto my Father. And whatsoever ye shall ask in my · name, that will I do, that the Father may be glorified in the Son. If ye ask any thing in my name, I will do *it*.

Kimball came to believe the words of the Master, as Mrs. Eddy believed them, and hers was a childlike confidence that everything unlike God is obedient to the prayer of understanding. To her, the words, "If ye ask any thing in my name, I will do it," are inseparable from the works; and the promise as redeemable today as at the moment of its utterance.

As redeemable as the promise to Esaias; redeemable, in Mrs. Eddy's teachings, to all those who come seeking His ways:

> And there was delivered unto him the book of the prophet Esaias. And when he had opened the book, he had found the place where it was written, The Spirit of the Lord *is* upon me, because he hath anointed me to preach the gospel to the poor;

he hath sent me to heal the broken-hearted, to preach deliverance to the captives, and recovering of sight to the blind, to set at liberty them that are bruised. . . .

And he closed the book, and he gave *it* again to the minister, and sat down. And the eyes of all them that were in the synagogue were fastened upon him.

And he began to say unto them, This day is this scripture fulfilled in your ears.

Mrs. Eddy required of her students that they be healers, and it was customary for them to travel about, teaching and gathering classes of their own. These students were the missionaries and, in considerable measure, their efforts accounted for the rapid early growth of the movement westward from Chicago. They encountered a great deal of hostility, but they established the teachings.

Typical of their work is this extract from an early report: ". . . She [the student] went to Mount Vernon, Iowa, and in a short time she had 100 patients. Many of them were foreigners, mostly Bohemians. She did not understand a word they said, but they understood the language of Truth, and they were all healed."

However, while spreading Christian Science, the missionary work contributed to discontent. There were no restrictions as to the number of classes a teacher might have, no restrictions on the number of pupils, and no regulations as to the number of states in which a teacher could function. Rivalry developed and, with rivalry, disagreement over the teachings and the shifting of students between the teachers.

Aware of the growing discord, Mrs. Eddy suggested:

> As the cause of Christian Science is extending
> rapidly all over our country, and the Christian Sci-
> entists' Association of Boston is exclusively a so-
> ciety of the Massachusetts Metaphysical College, I
> deem it advisable that an organization be formed
> on a broader basis, by which all Christian Scien-
> tists and their students may come together; and I
> would recommend that steps be taken by my stu-
> dents, throughout the United States, to organize a
> National Christian Scientists' Association.[2]

On January 6, 1886, the Christian Scientists' Association
of the Massachusetts Metaphysical College met in Boston
and prevailed upon Mrs. Eddy to withdraw her request to
retire as president and discussed, with her, the proposal
she had made for a national Association. On January 29,
a preliminary meeting was held at which it was agreed to
establish branch Associations; and arrangements were made
for a joint meeting of the Boston Association and the branch
Associations in Chicago.

The time and place of meeting were set as February 10,
in New York, and the purpose was to have a type of organization that would best "bring together and place upon an
equal footing with one another in Christian Science, all
students thereof (whether they have been personally taught
by the founder of the order, or have received their instruction from some of her students) and so promote unity and
brotherly love." [3]

Thirteen states, in addition to Massachusetts, were repre-

[2] *Christian Science Journal*, January 1886.
[3] *Christian Science Journal*, March 1886.

sented at this meeting. The states were Maine, New Hampshire, Rhode Island, New York, Michigan, Ohio, Illinois, Kentucky, Wisconsin, Missouri, Iowa, Nebraska, and Colorado. Also in attendance were Christian Scientists from the District of Columbia.

The organizing of a National Association did not bring about the "unity and brotherly love" Mrs. Eddy hoped it would.

At the time there was a great deal of interest among Christian Scientists in all literature pertaining to metaphysics, including all manner of esoteric literature and in everything that was written about the life and times of Jesus.

Ben Hur was avidly read and discussed; *The Light of Asia,* a poem by Sir Edwin Arnold, surpassed even the popularity of *Ben Hur* and was so warmly accepted that some students urged Mrs. Eddy to abandon prose and rewrite *Science and Health* in verse; an editor of the *Journal* wrote what he hoped would be endorsed as a companion book to *Science and Health* and, with no authority but his own, used the columns of the *Journal* to advertise a mixture which, whatever else it was, was not Christian Science.

Hoping the enthusiasm of her followers for other literature would subside, Mrs. Eddy did not interfere.

In 1886, she had retired as editor of the *Journal* and had turned over management of the publication to the Christian Scientists' Association. There was the daily watching over, and directing, the work in the field. Her correspondence with students was large, sometimes as many as forty or fifty letters a day and seldom less than a dozen, all of which she wrote by hand. She was constantly revising and refining *Science and Health;* she lectured in the Massachusetts Metaphysical College; as president of the college and as president of the Christian Scientists' Association, she had duties that required personal attention; there were her appearances — now occasional — as pastor at Sunday services in Chickering Hall; there was the management of her household.

It was her wish that her pupils should fend for themselves; she was aware of the growing disunity. A good many complaints were being circulated. Being bandied about was the charge that she was too strict in her teachings — that *Science and Health* was "too difficult to comprehend"; it was being said "There are others who are better able to prepare a textbook, and they should do it" — it was being argued that "the Massachusetts Metaphysical College should have teachers who were surgeons and medical doctors so students in Christian Science would be able to recognize the exact nature of the disease to be treated" — there was a strong demand that "hypnotism and spiritualism should be included in the subjects that are studied so as to widen the popular appeal of Christian Science" . . . and the opinion was beginning to be heard that Mrs. Eddy had carried the movement as far as she could, that the time was near when she should be displaced by an individual, or a group, chosen by themselves from among themselves.

The discontented could not seem to understand that Mary Baker Eddy was writing of graver matters than hypnotism and spiritualism and the opinions of medical men.

They could not seem to realize it was not she who was strict.

It was spiritual law that was strict.

In her teachings she was no more strict than is the schoolmaster who requires that students understand the precision that governs arithmetic before allowing them to graduate into the equal precision that governs algebra or physics or trigonometry. As with mathematics, so with awakening understanding of the law.

Was it not Pythagoras who required that his pupils have their minds disciplined by mathematics before admitting them to the higher thoughts of his classroom? And if, as someone has said, "Time is the mercy of eternity," then is not eternity mercifully broken up into crumbs of hours, of days, and of years until the moment comes when we are able to partake of the stronger food of timelessness?

In protesting that *Science and Health* was "too difficult to comprehend," the faultfinders were on ancient ground. The words of another were difficult of comprehension. "The Most High dwelleth not in temples made with hands." Stephen was stoned for saying that; and before Stephen, long before Stephen, Moses carried a Commandment to his people: "Thou shalt have no other gods before me."

The people did not understand.

The idea that they were a chosen people took root.

God belonged to them, and to them alone, just as now Christian and Buddhist, Jew and Mohammedan look with pity, or scorn, upon one another, not seeming to understand that what is in dispute is form, not God — nor seeming to realize if there is more than one God, there is none.

This fact — the oneness of God — seems to be a most difficult fact for the world to understand. Repeatedly, in her teachings, Mrs. Eddy dwelt upon it, dwelt upon its meaning, dwelt upon its significance, declaring, "This all-important understanding is gained in Christian Science, revealing the one God and His all-power and ever-presence, and the brotherhood of man in unity of Mind and oneness of Principle." [4]

⁴ *The People's Idea of God*, p. 13.

Basing her teachings solely on the principle that all are children of God, Mrs. Eddy was in the spiritual presence of Another who, speaking out from that same fundamental, established on earth the rights of man over the claims of Jew or Gentile, Mohammedan, Buddhist, or atheist — over the claims of everything not of God.

But there was plausibility in the contention that *Science and Health* was not easy to read, and that parts of it were obscure. Mrs. Eddy was writing on a subject most difficult to put into words; there was her growing perception; there was the other fact that she wrote at great speed, seldom taking the time to go back over what she had written to make corrections.

There was a standing order in the Christian Science publishing offices that her contributions were to be edited, and the offices' files of those years disclose sharp rebukes for failure to heed her instructions which, substantially, were: Edit carefully, but do not change the thought.

To reduce the number of errors in her writings, she went to the University Press and employed a proofreader to serve in a like capacity for her. His name was James Henry Wiggin.[5] He was a retired clergyman and, while he never became a Christian Scientist, he did write a great deal in de-

[5] In later years, after leaving Mrs. Eddy's employ, Wiggin was widely publicized as having revised and rewritten *Science and Health;* and as having originated Mrs. Eddy's unique style of expression; Wiggin's principal job was that of proofreader. There were occasions when he suggested changes. If the suggestions pertained to the teachings, they were never accepted, but there were occasions when changes in phrasing were accepted. As for having originated Mrs. Eddy's style of expression, that style appears in her earliest writings. This Wiggin rumor probably was started by Mrs. Josephine C. Woodbury, a student who was dismissed from the movement.

fense of the teachings under the pseudonym of Phare
Pleigh.

Having a proofreader who was a retired clergyman did
not lessen opposition to Mrs. Eddy from within the movement, or opposition to her teachings from without it.

Critics within the movement used the attacks by the clergy
to persuade the wavering that the teachings were too narrow, the teacher too extreme; and the further the critics and
the wavering got away from the oneness of the relationship
between God and man, with that oneness being wholly
spiritual, as maintained by Mrs. Eddy, the more objectionable her teachings became to them.

Most of the clergymen who were admitted to the college
were derisive because, as said before, in the teachings there
was nothing in common with what they called education.
And, of course, there was a vast difference in what she
taught, and in what they had been taught. Whereas they
had gone to college, she had gone to the Bible. In going to
the Bible, she sought to cut through all the text and context
that had grown up between Him and His teachings, and by
this very act she made it difficult for the scholarly to remain
her students.

In her teachings she appealed not to the subtleties that
delight the initiate, but to a devotion that explains itself.

Others came, learned a little, and left to absorb themselves with mesmerism, spiritualism, clairvoyance, medium-
ship, or mind reading. In their desire to make money they
took up with every passing popular notion, but called
themselves Christian Scientists. Many of them made substantial sums of money by their dilution of the teachings
whereas students faithful to the teachings often faced hard
times.

The deviators and the diluters gave Mrs. Eddy much to contend with, and made Christian Science a thing of poor repute. Newspapers, first critical, then friendly, again were critical.

It had been but a few years since there were headlines telling of the arrest of Asa G. Eddy on a charge of murder — and not long since public notoriety was the lot of Mrs. Eddy herself, what with having been hanged in effigy, charged with witchcraft, and accused of operating a house of prostitution. The charge now was that she was a thief.

Julius A. Dresser, who in 1882 had been a patient in Dr. Vail's hydropathic hospital in Hill, New Hampshire, and who had introduced Mrs. Eddy to Phineas P. Quimby in Portland, was living in Boston after a protracted stay in California where, with his wife, he had practiced healing after the fashion practiced by Quimby. Hearing of Mrs. Eddy's work he returned to Boston, visited Sunday services in Hawthorne Hall in early 1883, took note of the attendance, made inquiries as to the sale of *Science and Health,* and, without making his presence known to Mrs. Eddy, decided on an attack.

Under date of February 8, 1883, he wrote a letter to the *Boston Post,* using the initials "A. O." In this letter he accused Mrs. Eddy, although not by name, with "healing through a mental method which [she claims] to have discovered [but] did, in reality, obtain [her] first thoughts of this truth from Dr. Quimby, and [has] added [her] own opinions to the grain of wisdom thus obtained, presenting to the people a small amount of wheat with a great quantity of chaff."

On February 19, in the same newspaper, a reply was published over the initials "E. G." In part, this reply read:

. . . Dr. Quimby's method of treating the sick was manipulation, after immersing his hands in water he rubbed the head, etc. He never called his practice a mental method of treating diseases to our knowledge, and we knew him and his history. We asked him several times if he had any system, aside from manipulation and mesmerism of treating disease, and he always evaded the subject. We were his patient, but he never gave us any further information relating to his practice, but always said it was a secret.

. . . After treating the sick he would retire to a side room and note with pen the especial case and such other paraphrase as he thought best. This copy he gave to certain individuals to bring out, or, as he said, "put in shape." His scribblings were fragmentary, but sometimes very interesting. He requested us to transform them frequently and to give them different meanings, which we did. He never took a student, to our knowledge, or gave information that was practical with his healing. He called his scribblings essays, but never the "Science of Health."

Science and Health is the work of Mrs. Mary B. G. Eddy, issued in 1875. She discovered the science of healing embodied in that work, after years of practical proof through homoeopathy, sealed her proof by a severe casualty, from which she recovered through the exercise of mental power over the body, after the regular physicians pronounced her case incurable. . . .

Five days later Dresser used the *Boston Post* to make a direct attack on Mrs. Eddy:

. . . If "E. G." was ever a patient of Dr. Quimby's, as she claims, and "knew the history," she knows that her article above referred to is false from beginning to end. The undersigned is a quiet, humble citizen of Boston, who seeks no controversy with anybody. But when he knows positively that truth is being outraged and dragged in the dirt, he will step forward and uphold the truth and let error become, as it always does, its own destroyer. As "E. G." has maligned and belittled a good man, who gave his life for the cause of truth, and actually died for sick people, I will call as one witness the same Mrs. Eddy whom "E. G." speaks of.

This lady was a patient and a student of the late Dr. P. P. Quimby of Portland, Me., in the winter of 1862 and '63. She was then known as Mrs. Patterson, wife of Dr. Patterson, dentist. The writer of the communication was a patient and student of Dr. Quimby's at different times, from the year 1860 to 1865, including the period when Mrs. Patterson-Eddy was acting in the same capacity. There are other persons now in Boston who were likewise patients of Dr. Quimby at the same time, and who understand all the facts herein related.

Mrs. Patterson-Eddy knows positively that the assertion of "E. G." in last Monday's *Post* are a tissue of falsehoods. There are only some shades of truth on mere minor points contained in "E. G.'s" article. Mrs. Patterson-Eddy knows the late Dr. P. P. Quimby of Portland, Me., was actually and solely originator and founder of a mental method of treating diseases. . . .

She knows also that he called his peculiar theory the science of health, and that from him she got this name for the doctrine incorporated in her books. Dr. Quimby never had regular students, but to such of his patients as could understand him he freely explained his life-giving doctrine, for it was no secret, and such ones had access also to a portion of his writings, and copied them, as did Mrs. Patterson-Eddy. Such persons as her-

self and others of an inquiring mind were therefore in a sense
students of the doctor, and they made the most of their opportunities. . . .

The reply was immediate, and was signed by Mrs. Eddy:

> We had laid the foundations of mental healing
> before we ever saw Dr. Quimby; were a homeopa-
> thist without a diploma, owing to our aversion to
> the dissecting room. We made our first experi-
> ments in mental healing about 1853, when we
> were convinced that mind had a science which, if
> understood, would heal all diseases. We were then
> investigating that science, but never saw Dr.
> Quimby until 1862. . . .
> We never were a student of Dr. Quimby's and
> Mr. Dresser knows that. Dr. Q. never had students
> to our knowledge. He was a humanitarian, but a
> very unlearned man. He never published a work
> in his life; was not a lecturer or teacher. He was
> somewhat of a remarkable healer, and at the time
> we knew him he was known as a mesmerist. We
> were one of his patients. He manipulated his pa-
> tients, but possibly back of his practice he had a
> theory in advance of his method, and, as we now
> understand it, and have since discovered, he min-
> gled that theory with mesmerism.
> We knew him about twenty years ago and aimed
> to help him. We saw he was looking in our direc-
> tion and asked him to write his thought out. He
> did so, and then we would take that copy to correct,
> and, sometimes, to transform it that he would say it
> was our composition, which it virtually was, but

we always gave him back the copy and, sometimes, wrote his name on the back of it. . . .

After recounting her own healing in Swampscott, Mrs. Eddy acknowledged she had written to Dresser for help, as he claimed she had, because "the physician attending me said I had taken the last step I ever should, but in two days I got out of bed *alone* and *will* walk." She recalled that the fear of her friends that she really had not recovered from "the terrible spinal" trouble from which she had "suffered so long and hopelessly" had communicated itself to her; and went on to explain:

> . . . In one of these moments of fear we wrote Mr. Dresser. . . . We sought for once the encouragement of one we believed friendly, also with whom we conversed on Dr. Q's method of healing, and when we had said to him "it is a mystery," he replied to the effect that he believed no one but the Doctor himself knew how he healed.
>
> But lo! after we have founded mental healing and nearly twenty years have elapsed during which we have taught some 600 students and published five or six thousand volumes on this subject, already circulated in the United States and Europe, the aforesaid gentleman announces to the public, Dr. Quimby [is] the founder of mental healing. . . .

The exchange of letters attracted attention, and added to the growing disaffection within the movement.

Capitalizing on both, Dresser began a vigorous campaign to establish Phineas P. Quimby as the "originator and founder" of Christian Science. Help came to him from

Warren F. Evans, a Salisbury, Massachusetts, clergyman who had been a patient of Dr. Quimby's. The clergyman, long interested in mental healing, was the author of a number of books on the subject [6] and viewed with annoyance Mrs. Eddy's efforts.

Dresser and Evans set about to gather into one group all Quimby patients, and to establish a Quimby school of thought, with Dresser as its spokesman. They attracted one hundred to two hundred persons, including some of Mrs. Eddy's students, and in the spring of 1887 Dresser published *The True History of Mental Science*. This book which, largely, was an expansion of the letters in the *Boston Post,* drew a reply from Mrs. Eddy in the *Christian Science Journal* of June 1887:

> The most unselfish motives evoke the most in-gratitude; yet it is only by such motives that the best results are achieved. My final discovery of the Science of Mind-healing was the outgrowth of my motives and method.
>
> A dozen years before meeting Mr. Quimby, I healed desperate cases of disease with unmedicated globules. This was then my *modus operandi,* arising from such ignorant therapeutics; but it was by no means Christian Science Mind-healing. The lost chord of Truth (healing, as of old) I caught consciously from the Divine Harmony, vibrating its own sweet music. It was to me a revelation of Truth, — God; and Science, explaining the Prin-

[6] *The Mental Cure* (1860); *Mental Medicine* (1872); *Soul and Body* (1875); *The Divine Law of Cure* (1881); *The Primitive Mind Cure* (1885); *Esoteric Christianity* (1886). Dr. Evans also operated a sanitarium in Salisbury, calling it the "Evans Home."

ciple of this Divine Harmony, enabled me to understand it, and to systematize and demonstrate Truth.

It was after the death of Mr. Quimby, and when I was apparently at the door of death, that I made this discovery in 1866. After that, it took about ten years of hard work for me to reach the standard of my first edition of Science and Health, published in 1875.

Before understanding and settling the great question of my discovery, I wrote to Mr. Dresser, who had tried Mr. Quimby's cure by manipulation, and asked him if he could help anybody, or tell how Quimby healed. He replied, in a letter which I have, to the effect that he could not, and was unable to heal his wife of a slight ailment; adding, that he did not believe anyone living knew how Mr. Quimby healed the sick.

As long ago as 1844, I was convinced that mortal mind produced all disease, and that the various medical systems were in no proper sense Scientific. In 1862, when I first visited Mr. Quimby, I was proclaiming — to druggists, spiritualists and mesmerists — that Science must govern all healing.

When, therefore, I believed that Mr. Quimby had healed me, I naturally wrote and talked as if his method must be genuine Science, and I was too proud to believe it could be aught else.

Afterwards, I suffered a relapse; then I saw my bitter mistake. I then realized the harmful influence, mentally and physically, of such a false, human concept. This I hastened to acknowledge. In proportion as the mischief of misconceived mental bases and methods of treating disease were discovered, I took back my words, uttered in ignorant enthusiasm, and stated the Truth as it is in Science.

Misinterpretations and misapplications of Truth constitute all error; and error can only be destroyed by the correct interpretation and application of Truth. The animal poison imparted through mortal mind, by false or incorrect mental physicians, is more destructive to health and morals than are the mineral and vegetable poisons prescribed by the matter-physicians. This acknowledgement brings the wrath of mediums and mesmerists upon me, but never warps my purpose to enlighten mankind. . . .

Encouraged by Dresser, George A. Quimby began assembling his father's papers with a view to publication. Hearing of this, Mrs. Eddy offered to pay the cost of publication and to turn over the proceeds of the sale of the book, under these conditions:

Mr. George A. Quimby, son of the late Phineas P. Quimby, — over his own signature, and before a witness — stated, in 1883, that he had in his possession at that time *all* the manuscripts written by his father. I hereby declare to expose the falsehoods of parties publicly intimating that I have appropriated matter belonging to the aforesaid Quimby, that I will pay the cost of printing and publishing the first edition of these manuscripts, with the author's name attached:

Provided, — that I am allowed first to examine such manuscripts, and that I find they were Mr. P. P. Quimby's own compositions, and not mine, that were left with him many years ago — or that they have not since his death, in 1865, been stolen from my published works; and also, that I am given the right to bring out this one edition under copyright of said owner of said manuscripts, and that all the money accruing from the sale of the book shall be paid to said owner. Some of Mr. Quimby's purported writings, quoted by J. A. Dresser, were my own words, as nearly as I can recollect them.

There is a great demand for my book *Science and Health*. Hence Mr. Dresser's excuse for the delay in publishing Quimby's Manuscripts, namely, that this age is not sufficiently enlightened to be benefited by them (?) is lost; for if I have copied from Quimby, and my book is accepted, this acceptance creates a demand for his writings.

MARY B. G. EDDY

The offer, which was made in the *Journal* in June 1887, was published in Portland, Maine, newspapers, and was declined by Quimby. He was fearful, so he replied, that his father's writings would be "altered or destroyed." The manuscripts were published in 1921, and include this statement: "The religion which she [Mrs. Eddy] teaches certainly is hers; for which I cannot be too thankful; for I should be loath to go down to my grave feeling that my father was in any way connected with Christian Science. . . ."

Ordinarily, George A. Quimby's declaration would be sufficient to establish Mrs. Eddy's authorship. But a shelf of books and pamphlets and essays has been published asserting, as did Dresser, that Phineas P. Quimby was the originator and Mary Baker Eddy the plagiarist.

When Mrs. Eddy went to Portland to see Quimby in 1862, she was forty-two years old. An invalid much of her life, she had studied medicine (homeopathy) hoping to find health. Discouraged, she was turning again to the thought that first came to her in 1844, this thought being that if she was to find healing it would be in the Bible.

In Quimby she met a man, a kind of man, who did not believe in medication and who, through mental work, was a healer. This made a great impression on her. Deeply religious, she saw, or thought she saw, in the Quimby healings something more than mesmerism and manipulation.

One day she said to him that God, not mesmerism, not manipulation, and not Quimby, was the healer.

Of a religious nature himself, although not a Bible student, Quimby was impressed. They often talked about healing, and Quimby asked her to put into words the beliefs that were beginning to take shape in her mind. She did, and left these writings behind when, after her relapse, she discontinued the treatments and returned to Swampscott.

However, despite Quimby's failure to heal her, there is no question but their conversations together had much early influence on her. A gentle woman and a grateful woman (almost childishly grateful for kindnesses shown to her in her years of search) , Mrs. Eddy never lost her warm feeling of friendship for the Portland healer. In the early years of her quest she wrote many things. These writings were distributed. Some never were returned to her. It is quite possible some of them found their way into Quimby's hands because they had mutual friends, and because he was interested in her Bible studies.

There is a similarity in some of the so-called "Quimby manuscripts" to her writings, but examination of all of Mrs. Eddy's writings, and all of Quimby's writings, will dismiss doubt and erase speculation over their authorship.

From the day when Mary Baker Eddy began to get away from the "feeble attempts to state the Principle and practice of Christian healing," [7] her writings bear little resemblance not only to the disputed words, but to the ones about which there is no dispute until, in honesty, George A. Quimby was able to say "the religion which she teaches certainly is hers."

Her request of George A. Quimby for permission to examine the manuscripts and his refusal because he was afraid they would be "altered or destroyed" are understandable.

She wanted to separate what she believed belonged to her from what she knew belonged to him. For his part, he had an intense personal dislike of Mrs. Eddy, and for her teachings. He could have resolved the matter by requiring the presence of a third person at the examination of the papers. Seemingly, this obvious way to protect them never occurred to him.

In connection with these Quimby manuscripts three other charges have been leveled at Mrs. Eddy.

One says she "established her copyright, while the Quimby material languished in desk drawers"; [8] one says she stole the title of *Science and Health* from Quimby; one says she obtained her science of healing from Quimby.

[7] *Science and Health*, Preface, ix.
[8] *Mrs. Eddy*, by Edwin Franden Dakin; copyright, 1929–1930.

The first charge can be traced back to Edward J. Arens and the court decision which punished him for infringement of copyright. He, too, attempted to set up the Quimby claim but, as told, refused to testify under oath in support of his claim. The second charge that Quimby was the author of the words *Science and Health* also falls short of validity. These words were used centuries before Quimby was born.

To accept the claim that Mrs. Eddy obtained her science of healing from Quimby is to reject all the words and works of the great Teacher. Nothing could be more separated from the truth than such an allegation.

Mrs. Eddy did not obtain her high affirmation of God from Quimby.

She obtained it by going to the Bible and listening. The great servants in the Kingdom of the Spirit have always done that: listened.

She heard, in the teachings of the One she believed, the explanation "of myself I can do nothing"; the statement He was in the Father and the Father was in Him; the declaration of His Sonship.

She first perceived, then understood, that in this high affirmation of God was the source of all authority.

To perceive, she had to put aside what was familiar in other teachings; and to understand, she had to listen — listen from within, *knowing* God never speaks outside of Himself.

Ritualists reject this, and conformists deny it, but ritualism and conformity are never parts of that humility which is always first to hear the music of Easter.

Where are the words that describe the Indescribable? What are they?

When every facet of the Law is but the beginning of another, words are but faint suggestions of the Great Gift. Even His words never do more than suggest, and make no pretension to anything but affirmation.

The Great Gift is not subject to analysis. Nor is it subject to theft.

That Mrs. Eddy should be vigorous in her denial of Dresser's charges is altogether appropriate.

Mental healers were in vogue and her teachings were not only confused with theirs, but appropriated by them. Nor was her anxiety over the confusion occasioned by any fear of loss of position, or loss of money, as so often has been charged by her enemies.

Her concern was over dilution — dilution in the minds of her students, dilution in the minds of *all* — of what she believed was required if all are to be disciples of the Son of God. As keeper of the gate, she would have been a poor guardian indeed had she done less than protect what she believed.

CHAPTER NINE

Preparation for Leadership

WITHOUT the ability to renew herself, it is hard to see how Mrs. Eddy and her teachings could have survived the middle and last years of the 1880's. They were years of confusion and rebellion.

There was confusion because there were all manner of excursions into the occult, with many of the excursionists advertising themselves as "practitioners of the very latest methods in Christian Science." There was rebellion because Mary Baker Eddy accepted "I and my Father are one" as being the conscience of the universe and the citizenship of the city of God.

Illustrative of what was being taught by some, as Christian Science, was this method of "spiritual healing": "1. Look at an object on the ceiling ten minutes; think of that object alone. 2. Write a proposition on a sheet of paper, as 'God is the only Reality.' Think it for ten minutes with your eyes fixed upon the paper. 3. Begin to think a subject and give a dollar to the poor every time your mind wanders."

There were the "Go As You Please Treatments," which advertised: "Thought is substance, stuff, potency. Thoughts attract others that are like them. Concentrate your thoughts on a person and they will go to him like water through a fireman's hose."

There was:

Treatment 5, Will Treatment and Command

. . . Call the patient by name — SILENTLY — John Jones! In the name of God I bid you come out of your delusions. I command you to forget your sickness and pain sensations. I order you to stop your silly, sinful thinking about your physical diseases. I direct you to quit your inane, insane, iniquitous babble and drivel about your troubles and other people's troubles. I insist upon the abandonment of that gone-in-the-box, down-at-the-heel, woe-begone expression which you wear upon your face. I uncompromisingly and imperatively protest against that sickly, imbecile, flimsy feeling that you cannot live unless you tell everybody "O, how bad I feel!" In the name of GOD, John, I bid you be brave — enduring, full of grit, patient, hopeful, heroic. The Lord of the Universe expects every man to do his duty, and He is looking at you, John! Come now! All for God! Assert the majestic truth of your nature. Maintain the dignity of man. How grand a creature you are, John! The world could not whirl without you. Courage, now!

Also called "Christian Science" was this:

. . . The All-Mother sang you into being, you are music. In rhythmic mathematics is the plan of your virginal soul drawn; you are strong and divine; you are a globe of incomparable alabaster in which burns the exquisite lamp of womanliness (or manliness) lighted by the hand of the Eternal! And that you really could have sorrow! Could really feel pain! You, through whom flows the life river of the Arch-Genius of the Universe! Come out of the darkened cave of the sense. Achieve the eternal renaissance of the soul. Look into the abyss of reality. Do you not see afar the white Lotos, your self of self?

And this one, called "Prayer for a Dyspeptic," by Dr. Jean Hazzard, head of the New York School of Primitive and Practical Christian Science:

Holy Reality! We BELIEVE in Thee that Thou are EVERYWHERE present. We *really* believe it. Blessed Reality we do

not pretend to believe. WE BELIEVE. Believing that Thou art
everywhere present, we believe that Thou are in the patient's
stomach, in every fibre, in every cell, in every atom, that Thou
art the sole, only Reality of that stomach. Heavenly Holy Reality, we *will* try not to be such hypocrites and infidels, as every
day of our lives to affirm our faith in Thee and then immediately to tell how sick we are, forgetting that Thou art everything and Thou art not sick, and therefore, that nothing in the
universe was ever sick, or can be sick. . . . We know, Father
and Mother of us all, that the disease is of the Carnal, Mortal
Mind given over to the World, the Flesh and the Devil; that the
mortal mind is a twist, a distortion, a false attitude, the
HAMARTIA (Off-the-Trackness) of Thought. . . . Help us to
stoutly affirm with our hand in Your hand, with our eyes fixed
on Thee, that we have no Dyspepsia, that we never had Dyspepsia, that we will never have Dyspepsia, and that there is no such
thing, that there never was any such thing, and there never
will be any such thing. Amen.

In October 1886, Mrs. Eddy used the columns of the
Journal to strike directly at the spurious teachings.

. . . The growth of human inquiry and the increasing popularity of Christian Science, I regret
to say, has called out of their hiding places and set
upon us the poisonous reptiles and devouring
beasts of mortal mind. To these elements of ignorance, mad ambition, envy, strife, hate, and to
their Babels of confusion worse confounded, I call
a halt! And if the voice of Truth and Love be
heard above this din of error and hate, the stately
march of Christian Science will go on.

To protect the public, all my worthy students
receive certificates of degrees, that are renewed
annually, until they graduate with diplomas.

These credentials should be required . . . from all who claim to Practice or Teach Christian Science, Mind-healing . . .

Until the students graduate, they are incapable of teaching more than the first lessons of the Science of Mind. For them not to say this to all who apply to be taught is an error. As yet I have found no one able to explain correctly all my textbook *Science and Health*.

The claims of the counterfeiters were too fantastic to be overlooked. A Methodist, and an acknowledged authority on ecclesiastical law, the Reverend James Buckley brought national ridicule to Mrs. Eddy and her teachings, by writing in the *Century* magazine in July 1887. In his article Dr. Buckley used quotations from the writings of three of Mrs. Eddy's students,[1] added paragraphs written by Edward J. Arens, lumped them with excerpts from the practices of various cults, included a prayer by Hazzard, and entitled his article "Christian Science."

Because of the clergyman's prominence a great deal of discussion followed the appearance of his article and, in New York, the newspapers quoted Hazzard as saying, "Mrs. Eddy's philosophy really originated in the book *Bhagavad-Gita*."

In August 1887 the *Christian Science Journal* referred to Buckley's article, and to the newspaper interviews with Hazzard: ". . . The evident purpose of the article is not so much instruction as entertainment. The author means to tell a good story and he does it [but] the truth is sometimes so sandwiched that it momentarily resembles the thieves

[1] Elizabeth G. Stuart, Kate Taylor, Luther M. Marston, M.D.

crucified on either side . . . it is surely not fair to adduce Mr. Hazzard's extravaganza as 'an example of Christian Science.' "

Adding to the confusion were the ambitions of students who, becoming restless under Mrs. Eddy's insistence that there could be no deviation from Principle in Christian Science, set out to offer what their teacher offered — on easier terms.

Mrs. Mary H. Plunkett was one such, and joining her was Mrs. Emma Curtis Hopkins, an assistant editor of the *Journal,* who was expelled from the Christian Scientist Association on December 16, 1885.

When expelled, Mrs. Hopkins, who had been high in her teacher's confidence, took with her all of Mrs. Eddy's plans for her Church, her college, and her Association, including plans for the establishment of reading rooms and dispensaries. Communicating with Mrs. Plunkett, already a deserter, Mrs. Hopkins proposed that they duplicate Mrs. Eddy's efforts. Using notes she had made, surreptitiously, while attending lectures, Mrs. Hopkins prepared twelve lessons in what she called "Christian Science" and, together, the women spent a year gathering about them scores of former students of Mrs. Eddy, as well as hundreds of persons who were interested in metaphysics. Sharing the lessons Mrs. Hopkins had written, the women established a partnership. Mrs. Hopkins chose Chicago for her headquarters while Mrs. Plunkett chose New York.

In September 1887, Mrs. Plunkett gave a newspaper interview in which she said Mrs. Eddy was sick and had invited her to become associated in the management of the Massachusetts Metaphysical College. As quoted in Boston newspapers, Mrs. Plunkett said: "I called on Mrs. Eddy, found her sick, unable to go on with her class, and she invited me to return to the fold. I refused because I could not agree with Mrs. Eddy about teaching."

The interview caused quite a stir in Boston; and in October (1887) Mrs. Eddy wrote in the *Journal*:

> . . . The woman referred to did call on me, about the first of September, and sent up my servant with her card and a bouquet of flowers. I was in good health and spirits; and the entire substance of my conversation with her was a calm and kind rebuke of any false position taken in the name of Christian Science. The substance of her talk was a timid attempt to raise herself in my estimation. After she had left me, I remarked to my clerk:
>
> "This call was made for the purpose of subsequently misrepresenting what I had said, and you ought to have heard our conversation."
>
> Mrs. Mary H. Plunkett's report of our interview . . . is an utter falsehood, throughout. Nothing of the kind was said. It is not probable that I should ask a person to assist me in teaching Christian Science whom I regarded as too unsafe to be received into my Normal Class. Past experience had taught me her character, and I regret to add, that on the evening of her call I saw no improvement in her motives and aims.
>
> She is reported as saying that she paid "three hundred dollars for her tuition at the Massachusetts Metaphysical College, and that I then required two hundred dollars more to grant her a

certificate which she refused to pay." These are the facts relative to our business transaction.

When she entered the Primary Course, she claimed she did not have the money to pay for her tuition, and asked me to take some jewelry as part payment. I declined; but discounted one-third on her tuition, and she paid me just two hundred dollars. The only money I ever receive for certificates is twenty-five cents on each annually renewed certificate. I gave her no certificate, solely because she did not improve the opportunity she had in the class of receiving my instructions; and because I learned, with sad surprise, that only God's hand and lessons could so change her motives and morals as to make her receptive to Christian Science. My autumn term was referred to in our conversation; but I simply told her the Primary Class was postponed to accommodate some members of the bar who wished to enter my College, but were obliged to attend the September term of court.

There are sometimes to be met certain adepts who compel honest people to besmirch their own pens, and to spend their time in correcting injurious falsehoods. If you converse with these masqueraders, however cautiously and kindly, they are sure to go away and belie you, and repeat (professedly) what they want people to think that you have said.

This retards the cause of Christian Science. How shall we treat such defamers? If we refuse to meet them we lose a possible chance of doing good to this class of creatures. Even if we do not grant them interviews, they will improve other chances to do us evil. Charity receives many blows; but uncharitableness in ourselves is more to be feared than the blows.

The following month — November 1887 — Mrs. Plunkett had a publication of her own. It was called *Truth: A Magazine of Christian Science;* but after two issues the name was changed to the *International Magazine of Christian Science.* Mrs. Plunkett was the editor. Mrs. Hopkins was her assistant. The Unity Publishing Company, in which Mrs. Plunkett was identified as a partner, was the publisher. Called "the official organ of the International Christian Science Association," the magazine announced among its "intentions and objects" that it would "present a review of the current news concerning the progress of Christian Science."

Advertised in the publication as recommended reading for all Christian Scientists were about fifty books, including *Bread Pills* by C. M. Barrows; *Esoteric Christianity* by Dr. W. F. Evans; *Fifty Doses of Mental Medicine* by L. M. Merrman; *Personified Unthinkables* by Sarah Stanley Grimke; *What is Christian Science?* by Ursula Gestefeld, and another book under similar title by Albert B. Dorman.

Science and Health also was included as recommended reading, along with other writings of Mrs. Eddy,[2] but no mention was made of her as the founder of Christian Science, as president of the Massachusetts Metaphysical College, or as a teacher. In the publication, which was of comparable size with the *Journal,* was an announcement that

---

[2] *Christian Science (No and Yes)* ; *People's God; Rudiments and Rules of Divine Science; Unity of Good and Unreality of Evil.*

Mrs. Plunkett and Mrs. Hopkins had a stated hour for mental treatment with their students. It was called the Hour of Unison, and the time was from eight until nine o'clock each morning.

Under the direction of Mrs. Hopkins, colleges were organized in St. Paul, Minnesota, Louisville, Kentucky, and Milwaukee, Wisconsin. They were called the Hopkins Colleges of Christian Science. In Chicago was located the Hopkins Theological Seminary, where students were prepared for Christian Science Ministry, the First Course being devoted to "instruction in the principles and practice of Apostolic Healing," and the Second Course being "devoted to Theology and Practical Ministry." In New York, Mrs. Plunkett organized the National School of Christian Science.

Among those attracted to the women were Albert B. Dorman, of Worcester, Massachusetts, and Luther M. Marston, M.D., of Boston. Dorman brought with him a publication called *Messenger of Truth,* with one thousand five hundred subscribers; Marston brought his *Mental Healing Monthly,* with one thousand eight hundred subscribers. Combined, they gave the *International Magazine of Christian Science* a circulation larger than the *Journal.*

Each a student of Mrs. Eddy, Dorman and Marston departed from her teachings to form groups of their own. Dorman was opposed to the granting of diplomas by the Massachusetts Metaphysical College; Marston argued that Christian Science should include in its teachings such subjects as hypnotism, mesmerism, spiritualism, or whatever the subject of individual interest — "all should be taught," he maintained, "and if not taught, Christian Science should be antagonistic to none."

Mrs. Eddy pointed out to Marston that "the hypocrite

alone wishes to be known as antagonistic to no one, for he had no truth to defend." To this she added: "Error always united in a definition of purpose with truth, to give it buoyancy." [3]

For a time after leaving the teachings, Marston dropped the words "Christian Science" from his publication, but returned to their use upon learning their absence from the editorial columns had an adverse effect on his circulation. At the time of merging with the *International Magazine of Christian Science,* he was advertising his publication as being one that was "devoted to the exposition of Christian Science and divine truth."

About this same time he called upon all metaphysicians to meet with him in a national convention in Chicago, and included in his call all Christian Scientists living in the Midwest. The convention was held in 1888 and was presided over by A. J. Swarts, who in 1884 had said he had been a Christian Science practitioner for twenty years — "long before Mrs. Eddy ever heard of it, and she borrowed from me."

Hearing of this claim when she visited Chicago in 1884, Mrs. Eddy invited Swarts to attend five of her lectures to learn for himself that he was wrong. Swarts accepted her invitation and, following her return to Boston, began to use his newly acquired knowledge and to call himself a teacher in Christian Science.

In October 1884, he began issuing a magazine he called *Mind-Cure and Science of Life.* In the first issue he said: "Though the editor passed through the greater part of a course of instruction by Mrs. Eddy, of Boston, and can pass an examination in her books on *her system of healing,* it will

[3] *Christian Science Journal,* November 1885.

always be the truth that during the past twenty years he has cured many hundred cases by purely mental methods."

Working out of Chicago into the Western States, Swarts organized classes charging five dollars to twenty-five dollars (whatever he could get) for "seven lessons in Christian Science." He taught hundreds of persons and, at the same time, built up the circulation of his publication until it, too, was larger than the circulation of the *Christian Science Journal.* Reaching this point he went to Boston where, by letter, he proposed to Mrs. Eddy that they combine their efforts. Instead of being interested, Mrs. Eddy warned the public about him.

She knew about his classes in the Western States, his publication, about his visit to Syracuse, New York, a few months before, where he had announced in the newspapers that he would "undertake to cure, in seven treatments, 12 invalids suffering from diseases medical doctors call incurable"; and about how, in the same press announcement, he had invited the public to "select those who are to be healed."

Arrested, but freed when he convinced the court that his "system of cure did not come under any medical law of the State of New York," Swarts used the publicity to organize classes, to teach what he said was Christian Science, and to obtain subscriptions for his magazine. His aggressiveness attracted Marston and brought an invitation to visit Boston in May 1887 and join with Marston in gathering into one organization "all persons interested in Christian Science and other forms of mental healing." The organization, of course, was the one under the direction of Mrs. Plunkett and her assistant, Mrs. Hopkins.

It was at this time that Swarts sought an interview with Mrs. Eddy.

*   *   *

Altogether, there were nearly a score of publications identifying themselves as Christian Science periodicals. Repeatedly, Mrs. Eddy cautioned her pupils against promiscuous reading; and in the *Journal,* in March 1888, she cautioned again:

> . . . Homœopathy is the last link in material medicine. The next step is medicine in Mind. One of the foremost virtues of homœopathy is the exclusions of compounds from its pharmacy. I wish the students of Christian Science (and many who are not students understand enough of this matter to heed the advice) to keep out of their heads the notion the compounded metaphysics (so-called) is, or can be, Christian Science. They should take our magazine, work for it, and read it. They should eschew all magazines and books which are less than the best. "Choose this day whom ye will serve." My students should get the cobwebs out of their minds, which spurious compounds engender. . . .

This reminder to her students to devote their attention to better reading was objected to by some, it being asserted by them that Mrs. Eddy "is attempting to control our minds." What Mrs. Eddy was trying to do was to guide them. Plainly she wrote: ". . . they should eschew all magazines and books which are less than the best."

Civilized minds have long accepted that rule.

Former students did not neglect the opportunity to add to the resentment. They invented a good many stories, most of them malicious, and gave them wide circulation. They said she was "money mad" — so much so that whenever she occupied the pulpit in Chickering Hall she forced Frank E.

Mason, the assistant pastor, to pay her fifteen dollars from his own salary. This was not true. They said: "The *Journal* is a gold mine, and Mrs. Eddy is making a fortune out of it." Audits disclosed that in a financial sense the publication was just about breaking even.

They said: "Mrs. Eddy regularly employs a medical doctor to keep her well." The charge was believed by so many people that Mrs. Eddy issued a public statement: "I have neither called nor consulted a physician for myself for over twenty years, although I have averaged twelve hours work per day, with only two weeks' vacation in this time. . . ."

They said "Mary Baker Eddy has become a drug addict," and she replied to this by writing in the *Journal:* To quench the growing flames of falsehood, once in about seven years I have to repeat this, — that I use no drugs whatever, not even cofea (coffee), thea (tea), capsicum (red pepper); although every day, and especially at dinner, I indulge in homœopathic doses of natrium muriaticum (common salt). . . ."

Because of her wish to devote her time and her thought to her work as Discoverer, Founder, and Leader, and also because of her desire that instead of depending on her for guidance, students should seek the "guidance of Mind," Mrs. Eddy had announced in the *Journal* in 1885 that she did not take patients. In Boston, where in 1882 she had healed Hanover P. Smith, who had been deaf and dumb since birth,[4] this was an announcement that at this late time was being used by her enemies in charging "she has lost her power to heal."

[4] Before being brought to Mrs. Eddy by his mother, Smith was in an asylum for the deaf and dumb where medical doctors had pronounced him incurable.

To these charges Mrs. Eddy paid no attention; nor, and to the confusion of her enemies, did she cease to be the instrument of many healings.

In 1886, Mary H. Crosby, a student at the New England Conservatory of Music, came to see her following a diagnosis by a physician of an insurance company of a stomach condition. The next morning the condition had disappeared. . . . In 1886, while attending class in the Massachusetts Metaphysical College, Erwin L. Coleman, of Coleman, Nebraska, received a telegram informing him his wife was dying in childbirth. Mrs. Eddy assured him to the contrary. The woman the doctor said was dying lived to become a teacher in Christian Science.

Only one with a deep love of humanity and a deep feeling for humanity's need could have continued this lonely way. At a time when everyone, it sometimes must have seemed, was talking to her students, Mrs. Eddy was never, as she wrote on September 20, 1886, "in any way alarmed or discouraged. I was never less so. I know in Whom I have believed. . . ." [5]

She believed in God, and her effort was to get humanity to believe — to accept simple truth; to realize that every level of progress is mastered by the next step above it, and to take that step — to abandon the deception of material personality and acknowledge the reality of an eternal relationship — to know there are no cathedrals in the Kingdom of the Spirit, that God is not summoned by bell nor persuaded by incense — to learn that God is found, not in ceremony, but in silence; and that He comes alone, without need of advisers.

[5] Original letter in Archives of The Mother Church, Boston, Massachusetts.

Admitting to but one rule — to obey God, without having to know why — Mary Baker Eddy disclosed her fitness to be the Discoverer, and the Founder, and the Leader of Christian Science.

Soon after establishing her headquarters in New York, Mrs. Mary H. Plunkett became identified in the newspapers as "the high priestess of Christian Science." In her magazine, she explained that "Christian Science is the science of spirit. The science of spirit is the essence of all religions and philosophies. Spirit is causation, hence back of all the arts and sciences there is Christian Science, the science of the sciences."

With Mrs. Hopkins she established "Christian Science rest rooms" in New York, Chicago, and other cities, while under the imprint of the International Christian Science Association the two women published a series of "International Bible Lessons, Spiritually Interpreted." There follows an extract from one of the lessons:

The book of Exodus contains forty chapters. So named because it contains an account of the exodus, going out or departure of the tribes of Israel from Mind (Egypt) into Spirit, the promised land, or from embryonic growth into birth.

The first two chapters are like twenty-four elders, i.e., the twelve statements of being, masculine and feminine taken twice over, first the twelve masculine and then the twelve feminine.

These statements are as follows in order:

1. Principle	7. Love
2. Soul	8. Substance
3. Mind	9. Intelligence
4. Spirit	10. Omnipresence
5. Life	11. Omniscience
6. Truth	12. Omnipotence

This extract illustrates the confusion between the teachings of the two women and the teachings of Mrs. Eddy, and even while the "International Bible Lessons, Spiritually Interpreted," were being published, there appeared in the *International Magazine of Christian Science* in its issue of April 3, 1889, a "special notice," over the signatures of John J. T. Plunkett and Mary H. Plunkett, saying: "We . . . from the most profound conviction of duty, do jointly declare our marriage null and void. . . ."

The prominence of the Plunketts caused the newspapers to identify Christian Science with free love, and they sharply inquired if the laws of the land were to be ignored at the convenience of "the high priestess of this new cult, and her husband." Followers of Mrs. Plunkett were equally sharp with the newspapers, the prevailing opinion among them being that by agreeing to divorce, the Plunketts were submitting to "holy sacrifice."

This statement brought increased denunciation of Christian Science from the pulpits, and in the newspapers, while in the May, June, and July issues of the *International* were printed long articles explaining "Marriage and Divorce," according to the views of Mrs. Plunkett. In the June issue there was another "special notice": "Since our forms were made up, a matter of vital gravity to the Science has come before the public. It is too late for us to notice it this month, but the July number will contain a full account. Meanwhile, let us be slow in judgment, remembering that all great discoveries and reforms were first a private opinion; second, a little group of believers; third, a target for misrepresentation and abuse; and lastly a fact accomplished. Wait!"

In the July issue the "special notice" appeared in the

form of an announcement of the "spiritual marriage" of
Mrs. Plunkett to A. Bentley Worthington, treasurer of the
International Magazine of Christian Science as well as of the
National School of Christian Science.

The announcement of the "spiritual marriage" required
fourteen and one-half pages of type. It quoted liberally from
Science and Health and, twisting the meaning to suit the
need, concluded that "matrimony, which was once a fixed
fact among us, must lose its present slippery footing, and find
permanence in a more spiritual adherence. The mental
chemicalization, which has brought conjugal infidelity to the
surface, will assuredly throw off this evil, and marriage will
become purer when the scum is gone."

Editorially, the newspapers had a holiday with Mrs.
Plunkett's "spiritual marriage." In the *New York World*
and the *New York Sun* the bride was quoted as saying,
"when Mr. Worthington came into my presence I knew
instantly that he was my conjugal mate"; and she issued this
statement to all newspapers: "The Press, because of its
slight knowledge of Christian Science, has persistently
spoken of me as its 'High Priestess.' This is entirely unwarrantable and untrue. I am only an earnest and grateful student. Mary B. G. Eddy was my teacher, and the teacher
either directly or indirectly of all who are teaching pure
Christian Science. Her book, *Science and Health,* now in its
fortieth edition, is the most important book in the world
today, outside of the Holy Scriptures; in fact, its statements
are Holy Scriptures revealed. While she may sometimes
have seemed severe, with some of us, I am convinced that
but for her determined and oft-repeated warnings, many,
and I am not sure but all of us, because of our belief in
materiality, would have fallen back into mind-cure, or will-
cure healing, instead of rising to the purely spiritual. I am

only one of the many thousands who silently thank God every day for the truth revealed through Mary Baker Eddy."

This was a damaging statement, and a revealing one. Not since the interview in the Boston newspapers had Mrs. Plunkett associated her name with that of Mrs. Eddy's and at no time in her magazine had she identified Mrs. Eddy, or acknowledged her as a teacher, or as the author of *Science and Health*. The statement was damaging to Mrs. Eddy as, probably, it was intended; and it was revealing in its involvement of Mrs. Plunkett as, probably, it was not intended.

In the uproar which followed, the newspapers identified Worthington as being several times a married man, as having failed to divorce his previous wife, as being wanted by the police on a twenty-year-old embezzlement charge, and as masquerading under an assumed name. Worthington disappeared, and in 1889 the *International Magazine of Christian Science* suspended publication. At the same time, the National School of Christian Science ceased to exist.

Meanwhile, in 1885, and despite the attacks he had made upon her, Julius A. Dresser began the study of Christian Science that he might destroy Mrs. Eddy and her teachings. Also, in 1885, Louisa M. Alcott, author of *Little Women* and daughter of A. Bronson Alcott, issued a statement in which she said she had given "mind-cure" a thorough trial, and found it a failure.

Because of Miss Alcott's prominence, the newspapers, magazines, sectarian and medical press gave conspicuous attention to what many described as "Miss Alcott's experience in Christian Science," and little attention to a statement issued by the Massachusetts Metaphysical College on May 15, 1885, in which it was disclosed that Miss Alcott was treated by a Mrs. Anne B. Newman. Mrs. Newman was not a student of Mrs. Eddy, or a student of Christian Science. She was a member of one of many groups practicing mesmerism.

On May 24, 1888, the *Congregationalist,* which had been quiet for some time, returned to the attack, declaiming: ". . . To such empirical treatment [Christian Science] do Christian mothers commit their little children, with a blindness more blameworthy than that of the heathen matron who sacrifices her babe to the god of the Ganges"; and the *Journal of the American Medical Association* in its issue of June 16, 1888, editorialized: "Under the title 'Christian Science Manslaughter,' an item from Malden, Mass., of May 26, states that Judge Pettingill found a Mrs. Abbie H. Corner, a 'Christian Scientist,' guilty of manslaughter in causing the death of her daughter, Mrs. Lottie James, by neglecting to provide proper medical assistance at the time of her confinement on April 18. She was held in $5,000 bail. . . . And so it goes. It is about three years since this new fad had its birth in the East, and by the assistance of the newspapers spread over the country. For the newspapers, nothing was too good to say of it. Now that the easily foreseen result has occurred, the papers have discovered that all is not wisdom that cries aloud in the streets, and are as ready to publish derogatory items concerning the 'faith-cure' as they were at first hasty in flaunting its nonsense in the faces of sensible people. It will not be long before the now votaries of 'Christian Science' will be in need of a new fad." [6]

Mrs. Corner was not found guilty of manslaughter. She

[6] The first arrest of a Christian Science practitioner was in McGregor, Iowa, in 1887, when medical doctors prevailed upon the police to jail Mrs. Lottie Post and the county authorities to prosecute on a charge of practicing medicine without a license. Mrs. Post was twice convicted and fined before winning acquittal in a third trial.

was acquitted. Following an autopsy, medical testimony agreed that death would have ensued, the result of hemorrhages, had medical doctors been in attendance.

A year before Dresser began studying Christian Science, Mrs. Eddy had a student who was to give her a great deal of trouble. This student's name was Ursula N. Gesterfelt.

A Christian Science practitioner in Chicago from the time of her graduation in 1884, Mrs. Gesterfelt came to believe, in 1888, that as Mary Baker Eddy was the author of *Science and Health,* so was Ursula N. Gesterfelt its interpreter. Putting together eighteen lessons and twelve sections under the title, *Statement of Christian Science,* Mrs. Gesterfelt circularized Mrs. Eddy's students on June 8, 1888, offering her pamphlet for sale and saying: ". . . This work is not intended to supplant *Science and Health,* but is offered as a key to those who are unable to understand its meaning. The book, *Science and Health,* first published in 1875, was the first statement of Christian Science given to the public. Though many publications of the same nature are in wide circulation today, it still stands preeminent among them as the text-book of the Science, because its statements are positive, exact and unmixed with theory. It is yea, yea; nay, nay. At the same time it is a book difficult of comprehension, and much patient study of it, for many, does not suffice for an understanding of its meaning. . . ."

A mixture of mysticism, spiritualism, and interpolations from Mrs. Eddy's writings, the *Statement* found few readers. In anger, Mrs. Gesterfelt issued another pamphlet. This one she entitled "Jesuitism in Christian Science." It was a vicious, personal attack on Mrs. Eddy's leadership, to which Mrs. Eddy replied in the November 1888 issue of the *Journal:*

> . . . The picture she [Mrs. Gesterfelt] draws of
> me, in the above-named pamphlet ["Jesuitism in
> Christian Science"] is the subjective state of her
> own mind. . . . The reader recognizes at once that
> it is no portraiture of the Author of *Science and
> Health.* . . . My heart's desire is, that the mind of
> this woman be imbued with better thoughts, and
> her life uplifted. The only sense in which I employ
> the phrase "Loyal Students," she seems not to
> know. I mean those who are loyal to God, to jus-
> tice, to truth and Love . . . united indissolubly
> in the bonds of Christian Science. This bond is not
> *personality;* it is Principle. . . .

In Chicago at the same time was the Reverend Joseph
Adams. Born in England and in turn an Episcopalian, a
Congregationalist, a Methodist, and an Independent Congregationalist, Adams was assistant pastor in an Independent
Congregationalist church in Oakland, California, in the
early 1880's, when he wrote Mrs. Eddy for an interpretation of some of her teachings. There was correspondence
between them and, when Adams became involved in a dispute and was dismissed from the Oakland church, he went
to Boston.

On invitation of Mrs. Eddy, he attended Primary Class
and, on three occasions,[7] preached in Chickering Hall.

Returning to California, he attempted to establish himself as a Christian Science practitioner, was not successful,
and moved to Chicago. Here he became involved in a
wrangle over church organization with the Reverend
George B. Day, pastor of the Chicago Church of Christ,

[7] May 9, 16, and 23, 1886.

Scientist. Adams organized his own church, conducting services in Hooley's Theater, and in June 1887 began publishing the *Chicago Christian Scientist.*

For a time he used his publication in vigorous defense of Mrs. Eddy and her teachings. He, too, fell away. Although professing to practice Christian Science, millennnarianism took his fancy. He invited Mrs. Gesterfelt to his pulpit, and continued to invite her over the protests of the Chicago Christian Scientist Association, until, in spite of Mrs. Eddy's hope she could bring him back to her side, the Association expelled him as, previously, it had expelled Mrs. Gesterfelt.

That there should be many pretenders to Mrs. Eddy's leadership is not surprising.

She gave of her teachings to all who asked, as only the sure of foot can give a hand to those who stumble. She could not seem to accustom herself to the thought that among her students would be those of devious, covetous nature who would use what she gave to take advantage for themselves over others.

Filled with an idealism which said that the Bible is an open door through which all may pass, and that beyond the door is perfection, Mrs. Eddy could not fail to encounter tension that would force her into continuous struggle.

The presence of an assortment of publications identifying themselves with Christian Science was but one phase of the attempt to put an end to her, and to what she taught, in the middle and last years of the 1880's.

It was all part of her preparation for leadership.

CHAPTER TEN

Rebellion

IT WAS on June 6, 1888, at a meeting of the members of the Boston Christian Scientist Association in Meionian Hall (Tremont Temple) that opposition to Mrs. Eddy's leadership of the movement was beaten back, but not defeated.

That night Mrs. Eddy called a few loyal students to her home and talked with them, and two days later William B. Johnson, Secretary of the National Christian Scientist Association, was on his way to Chicago to attend the annual meeting of the national body. In an inner pocket of his coat was a letter:

BOSTON, *June 8, 1888*

MY DEAR STUDENTS:

Listen to this faithful student. Our vice-president in Boston is heading a *new* faction, ask Mr. Johnson about it who bears this letter.

As ever Your faithful Teacher,

M. B. G. EDDY

In Johnson's ears were instructions to seek out the Reverend G. P. Day, Mr. and Mrs. Bradford Sherman, Mrs. Elizabeth Webster, Mrs. J. H. Bell, Mrs. G. W. Adams, Mrs. Caroline D. Noyes, Mr. and Mrs. John Linscott, and Mrs. Hannah A. Larminie and acquaint them with the events of the meeting of June 6, and the events leading up to that meeting.

The story was familiar, but this time there was taking shape a very different rebellion from that of 1881. This time people of standing in Boston and in Massachusetts were involved.

Disagreement centered over using association funds for paying the legal costs attached to the defense of Mrs. Corner, in the manslaughter charge. The sum was two hundred dollars, and it was contended by many members that, as a body, the Association should meet the obligation. It was Mrs. Eddy's view that such action would establish a precedent. She favored individual subscriptions. This was done but after much controversy the action was rescinded, and the Association footed the bill.

There was opposition to Mrs. Eddy's wish to build a church in Boston.[1] Only about 25 per cent of the members of the organization believed there should be a church edifice. Many were unwilling to surrender their memberships in denominational churches; many were obsessed by the belief that edifices represented "old theology," and only a spiritual Church was appropriate.

Thoroughly practical, Mrs. Eddy did not have the hardihood to believe that Christian Science could continue to do its work without church organization. Then, as later, she advocated:

> . . . It is not essential to materially organize Christ's Church. It is not absolutely necessary to ordain Pastors, and to dedicate Churches; but if this is done, let it be in concession to the period, and not as a perpetual or indispensable ceremo-

[1] The first Christian Science church edifice was built in 1886 in Oconto, Wisconsin, a lumbering town on the shores of Green Bay. For description, see Appendix 5.

nial of the Church. If our Church is organized, it is to meet the demand, "suffer it to be so now." The real Christian compact is love for one another. This bond is wholly spiritual and inviolate. It is imperative at all times and under every circumstance, to perpetuate no ceremonials except as types of these mental conditions: remembrance and love, — a real affection for Jesus' character and example. Be it remembered that all types employed in the service of Christian Science should represent the most spiritual forms of thought and worship that can be made visible.[2]

There was personal criticism, a lot of it. They found fault because she wore jewelry — a ring; because of the dress she wore at Sunday services, saying it was velvet and, hence, a display of materiality; they said her home on Columbus Avenue was too pretentious to be in keeping with spiritual values; they found fault because, oftentimes, she laughed and was gay, told stories and joked with those about her.

"Christian Science," some of her students said in letters to the *Journal*, "is not clothed in silk and velvet, but in the soberest kind of dress — for only in the soberest kind of dress can it show its aloofness to all that is worldly and of the devil."

In a public gathering, Mrs. Eddy was asked, "How can a Christian Scientist afford to wear diamonds and be clad in purple velvet?" Her answer was:

This ring that I wear was given me several years ago as a thank-offering from one I had brought from death back to life; for a long time I could

[2] *Christian Science Journal*, March 1892.

not wear it, but my husband induced me to accustom myself by putting it on at night, and finally I came to see it only as a sign of recognition and gratitude to my Master, and to love it as such. This "purple velvet" *is* "purple" but it is velveteen that I paid one dollar and fifty cents a yard for, and I have worn it for several years, but it seems to be perpetually renewed, like the widow's cruse.[3]

This dismal approach to the teachings persisted. In the *Journal* there appeared a complaint from a reader: "I wish something might be said in the *Journal* to check the tendency to dress, and devotion to the laws of mortal mind as manifested in the fashions. The exhibition in this line staggers many of 'the people standing by,' who ask, 'Can this be the *Coming of Christ in the Spirit?*' "

Severity in dress and in manner marked a good many who said they were Christian Scientists, and it was not easy for Mrs. Eddy to persuade the doleful that the canticle which was heard over a manger so long ago was not a dirge.

A substantial number of the members of the Boston Christian Scientist Association was strongly assertive that a Christian Science practitioner should be familiar with medicine and, preferably, should be a graduate of a medical school. Leading in this contention were J. M. C. Murphy and W. H. Bertram, both students in the Massachusetts Metaphysical College. A wrong view, it had persisted and had retarded the growth of the movement and added to the burden of its Leader — as now these trusted students were adding to her burden by plotting against her.

[3] *Christian Science Journal,* February 1889.

It was a plot that caused Mrs. Eddy to change her mind suddenly and attend the Chicago meeting of the national Association, after having announced in the May 1888 issue of the *Journal:*

> . . . I shall not be present at the National Christian Scientist Association in Chicago, June 13; but my sympathies will go out largely to my students on that occasion. I even thank beforehand those who, with deathless love, are struggling Godward; and I warn those who are halting or are getting blind, neither to stop and rest on my personality for all they achieve, nor to abuse it; but to remember always that Love fulfills God's law, and destroys sin as well as sickness, and that there is no other door by which to enter into Christian Science. . . .

In June, through the *Journal,* she called for a full attendance at the meeting: "Let no consideration bend or outweigh your purpose to be in Chicago on June 13. Firm in your allegiance to the reign of universal harmony, go to its rescue. In God's hour the powers of earth and hell are proven powerless."

On the way to Chicago, Mrs. Eddy must have given a great deal of prayerful thought to the disputants in Meionian Hall on June 6; and, in Chicago, she was thrust into one of the great emergencies of her career.

The first day of the convention was devoted to business sessions. These were held in the First Methodist Church, then located at Clark and Washington Streets. Mrs. Eddy used the business meetings to complete her work of better organizing the national Association, and it was planned to devote the morning of June 14 to a public meeting in Central Music Hall [4] at which students would deliver a program of addresses on Christian Science.

Without Mrs. Eddy's knowledge, the plans were changed. Instead of a program of addresses by students, Mrs. Eddy was announced as the only speaker and it was not until she was in the hall and about to take a seat on the platform that she was told of the new arrangement. On the platform were one hundred of her own students; on the main floor were more than eight hundred members of the National Christian Scientist Association; crowding the sides of the hall and in the balcony were hundreds of visitors while just below the platform was a filled press table.

Writing in the *Christian Science Monitor* (June 14, 1938) Frederick W. Carr published, for the first time, an account of the occasion as recorded by Mrs. Laura E. Sargent: [5]

I had just entered the ante-room which led to the stage when Mrs. Eddy and her attendants arrived. A member [6] of the committee in waiting stepped forward and handed her a program. Mrs. Eddy looked at it and then said to him, "Why! what does this mean? I was told that the students were to address this meeting. I have not even a subject, and it is time for the meeting to open."

With a look of diabolical satisfaction on his face, this man replied, "Oh, that does not make any difference. You can do it," or words to that effect.

Mrs. Eddy made no reply but removed her bonnet and ar-

---

[4] State and Randolph Streets, the present location of the Marshall Field Building.

[5] Mrs. Sargent was Mrs. Eddy's companion for a number of years.

[6] Rev. George B. Day, pastor of the Chicago Church of Christ, Scientist. Not long afterwards Day withdrew from the movement.

ranged her hair in a mirror. I smoothed her lace collar and ventured to whisper in her ear, "God is your strength."

She then turned and took the student's arm and went on the platform.

While the audience was singing a hymn, Mrs. Eddy selected the 91st Psalm to read and then addressed the audience for over an hour with one of the most eloquent, inspired messages on "Science and the Senses," a brief synopsis of which is found in *Miscellaneous Writings* [p. 134].

The vast audience which filled the auditorium to the outer vestibule was held spellbound and not a sound from the people broke the impressive silence as Mrs. Eddy's voice rang out clear and distinct, carrying the conviction of Truth into the hearts of her listeners.

After the address was finished the people pressed forward for healing. A woman lifted her sick babe up above the heads of the people so Mrs. Eddy could see it. Others brought a paralytic to be healed.[7]

As Mrs. Eddy concluded, "the audience" — according to the *Chicago Times* — "arose enmasse and made a rush for the platform. There were no steps provided for getting on the rostrum but that did not deter those who wanted to shake hands with the idolized expounder of their creed. They mounted the reporters' table and vaulted to the rostrum like acrobats."

This address was the real introduction of Christian Sci-

[7] Referring, perhaps, to the same paralytic, Mrs. Emily Hulin wrote to Mrs. Eddy, and the letter was published in the *Christian Science Sentinel* (March 27, 1906): "At the conclusion of your address, I noticed a poor woman who had entered the auditorium on crutches and who was evidently crippled, stretch out her arms toward you in a beseeching manner. You looked at her with eyes full of compassion and love, as it seemed to me, and immediately she laid down her crutches and walked out as anyone in a normal condition would do. I cannot tell you of the awe that fell on me, or the impression I received, and I then determined to learn more of this wonderful truth. . . ."

ence to the West; and, as noted by Clifford P. Smith in his *Historical and Biographical Papers* (First Series, page 32), "Although not previously reduced to writing, this address can be rated as one of Mrs. Eddy's most notable utterances." The *Chicago Tribune* said it was an address which "depended largely upon its logic for its force," and told its readers that in Mrs. Eddy's voice "there is a ring of terrible conviction."

The *Chicago Inter-Ocean* reported:

Christian Scientists, as an organization, are of comparatively recent origin. . . . They stand for themselves, and are practical illustrations of the truths they teach. It must be admitted that the countenances of most of them showed evidence of high thinking, as if they had attained to that condition wherein the spirit has obtained ascendancy over the body.

The audience was composed of a goodly number of men and young women, but the women of middle age constituted the majority. Many of the latter were white-haired; their faces were cheerful and serene, and they looked very much as if they had come into possession of the most coveted secret of happiness, for which the sordid, selfish world without was struggling and contending in vain.

The Rev. Mary B. G. Eddy stands at the head of the movement in Boston, where she had a strong and enthusiastic following. Her admirers, however, are not confined to the East, but are everywhere, and her presence in Chicago has very generally called them together.

When she came upon the stage a silence fell upon the audience which rose as if by pre-concerted plan, but in reality from some mysterious influence that no one could explain. . . . She had the typical Boston face, pale and high spiritual. . . . She wore a black and white silk dress, and there was in her general appearance that exquisite darkness and daintiness which is also charactcristic of women in the Eastern states. Her voice is clear and exceedingly penetrating. . . .

The voluntary was followed by Scriptural reading and silent prayer, after which the old familiar hymn "Nearer my God to Thee" was sung, leaflets having been distributed to the audience at the door. . . .

Afterwards, at the Palmer House,[8] there was such a waiting throng that in the evening Mrs. Eddy yielded to the urgings of students and permitted a reception. Hurriedly, the management of the hotel set aside several rooms and decorated them with a profusion of flowers. Soon the rooms, the corridor leading to them, and the stairway leading to the corridor were filled with people, rich and poor jostling each other that they might see the woman whose words had healed so many.

In *The Life of Mary Baker Eddy,* Sibyl Wilbur wrote: "Mrs. Eddy drew back from the pressure of humanity and as she looked upon the flushed faces she seemed to shrink within herself, as if saying 'What came you here to see?' She turned to her secretary and companion for assistance, and almost immediately withdrew by a side door . . . from such scenes Mrs. Eddy has always shrunk with peculiar sensitiveness. As she had told her students when first coming to Boston, she now reiterated to her immediate helpers, 'Christian Science is not forwarded by these methods.' "

Mrs. Eddy returned to Boston to learn that, in her absence, thirty-four students [9] had withdrawn their support

[8] There is no record, as has been published a number of times, that Mrs. Eddy was refused hotel accommodations on her visit to Chicago in 1884.

[9] The students were: Mrs. S. E. Avery, Mrs. Maria A. Brown, Henry P. Bailey, Mrs. Henry P. Bailey, Mrs. C. A. Beecher, Miss I. A. Beecher, George A. Bradford, Mrs. Mary T. Bradford, Mrs. M. A. Batchelder, Wm. H. Bertram, Mrs. Sadie I. Bertram, Mrs. Abby H. Corner, Charles W. Crosse, Mrs. Sarah H. Crosse, Mrs. S. M. Cowan, Mrs. E. P. Clark, Albert B. Dorman, Mrs. M. J. Davis, Miss Mary Hampson, Mrs. A. D. Kennedy, J. M. C. Murphy, S. E. Kirby, George A. Miles, Mrs. E. E. Murphy, Mrs. C.

from the Christian Scientist Association of the Massachusetts Metaphysical College, and from the Church.

Among them were students influential in the affairs of Boston and of Massachusetts. She also learned that the recalcitrants had gained possession of the records of the Association and had placed them in the hands of an attorney. Capture of the records had been accomplished by sending one of their number to the home of the absent secretary with an announcement of an impending meeting, and the need for the records. Unsuspectingly, Mrs. Johnson had surrendered them.[10]

It was the intention of the plotting teachers to expel Mrs. Eddy from the Association, and from the Church, although how they were to accomplish this is not clear. Final authority in these matters was with Mrs. Eddy. Instead of using her authority, Mrs. Eddy instructed Johnson to communicate with the rebels and all other members of the Association by letter, announcing a special meeting "of the C. S. Association for the purpose [of giving] certain members opportunity to comply with the Constitution, Article 2, section 1, and the By-Laws on Fellowship, Section 1," which read . . .

Article 2, Section 1, of the Constitution:
Members hereby pledge themselves to live peaceably with all men, so far as is consistent with

---

R. Marshall, Mrs. M. R. Nutter, Mrs. N. H. Parker, Mrs. E. L. Palmer, Mrs. Mary A. Poole, Horace N. Poole, Mrs. R. J. Robinson, Mrs. B. J. Swett, Charles A. S. Troup, and Walter J. Vinal.

[10] The records were not returned until nearly a year later. On June 8, 1889, or thereabouts, George J. Tufts, counsel for the rebelling teachers, gave up the records, and the Association agreed to refund contributions made by individuals in assisting Mrs. Corner.

justice, and truth, and do unto others as they would that others should do unto them. To remember the Ten Commandments, and never to interfere with the rights of Mind. It is expected that all members will express their views, by voting for or against any question. It shall be the privilege of all members to act independently, and exert an influence to restrain error and promote truth. Unwillingness to do this, will be considered as disqualifying them for Christian Science.

The By-Law on Fellowship, Section 1:

It shall be the duty of Christian Scientists to befriend and help each other in times of need, and, so far as is consistent with justice and truth, to defend the reputation of members of this Association. If they have aught against other members, it shall be their duty to faithfully tell them of it, and so seek a reconciliation.

In the letter which Johnson wrote under instructions on August 22, 1888, he quoted Mrs. Eddy as saying:

I have no conception of what some members of the Association are hinting against me, and I will be present on the 27th inst. to hear what they have to say. Conscious of my own integrity in all things, I call on the members of our Association who have aught against me, to tell me of it, and even after they have broken this rule of the Church of Christ, and the commandments of God, and not "first having told their brother his fault, I will give them another opportunity to deal justly." This same injustice to others has been bitterly complained of to me by the very members who are now dealing with me thus.

I have earnestly counselled my students not to be guilty of this great wrong which has caused much discord. I have set them a different example, and told them first their faults and avoided telling them to others. I will now give them one more opportunity to deal justly, and I will listen patiently, and charitably to all they have to say against me, and in return I will ask only this: that those who have freely spoken of their great obligations to me, will now be simply just to me. . . .

At the first special meeting called in behalf of Mrs. Corner, I was absent, not because I was unwilling to help her, but because she needed no help, and I knew it. I was not at the second special meeting because it was impossible for me to be and to go to the meeting of the National Association at Chicago; also I wanted this conspiracy to come to the surface, it has. . . .

On June 27 it was apparent the break was wide. The rebelling students ignored their teacher's plea to those "who have aught against me, to tell me of it" by not attending the meeting. Their absence made an open secret of their determination to have a plan of worship less strict, under a Leader less watchful. That evening, in a moment of despair, Mrs. Eddy confided in a pupil, "I do not believe I have twelve loyal students left," [11] expressed herself as seeing little

[11] In Boston there were fourteen students who displayed their loyalty by using the *Christian Science Journal* to advertise themselves as Christian Science practitioners: Julia S. Bartlett, Mary F. Berry, Erwin L. Colman, Janet T. Colman, Captain Joseph S. Eastaman, Mary F. Eastaman, William B. Johnson, Frank E. Mason, Mary B. Moarn, Mary W. Munroe, Mary C. Piper, Laura A. Rand, Hanover P. Smith, and Josephine C. Woodbury.

hope for her Church in Boston, and indicated she was thinking, most seriously, of moving to Chicago and continuing her work from there.

A night of prayer turned her despair into determination not to be driven from the state where she began her teachings.

Her articles in the *Journal* began taking on a different tone; her choice of students became more selective. Where once she was willing to teach all, now she chose only some of those who came. No longer was she free with her confidences; now she did not go beyond the tested in the assignment of things to be done. With her mind on students in cities other than Boston, she wrote in the *Journal,* in July 1888:

> You, my beloved students, who are absent from me, and have shared less of my labors than many others, seem stronger to resist temptation than some of those who have had line upon line and precept upon precept. This may be a serviceable hint, since necessities and God's providence are foreshadowed. I have felt for some time that perpetual instruction of my students might substitute my own for their growth, and so dwarf their experience.

It was in this period that Mrs. Eddy's extraordinary executive ability began to express itself. The clergy was sure, and said so, that the division within was the long-predicted collapse of "a theory [where] the Deity is degraded by misrepresentations of His character and work." [12] With seventy members, in addition to the thirty-four students, having

[12] *The Congregationalist,* May 24, 1888.

withdrawn their support, Sunday services in the Church of Christ, Scientist, were so poorly attended that the communicants huddled together in the center of Chickering Hall.

But despite the almost complete loss of her Boston following, Mrs. Eddy decided to open a public salesroom for the distribution of Christian Science literature, and she chose a location in the heart of the business district. Renting two rooms in the Hotel Boylston,[13] she established in these quarters in October 1888 a Christian Science reading room.

The partition was taken out and the two rooms made into one, thus providing a place large enough to accommodate fifty persons. In addition to a reading room the place was used as a publication office and, also, as a meeting place for the Christian Scientist Association. On Friday evening, services were held there. A small table was set against the wall at the far side, with chairs arranged in front. Occasionally, Mrs. Eddy sat at the table and conducted services, but, usually, a student was in charge.

As she could find them, Mrs. Eddy began using men in responsible positions. She named Frank E. Mason, assistant pastor, as manager of the *Journal,* made Captain Joseph S. Eastaman [14] a confidential business adviser, and appointed Ebenezer J. Foster [15] teacher of obstetrics in her College.

[13] The Touraine Hotel is now on this site.

[14] A retired sea captain, Eastaman approached Mrs. Eddy after services in Hawthorne Hall, explained that his wife was an invalid, and asked for help. To his amazement, Mrs. Eddy suggested that *he* supply this help. Disbelieving, Eastaman entered one of her classes and, while still a student, began treating his wife. She showed almost immediate improvement and, on Mrs. Eddy's invitation, accompanied her husband to his last Primary Class.

[15] Foster, a graduate of the Hahnemann Medical College, Philadelphia, was attracted to Christian Science by the healing of a friend and, in 1887,

In the columns of the *Journal,* she informed the public that "the late much-ado-about-nothing arose solely from mental malicious practice, and the audible falsehood, designed to stir up strife between brethren, for the purpose of placing Christian Science in the hands of aspirants for place and power. These repeated attempts of mad ambition may retard our Cause, but they can never place it in the wrong hands and hold it there, or benefit mankind by such endeavors." [16]

That she might have less interruption, Mrs. Eddy moved to 385 Commonwealth Avenue, declared her intention to use the house as a parsonage, and announced that she would give all money accruing from the sale of *Science and Health,* and her other writings, to the advancement of Christian Science. Her textbook (28th edition, revised, published 1887 [17]) contained 590 pages, an index,[18] and the following chapters: "Science of Being," "Footsteps of Truth," "Creation," "Marriage," "Physiology," "Animal Magnetism," "Wayside Hints," "Imposition and Demonstration," "Healing and Teaching," "Platform of Christian Scientists," "Re-

---

he enrolled in the Massachusetts Metaphysical College. Ingratiating himself into her confidence, Foster became Mrs. Eddy's adopted son on November 5, 1888, and changed his name to Foster Eddy.

In the early part of the same year, Mrs. Eddy's own son, George W. Glover, brought his family to Boston at his mother's request. Mrs. Eddy made a strong effort to bring him to her side, but failed. Glover's interest was in speculation in Western lands. His sole interest in his mother appeared to be confined to the limit of how much money he could persuade her to give him, and she gave him thousands of dollars.

[16] September, 1888.

[17] A number of editions were published in which there were no revisions from previous editions.

[18] The index was prepared by J. H. Wiggin in 1885 and was the forerunner of the *Concordance* now in use.

ply to a Critic," "Recapitulation," "Key to the Scriptures," "Genesis," "Prayer and Atonement," "The Apocalypse," and "Glossary."

Heading some chapters were quotations from non-Biblical sources, and when a student inquired, Mrs. Eddy stated her reason: ". . . I baited my hook with those passages to reconcile other readers than those who understand. . . . And my device works admirably. The authors of those sayings are not hated as I am, and because they say some things as I do, the world will listen to my sayings in that chapter." [19]

In November 1888 Mrs. Eddy surprised her critics and her followers, both, with an announcement that in the future no students would be admitted to Normal Class in the Massachusetts Metaphysical College unless they had completed Primary Class; and, instead of twelve, there would be seven lectures. In the *Journal* in the previous March she had warned: ". . . After the next class [Mrs. Eddy] will receive no Normal students who have not been previously prepared by herself in the Primary Course. She very much regrets this necessity, but finds it her duty to do this, so great is the demand for *thoroughly qualified teachers*."

Now in November her announcement was a surprise because, considering the rebellion of a few months before, few expected she would keep to her announced course. What those who were surprised did not realize was that by selecting only "students prepared by herself," and reducing the number of lectures from twelve to seven, she was lifting her students, and her teachings, out of the confusion that was threatening to surround them. By selection, and by concentration, she was able to instruct and reinstruct in a man-

[19] Original letter in Archives of The Mother Church, Boston, Massachusetts.

ner that would do much to offset what more than thirty
colleges and academies and nearly a score of publications
were now advertising as Christian Science. And, directly,
there was to be another pretender.

In January 1889 appeared the first issue of the *Boston
Christian Scientist*. Although not so identified, Mrs. Sarah
Crosse, former editor of the *Journal*, was the editor of the
new publication and her associates in the venture were the
other rebel graduates of the Massachusetts Metaphysical
College. In the first issue, the newcomer stated it hoped to
be "helpful, interesting and instructive to all Christian Scientists."

Having taken with them when leaving — as did Mrs.
Plunkett and Mrs. Hopkins — copies of the mailing lists
of the *Journal*, as well as membership lists of the two Associations, samples of the *Boston Christian Scientist* were sent
to Mrs. Eddy's students, along with subscription blanks.
Mrs. Eddy's reaction was prompt.

In the February issue of the *Journal*, she wrote:
". . . This periodical is appropriately published . . . anon-
ymously. The handkerchief of St. Paul conveyed healing
to those who received it, but these mischievous periodicals
. . . are the intended media of malicious animal magnetism to the homes that do not send them away," and she suggested that all her students "return the aforesaid periodical,
through the mail, to Sarah H. Crosse, 19 Berwick Park,
Boston, Mass."

Excepting for this prompt action, Mrs. Eddy gave little
notice to the efforts of the Boston dissidents. For some time
her mind had been turning to church work and church
organization. She saw its lack "as the one weak place in our
Cause, one which should be the strongest," and, in February

1889, she went to New York to see for herself the organizational work of Mrs. Laura Lathrop,[20] Mrs. Augusta E. Stetson, who of her own volition followed Mrs. Lathrop to New York, and Mrs. Snider.

Mrs. Eddy made the occasion of this visit to New York City an opportunity to speak in Steinway Hall. The following day — February 16 — New York newspapers were in disagreement over Mrs. Eddy's appearance, her introduction, what she said, and how she was received.

The *New York Times* reported: ". . . When an organist had played a selection the Rev. Mr. Ager (a Swedenborgian minister) arose solemnly and made a cautious little speech, in which he disclaimed knowledge of or responsibility for the lesson about to be taught by the 'Rev.' Mary Baker G. Eddy. He was there simply to introduce the lecturer, and he did. When the apostle arose the fall of a pin could have been heard in the hall so rapt was the attention. She stood for a moment surveying her audience, her keen and sunken black eyes peering weirdly from her colorless face, and her dark hair brushed severely down on her temples. Then she began to speak in a shrill, thin voice that was frequently indistinct. What she said was almost unintelligible, but her auditors hung upon every utterance as though it had divine significance. . . . When she finished and resumed her chair the audience never moved. It looked at her and then looked at itself. Its faith was great, but its intelligence was mystified. The 'Rev.' Mrs. Eddy was not a little astonished herself.

---

[20] Until June 1886, the only advertised Christian Science practitioners in New York City were Mr. and Mrs. J. Allen Campbell. Soon five more of Mrs. Eddy's students were active and Mrs. Eddy sent Laura Lathrop to organize the work, and establish a church. The work was organized and the first church services were held on December 4, 1887. Jealous of Mrs. Lathrop, Campbell joined the Boston seceders in September 1888.

She arose and gravely bowed. The audience still refused to stir. Then she got up and walked off the stage and out of sight, followed by the Rev. Mr. Ager. At this a little murmur rippled over the assemblage. . . . 'What is it all about?' asked an unbeliever. No one could explain, but from all sides came the assurance that it was 'simply splendid.' Still the audience would not depart. It stood about in groups until the 'Rev.' Mrs. Eddy reappeared on the stage. Then it rushed enmasse for her, and, hanging over her chair, poured its praises in her ears while it grasped her hand. This was not very material, but it was the most tangible thing the audience discovered during the evening."

The *New York Sun* reported: ". . . An organist played a soft prelude, and Mrs. Eddy . . . was escorted to the platform by the Rev. J. C. Ager of Brooklyn. . . . Mr. Ager introduced her with a careful announcement that he had little knowledge of the subject itself; that he had observed it, as it were, from a distance, but he had watched it as a thoughtful man, and he introduced her as the originator of a religious movement which has, it seemed to him, a wider and deeper influence on human thought than any movement in recent times. . . . Mrs. Eddy closed her lecture shortly after 9 o'clock. Then many of her personal friends crowded to the platform to greet her cordially. Many of the ladies had been her patients, and professed to see great beauty in the lecture. Many strangers to the alleged science, however, were unable to make head or tail of it. . . ."

The *New York World* reported: "Over a thousand ladies and gentlemen assembled last night at Steinway Hall and listened to a lecture by Rev. Mrs. Mary Baker G. Eddy, of Boston, President of the Massachusetts Metaphysical College, on the subject of 'Science in Christianity.' Miss [Mrs.]

Eddy is a pleasant little woman, with dark hair and dark eyes, and does not look more than forty years old. . . . In speaking of Christian Science, Mrs. Eddy said that its starting point was in God, and there was no power beside Him. 'If God is all,' she said, 'there is no place for sin, sickness and death. The man whom God made neither suffers, sins or dies. . . . Christian science,' continued the lecturer, 'teaches us that Jesus really showed us the way to God, to the true life of man, which is spirit. Is materia medica a science? I have not found in it the character of invariability that belongs to science. I have found by actual experiment that as the drug is attentuated its power is increased until, when the drug is all gone and there is only mind, its greatest efficacy is reached.' . . . This remarkable statement stood near the close of her brief address. . . ." And, singling it out, the *World* headlined it, *Important if True*.

As the newspapers indicated, there were few in New York who saw their own work defined in her words and, in her, a teacher of great originality.

CHAPTER ELEVEN
A Decision of Great Importance

THE CENTRAL EVENT of Mary Baker Eddy's evangelical career was her protection of her teachings, and March 5, 1889, was one of the memorable days in the history of Christian Science. On that day, in a "leave-taking" report of a Primary Class at the Massachusetts Metaphysical College, Mrs. Eddy wrote:

> I want to say, too, to my students everywhere, whether they have attended my classes or have received instructions through reading my books, that they can become members of the "mother church" here in Boston, and be received into its communion by writing, without their personal appearance. If you are united with us in thought and affection, you know in Science that you are not absent from us. I carry you all in my affections.

This declaration was published in the April issue of the *Christian Science Journal*, and was the first public indication that she was thinking in terms of a "Church Universal."

On that same day of March 5, 1889, a student inquired as to the relation of the Christian Science Church to other Christian Churches, and as to organization within itself. Mrs. Eddy answered, plainly choosing words that would carry beyond the walls of the classroom:

> . . . I want to promote the union of the church.
> . . . The Christian church is sacred to me; just as

the Jew held all that had the name of God written on it, so all that calls itself by the name of Christ, I love and hold sacred. How shall we best promote union with Christ, and draw all the churches that are called by that holy Name nearer to him?

I look to Christ for guidance. Jesus did not carry his church, the Jewish, with him. He could not build on their foundation; neither can we. They are founded on personal sense and credal doctrines about God. How can we proceed on our way without the life of Christianity, the recognition of God, Good, as all? . . . We cannot afford to remain in the fetters of a personal sense of God. Then we plant ourselves on matter rather than Spirit. But we must plant ourselves on Spirit, and must say as Martin Luther said, "Here I stand, I cannot do otherwise, so help me God, Amen."

There is no compromise here. We must go forward. What holds the churches from acknowledging that our church, built on Christ, is evangelical? It is pride, the pride of antedated possession. But this is not a lawful pride. I repeat that I love the old church organization that has kept alive the name of Christ, but I want to see it founded on God, and a God who is Spirit, not matter; who is Good, not evil; a God who is Supreme over *all,* superior to sickness, sin and death included; that *is* a present help in *all* times of trouble; that, just when we want Him most, does not turn us over to matter and an M.D. for our refuge.[1]

* * *

[1] *Christian Science Journal,* April 1889.

This, too, was an announcement of great importance to Christian Scientists. It presaged a time, now not far away, when there would be no dilution of membership in a Church of Christ, Scientist, by allegiance to a church of another denomination.

"I joined a church thirty years ago; its creed and doctrine have become nothing to me. Shall I ask a letter of dismission and credence, with this feeling that as an organization it does not represent Christianity, or shall I say simply to my church what the fact is, and ask for a severance of the church relation and dismissal?"

This question was asked Mrs. Eddy on March 5, 1889; she replied:

By all means simply ask the letter of recommendation, then you have done your duty as an individual member. When my adopted son, Dr. Foster Eddy, applied to his church in Vermont for such a letter to the Church of Christ, Scientist, here, it was not only given, but with a cordial recommendation and expression of regret.

I wish you could see, as I do, the gain in three years in the attitude of the churches and the public toward Christian Science Churches. Then they would have spurned such recognition. My own case, however, was an exception. I received such a letter seventeen years ago from the Congregational Church to which I belonged for forty years.

In 1892, this suggestion by Mrs. Eddy became a rule for membership in her Church.

Also, on March 5, 1889, there was another important

question, and answer. It concerned the duties of pastors in Christian Science churches. Until February 1, 1889, the use of the term Reverend, or Doctor, was optional with students if they were called upon to occupy pulpits. In February a rule was adopted which stipulated that "all students of Christian Science must drop the titles of Reverend and Doctor, except those who have received these titles under the laws of the State." Mrs. Eddy proposed this rule, and advised, "My beloved brethren will some time learn the wisdom of this By-Law."

In Primary Class on March 5, a student inquired "as to the reception of members from other churches by a pastor who, like myself, is not ordained."

> The ordination of the pastor is not an essential to the reception of members from other churches [replied Mrs. Eddy]. The old membership ceases when the new begins. The pastor is not the church; it is the church that they come into, and that does not depend on the pastor. You are delegated by the church to perform this duty, and your action has as much validity as the action of a chairman or a moderator of any meeting who is appointed *pro tem*. The person, any person, so delegated can receive new members just as effectively as an ordained pastor.

Up to February, and for the sake of appearance, Mrs. Eddy had made no objections to the use of titles by those serving as pastors in her Church. There were even times when she encouraged such use. That was over now. It was evident that her thought was turning away from individuals, and turning to an impersonal pastor.

There were sixty-five students in the Primary Class which had its "leavetaking" on March 5, and a few days afterwards Mrs. Eddy left Boston for Barre, Vermont. It was a time of grave thoughts. Much remained to be done if there was to be safety for her Church, and for her teachings. She was seeking relief from the demands upon her, and guidance in her desire to live apart from the commotion of material organization.

With her departure rumors multiplied until she felt compelled to use the July 1889 *Journal* to say:

> . . . Inquiries are coming in from the "four-quarters" — For what purpose has Mrs. Eddy relinquished certain lines of labor in the field of Christian Science and called others to the work? Is she writing her history? or completing her works on the Scriptures? She is doing neither, but is taking a vacation, her first in twenty-five years. She is taking no direction of her own, or others, but her desire is that God may permit her to continue to live apart in the world, free from the toil and turmoil in which her days have been passed for more than a quarter century.

Completing her stay in Barre, Mrs. Eddy sent her foster son to Roslindale, a suburb of Boston, to locate a suitable dwelling. He did not succeed, and Mrs. Eddy moved to Concord, New Hampshire. She rented a house at 62 State Street, and used the columns of the *Journal* to inform the field:

> Take Notice: No correspondence relating to any matter of organization, or aught connected with Church, Christian Scientist Associations, or mat-

ters relative to individuals — in fine, no question relating to our cause except those involving the real essence or animus of Christian Science, will be considered by Mrs. Eddy, Dr. Foster Eddy, or Mr. Frye.

She also sent a letter to Julia Bartlett saying:

> Now I repeat that whatever questions in any of the C. S. organizations come up — no reference be made to me, for I hereby state that I *will not* entertain the question nor consider it, and why?
>
> Because under the counteracting mental influences, if I do this, my counsel is liable to be either carried out too late, or misunderstood, or carried out only in part, and because of all these things the wisdom and necessity of it is not seen nor the good it might do accomplished, and many will say she is a "hard master." I have borne this many years and think at this period of my retirement it should be seen that this is why I left the field. Again my students must learn sooner or later to *guard themselves,* to *watch* and not be misled.
>
> I appreciate your tasks far more than you can mine and have rewarded you by incessant care of you for many years. It is a *grave mistake* not to do *quickly* all that is worth doing, *delay,* gives all away, under our circumstances.[2]

Having begun her teaching without rules, and without experience, it was clear that Mrs. Eddy had come to believe

[2] Original letter (dated July 21, 1889) in the Archives of The Mother Church, Boston, Massachusetts.

that individual progress in Christian Science was determined by the investment the individual made of himself in his search for truth. This belief can be found in her statement that "the spiritual sense of truth must be gained before Truth can be understood"; [3] and it can be found in her declaration, "It is the genius of Christian Science to demonstrate good, not evil, — harmony, not discord; for Science is the mandate of Truth which destroys all error." [4]

By investing all of herself in what she taught, she became persuaded that the greater the need of people for human leadership, the less competent these same people become; and she saw that a fault of her Church, her Association and in her college was the tendency of many of her students to confuse her human personality with her spiritual teachings.

That was what happened in 1881, when eight students withdrew their names from the Association and the Church; that was what happened in 1888 when thirty-four students broke away in open rebellion; that was what was happening now with "inquiries coming in from all the 'four quarters.' " In issuing her instructions denying consultation, she was requiring that her students "guard themselves"; and by withdrawing from active membership she was learning that such absence on her part "developed higher energies on the part of true followers, and led to some startling departures on the other hand." [5]

Three months had passed since Mrs. Eddy used the columns of the *Journal* to express her thought of a "mother

---

[3] *Science and Health*, p. 272.
[4] *Miscellaneous Writings*, p. 283.
[5] *Christian Science Journal*, July 1889.

church" and to speak out against dilution of membership in a Christian Science Church. During those three months she watched, carefully, the reaction of her followers. Many still were in opposition to organization, but there were fewer than the three out of four who, a year before, argued against its use.

Instead of disputing with them, Mrs. Eddy permitted what she had written to rest. She agreed with the high thought that the greatest stimulant to spirituality is not in church organization, but in its absence — but she saw, if they did not, that some statements of truth have to await the proper time and the proper place before being expressed. She saw, if they did not, that in the long years of the future there would be forces in the world that would destroy Christian Science unless there was an organization to protect it in all human contacts.

To better accustom her students to organizational effort, Mrs. Eddy next announced at the Easter services in 1889 that:

> . . . a Christian Science Mission and Free Dispensary would be opened . . . for work among those unable to pay for healing and prevented from hearing the Glad Tidings unless taken to them by messengers of Truth. . . .
>
> This line of work opens a new era in the history of Science. It will help to raise the vocation of Scientists from being looked on by the world as primarily a means to a livelihood. Most Scientists today are doing a large part of their work with no consideration, but the love of the Master. Mission work will draw the world's attention more dis-

tinctly to the humane character of Science than any
degree of generosity and self-sacrifice in the routine
of a private practice could do.

The free dispensary was opened at 3 Boylston Place. Students treated such cases as came and, using the address as
their headquarters, went into the slums of the city to serve
the sick. They encountered a great deal of disbelief, and they
encountered a great deal of resistance, but they gave help
to so many sick people that the Christian Science Dispensary
Association was organized on May 31.[6]
On that same Easter Sunday, Mrs. Eddy also announced
that, because of greatly increased attendance, and beginning
April 26, Friday evening services would be held in Steinert
Hall, instead of the Hotel Boylston. She expressed the wish
that these services be called Public Meetings, and that they
consist of an address, a relating of experiences in Christian
Science, and a discussion of questions from the audience.[7]
In the late spring and in her desire to "live apart in the
world," she resigned the pastorate of her Boston church, resigned the presidency of the National Christian Scientist Association, and turned over the ownership and management
of the *Christian Science Journal* to the national association.[8]

It was on May 28 that she dispatched her letter of resignation as pastor:

[6] Dispensaries were opened in a number of cities, but the rapid increase
in the number of practitioners greatly lessened their usefulness. After a
few years they were closed.

[7] Midweek services were continued on Friday evening until June 10,
1898, when they were changed to Wednesday evening.

[8] Control of the magazine was vested in a Publication Committee
consisting of Joseph Armstrong, Edward P. Bates, William G. Nixon,
Augusta E. Stetson, and Caroline D. Noyes.

To the Church of Christ, Scientist, Boston

Beloved Brethren: —

For good and sufficient reasons I again send you my resignation which must be final of the Pastorate of the Church of Christ, Scientist, Boston, and recommend that you secure a Pastor to enter upon this labor in early autumn, one who will take full charge of this dear church, look after its interests, receive and attend to applications for membership, hold regular communion service, and in all respects discharge the duties of a Pastor. Also I beg that you will give such an one a sufficient salary to enable him to give his whole time to the duties which belong to this responsible office.

Yours in the bonds of Spirit,

Mary B. G. Eddy, Pastor

Having reached some conclusions regarding the organization of churches, Mrs. Eddy chose June 13 as the day on which to write to the National Association, which was in convention in Cleveland:

I earnestly, hereby recommend that you appoint a committee to look after church work and organization. Give it free discussion. The churches should be organized under the title of "Church of Christ, Scientist." They should have an independent form of government, subject only to the moral and spiritual perceptions, and the rules of the Bible and Christian Science as laid down in Matt. 18:15, 16, and 17. . . .[9]

[9] The National Christian Scientist Association was the only body that could deal with the "church work and organization" desired by Mrs. Eddy.

In Cleveland, after a great deal of discussion — which was led by L. P. Norcross, pastor of the Oconto (Wisconsin) church — a committee was appointed to do as Mrs. Eddy wished, after Norcross had wondered if it was "idle boasting to predict that we will have fully a hundred churches in this new faith — when, in the providence of God, we gather again for the yearly meeting of our Association."

At this convention, and after naming Foster Eddy as President, the Association acted on another important recommendation by Mrs. Eddy.

Up to this time, Sunday services had been held in the afternoon, so as not to intrude on those who still retained their memberships in denominational churches and who, also, attended morning services in those churches. Feeling the time had come when Christian Scientists should drop the idea that hers was "subordinate, or supplementary to any other religious system," she requested the National Association to adopt resolutions changing the time for Christian Science services to Sunday morning. It was done; and this was the first of her March 5 representations to be put into effect.

Following the Cleveland convention, Norcross assumed

When the Association was organized in 1886, the number of Christian Science churches was so small that it was not considered necessary to bring them into a centralized body and the Association was set up as the governing body of the movement. In its Constitution was this Article:. "This National Christian Scientist Association has exclusive jurisdiction in granting charters. No Students' Christian Scientist Association can be formed or continue to exist without its sanction. It possesses the sole right and power of granting charters; of receiving appeals and redressing grievances arising in Students' Christian Scientist Associations; or originating and regulating the means of its own support; and of *doing all other acts conducive to the interests of the Order.*" (Italics supplied.)

the pastorate of the Boston church and F. E. Mason transferred to Brooklyn, New York.

But, while she had recommended it, Mrs. Eddy was not
satisfied to leave the Church in the custody of the National
Christian Scientist Association. In three years the Association had grown into a membership of five hundred. Unlike
the Christian Scientist Association of the Massachusetts
Metaphysical College, whose membership was confined to
her own students, the national Association included pupils
of all teachers, including some whose teachers were loyal no
longer. Mrs. Eddy's concern was with the deception of
numbers.

This was the deception which brought temptation to
assert authority, to form cliques, to indulge in politics;
and a year later she was reminding them once more of those
temptations:

> You must give much time to self-examination
> and correction; and you must control appetite,
> passion, pride, envy, evil-speaking, resentment,
> and each of the innumerable errors that worketh
> or maketh a lie. . . . For students to work together
> is not always to co-operate, but to co-elbow! [10]

Although presently the desire to revise *Science and
Health* held the highest place, her church was never away
from her thought.

Since that night in Lynn, in 1872, when she was walking
home from the railroad station after the rejection of her
first manuscript of *Science and Health* by a Boston pub-

[10] The *Christian Science Journal,* July 1890.

lisher, she had pondered deeply of worship without servility in a church in which nothing stood between God and man.

As the physicist who, although he has never seen it, knows the electron better through its effects than he knows the pencil he uses to write his calculations, so did Mrs. Eddy know God better than she knew the members of her own household, although she saw them every day. She felt His presence. That was enough and, from the moment of her discovery, the fundamental idea in her teachings was to turn the attention of all who listened to the vital relationship between God and man.

Conscious of her own affinity with Him, she submitted to instructions within herself.

Instead of copying the past and mechanically repeating wonderment over His miracles, she declared them miracles only to the spiritually blind.[11] A bold conception, it was in keeping with the gentle assurance, "I am the door";[12] but it brought hate, and it brought abuse and great misunderstanding.

Yet these things, hate and abuse and misunderstanding, were things that never seemed to touch her; she seemed to feel only His hand upon her shoulder.

Careful in her leadership, and careful not to lead too fast, Mrs. Eddy, in August, suggested a new use for *Science and Health*. She suggested that it be made a definite part of the Sunday services. Her letter to the Boston congregation follows:

[11] "All men and women, in proportion as they are true disciples of the Truth, can heal and be healed, even according to the Master's word." (*Science and Health* p. 232, 28th edition, revised; copyright, 1887.)
[12] John, 10: 9.

ORDER OF CHURCH SERVICE

TO THE CHURCH OF CHRIST, SCIENTIST, BOSTON:

BELOVED BRETHREN, — I recommend that you lay aside all that is ceremonial even in appearance in our Church and adopt this simple service.

Before the sermon read one hymn, sing once. Read selections from a chapter in the Bible, and if agreeable to pastor and Church, a corresponding paragraph from *Science and Health*. Repeat alternately the Lord's Prayer, the pastor repeating the first sentence and the audience the following one. Unite in silent prayer for all who are present. Close with reading hymn, singing, silent prayer, and the benediction.

Yours lovingly in Christ,
MARY B. G. EDDY [13]

There were two reasons for the use of *Science and Health* in the services. It identified the church; it made the textbook a part of the services.

Up to this time there was only occasional mention of *Science and Health* in the church service. Pastors now were expected to quote from it in explaining the Bible before preaching their sermons, the purpose being to offset interpretations that were too expansive, or personalities that were too extravagant.

Already, in effect, Mrs. Eddy had counseled her students: Error will urge two extremes; the first to act too far in advance of our understanding, and to strike a blow too soon, and bring on a crisis that we are not fully prepared to meet and master. We must not mistake self-sufficiency, pride in

[13] *Christian Science Journal*, August 1889.

the letter of Christian Science, and our finite conception of the fitness of things for spiritual intuitions. . . .[14]

Suggesting the pulpit use of *Science and Health* was Mrs. Eddy's way of informing her church congregations that she did not intend leaving Christian Science to the vagaries of personal interpretation, or to the protection of human hands. She saw that any personal translation of her words must be avoided. Between the covers of her textbook were her teachings and, as stated on the cover of this textbook, in these teachings was the Key to the Scriptures. She intended they should not be used for the picking of any strange locks.

She cautioned, often, against reliance on material personality. Having in mind, apparently, those who diluted her teachings and set up schools of their own, she wrote to Joseph Adams in Chicago, on October 3, 1888, saying, "My personality asserted and aimed at by others has been under my feet twenty-two years; but the foes of Christ, marshalled under the signals of Christian Scientists seem to see my personality very vividly and are constantly firing at it, although they never hit me."

In *The First Church of Christ, Scientist, and Miscellany* (pages 118–120) is published a letter she wrote to a clergyman declining his request to call on her "in person," and explaining: "Those who look for me in person, or elsewhere than in my writings, lose me instead of find me. I hope and trust that you and I may meet in truth and know each other there, and know as we are known to God. . . . Forgive, if it needs forgiveness, my honest position."

* * *

[14] Meeting of Christian Scientist Association of the Massachusetts Metaphysical College, April 1889.

Having taken the first step in establishing her Church as a spiritual entity, and in a continued effort to get her teachings outside of organization, Mrs. Eddy turned her attention to the Christian Scientist Association of the Massachusetts Metaphysical College. On September 23, 1889, she wrote its members:

BELOVED STUDENTS:—

I have faithfully sought the direction of Divine wisdom in my advice herein given, namely, that you vote To-day to dissolve this organization.

1st. Because the teacher who organized this first Christian Science Association has retired from her place in the College, and no longer prepares the students for entering this Association.

2nd. Because new students whom others have taught may not receive the reception that her students have received from this associated body. They may not consider them students of the same grade, and this may incite improper feelings between my students and the students of other teachers. I regret to say that there has been much discord in the past between students connected with this Christian Science Association, and it would seem more natural for them to harmonize than different grades of students; hence the precedent does not favor the hope for future harmony.

3rd. Because it is more in accord with Christian Science for you to unite on the basis of Love and meet together in bonds of affection, from unselfish motives and the purpose to benefit each other, and honor the cause. Therefore I strongly recommend this method alone, of continuing without organization, the meeting together of the students of the Massachusetts Metaphysical College.

I most earnestly desire that the present reputation of my College shall be sustained, and go into history honoring God and whomsoever He hath anointed with peace on earth and love for the whole human family.

Affectionately your Teacher,

MARY B. G. EDDY

The students met on that same day and, after voting to "continue to meet on the first Wednesday of each month" and to continue to pay the "same sum of money, quarterly, as heretofore . . . for the purpose of paying incidental expenses . . . a communication from our Teacher was adopted by a unanimous vote. By which act the Christian Scientist Association of the Massachusetts Metaphysical College was dissolved at three o'clock and ten minutes, P.M."

Inasmuch as restrictions kept the membership confined to Mrs. Eddy's students, there was in the Constitution — unlike the constitution of the National Christian Scientist Association, which permitted withdrawal by "any member who is dissatisfied with the demands of Christian Science" — a provision stating that "all persons entering the Association become life members, though they may be expelled for violation of the Constitution, or By-Laws." [15]

[15] According to the records of the Association, when on September 5, 1889, Mrs. Eddy requested permission to withdraw her membership, Calvin Frye moved a suspension *pro tem* of this provision (Section 4, Article 1) in the Constitution, and it was unanimously approved. The Association records also disclose that in 1889 Mrs. Eddy made five efforts to disengage herself from organizational responsibilities. She resigned the editorship of the *Journal*, the pastorate of the Church in Boston, the presidency of the

Her concern that, unless dissolved, there might come into the Association "improper feelings between my students and the students of other teachers" foresaw what did happen several years afterwards.

Having succeeded to the presidency of the National Christian Scientist Association, Foster Eddy was given a teacher's role in the college. He taught Primary, Normal and Obstetrics Class through one term. General Erastus N. Bates also was a teacher in the Massachusetts Metaphysical College.[16]

Bates taught a Primary Class, was moderately successful, but the demand was for Mrs. Eddy.[17] Recognizing the impossibility of yielding to it, she called a special meeting of the Massachusetts Metaphysical College Corporation on October 29, 1889, at which "after due deliberation and earnest discussion it was unanimously voted: That as all debts of the Corporation have been paid, it is deemed best

---

two Associations, and her position as teacher in the Massachusetts Metaphysical College.

[16] Bates was in poor physical condition when he was discharged from the army at the close of the War Between the States. Medical men finally told him they could do no more than offer him an invalid's life for his remaining years. Out of gratitude for being healed through Christian Science, Bates sought out Mrs. Eddy, became her student, and devoted his life to her Cause.

[17] In a letter printed in the *Boston Traveler*, Mrs. Eddy informed the public of her "desire to revise my book, 'Science and Health with Key to the Scriptures,' and in order to do this I must stop teaching. . . . The work that needs to be done, and which God calls me to do outside my College work, if left undone might hinder the progress of our cause more than my teaching could advance it; therefore, I leave all for Christ."

When she decided to close the College there were more than three hundred applications on her desk, with each day adding to the total. In *Retrospection and Introspection* (p. 47) she spoke of this period, saying: "The apprehension of what has been, and must be, the final outcome of material organization, which wars with Love's spiritual compact, caused me to dread the unprecedented popularity of my College."

to dissolve this Corporation, and the same is hereby dissolved." [18]

In the resolutions of dissolution it was explained "the hour has come wherein the great need is for more of the spirit instead of the letter, and *Science and Health* is adapted to work this result. . . ." Copies of the resolutions were distributed among Mrs. Eddy's students and, following C. A. Frye's signature as Clerk, Mrs. Eddy attached this note:

> BELOVED STUDENT: You are again called to accept, without a present understanding, a marked providence of God. Our Master said: "What I do thou knowest not now, but thou shalt know hereafter."
>
> Trust Him in this unlooked-for event, and He will sooner or later show you the wisdom thereof. I have acted with deliberation. For the past two years this change has seemed to me the imperative demand of Christian Science in consonance with the example of our Master. Trusting that you also will discern the wisdom of this advanced step and coincide with this act of the Corporation.
>
> I am affectionately yours,
> MARY B. G. EDDY

With her college closed and her Association dissolved, Mrs. Eddy turned again to her great purpose. In February, there had been but two notices of church services in the *Journal;* now, in the late autumn, there were near-one hundred. Aware that the authority of God does not depend upon the authority of numbers and wanting The Mother Church

---

[18] For complete text of resolutions dissolving Massachusetts Metaphysical College Corporation see *Retrospection and Introspection,* pp. 48–49.

to be a structure of spiritual development, distinct from any branch organization, she wrote on November 23:

> MY DEAR STUDENT:
>
> This morning has finished my halting between two opinions.
>
> This Mother Church must disorganize, and now is the time to do it and form no new organization but the spiritual one.
>
> Follow Christ Jesus's example and not that of his disciples. Theirs has come to naught in science ours should establish Science but not material organizations. Will tell you all that leads to this final decision when I see you.
>
> Lovingly,
M. B. G. EDDY

The following day, November 24, this notice was sent to the members of The Church of Christ, Scientist, Boston:

> The annual meeting of the Church of Christ, Scientist, will be held in the Christian Science Read-Room, No. 210 Hotel Boylston, 24 Boylston Street, Monday, Dec. 2, 1889, at 7:30 P.M.
>
> At this meeting the question will be laid before the Church — to consider the advisability, and to take action thereon, of dissolving the organization of the Church on the basis of material and human law, and of remaining together henceforth on a plane of spiritual law in accordance with the higher teachings we are constantly receiving.
>
> By order of the Business Committee,
> WM. B. JOHNSON, Clerk

On December 2, 1889, the church Board met and adopted the following resolutions, unanimously:

(1) That the time has come when this Church should free itself from the thraldom of man-made laws, and rise into spiritual latitudes where the law of love is the only bond of union.

(2) That the Regulations and By-Laws of this Church be and are hereby declared to be, in all their articles and clauses except that part of Article 1 which fixes its name, null and void.

(3) That the Corporation be and is declared dissolved and that the present Clerk of the Church is hereby requested to take necessary steps to give legal effect to this resolution.

(4) The members of this Church hereby declare that this action is taken in order to realize more perfectly the purpose of its institution as an organization viz. growth in spiritual life and the spread of the "glad tidings" — and that they will continue as a Voluntary Association of Christians knowing no law but the law of Love, and no Master but Christ in the exercise of all the ministrations and activities heretofore performed as a Church of Christ, Scientist.

(5) That the members of this church make loving recognition of the services and guidance of the founder and late pastor of the church, and also the expression of their grateful thanks to those who in the capacities of assistant pastor or otherwise have fostered its growth.

*　*　*

This was a year of great change — and great accomplishment!

Behind Mary Baker Eddy's desire for "no new organization but the spiritual one" was the now-reached conviction that the distractions of material organization and ceremony and personal ambition are what keep mankind from seeing the eternal truths. Believing life to be a gift which man holds as a mark of his Relationship, her whole purpose was to design a Church that would aid man in his great quest — the understanding and service of God.

In announcing her intention of establishing her Church on a spiritual basis, her purpose was a Church in which all would have responsibility. She saw in the trial and crucifixion things that could be organized — private posse, torches, weapons, arrest, ecclesiastical court, legal formalities, military escort, the death march; she saw in the Sermon on the Mount, and in the Lord's Prayer, things that could not be organized:

> Blessed *are* the poor in spirit: for theirs is the kingdom of heaven. Blessed *are* they that mourn: for they shall be comforted. Blessed *are* the meek: for they shall inherit the earth. Blessed *are* they which do hunger and thirst after righteousness: for they shall be filled. Blessed *are* the merciful: for they shall obtain mercy. Blessed *are* the pure in heart: for they shall see God. . . .

These, she believed, are things that have to be understood and practiced — being Spiritual; they are, she taught, qualifications necessary for admittance into His high company.

CHAPTER TWELVE

A Story of Prayer

IN APPEARANCE, on January 1, 1890, Mary Baker Eddy was starting all over. She had closed her college, dissolved her Association, and disorganized her church. Actually, the land had been cleared: the soil was fertile, and was ready for the planting.

Among those Mrs. Eddy hoped would be tillers of the soil was Josephine C. Woodbury. Sick, Mrs. Woodbury first visited Mrs. Eddy in Lynn, in 1879. She was healed and, after attending a Normal Class in 1885, became an assistant editor of the *Journal* and a frequent contributor. Following Mrs. Eddy's resignation as pastor of the Boston church on June 21, 1889, Mrs. Woodbury offered to serve as preacher. Meeting refusal by the Church Board, she became critical of Mrs. Eddy and left Boston to carry her criticisms into Maine and Quebec.

Toward the end of 1889 she visited Mrs. Eddy in Concord and was told, so she wrote, to "go home and be happy. Commit thy ways unto the Lord, Trust Him and He will bring it to pass."

Back in Boston, Mrs. Woodbury began telling all who would listen that "I am closest to our Leader." [1] Soon she had a small and zealous following — a following so zealous

---

[1] Mrs. Eddy publicly used the term Leader in connection with herself in June 1879, and an editorial in the *Christian Science Journal* in January 1888 began its general use.

that it did not question her explanation of an event of June 11, 1890: "There was born to me a baby boy: though, till his sharp birth-cry saluted my ears, I had not realized that prospective maternity was the interpretation of the preceding months of poignant physical discomfort, not unreasonably attributed to other physiological causes and changes — growing out of my age and former reliance upon medical opinion — and pointing in the direction of some fungoid formation."

A few weeks later — on July 4 — the baby, named the Prince of Peace, was baptized at Ocean Point, Maine. Surrounding a salt-water pool — named Bethesda, by Mrs. Woodbury — were thirty of her students who, as Mrs. Woodbury also wrote, "joined in a spontaneous and appropriate hymn" as the child was immersed three times. In a frenzy and plainly out of balance mentally, Mrs. Woodbury declared her offspring "an immaculate conception," proclaimed it had come to "redeem the world," and announced that Mrs. Eddy was its father.

The whole thing was so profanely ridiculous that Mrs. Eddy sought to ignore it. This she was not able to do. Mrs. Woodbury was excommunicated.

Desiring even more newspaper attention than she was getting, Mrs. Woodbury revealed herself as a second Mary, and called upon her small following to bring gifts — gifts of new gold coin, gifts of food, of clothing, of a home [2] for the Prince of Peace. That the dead might be raised, she closed the child in a room with a corpse, but the experiment failed. She sent her followers to "mesmerize" Sunday services at Chickering Hall.

[2] 412 Newbury Street, close by 385 Commonwealth Avenue, which was owned by Mrs. Eddy.

Following so closely the antics of Mrs. Plunkett, the mania of Mrs. Woodbury supplied the enemies of Mrs. Eddy with additional opportunities to destroy her work. Being enemies, they disregarded the obvious fact that whatever the mistakes of Mrs. Plunkett and of Mrs. Woodbury they were not Mrs. Eddy's mistakes, nor were they happenings in accordance with her teachings. In the years since, critics have not overlooked the improprieties of these two students; nor have they overlooked the improvisations of Joshua F. Bailey.

In the spring of 1889, when Mrs. Eddy indicated her intention of divesting herself of organizational responsibilities, Bailey, an assistant on the *Christian Science Journal,* went to her with the proposal that she give him the publication as his personal property. She declined, but this did not prevent Bailey from using the publication as his own.

Becoming editor, Bailey (in July 1890) used the *Journal* to announce "All quotations from the *New Testament* printed in the *Journal* hereafter will be made in accord with Rotherham's version" [3] and recommended that this translation of the New Testament "be the inseparable companion of *Science and Health* in the closet, the class-room and on the platform. . . ."

Given little support in his enthusiasm for Rotherham, Bailey's next recommendation was that newcomers in Christian Science put aside their Bibles, "for three months or more," and wrote this recommendation which appeared in the October 1890 issue of the *Journal:* " 'Out of the abundance of the heart the mouth speaketh.' The words of the old theology puts us in spite of ourselves in the current of

[3] This version of the New Testament was translated in 1872; the Rotherham translation of the Old Testament was published in 1902.

that thought. 'All is Mind.' A beginner in Christian Science, for this reason, progresses more rapidly if the Bible is laid aside for a time. A student — in the tongue of the world called 'a patient' — who says to a Scientist, 'I take so much comfort reading my Bible,' if guided wisely will be answered, 'Let your Bible alone for three months or more. Don't open it even, nor think of it. But dig day and night at *Science and Health.*' "

Published over the signature of the editor of the *Christian Science Journal,* the announcement was a sensation in the religious world. It was denounced from the pulpits, in the newspapers, by the religious press, and it brought strong protests from Christian Scientists. In apparent dismay, Bailey retreated from one position into another, equally vulnerable. In the November issue of the *Journal* he advised Christian Scientists: ". . . Burn every scrap of 'Christian Science Literature' so called, except *Science and Health,* and the publications bearing the imprint of the Christian Science Publishing Society of Boston; return to the diligent study of *Science and Health* and the Bible; preach Christ as there unfolded; direct all inquiries to the same, as the only sources of truth, and warn the public, at every opportunity, against the refuge of lies."

In almost no time the Publication Committee of the National Christian Scientists Association was busy reading letters and listening to protests that the sermons preached in Christian Science churches and the lessons taught by Christian Science teachers were not the "refuge of lies."

The Publication Committee acted. Bailey's resignation as editor was requested, and in the December issue of the *Journal* the Publication Committee published this notice:

BOSTON, MASS., *Nov. 22, 1890*

At a meeting of the Publication Committee this day held, it was unanimously voted that the sentiments expressed in the October *Journal* page 318, lines 20–21 (quoted above) and the November *Journal,* page 359, lines 34–36 (quoted above) were unauthorized, unwise, and not the thought of the Committee. Also, that at present it is not advisable to issue a Children's Quarterly.[4]

ALFRED LANG,
CHAIRMAN, PUBLICATION COMMITTEE

Leaving the editorship of the *Journal,* Bailey persuaded the Publication Committee into forming a "General Association for Dispensing Christian Science Literature." In May 1891, he published a notice in the *Journal* requesting all Christian Scientists to join in the work, and managed to create an impression that if they did not purchase a copy of the new edition of *Science and Health,* when it was published in January, they were disloyal to their Leader.

News of the indiscretion came to Mrs. Eddy's ears in June, and in the July issue of the Journal she published this "Card":

Since my attention has been called to the article in the May *Journal,* I think it would have been wiser not to have organized the General Association for Dispensing Christian Science Literature.

1. Because I disbelieve in the utility of so widespread an organization. It tends to promote monopolies, class legislation and unchristian motives for Christian work.

[4] This was an idea Bailey developed for use in Sunday School.

2. I consider my students as capable, individually, of selecting their own reading matter, as a committee would be chosen for this purpose.

I shall have nothing further to say on this subject, but hope my students' conclusion will be wisely drawn, and tend to promote the welfare of those outside, as well as inside this organization.

MARY B. G. EDDY

Accompanying the "Card" was a "Notice":

Having awakened to the fact that material means and methods cannot be incorporated in the practical demonstration and work of Divine Science and especially in the circulation of Christian Science literature, I hereby recall the request made in the May *Journal,* namely, "that Scientists organize in the systematic distribution of Christian Science literature," and hereby declare the General Association for Dispensing Christian Science Literature dissolved from date.

CAROL NORTON,
General Secretary

NEW YORK, *June 26, 1891.*

Bailey's improvisations still pursue Mrs. Eddy's teachings. Critics continue to quote him as an authority for the contention that in Christian Science the Bible is in a secondary position to *Science and Health* and to support the argument by saying what Bailey wrote could not have been printed in the *Journal* without her consent. This, of course, is not true. From the time of its appearance, a good many things were published in the *Journal* that did not have Mrs. Eddy's sanction; and especially was this true after June 1889, when she turned over the publication to the control of the National Christian Scientist Association.

She was not aware of Bailey's statements in the October and November issues of the publication until long after their appearance. Her days were taken up with the writing of her new edition of *Science and Health,* the reading of proof, and the changing over of her church into a spiritual organization.

In the *Journal* of January 1890, she had expressed a desire to be undisturbed in her tasks:

> No letters containing inquiries as to the management of other people's affairs will be read or answered by me or by my secretary from this date, and no interviews for the purpose above named will be granted. The individual privilege sacrificed for twenty years I now claim. Having relinquished hitherto my own personal peace, time and opportunity to help others — to cast my mite for all who needed it into the scale of justice, wisdom and love, proportionately to my understanding, and leave it for them to maintain the true poise — experience has shown that thus the balance was often lost, and blame always attached to me. . . . Some students are saying and doing things in my name, while thinking and acting contrary to my judgment and counsel. This conduct deceives the world and stultifies the growth of students. . . .

These were times when it was impossible for Mrs. Eddy to see many persons. As she wrote one student who requested an interview, "It is now impossible for me to give one hour to aught but what I have on hand." [5]

In refining *Science and Health,* much of her thought was given to the chapter entitled "Animal Magnetism." The frequent use by her students of the words — "animal magnetism" — had long concerned her. As far back as October 11, 1882, at a meeting of her students in Boston, she had rebuked them: "There is a great excess of talk about error (mesmerism). All there is to mesmerism is what we make of it."

In the summer of 1890 the words were in such frequent use that in the August issue of the *Journal,* she again warned:

> The discussion of malicious animal magnetism had better be dropped until Scientists understand clearly how to handle this error — until they are not in danger of dwarfing their growth in love, by falling into this lamentable practice in their attempts to meet it. Only patient, unceasing love for all mankind — love that cannot mistake Love's aid — can determine this question on the Principle of Christian Science.
>
> MARY B. G. EDDY

Five months afterwards, and with the appearance of the new edition of *Science and Health,* her students discovered that she had reduced the length of the chapter by about one half. To those who had accustomed themselves to using "animal magnetism" as an excuse for their own misdeeds, the new chapter was a keen disappointment. However, most of the students understood the significance of the change.

[5] Letter to Joseph Adams, Chicago, March 1890.

Meanwhile, instead of acceding to her wishes to be undisturbed, many of her students continued to besiege her with messages and letters — so many, that in the September 1890 issue of the *Journal* she gave strong emphasis to her request for solitude:

    1. I shall not be consulted verbally, or through letters, as to whose advertisements shall or shall not appear in the *Christian Science Journal*.

    2. I shall not be consulted verbally, or through letters, as to the matter that should be published in the *Journal,* and *C. S. Series.*

    3. I shall not be consulted verbally, or through letters, on marriage, divorce, or family affairs of any kind.

    4. I shall not be consulted verbally, or through letters, on the choice of pastors for churches.

    5. I shall not be consulted verbally, or through letters, on disaffections, if there should be any between the students of Christian Science.

    6. I shall not be consulted verbally, or through letters, on who shall be admitted as members, or dropped from the membership of the Christian Science Churches or Associations.

    7. I am not to be consulted verbally, or through letters, on disease and the treatment of the sick; but I shall love all mankind — and work for their welfare.

But, in spite of the distractions that threatened to overwhelm her, the world was beginning to see Mary Baker Eddy in her gathering stature — not as a solitary figure, but as a Leader devoting herself to the building of a religion in which love is not a sentiment — but is power, is authority, and the rule of right in human life.

In the *Journal,* in February 1890, it was stated:

> The dissolution of the visible organization of the Church is the sequence and complement of that of the College Corporation and Association. The College disappeared "that the spirit of Christ might have freer course among its students and all who come into the understanding of Divine Science"; the bonds of organization of the Church were thrown away, so that its members might assemble themselves together and "provoke one another to good works" in the bond only of Love.

When she threw away the "bonds of organization," Mrs. Eddy revealed her conviction that new provisions were needed for the government of her church.

By the autumn of 1891, most of the offshoots and imitators were gone. Nearly all the self-styled Christian Science colleges and academies had closed; nearly all the so-called Christian Science publications had suspended. The *Boston Christian Scientist* ceased publishing in December 1890; the *Chicago Christian Scientist* was still appearing, but would disappear before the year was over; Mrs. Hopkins, who had localized her efforts in the Midwest, still had her colleges but in another year they, too, would be gone.

Although seeking "no new organization but the spiritual one," Mrs. Eddy was fully aware that her church had to be built on a proper legal foundation; and fully aware that in the new organization there must be responsibility that would be subject only to delegation, and never to seizure. How she worked it out is a story of prayer, which included a program of church services as impersonal in performance as the faith it represents.

In May 1890, and doubtless with great interest, Mrs. Eddy read a report from Caroline D. Noyes, of Chicago: ". . . Recognizing that the truth expressed in *Science and Health* is both our teacher and our healer, we resolved to take it into our pulpit and make it our preacher also, by reading selections from it together with appropriate passages from the Scriptures in place of a sermon. . . . In two months both church and Sunday school have doubled in numbers. . . . We do not desire to convey the impression that there are no circumstances under which a pastor or speaker may not be necessary, nor imply that it is not well to have one. . . . It is apparent . . . that the numerous groups of Scientists who are waiting for a pastor or speaker, to establish services, can proceed at once with possibly greater advantage to themselves than could be realized with a speaker. They are certain to gain strength through reliance on their own efforts, and from participation in the worship. . . ."

However, Mrs. Eddy knew that the thousands who were hearing her teachings for the first time were not ready for such a drastic change in church services. With an influx of clergymen, and laity, of many denominations there were nearly two hundred Christian Science church organizations scattered about the country.[6] She knew the need was to

---

[6] In November 1889, there were eighteen Christian Science churches, and fifty-nine Christian Science societies; in September 1892, there were fifty-five Christian Science churches, and one hundred and fifteen Christian Science societies.

bring the newcomers into gentle acceptance of her teaching that "everything God created, He pronounced good. He never made sickness. . . ." [7]

She knew about the belief, held by some, that "the way to keep well, or to get well, is to copy by hand from *Science and Health*." She was aware that others slept with her textbook under their pillows. She rebuked these superstitions, often. She was concerned lest there be indiscriminate copying from *Science and Health,* and declaring from the platform in her church that such paragraphs were explanatory of an equally indiscriminate selection of scriptural verses. She knew that few of her followers were far enough advanced to make proper selections from the two books, the Bible and the textbook, *Science and Health;* and she knew about both as she wrote about the illustrations in her work, *Christ and Christmas:* "The illustrations were not intended for a golden calf, at which the sick may look and be healed." [8]

In recognition of Mrs. Eddy's concern over any misuse of her teachings, Sarah J. Clark, who succeeded Bailey as editor of the *Journal,* advised all contributors in the April 1891 issue: "In preparing your article for publication, eliminate all quotations from our text-book, *Science and Health;* also avoid giving the thought with a change of a few words, as thought thus expressed is not our own, but belongs to the individual consciousness that has brought it out through actual experience. It may be well not to explain the Bible as much as we have formerly done, until a higher plane is reached."

A clearer statement was needed, and in the August 1891 issue of the *Journal,* after recalling that she had given "the

[7] *Miscellaneous Writings,* p. 247.
[8] *Christian Science Journal,* February 1894.

Church of Christ, Scientist, of Boston . . . permission to cite in the CHRISTIAN SCIENCE QUARTERLY from my work *Science and Health,* passages giving the spiritual meaning of Bible texts," Mrs. Eddy reminded her followers that "this was a special privilege, and the Author's gift."

She explained that permission was necessary because copyrights protected her writings, and said, "It is not right to copy my book and read it publicly *without my consent,*" but offered "as a gift to my noble students — working faithfully for Christ's cause on earth — the privilege of copying and reading my works for Sunday service, provided they each and all destroy these copies at once, after said service. Also, that when I shall so elect, and give suitable notice, they desist from further copying my writings, as aforesaid."

To this she added, "This injunction . . . is intended to forestall the possible evil of putting the divine teachings contained in *Science and Health* into human hands, to subvert or to liquidate." [9]

The practice of reading "Bible Lessons" at Sunday services became so general that at a meeting of the Christian Scientist Association of the Massachusetts Metaphysical College in October 1891, the subject came in for long discussion, as indicated by the Association's records: "Much was said in favor of the Bible Lessons, of how much they had accomplished in the Sunday services, in place of sermons. . . . Questions were asked regarding the best method for studying these lessons and the experiences given. To the direct question as to the wisdom of writing the references, quite a general expression was given of a higher understanding, a greater unfolding of truth in the study, from the read-

[9] For full text, see *Miscellaneous Writings,* pp. 298-303.

ing of the references from the Bible and *Science and Health,* both in the home study and in the Sabbath School class."

The October 1891 *Journal* responded to many questions by publishing the following "Notice":

> QUESTION: — "Shall we continue to read in the pulpit, on Sunday, extracts from *Science and Health?*"
>
> If you comply with my terms relative to these Sunday services, published in the August issue of this year's *Journal,* you should. I have consented to this as above, and see no other causes than those designated in August *Journal* for changing the form you had already adopted for your Sunday services. I gave no permission for you to use my writings as aforesaid, except it be in place of a sermon delivered in your established pulpits.

Mrs. Eddy's words were explicit. If a church — such as the church in Chicago, about which Mrs. Noyes had written — was using the Bible and *Science and Health* in place of a sermon by a pastor, it was free to do so; if not, she gave no opinion, but did make it clear that the privilege of copying was confined solely to those occupying "established pulpits."

After watching closely the use of "the Bible and *Science and Health* in place of a sermon by a pastor" through two more months, Mrs. Eddy extended the radical action she began in August 1889. In December 1891, in a sweeping order, she established the Bible and *Science and Health* as the only preachers in her church. It was a new "Order of Church Services," and it removed from Christian Science churches all human personality, including her own — leaving only the Bible and *Science and Health with Key to the Scriptures* as the source of the sermons.

That there be uniformity among Christian Scientists in their Church services, I submit the following Order of Exercises:

Anthem.

Pastor announces that he will read from the Bible and from *Science and Health*.

Reading.

Lord's Prayer and Spiritual Version repeated alternately.

Pastor commences the first line of the Prayer, and repeats it with the Church; then he responds to it with the version. Next, the Church repeats the second line of the Prayer and Pastor responds, and so on to the end.

Pastor reads Hymn.

Singing.

Sermon.

Collection.

Pastor reads Hymn.

Singing.

Benediction.

Mary B. G. Eddy

This new order of services included several changes. The first change, of course, was the use of the Bible and *Science and Health*. Prior to this time, reading from the two books was secondary to the sermon; now they preceded the sermon, as such. The inclusion of "the Lord's Prayer and Spiritual Version" as an integral part of the services was another great change. Mrs. Eddy's spiritual interpretation of the Prayer first appeared in the first edition of *Science and Health*.

Through succeeding editions she evidenced her growing perception of what she understood the Master's words to mean; and she had received so many letters of gratitude that she believed the time had come for its use in church services.

The Prayer with its spiritual interpretation, as contained in the 1891 edition of *Science and Health,* follows:

> Our Father, which art in Heaven,
> (*Our eternal supreme Being, all-harmonious,*)
>
> Hallowed be Thy name.
> (*Forever glorious.*)
>
> Thy kingdom come!
> (*Ever-present and omnipotent!*)
>
> Thy will be done in earth, as it is in Heaven.
> (*Thy supremacy appears as matter disappears.*)
>
> Give us this day our daily bread;
> (*Give us each day the living bread;*)
>
> And forgive us our debts, as we forgive our debtors.
> (*And Truth will destroy the claims of error.*)
>
> And lead us not into temptation, but deliver us from evil;
> (*Led by Spirit, mortals are freed from sickness, sin and death;*)
>
> For Thine is the kingdom and the power and the glory forever. *Amen.*
> (*For Thou art all Substance, Life, Truth, and Love forever. So be it.*)

The substitution of a Reader for a pastor, and the introduction of the "Spiritual Version" of the Lord's Prayer, were not the only changes Mrs. Eddy had in mind. If there was to be uniformity in the services, there was need for a hymnal that would be in keeping with the teachings. A number of so-called Christian Science hymnals were available, but none was satisfactory. Among them were: *Fifty Christian Science Hymns* by Joseph Adams; *A Collection of Familiar and Original Hymns and Tunes Rendered Scientifically for Christian Science Services* by Ursula Gestefeld; *A Christian Science Hymn and Tune Book* by Hannah Moore Kohaus; and *Hymns for Christian Science Church and Sunday School Service* by Jessie Day. The last-named was advertised, for a time, in the *Journal.*

In the summer of 1890 Mrs. Eddy suggested the appointment of a committee to select the contents of a hymnal for her Church and, on August 5, 1890, the Publication Committee of the Christian Science Publishing Society announced the appointment of Professor Lyman Brackett, Julia Bartlett, William B. Johnson, Susie M. Lang, Mrs. Charles Thomas, E. H. Hall, and W. G. Nixon as "a committee to compile a church hymnal for the use of Christian Scientists."

In October 1892, the hymnal was ready. One source of material was the *Journal,* back numbers being searched for poems that could be set to music. A number of appropriate poems were found; and a number that, otherwise, would have been suitable were rejected because, since their publication, the authors had proved themselves disloyal. To give variety to the hymnal, each approved hymn was supplied with three different melodies.

For the most part the melodies were simple. Professor Brackett, who was responsible for them, had to keep in mind that in nearly all Christian Science churches the organist, or pianist, was a volunteer, and seldom an accomplished musician. Nevertheless, there were many objections. Being tuneful, it was said they were not appropriate for church services. However, it was not long before the criticisms were lost in the enthusiasm for congregational singing.[10]

It had long been Mary Baker Eddy's hope that the world would respond to her in truth, and not in emotion; understand her in spirit, and not in intellect. She saw belief in material personality as mistaken as belief in matter, and trust in either as the chain which imprisons mankind. Belief in material personality brought adulation, which was a blunder; or it brought hate, which was a mistake.

She saw these things, adulation and hate, in the religions of the world — saw too much of them, and too little obedience to the Word.

By establishing the Bible and *Science and Health* as the only preachers in her church, she called for obedience only to the teachings.

It was a decision of great importance then, and a decision of transcendent importance later.

Then, it was the decision that brought uniformity to "Christian Scientists in their Church services"; later, it was the decision that established the By-Laws and the government of The First Church of Christ, Scientist, in Boston, Massachusetts.

[10] In 1897, Mrs. Eddy suggested to the Christian Science Board of Directors that when a revision of the hymnal was made she hoped it would include "I Need Thee Every Hour," "Eternity," and "I'm a Pilgrim, and I'm a Stranger." In 1898, when the revision was undertaken, the three hymns were included.

CHAPTER THIRTEEN

"Who Owns God's Temple?"

Having, in 1889, dissolved the Christian Scientist Association of the Massachusetts Metaphysical College, Mrs. Eddy, in May 1890, requested the members of the National Christian Scientist Association at their convention in New York also to dissolve or, failing, to recess for three years.

In a letter clear in its recognition of individual responsibility, Mrs. Eddy advised the members of the National Association:

> . . . The time it takes yearly to prepare for this National Convention is worse than wasted, if it causes thought to wander in the wilderness, or ways of the world. The detail of conforming to society, in any way, costs you what it would to give time and attention to hygiene in your ministry and healing.
>
> . . . For students to work together is not always to co-operate, but sometimes to co-elbow! Each student should seek alone the guidance of our common Father — even the divine Principle which he claims to demonstrate — and especially should he prove his faith by works ethically, physically and spiritually. Remember that the first and last lesson of Christian Science is love, perfect love, and love made perfect through the cross. I once thought that

in unity was human strength; but have grown to
know that human strength is weakness — that in
unity with divine might alone is power and peace.

The Association voted to recess for three years, and this
was an action that provided an opportunity for Joshua F.
Bailey and Augusta E. Stetson.

Not right away, but with the Association in recess, ques-
tions were asked as to the ownership of the *Christian Science
Journal;* and, on November 1, 1892, when William G.
Nixon [1] resigned as Manager and Publisher, Bailey and
Mrs. Stetson began planning to get possession of the pub-
lication.

They were attracted by something Nixon stated in his
letter of resignation: ". . . On assuming my duties as publisher, there was not a dollar in the treasury, but, on the
contrary, the Society owed unpaid printing and paper bills
to the amount of several hundred dollars, not to mention a
contingent liability of many more hundreds represented by
unearned *Journal* and *Series* subscriptions paid by subscribers in advance, which sum of money had been disbursed
in the course of business prior to my coming. Today there is
cash in the treasury to the amount of over six thousand dollars ($6,000) with all our bills paid to date. . . ."

Nixon's statement, "On assuming my duties as publisher,
there was not a dollar in the treasury," was a direct attack
on Mrs. Eddy, and his boast that "Today there is cash in the
treasury to the amount of over six thousand dollars ($6,000)
with all our bills paid to date," attracted so much attention
that Joseph Armstrong, who succeeded Nixon, issued a state-

[1] Nixon was appointed to manage the *Journal* following Mrs. Eddy's
gift of the publication to the National Christian Scientist Association in
1889.

ment containing an auditor's report, which carried the approval of the Publishing Committee.

The audit disclosed:

ASSETS

On deposit at Old Colony Trust Co.. .	$8,032.92	
Due on Ledger accounts	159.96	$8,192.88
Cost of furniture and fixtures	879.07	
Cost of Bibles in stock	214.12	
Estimated cost of Tracts in stock . . .	550.00	
Estimated cost of Quarterlies in stock .	37.50	
Estimated cost of Dictionaries and other books	80.00	1,760.69
		$9,953.67

There is in stock a quantity of old *Journals* and *Series*[2] on which we can make no estimate.

LIABILITIES

Journal and subscriptions paid and unearned which expire on and after Feb. 1893	$3,531.85	
Quarterly	668.78	
Advertising	823.95	
Due customers on ledger	263.84	
Bills not paid	2,253.01	
Balance	2,362.24	$9,953.67

There are some old bills outstanding against the Society which have not been presented and we do not know what they amount to. The above statement shows what would be the condition of said Society if it should cease doing business at the above date

[2] A small periodical, the *Christian Science Series*, was published semimonthly from May 1, 1889, until May 1, 1891. It contained twelve pages, and consisted of articles and poems, many of them reprints from the *Christian Science Journal*.

(January 1, 1893) and return to the subscribers *pro rata* the amount of their subscriptions and advertisements which have not yet been earned.

J. ARMSTRONG, PUBLISHER

Approved: E. B. HULIN
E. P. BATES
M. ANNA OSGOOD
DAVID ANTHONY

Accompanying the audit was a statement:

It has been the impression of many of the students that there was a large surplus in the hands of the Publishing Committee. You will observe by examining the above statement of the Publisher (the first made in our history) that we are simply in a healthy financial condition. The assets aside from the cash are liable to a large percentage of shrinkage, and the liabilities will be increased somewhat by bills which had not been presented at the date our Publisher (Mr. Armstrong) assumed the duties of this office. We call attention to the fact as indicated above that the actual cash balance is very small, yet it is sufficient to carry on the business and meet all current obligations.

E. P. Bates
E. B. Hulin
M. Anna Osgood
David Anthony
Of the Publishing Committee [3]

The failure of the auditor's report to substantiate Nixon's boast did not lessen the desire of Bailey and Mrs. Stetson to own the *Journal.* They saw the publication primarily as a money-making proposition, and not, as Judge Septimus J. Hanna, when he was editor, said of it, "An organ through which the utterances of the students and friends of Christian Science may from time to time be [published] . . . but

[3] *Christian Science Journal,* March 1893.

more important . . . is the other fact that through its columns our beloved Leader may and does give forth her words of encouragement, guidance and admonition. . . ."

But, whatever the hopes of Bailey and Mrs. Stetson, they were hopes that disappeared on September 20, 1893. On that day, at the first meeting of the National Christian Scientist Association since its recess vote of three years before, a letter was read:

> My dear Students: — I have a unique request to lay before the National Christian Scientist Association. It is this: Will you decide by vote, whether or not I already am the owner of the *Christian Science Journal,* which seems to have fallen into my hands by reason of your prior vote to disorganize this Association? But however this may be, I see the wisdom of again owning this Christian Science waif. Therefore, I respectfully suggest to this honorable body the importance of voting on this question.
>
> Affectionately yours,
> Mary B. G. Eddy

On the same day, "It was moved, seconded and unanimously carried, that the meeting be considered the adjourned meeting of the National Christian Scientist Association, and that the body should adjourn to meet again in three years from this date.

"It was also moved, seconded, and unanimously carried: That it be declared by this Association of Christian Scientists to be its understanding that the *Christian Science Journal* is now owned by Rev. Mary Baker G. Eddy, its donor and original proprietor. There was then read an instrument signed by Mrs. Eddy, in which she redonated to this Association the *Christian Science Journal*. It was moved, seconded, and unanimously carried that the offer be accepted with gratitude and thanks subject to the conditions contained therein. . . ."

In an article in the November 1893 issue of the *Journal*, it was told that Mrs. Eddy took this unusual way "to make doubly sure that it [the *Journal*] belonged to her, and that no person had, or could have, any legal claim on the *Journal*"; and, in the same issue, Mrs. Eddy published this "Notice":

> MY BELOVED CHRISTIAN SCIENTISTS: — Please send in your contributions as usual to our *Journal*. All is well at headquarters and when the mist shall melt away you will see clearly the glory of the heaven of love within your own hearts. Let this sign of peace and harmony be supreme and forever yours. . . .

There were other occasions when Mrs. Eddy gave her students lessons in economics. A very important occasion when she did this was in the building of The Mother Church.

In 1885, with Hawthorne Hall becoming crowded, members of the Christian Scientist Association of the Massachusetts Metaphysical College began making contributions toward the building of their own edifice. In June 1886, the contributions totaled $2000, and it was proposed that the money be used in making a down payment toward the purchase of a lot in the Back Bay district of Boston. The cost of the property under discussion was $6800. The owners were willing to accept $2000 as a down payment, and to extend a three-year mortgage, payable on July 1, 1889, for the balance of $4800.

Mrs. Eddy advised against buying church property, and placing a mortagage on it — advising her students, as she later wrote, that a church is "God's gift, foundation and superstructure," and being so, she insisted it was something in which "no one could hold a wholly material title." [4]

She reminded them that the spontaneity of supply is the normal fact in spiritual law, and assured them that, in accordance with this law, funds would be available with the coming of the proper time to build the church.

But the wish to buy a lot, to place a mortgage on it, and, by traditional methods, to raise money to pay off the mortgage was stronger than their teacher's counsel. The students bought the property by paying out the cash, and signing the mortgage.

Planning ways to pay off the mortgage, they decided to hold a church fair. Again Mrs. Eddy sought to dissuade them from traditional methods, preaching to them on Communion Sunday, June 19, 1887, in Chickering Hall, substantially as follows:

> "Children, have ye any meat? They answered him, No." . . . Notwithstanding the privileges the disciples had enjoyed with their Master; who had qualified them to be fishers of men, they, who had been called from their nets, as soon as they had lost sight of him, relapsed, turned back to their nets, and were ensnared in them again.

[4] *Christian Science Journal*, July 1892.

"They toiled all night and caught nothing." It is always darkest before dawn. The night was far spent. They had sailed forward and backward over the dark waters, vainly searching for gain — reminding us of Job's experience, where he says: "I go forward, but He is not there; and backward, but I cannot perceive Him." As they drew nigh to the shore, they heard the loving voice of their Master, saying: "Children, have ye any meat? They answered him, No!"

Then he directed them to cast their net on the right side of the ship. This . . . is the important thing to understand, which is the right side? Is it the material or is it the spiritual side of life and its pursuits? They found after they had learned by bitter experience their mistake, and yielded obedience to Christ's command — that success followed; for now heeding his direction, they cast their net on the other side, and gathered an abundance of fish.

One who loved his Teacher was the first to recognize the stranger on the shore. . . . Peter did not attempt to walk over the wave as once he did, when Jesus was nearer to him, but was willing to beat against the wave; so, plunging into the water, he swam for the shore.

Upon their arrival they found that Jesus had provided for their wants, for "they saw a fire of coals, there, and fish laid thereon, and bread;" and Jesus supped with them. Whence came this supply of food, which he had prepared for them? Was it not a spiritual feast, even the "bread that cometh down from Heaven"? After they had partaken of this — the last supper . . . we find the disciples so enlightened and strengthened in Spirit that they never returned to their old pursuits, but were steadfast in following his teachings, proclaiming the "glad tidings of salvation. . . ."

The sermon was received, but not heeded. She then offered to buy the property, thus relieving them of responsibility for the mortgage. In their enthusiasm for a fair, they declined. Rather than interfere further, Mrs. Eddy withdrew her opposition.

The fair was held on December 19–21, in Horticultural Hall, then at Tremont and Bromfield Streets. Mrs. Eddy attended, and the affair was so successful that almost the entire amount needed to pay off the mortgage was raised. Then, within the month, the treasurer of the church building fund disappeared. With him disappeared the more than $5000 profit from the fair. The committee hesitated before telling Mrs. Eddy of the defalcation. Finally, they did go to her. She requested that they make no attempt to bring about the arrest of the missing treasurer. She gave it as her opinion that "he was an honest man," and observed that his own awareness that he was a thief was sufficient punishment.

Her wish was acceded to, and she then implored the committee and the congregation of her church to stand fast in the knowledge that if it was right that the church should rest on a spiritual foundation, a way would be found by which title to the property would not be lost.

Months passed. The months became a year, two years, two years and five months. It was the end of November 1888. In the distraction of the rebellion of the Boston teachers, the confusion and the ridicule brought on by Mrs. Plunkett, and the theft of the proceeds of the church fair, much of the interest in buying the lot and building a church was gone. There was little money — about five hundred dollars — in the church building fund, and there were rising objections to the building of an edifice. Beginning to be heard was the argument, "It is unscientific and not in strict keeping with Christian Science to build a material structure."

At the end of November 1888, Mrs. Eddy engaged Baxter E. Perry, a Boston attorney, gave him a check, and instructed him to purchase the mortgage on the lot in Back Bay. This was done on December 4, 1888. With word from Perry of the completion of the transaction, Mrs. Eddy quietly waited.

July 1, 1889, the day on which the mortgage was due, came and went — with no word from Alfred Lang who, in February 1889, had become treasurer of the church building fund. July passed. Still there was no word. Then, acting in accordance with Mrs. Eddy's wishes, the lawyer notified Lang that foreclosure proceedings had been instituted, and the lot would be advertised for sale at public auction on August 3. This was done. Lang did not appear; nor did any member of the congregation. Acting as Mrs. Eddy's representative, the sole bidder for the property was George Perry, son of the attorney. His bid was approximately $5000. Title to the lot was conveyed to him on August 6, 1889.

Not knowing that, technically, the property was not in Mrs. Eddy's possession, seven students [5] met in Boston on October 5, and authorized William B. Johnson to write a

[5] Julia S. Bartlett, Captain and Mrs. Joseph S. Eastaman, William B. Johnson, Ira O. Knapp, Mrs. M. W. Munroe, and the Reverend L. P. Norcross.

letter requesting "permission to build a church upon the lot of land at the corner of Falmouth and Caledonia Sts." Under date of October 9, Mrs. Eddy informed the students that she had put the land "into honest hands for you to redeem," but instructed them not to "attempt building a church. If you do you will fail and again lose your money. . . . You are not strong enough in God to stand."

Throughout this period, Mrs. Eddy was working out a way by which all (including all dissenters from her teachings) who had made contributions to the building of the church edifice might share in the ownership of the title. She took another step toward this goal on December 10, 1889, when, at a private sale, Ira O. Knapp became the legal owner of the lot. In making the purchase, Knapp gave Perry a check signed by Mrs. Eddy. This check, of course, was returned to Mrs. Eddy after title to the property was surrendered by Perry's son in favor of Knapp.

Mrs. Eddy then instructed her attorneys in Concord, New Hampshire, to draw up a deed of trust. Under terms she outlined, Knapp was required to transfer title of the lot to three Trustees. After the deed was drawn, Knapp took it to Boston, where Attorney Perry refused to execute it, saying it was defective, whereupon Knapp sought another attorney. This lawyer completed the details of making the deed of trust, as drawn, a legal instrument.

This document was a complete break with a tradition that builds cathedrals, temples, and monuments in accordance with human ideas of what is appropriate to His name.

To Mrs. Eddy, this one church edifice, The Mother Church for *all* Christian Scientists, must be that of a Church — governed by Truth — a Church which, recognizing only the divine sentiments in man, brings man out from under doctrinal servitude and into the freedom of the spiritual kingdom.

Her definition of *Church* being "the structure of Truth and Love," it was natural for her to believe that ownership is with God — and to teach that a church is not land, not brick, nor stone, nor mortar, but a structure that is holy in conception and spiritual in revelation.

By using what she afterwards called a "circuitous, novel way" for transferring ownership of the property, Mrs. Eddy had in mind the fact that while she had dissolved her church organization in 1889, she had not surrendered the church charter she had taken out in 1879. Aware that there were members who still were belligerents, and suspecting they were seeking other ways to destroy her work, she devised the method of sale to hold them, and their counterparts, in check. Within three years after the transfer of the lot by Knapp to the Trustees, precisely the situation she anticipated made its appearance.

Dissatisfied with the terms of the deed of trust that Mrs. Eddy's Concord attorneys had drawn, the Trustees challenged the deed — in an effort, so the Directors charged, to "get money from students sufficient to buy a lot and then build a church edifice of their own under no restrictions, that . . . the true Scientists be again robbed, and our Cause suffer throughout the land." [6]

It was a bitter quarrel, in which — as Mrs. Eddy wrote — "mortal man sought to know who owned God's temple."

In the deed of trust, Mrs. Eddy named David Anthony, Joseph S. Eastaman, Eugene H. Greene, William B. John-

[6] Letter, dated May 3, 1892, and sent to the field by the Board of Directors after being approved by Mrs. Eddy.

son, and Ira O. Knapp to the Board of Directors of the
Church of Christ, Scientist, with Knapp presiding as Chairman. Under the terms of the deed, the Directors were authorized to maintain church services, name a pastor for the
church, organize the church whenever they so desired, to
fill Board vacancies, and, if they so desired, to increase their
number to seven.

In the deed Alfred Lang, Marcellus Munroe, and William
G. Nixon were named members of a Board of Trustees and,
under the deed, the Trustees held title to the lot, but only if
a church edifice was erected upon it. The deed stipulated
that building operations must begin when subscriptions
totaled $20,000, and required the posting of a bond in
amount of $5000 by the treasurer as a guarantee of the ful-
fillment of his duties. Applicable to Directors and Trustees,
alike, was this paragraph:

If any member of the Board of Trustees or of the Directors
shall bring any business matter before the Rev. Mary B. G.
Eddy relating to this fund, or the building of said Church
or any other business matter relating to any of the transactions
connected therewith, he or she shall be liable to forfeit his or
her place as Trustee or Director, and on complaint of the Rev.
Mary B. G. Eddy to the Secretary of either the Trustees or Directors a meeting of the Board shall be called and the name . . .
of the offending member shall, if she shall so request, be
dropped from the Trustees or Directors.

In the *Journal* in January 1890, under the title "Good
News," it was announced:

The lot of land on the corner of Falmouth and Caledonia
Streets, now valued at fifteen thousand dollars, has been sold to
Trustees on the condition that a church edifice shall be built
thereon, for Christian Scientists. The building is not to be *begun* until $20,000 has been raised for this purpose. All friends

of the Cause are asked to contribute to the building of this
Church, with the assurance that the Treasurer, Mr. Alfred
Lang, of 279 Broadway, Lawrence, Mass., is under bonds for
the faithful performance of his duties, and that not a dollar
of the sums donated will be spent until $20,000 has been se-
cured. All amounts will be accounted for, and reported in the
Journal quarterly, and due acknowledgements made for all re-
mittances as received.

With announcement of the plan, it soon was apparent
that the $20,000 needed to begin construction work would
be subscribed. Everywhere there was a student loyal to the
teachings, there was a contribution and a growing sentiment
that the new structure should be a memorial to Mrs. Eddy.

It was a sentiment that gained momentum in August
when, without a dissenting vote, it was resolved by the members of the Christian Scientist Association of the Massachusetts Metaphysical College that

. . . the early erection of a church edifice is not only desirable and possible, but that the spirit of Love now becoming
more and more manifest will bear fruit after its kind, and that as
a result a Memorial of Love will — must — be erected.

No intimation that a topic of this nature would be presented
for discussion has been given, and, as a consequence, only an
average attendance was present; yet within a few moments, with
no vestige of begging or pleading, $2,600 payable within the
year or as needed, were pledged by less than one dozen Scientists. This was an admirable outcome of a few minutes of
well-directed thought, though but a small part of the sum the
people of the Boston Church alone stand ready to pledge toward
this enterprise lying so near the hearts of us all.

Why not build this church the coming year? Why not make
it strictly a Memorial Church, representing the voluntary offerings of Scientists from ocean to ocean, from Lake to Gulf?
What people have greater cause for thanksgiving? And where so
fitting a site for the erection of such a building, as in the heart

of the very city where the Founder and Teacher of this Science has had the hardest battles to wage against error; where at its early inception she stood alone, sole advocate and defender of the Cause that is to bless infinitely the universal family. . . .

In the November 1890 *Journal,* Mrs. Eddy put a stop to the proposal by informing Christian Scientists everywhere:

> I object to such a departure from the Principle of Christian Science, as it would be, to be memorialized in a manner that should cause personal motives for building the First Church of Christ, Scientist, in Boston.
>
> Contributions to this Boston Building Fund should be made on a higher plane of thought.
>
> The lot of land that I gave this church was for the purpose of building thereon a house for the worship of God, and a home for Christian Scientists.
>
> The true followers, who worship "in Spirit and in Truth," will contribute to this Building Fund from a similar motive, and thus abide by the Principle of Christian Science which we acknowledge.
>
> MARY B. G. EDDY

With the abandonment of the idea for a Memorial Church, another took its place. The new idea called for the building of a structure that would be a combination church and publishing office, with emphasis on publishing. This was a period when there was a strong public demand for all printed matter pertaining to metaphysics — the period, previously mentioned, when the General Association for Dispensing Christian Science Literature was active. Anxious for the publishing group to be in a position to take advantage of the public demand, Nixon persuaded his fellow Trustees into the point of view that propaganda was first in importance in the furtherance of Christian Science.

Also, he influenced one of the Directors into this point of view for, in the spring of 1891, Joseph S. Eastaman urged that in planning the new building allowances should be made for the housing of all Christian Science activities under one roof.[7]

Apparently, Eastaman did not realize that his proposal was a violation of the deed of trust, in its stipulation that on the lot should be erected an edifice "to be called the Church of Christ, Scientist." Nor, apparently, did Foster Eddy realize it, because, in the June 1891 issue of the *Journal,* he wrote: "I am most heartily in accord with the article in the May *Journal* . . . Christian Science Publishing House. . . . We must have a foundation, a starting point, and here it is. Now brethren, let us build solidly and well. . . . I . . . send my check. . . ."

On February 3, 1892, at a meeting of the Christian Scientist Association of the Massachusetts Metaphysical College in the Hotel Boylston, Treasurer Lang reported a balance of $23,172.08 in the building fund, and Nixon expressed his opposition to the stipulation in the deed of trust that required building operations to begin when subscriptions reached $20,000.

Nixon feared this amount was insufficient, hoped for $60,000, and said that as "every teacher and practitioner over the country came into intelligent touch with the needs and aims of the publishing society; as each sees that the

[7] Plans for the new building, including publishing offices, were announced in the *Christian Science Journal* in its March 1892 issue. For description, see Appendix 6.

proposed edifice means vastly more than a church for the use of Boston Scientists, the activities of each would be enlisted in its behalf, and substantial testimonials would follow."

His words were found persuasive and the Directors, while not willing to wait until $60,000 was subscribed, did agree to postpone the starting of building operations until $30,000 was available. They hoped this amount would be on hand by April.

Following the joint meeting with the Directors and members of the Association, the Trustees held a meeting of their own at which they decided to seek the advice of a lawyer as to the soundness of Knapp's title to the property. They were told that "no individual, or body, has a title to the property." They inquired as to the possibility of perfecting such a title, were assured it could be done, as a first step toward that end, were asked to secure permission for the attorney to examine the church records. The request was made, and was refused by the Directors. Lang then wrote to Mrs. Eddy.

In this letter and after recalling the lawyer's advice, and the refusal of the request to examine the church records, Lang commented: "What a condition we are in! We must give to Caesar the things that are Caesar's. We must conform to the laws of our country in our business transactions. Really the work of perfecting this devolves upon yourself and the Church."

Continuing, in this letter of March 19, 1891, Lang advised his Teacher;

I think you may feel assured that we, the Trustees, will release the property to the new Trust, or Directors, that you named, said Directors holding the fee in the whole property but reserving to the Publishing Society a life lease of so much of the property as the publishing house occupies in case it is built upon, and should it ever be sold the Publishing Society to receive the pro rata value of the publishing building which would be but a small part of their gifts. As four-fifths of all the money I received came from outside the Boston Church, I feel quite sure you will see this to be just. We, the present Trustees, must act together and unanimously, or we can't effect the object we are seeking.

Please allow me here to say that I should regard it as very unfortunate if we or yourself should break faith with brother Nixon. I regard him as one of the truest men within my acquaintance. I know he has the good of our Cause at heart. I shall rejoice if the course which you have outlined shall take legal form and be perfected. We can do nothing to building until it is so made. If we should fail in this, it would be one of the hardest blows that has ever hit Christian Science since I knew of it. I do most earnestly desire that there be no delay. I also keenly realize the sacredness of the trust and the responsibility devolving upon me in holding this large fund, so lovingly bestowed by some thousands of persons, much the greater part being poor.

After referring to the bank deposit, Lang wondered what the subscribers would "say of us, after proclaiming as we have, that we have a lot of land given by yourself, if we should be obliged to say, we have no land to build upon?"

Lang closed his letter by thrusting sharply at Mrs. Eddy, and the Directors:

"It occurs to me that by force of circumstances, not from choice, touching this question, you are still the power on the throne, not behind it."

By letter, on March 23, Mrs. Eddy warned the Directors:

All that I have counselled has worked well for Church and Cause. Your only danger now lies in the past being repeated. Another *faction formed* to pick off my soldiers, to make the leader of it a traitor. . . . *Watch,* the hour is ominous, when any student goes against my advice and still gives orders in my name.

. . . I wrote you, Miss Bartlett and others, not to organize a church! Then it was reported that I gave the order to organize, but I did not. Now your salvation as a people whose God is the Lord lies in being wise as a serpent.

Again I repeat, do not . . . change your present materially disorganized — but spiritually organized — Church, nor its *present form* of Church *government.* . . . The lot I paid for, the taxes on it, the expense of Lawyer, etc., are all straight, *legally* and forever settled. No man can make it otherwise any more than evil can destroy Good.

Affectionately,

M. B. G. EDDY

Nixon and Lang went to the Directors a second time in an effort to get possession of the church records. Again they failed, and Nixon then submitted the deed of trust to the Massachusetts Title Insurance Company, in Boston, for examination.

He was informed, so he told his fellow Trustees and the Directors, that: (1) lacking the words "to their heirs, and assigns" the property would revert to Knapp and his heirs upon the death of last Trustee; (2) Flavia Stickney Knapp had not relinquished her dower rights and could be considered a legal heir; and (3) inasmuch as there had been no formal church organization since December 2, 1889, the trust as set up by Mrs. Eddy was in the nature of "a public charity," and, therefore, the lot at the corner of Caledonia and Falmouth Streets was under the control of the Supreme Court of the State of Massachusetts because, so the finding went, there was no church organization qualified to hold property.

The Massachusetts Title Insurance Company itemized other clauses it considered questionable, and it was with more than a little satisfaction that the Trustees forwarded the information to Mrs. Eddy. They received word from her to take counsel with Attorney Perry. They did. Perry agreed with the findings of the title company, and advised the Directors to reorganize the church so as to make it a corporate body, and convey title to the property to this corporation.

In effect, Perry told the Directors: "Under the terms of the deed of trust, you are empowered to reorganize the Church. Do this, and then have Knapp obtain his wife's release of her dower rights. With this done, Knapp can surrender all rights in the property by merely signing it over to the Church, instead of to the Trustees. Then, and not until then, will you have a legal document."

Knapp refused to do what the lawyer advised, and the Trustees demanded. He sought Mrs. Eddy's counsel and, following her suggestion, went to Perry's office, where he expressed a willingness to revise the title to include the words "to their heirs, and assigns," but, beyond that, refused to act. Supported by other Directors and speaking as their Chairman, Knapp declined to agree to any reorganization of the church, or to consent to any abridgement of the deed of trust.

Standing firm in Mrs. Eddy's instructions of March 23,

it was the position of the Directors that, because the church charter had not been surrendered when the church organization was dissolved, any immediate reorganization might bring on greater legal difficulties with those who had been expelled from membership.

It was the position of Mrs. Eddy that, despite the opinion of legal experts, the deed of trust was not in the nature of "a public charity," and the lot was not under the control of the Supreme Court of the State of Massachusetts. She insisted that her action in transferring property to a Board of Trustees to be held in trust for the benefit of the church membership was a legal proceeding.

In possession of the deed to the property, the Trustees refused to accept Knapp's proposed revision, or to heed Mrs. Eddy. Instead, they began accusing her of being arbitrary, and made public inquiry as to "Who owns God's temple?"

In April 1892, Nixon left Boston on a trip through the Western States for the purpose of persuading Christian Scientists to agree to the use of their subscriptions, now amounting to about $30,000, in purchasing another lot — and building on it a church that would not be subject to the restrictions laid down by Mrs. Eddy.

Acting for the Directors, Johnson wrote a general letter to the field. Under date of May 3, 1892, the letter said, in part:

. . . The factionists in Boston are determined to make the Trustees buy another building lot with the money that has been contributed, and build thereon a church free from the restrictions in the Trust deed. So many of our church members were belligerents when it was disorganized, that this form of deed and circuitous way of conveying the land was deemed the remedy against future broils, and so far has proved to be a restriction on error.

. . . Their main plot at present is to get money from students sufficient to buy a lot and then build a church edifice of their own under no restrictions, that the reign of heterodoxy may have foundation in Boston, the true Scientists be again robbed and our Cause suffer throughout the land. . . . Mr. Lang and Mr. Munroe seem completely blinded. It is said that Mr. N. has always hated the Church government as it is stated in this deed, but he claims the legal points are what hinder his starting to build.

. . . He is now on a *tour* in the *West*. It is no longer safe to contribute or allow to be contributed, if you can prevent it, another dollar till the Trustees put the $30,000 they now have on hand into a building on the lot that our Teacher has given for this purpose, a lot which is now considered worth about $20,000 and if they delay to build and still take contributions then we must ask them to return our money, or stop taking money if they are not legally Trustees. . . .

Johnson's letter compelled Nixon to return to Boston where, with Lang and Munroe, he renewed his effort to force a reorganization. With the help of a number of the teachers who had rebelled in 1888, he succeeded in persuading a majority of the church membership into voting favorably on his proposal. When told, on May 10, of this action, Mrs. Eddy cautioned the members, informing them that, by reorganizing, they were in danger of losing their form of church government, as well as title to the property.

At the same time, however, she declined to stand in the way of their wishes, saying, "Let the church reorganize . . . let her pass on to her experience, and the sooner the better. When we will not learn in any other way, this is God's order of teaching us. His *rod alone* will do it."

Sobered by their Leader's words, the congregation re

versed itself, voted to accept the deed of trust, and, on June 1, passed resolutions instructing the Trustees to begin building operations without delay. The Trustees responded by dispatching a circular letter to the field in which they declared themselves "of the opinion that, had they had free access to Mrs. Eddy during the past three months, and had no one to deal with other than herself, this imperfect title would have been in a way to cure, and the church edifice would ere this have been begun. . . ."

The Directors made an immediate reply, saying, "if the Deed was not strictly sound and Mr. Nixon knew it as he said he did from the first, he had no right to get your money for building on land to which he had not a clear title."

Continuing, the Directors stated: ". . . When Mrs. Eddy was led to fear there was a flaw in the deed she begged the Trustees to put your money in the building and then have the title made sound. For if the Deed is broken before this is done the Trustees can claim the money which they have deposited in their own names and nobody but themselves can take it out of the banks. This was why she urged them to go to building or else stop calling for building funds, until they had a clear title. Mr. Knapp is ready to give a sound title to the land on the terms of his Deed, and as Mrs. Eddy wished to give it; but they will either have it on their own terms or, as they say, no title at all, and yet continue to receive your money."

Meanwhile, the Trustees made wide distribution of a ballot requesting permission to continue their opposition to building operations unless contributors representing $20,000 of the subscriptions on hand indicated, in a witnessed statement, their opposition. In the July issue of the *Journal,* Mrs. Eddy called upon the Trustees: "Delay not to build our church in Boston; or else return every dollar that you have no legal authority for obtaining — to the several contributors and let them, not you, say what shall be done with their money."

Before the end of August, contributors had requested the return of more than $20,000.

The demand to the Trustees to "delay not to build our church . . . or else return every dollar that you have no legal authority for obtaining," was contained in an article which Mrs. Eddy wrote about her purpose in the giving of the land. Under the title of "Hints for History," [8] in the *Journal* in July 1892, Mrs. Eddy said:

> On December 10, 1889, I gave a lot of land, — in Boston, situated near the beautiful Back Bay Park, now valued at $20,000 and rising in value — for the purpose of having erected thereon a Church edifice to be called the Church of Christ, Scientist. I had this desirable site transferred in a circuitous, novel way, the wisdom whereof a few persons have since scrupled; but, to my spiritual perception, like all true wisdom, this transaction will in future be regarded as greatly wise, and it will be found that the acts of Christian Scientists were in advance of the erring mind's apprehension.
>
> As with all former efforts in the interest of Christian Science, I took care that the provision for the land and building were such as error could not control. I knew that to God's gift, foundation and superstructure, no one could hold a wholly material title. The land and the Church standing on it

[8] The text, revised by Mrs. Eddy to give it permanent form, appears in *Miscellaneous Writings*, pp. 139–142.

must be conveyed through a type representing the true nature of the gift; a type morally and spiritually inalienable, but materially questionable — even after the manner that all spiritual good comes to Christian Scientists to the end of taxing their faith in God, and their adherence to the superiority of the claims of Spirit over matter or merely legal titles.

No one could buy, sell or mortgage my gift as I had it conveyed. Thus the thing rested, and I supposed the trustee deed was legal; but this was God's business not mine. Our Church has prospered by the right hand of His righteousness, and contributions to the Building Fund generously poured into the treasury. Unity prevailed, till mortal man sought to know who owned God's temple, and adopted and urged only the material side of this question.

Note this: The lot of land which I donated, I had to redeem from under mortgage. The foundation on which our Church was to be built had to be rescued from the grasp of legal power, and now it must be put back into the arms of Love if we would not be found fighting against God.

The diviner claims and means for upbuilding the Church of Christ were prospered. Our title to God's acres here, will be safe and sound — when "we can read our title clear" to heavenly mansions. Built on the rock, our Church would stand the storm; the material superstructure might crumble into dust, but the fittest would survive — the spir-

itual idea would live a perpetual type of the divine
Principle it reflects.

Our Church of Christ, our prayer in brick,
should be a prophecy and monument of Christian Science. Then would it speak to you of the
Mother Church that you built for her through
whom was revealed to you God's all-power, all-
presence, and all-Science.

This building begun, would have gone up and
no one could suffer from it, for no one could resist
the power that was behind it, and against this
Church and temple "the gates of hell could not
prevail."

All loyal Christian Scientists hailed with joy this
type of universal Love. Not so with error which
hates the bonds and methods of Truth, and shud-
ders at the freedom, might and majesty of Spirit,
even the annihilating law of Love.

I vindicate both the law of God, and the laws of
our land. I do believe, yea, I understand that with
the spirit of Christ actuating all the parties concerned about this legal quibble, that it would be
easily corrected to the satisfaction of all. Let this
be speedily done. Do not, I implore you, stain the
early history of Christian Science by the impulses
of human will and pride; but let the divine will
and the nobility of human meekness, rule this business transaction in obedience to the law of God,
and the laws of our land.

As the ambassador of Jesus' teachings, I admonish you, Delay not to build our Church in
Boston; or else, return every dollar that you your-

selves declare you have had no legal authority for obtaining — to the several contributors, and let them, not you, say what shall be done with their money.

Of my first Church in Boston, oh! recording angel, write: God is in the midst of her, how beautiful are her feet, how beautiful are her garments, how hath He enlarged her borders, how hath He made her wilderness to bud and blossom as the rose!

Having lost no opportunity to declare a Church as being "a structure of Truth and Love," and believing it needed no proof of corporate papers to establish its existence, Mrs. Eddy, at the same time she was calling upon the Trustees to "delay not to build," was having the statutes of Massachusetts searched in an effort to find legal approval for her conviction that her Church could be free of corporate limitations, and still hold property.

The searching lawyers found approval in Section One, Chapter 39, of the Public Acts of Massachusetts, and this provision: "The deacons, church wardens, or other similar officers of churches or other religious societies, and the Trustees of the Methodist Episcopal churches appointed according to the discipline and usages thereof, shall, if citizens of this commonwealth, be deemed bodies corporate for the purpose of taking and holding in succession all the grants and donations, whether of real or personal estate, made either to them and their successors, or to their respective churches, or to the poor of the churches."

This little-known law proved Mrs. Eddy right — and, at

the same time they notified her of their successful search, the attorneys informed her that in soliciting subscriptions for a combined church and office building, the Trustees had violated the terms of her deed of trust. It was Mrs. Eddy's first knowledge of the breach in the agreement. She summoned the Trustees to Concord, and, at the same time, requested the presence of Knapp and Foster Eddy. When all were assembled she inquired, in substance, of her Concord attorney, Frank S. Streeter: "Does advertising for funds to build a publishing house in connection with a church give any title to church property?"

Before Streeter could reply, Nixon snapped, "It does not!"

The lawyer voiced vigorous disagreement, and questioning by him disclosed that Lang had failed to post a bond as a guarantee of his duties as treasurer of the building fund.

Before the meeting was ended, the Trustees agreed to return all the contributions they had received — and the deed of trust under which they had functioned was canceled.

On August 19, upon payment of one dollar, Ira O. Knapp and Flavia Stickney Knapp gave a quit-claim deed of the lot at Caledonia and Falmouth Streets, in Boston, to Mrs. Eddy. For the first time since its purchase in 1886, the property was in her name.

With the title in her possession, Mrs. Eddy, on August 22, dispatched letters to twelve Christian Scientists requesting that they meet in the home of Julia Bartlett at twelve o'clock, noon, on August 29, 1892, for the purpose of organizing in Boston The First Church of Christ, Scientist.[9]

[9] It was Mrs. Eddy's wish that in the others the prefix "The" be dropped. In each case her request was granted, and a clear field was given for the establishment of the only Christian Science church having "The" as a prefix — thus, "The First Church of Christ, Scientist, in Boston, Massachusetts."

In July, 1892, Mrs. Eddy wrote a letter to Oconto, Wisconsin, and sent a representative to New York. The letter and the representative had similar missions. Only in Oconto and in New York were churches identified as The Church of Christ, Scientist.

CHAPTER FOURTEEN

According to the Promise

HAD MARY BAKER EDDY died in this period of her career, there is little doubt that she would be lost among the crowded dead, and her teachings lost with her. Her church was disorganized. Except for her, there was no one to light the lamp. Nor, was she sure, although she had chosen twelve to organize The First Church of Christ, Scientist, in Boston, Massachusetts, that even now her students heard the cry of the Psalmist, "Unless the Lord build the house, they labour in vain that build it."

She still was not satisfied there was full acceptance, even among the most tested, of her words:

> It is not essential to materially organize Christ's Church. It is not absolutely necessary to ordain Pastors, and to dedicate Churches; but if this be done, let it be in concession to the period, and not as a perpetual or indispensable ceremonial of the Church. If our Church is organized, it is to meet the demand, "suffer it to be so now." The real Christian compact is Love for one another. This bond is wholly spiritual and inviolate.
>
> It is imperative at all times and under every circumstance, to perpetuate no ceremonials except as types of these mental conditions: remembrance and love, — a real affection for Jesus' character and

example. Be it remembered that all types employed in the service of Christian Science should represent the most spiritual forms of thought and worship that can be made visible.[1]

The doubt that there was full acceptance of her words is disclosed by contents of the call that went out on August 22:

TO ——

    You are hereby notified that the first meeting of the subscribers to an agreement to associate themselves with the intention to *constitute a Corporation* [italics supplied] to be known by the name of THE FIRST CHURCH OF CHRIST, SCIENTIST, dated August 17th, 1892, for the purpose of organizing said Corporation, by adoption of the by-laws and election of officers and the transaction of such other business as may properly come before the meeting, will be held on Monday, the 29th day of August, 1892, at 12 o'clock M., at No. 133 Dartmouth Street, Boston, Mass.

                    WILLIAM B. JOHNSON
        one of the subscribers to said agreement [2]
BOSTON, MASS., *August 22, 1892*

When the meeting was held on August 29, the twelve were told that a corporation would not be organized; in-

[1] *Christian Science Journal,* March 1892.
[2] At Mrs. Eddy's request, this agreement was never filed. The stated purpose of the projected Corporation was "to establish and maintain the worship of God in accordance with the doctrines and teachings of Christian Science as contained in a certain book called Science and Health, by Rev. Mary Baker G. Eddy. The sixty-ninth edition is particularly referred to, and in such subsequent editions thereof as the Rev. Mary Baker G. Eddy may edit. . . ."

stead, they were acquainted with a new deed of trust,[3] drafted but not executed, under which Mrs. Eddy transferred title to the lot to four donees who comprised a new Board of Directors. The members of the new Board were: Ira O. Knapp, William B. Johnson, Joseph S. Eastaman, and Stephen A. Chase.

Considering the many disappointments, long thought must have been behind the choosing of the twelve whose duty it was to establish The First Church of Christ, Scientist, in Boston.

Besides the four Directors, the twelve were: Julia Bartlett, Ellen L. Clarke, Janet T. Colman, Mary F. Eastaman, Ebenezer J. Foster Eddy, Eldora O. Gragg, Flavia S. Knapp, and Mary W. Munroe. Each was the personal selection of Mrs. Eddy, and — of great importance in the new order of her Church — each of the Directors was appointed by her.

Her desire was that the Directors serve her cause and, having appointed them, she accepted responsibility for them. Hers being the sole decision to appoint, she asked for no ratification; nor do the records disclose any suggestion, or inquiry, from the remaining eight original church members regarding ratification. Having watched, and guided, and guarded all twelve, she trusted them; and they trusted her. Particularly was this true of the Directors, her action indicating that having first trusted them as students, she now trusted them with the land and, trusting them with the land, trusted them as Directors.

By appointing them herself and making them responsible to her, just as she was responsible for them, Mrs. Eddy broke with the commonly accepted form of church government.

[3] The new deed of trust was executed on September 1, 1892. For text, see Appendix 7.

She made membership in her Church a condition of invitation — invitation that included acquiescence with the establishment of the Christian Science Board of Directors as defined in the new deed of trust.

In the new deed of trust, the Christian Science Board of Directors became "a perpetual body," but in the new order of the Church, the position of a Director became one of place and responsibility. The basic idea in the organization Mrs. Eddy was envisioning was a Church operating in its natural field — and, its natural field being spiritual, its only authority is God.

By appointing the Directors herself, the likelihood is that Mrs. Eddy reduced the occasion of envy in her Church; and it is certain she prevented the encroachment of politics. Had she not established under the little-known statute, and had the members been permitted to decide, the probabilities are they would have clung to the familiar type of church organization, forgetting that, when a Church departs from its spiritual base, it tends to fall more and more into ritual.

And did not Mrs. Eddy speak of this when, in the previous March, she wrote, "The real Christian compact is Love for one another. This bond is wholly spiritual and inviolate"?

Fearful of the personally ambitious — for, even now, there were those who, learning of the provisions in the new deed of trust, were attempting to force upon her the idea of reorganizing the Church and electing Directors from the membership — Mrs. Eddy called upon the twelve she had chosen to meet and agree upon twenty others who, like themselves, would become "First Members of THE FIRST CHURCH OF CHRIST, SCIENTIST, IN BOSTON, MASSACHUSETTS."

While they were doing this, Mrs. Eddy used the September issue of the *Journal* to announce:

> I have given . . . a *sound* title to the lot of land in Boston, on which to build a Church edifice for the benefit of Christian Science.
>
> For particulars relative to the Building Fund you must communicate with Mr. Alfred Lang, 279 Broadway, Lawrence, Mass., and William B. Johnson, 41 G St., South Boston, Mass.

On September 16 a letter was mailed to all Christian Scientists and to all others who had contributed to the Church Building Fund:

DEAR FELLOW CONTRIBUTORS:

Doubtless you are already informed by the former Board of Trustees, through a circular letter with the return of your contribution to the Church Building Fund, that the title to the Church lot has been returned to the donor, Mary Baker G. Eddy, and that she has again conveyed the title to "certain persons."

We therefore inform you that Mary Baker G. Eddy has deeded said land to Ira O. Knapp and Wm. B. Johnson of Boston, Mass., Joseph S. Eastaman of Chelsea, Mass., and Stephen A. Chase of Fall River, Mass., who are, by the lawful terms of said deed, a corporate body designated the "Christian Science Board of Directors," to hold said land in trust for the purpose of erecting thereon a church edifice, as originally designed by the donor of said land.

The above named directors are now formally organized, with Ira O. Knapp as President, Wm. B. Johnson, Secretary, and Stephen A. Chase, Treasurer. Therefore, in the name of "Christian Science Board of Directors," and for the good of the Cause, we kindly solicit the return of your contribution, with any additional offering you may see fit for the aforesaid purpose, to Stephen A. Chase, Treasurer, P.O. Box 136, Fall River, Mass.

For further particulars, we refer you to a copy of said Deed, which will appear in the October number of the *Christian Science Journal*.

(Signed) IRA O. KNAPP   JOSEPH S. EASTAMAN
WILLIAM B. JOHNSON   STEPHEN A. CHASE

The two announcements brought such a large response that, instead of waiting two or three months, as she had planned, Mrs. Eddy requested the chosen twelve to meet — quietly — in Boston on September 23, 1892, for the purpose of organizing the new church, and vote into membership the twenty they had selected, and Mrs. Eddy had approved.

The meeting was held and on that September 23, 1892 — a day which broke clear and warm after two nights and a day of strong winds and driving, heavy rain — The Mother Church, The First Church of Christ, Scientist, was founded.

The minutes of this historic meeting read:

BOSTON, MASSACHUSETTS, *Sept. 23, 1892.*

Eleven persons, namely: Dr. Ebenezer J. Foster Eddy, Mr. Stephen A. Chase, Mr. Joseph S. Eastaman, Mr. William B. Johnson, Mr. Ira O. Knapp, Miss Julia S. Bartlett, Mrs. Mary W. Munroe, Mrs. Ellen L. Clarke, Mrs. Mary F. Eastaman, Mrs. Janet T. Colman, Mrs. Flavia S. Knapp, Mrs. Eldora O. Gragg met this day at No. 133 Dartmouth Street, Boston, Massachusetts, at 12 o'clock M. Dr. E. J. Foster Eddy was chosen chairman, and William B. Johnson, secretary.

The meeting was opened with silent prayer, followed by the Lord's Prayer repeated in unison;

after which the following business was transacted:

The following motion was read by the chairman, seconded, and voted: That all who are present, and Mrs. Ellen L. Clarke, who is absent, are First Members of "The Church of Christ, Scientist," in Boston, Massachusetts.

Voted: That the secretary shall add Mrs. Ellen L. Clarke's name to the list of names of those present, which was done.

On motion of Mrs. Janet T. Colman, seconded by Mrs. Eldora O. Gragg, Dr. Ebenezer J. Foster Eddy was elected president of "The First Church of Christ, Scientist," in Boston, Massachusetts.

Mrs. Mary F. Eastaman moved, Stephen A. Chase seconded, and it was voted that William B. Johnson be the clerk of "The First Church of Christ, Scientist," in Boston, Massachusetts.

Voted: On motion of Stephen A. Chase, seconded by Ira O. Knapp, that Mrs. Mary F. Eastaman be the treasurer of "The First Church of Christ, Scientist," in Boston, Massachusetts. The foregoing votes were unanimous.

A list of names was read by the clerk of persons proposed for membership with this Church, as follows: Mr. Calvin A. Frye, Mr. Edward P. Bates, Mr. Eugene H. Greene, Mr. David Anthony, Mr. Hanover P. Smith, Mrs. Joseph Curtis Otterson, Mrs. Grace A. Greene, Mrs. Caroline S. Bates, Mrs. Emilie B. Hulin, Mrs. Caroline W. Frame, Mrs. Elizabeth P. Skinner, Mrs. Augusta E. Stetson, Mrs. Henrietta E. Chanfrau, Mrs. Emily M. Meader, Mrs. Berenice H. Goodall, Mrs. Annie

V. C. Leavitt, Mrs. Laura E. Sargent, Mrs. Ann M. Otis, Mrs. Mary F. Berry, Mrs. Martha E. S. Morgan.[4]

Unanimously voted: That all those persons named in the list read by the clerk, are elected First Members of "THE FIRST CHURCH OF CHRIST, SCIENTIST," in Boston, Massachusetts.

Voted: That the clerk is requested to notify each of the members of their election as follows:

"You are hereby notified that you are elected one of the First Members of 'THE FIRST CHURCH OF CHRIST, SCIENTIST,' IN BOSTON, MASSACHU-SETTS."

Before they named the twenty new First Members, the original twelve were charged by Mrs. Eddy not to "name anyone having a tablet." By this she meant they were to reject anyone bearing gifts. Since the suspension of the *Boston Christian Scientist* rebel teachers, and their students, had been returning to church services, and some were requesting re-establishment in positions of influence. They offered contributions to the building fund and were welcomed at church services, but they were not trusted with membership until their sincerity was "proved by their

[4] After the admittance of these twenty, each new member was supplied with a seven-page book containing "the Tenets and the Rules," and this information: "On the twenty-third day of September, 1892, by advice of our beloved Teacher, Rev. Mary Baker G. Eddy, twelve of her students met and formed a Christian Science Church, and named it, THE FIRST CHURCH OF CHRIST, SCIENTIST. At this meeting twenty other students of Mrs. Eddy were elected members of this Church, which with the twelve who formed the Church, are to be known as 'First Members.' Church Tenets formulated by Mrs. Eddy were adopted, also Rules for the government of the Church."

works." The probationary period was not quickly over; for some it extended until well into the new century, and none was ever named as a First Member.

The minutes of the historical meeting of September 23, 1892, also contain the Tenets of the Church, and the Rules for its government.

In reference to the Tenets, the minutes read:

> Tenets to be subscribed to by those uniting with "THE FIRST CHURCH OF CHRIST, SCIENTIST," in Boston, were read by the President. The Tenets were adopted, and ordered to be written in a book containing the records of this Church.

TENETS

OF

THE FIRST CHURCH OF CHRIST, SCIENTIST

BY

REV. MARY BAKER G. EDDY

To be signed by those uniting with "THE FIRST CHURCH OF CHRIST, SCIENTIST."

1. As adherents of Truth, we take the Scriptures for our guide to eternal life.

2. We acknowledge and adore one Supreme God.

We acknowledge His Son, the Holy Ghost, and man in His image and likeness. We acknowledge God's forgiveness of sin, in the destruction of sin, and His present and future punishment of "whatsoever worketh abomination or maketh a lie." And the atonement of Christ, as the efficacy of Truth and Love. And the way of Salvation as demonstrated by Jesus casting out evils, healing the sick, and raising the dead — resurrecting a dead faith to seize the great possibilities and living energies of the Divine Life.

3. We solemnly promise to strive, watch, and pray for that Mind to be with us which was also in Christ Jesus. To love the brethren, and, up to our highest capacity to be meek, merciful, and just, and live peaceably with all men.

As in her other writings, so in the Tenets: there were changes, the result of increasing inspiration. But, whatever the changes, in them were four words that never changed. The four words were, "As adherents of Truth" — and, no matter how phrased, the pledge that followed always accepted the Scriptures as being the inspired Word. In her ceaseless search for Truth, Mrs. Eddy constantly used different words and different phrasing to affirm her conviction that as He was the Son of God, so are we the children of God.

In closing the meeting of September 23, Rules governing the affairs of the Church were adopted:

1. The annual meeting of THE FIRST CHURCH OF CHRIST, SCIENTIST, IN BOSTON, shall be held on the first Tuesday evening in October of each year, for the choice of officers for the ensuing year, for listening to the reports of the treasurer, secretary, and committees, and for the transaction of any church business that may come before the meeting.

2. Quarterly meetings of this Church shall be held on the Saturday evening next preceding the Communion Sunday in each quarter, beginning

with the Saturday next preceding the first Sunday in January, 1893.

3. Applications for membership, coming from the students' students, must include the names and recommendations of their teachers. All applications for membership must be addressed to the pastor or the clerk of the Church. If to the pastor, he shall hand the letters to the clerk, who shall read them at the quarterly church meeting, and the First Members shall vote on admitting these candidates. Candidates for membership with this Church shall be elected by a majority vote.

4. The names of the members elected at a quarterly meeting of this Church shall on the following Sunday be read from the pulpit and the communion service be held.

5. The communion shall be observed by this Church on the first Sunday in October, January, April and July — by special exhortation, hymns, singing and silent prayer.

6. Members of this Church cannot be members of other churches except they are of the same denomination as this Church.

The clerk was authorized to procure a suitable book in which to keep the records of this Church.

The meeting then adjourned, subject to a call from the clerk of the Church at 2:15 P.M.[5]

In omitting a disciplinary rule, Mrs. Eddy was hoping her Church would be — and remain — a harmonious whole and, until such a rule was needed, she preferred its absence.

[5] When she chartered her first church in 1879, Mrs. Eddy wrote twenty rules of membership.

She had no problem such as she faced in 1879 when most of the church members were beginners. With membership now restricted to selected students, Mrs. Eddy was able to confine the Rules to a few simple regulations, and to depend upon the Tenets for increased spiritual perception.

Mrs. Eddy's determination to protect her new Church from the dissension that so ominously threatened its predecessor is shown by Rule 3 — which required that "applications for membership, coming from the students' students, must include names and recommendations of their teachers . . . and the First Members shall vote on admitting these candidates." At the time there were about three hundred active members in the church that was chartered in 1879. Mrs. Eddy first chose twelve, then twenty more, and, on October 5, 1892, approved fifty-nine others as being "fit for membership in her new church."

In making the selections of First Members, Mrs. Eddy chose only from among her own students, although Foster Eddy strongly disagreed, having argued in favor of some of his own. Naturally, with less than two weeks separating September 23 and October 5, invitations were confined largely to students living in the Eastern States. After October, Mrs. Eddy reached out to all parts of the country, so that by December, and the time of the second quarterly meeting, there were 349 applicants awaiting membership. A year later, the total was 1502.

It was at the quarterly meeting in December 1892 that Nixon's control over the *Journal* was ended. Responding to Mrs. Eddy's wishes, the First Members voted unanimously in favor of confining the advertising columns of the publication to teachers and practitioners who were members of The Mother Church. Up to this time, Nixon had opened the advertising columns of the *Journal* to practitioners and teachers who were not strictly followers of Mrs. Eddy. This refutation of his policy, coupled with Mrs. Eddy's failure to invite him into membership in her Church, although his wife was invited, caused Nixon to resign as publisher of the *Christian Science Journal.*

It was because of Nixon that Mrs. Eddy was careful in her use of the *Journal* in announcing plans for the new church. She was doubtful about what might be done with her communications. Knowing of Nixon's disposition to seek favor with the belligerents among her students, she withheld announcement of the establishment of The First Church of Christ, Scientist, from the October issue of the publication. She was not willing to give Nixon the opportunity to put her new Church in a poor light.

She intended that nothing should happen to hinder the development of this, her Church. She felt it was her Church because it was His Church — and it could remain His Church only so long as she kept the door closed on quarrels and disbelief; she knew if she permitted the door to open even a little, it soon would be opened wide.

But she did use the October issue of the *Journal* to announce "to the contributors of the Church Building Fund in Boston," that "certain legal proceedings with reference to the title to the church lot in Boston, which I donated . . . about three years ago for the specific purpose of building thereon a church edifice, have been taken, which, I am advised by my legal advisers, reverted the title to me. As soon as this end was accomplished I executed a trust deed of the lot . . .

"I conveyed said lot through Mr. Perry, and Mr. Knapp, of Boston. In Mr. Knapp's deed of trust to Mr. Lang, Mr.

Munroe and Mr. Nixon, no provision was made for publishing rooms. A few weeks ago, my lawyer showed me a circular letter, that had been issued without my knowledge, calling on the public for funds wherewith to build a church, and publishing rooms, upon said lot."

Then followed some sharp words, directed at Nixon:

> In July 16, 1892, I asked my lawyer in the presence of the Trustees, Mr. Knapp and Dr. Eddy (and the latter will testify that I objected from the beginning to having a church occupied for aught else but church work) if advertising for funds to build publishing rooms gave any title to the church property? Mr. Nixon said that it did not, but the lawyer replied emphatically that it did. After that I said no more about commencing to build the church.
>
> As much of the Building Fund was received, after this illegal call, the Directors and Trustees have thought best to return this fund to the contributors. It is plain that their money should not be used without their knowledge as to the specific purpose for which the church lot was donated. Before seeing the circular letter, I had advised Mr. Lang to commence building the church, at the same time we would conjoin in making the title sound. The Trustees then declined to do this, but afterwards united with me in its accomplishment — and we now have a sound title, but are minus funds.
>
> My lawyer has advised, under the circumstances,

to return the money to the contributors, for them to send back to the new Board of Directors, to be used according to the original purpose. In coming back, may the talents be doubled, and so blessed that the Building Fund shall be increased to sixty thousand dollars. . . . I am confident that all loyal Christian Scientists will gladly consecrate our church to a more dignified end, than an exchange, or a place for business bickerings, bag and baggage! — a church to be erected on a lot given, and regiven to them under such difficult circumstances, by the . . . author of *Science and Health.*

This sad delay to build, this necessity for returning the money so tenderly and generously bestowed, this lack of faith in God's providence and omnipotence, this straining at a gnat in one legal direction and swallowing a camel in another, have not been blessed by Divine Love. But now that the end has come, let us love one another, and, in the words of St. Paul — "Thank God and take courage."

The glorious object you have attempted to achieve must not be abandoned until it be accomplished. It is far too vital to the present and future welfare of Christian Science to be left undone . . . .

The task Mrs. Eddy set upon her followers was not one of ordinary logic. It was one of complete faith.

Hers were teachings that were finding scant support in a world that had reduced the words of Jesus largely to questions of ceremony. Almost entirely, hers was a movement of the poor; almost entirely, it was a movement of women. But her followers found in her words assurance they could not fail, even though the call now was "in coming back, may the talents be doubled. . . ."

In his small book, *The Mother Church,* Joseph Armstrong [6] wrote of the building of this church as being an undertaking "which must be given its place in history." In his book, Armstrong said: ". . . Something was accomplished which must be accepted by mortals as a part of the world's history. The fair and impartial accounts of the church, as given by the press at the time of the dedication, illustrate this point. Just as a large part of mankind have accepted the lives of Jesus and his apostles as historic facts, however little this may affect their living; just as proofs of astronomical facts, reversing the evidence of the senses, are universally undenied — so the erection of this church is so great a demonstration of Christianity and Science as to leave on the world's thought an undeniable mark which must be given its place in history."

In September 1893, this was the situation:

The building plans the Directors had accepted called for an expenditure of approximately $200,000. On hand was a sum approximating $40,000. Contributions had practically ceased.

The terms of the deed prevented the borrowing of any money through a mortgage on the property. In the deed also was a provision that forbade the making of any promises of payment beyond the funds in hand. The penalty for so doing was forfeiture of title to the land; and, to make sure

[6] In 1893, Armstrong succeeded Eastaman as a member of the Christian Science Board of Directors.

there was no violation of this clause, the Directors imposed upon themselves a rule under which they made calculations based solely on their bank balance.

The approved building design provided for all use of the lot, and two sets of plans had been drawn. One set was for a brick edifice; the other set was for an edifice of stone. Stone cost more, but the Directors chose it, and, to honor Mrs. Eddy's native state, began talks with New Hampshire contractors to supply the material. They learned that prices were reasonably stable, but when they looked into construction costs in Boston they discovered an increase of nearly one-third because of the adoption of a new building code in Boston. Under this new code, plans for all new buildings had to be approved by the City Engineer. In addition, a building permit could not be issued until the builder had accepted drawings for a completed structure.

Confronted by this seemingly impossible situation, the Directors went to see Mrs. Eddy. They told her there were insufficient funds on hand to assure success, but she urged them to go ahead, and steadied them by her confidence that money would be forthcoming as needed.

Returning to Boston from Concord they received word from the architect that he was dissatisfied. Instead of receiving a percentage of the cost of the building, with one half payable when construction contracts were signed, and the remaining half upon completion of the edifice, he insisted upon a substantial sum in advance. After discussion, the Directors bought the plans, and retained the architect as consultant.

In the plans, the roof was drawn in outline. Under the building code, it was required that exact details of construction be included. In order to obtain specifications for roof construction, the Directors advertised for bids. None of the bids was wholly satisfactory but, to prevent delay, the contract was awarded to the lowest bidder. The bidder refused to keep his agreement.

Going to the City Engineer, the Directors explained the difficulty. Their earnestness must have been convincing because the city official waived the requirement for full specifications, and issued the building permit.

In October,[7] the Directors let contracts for excavation, pile driving, and stone foundations. The work was completed before the arrival of heavy winter weather, and the excavation carefully boarded over to await the coming of spring. All bills were paid. Contributions had started coming in again.

Meanwhile, the Directors were in receipt of a communication from Mrs. Eddy, suggesting that the edifice be completed in 1894, instead of by September 1, 1897, as the terms of the deed of trust permitted. This meant if the church was to be completed in 1894, contracts for building the walls had to be signed without delay.

Calling in the builders while the foundation work was still in progress, the Directors asked for estimates on the cost of walls, including brick with stone exterior, along with the necessary steel, or iron, beams. The price was beyond their means. While struggling with their desire to meet Mrs. Eddy's wishes and, at the same time, live within the terms of the deed of trust, they received another communication from their Teacher.

She suggested that in contracting for the walls they include a provision giving them the right to stop work at any time the walls had been completed above the level of the

[7] October 19. Cost of the work was $7158.

auditorium floor — if they "could find parties who would enter into such an unusual arrangement."

The proposal was made, the contractors were agreeable, and the contract was signed on December 6, 1893. The contract figure for building the walls was $57,000; on hand was about $44,000. In this agreement it was provided that if there were no work stoppages the walls would be completed by August 1, 1894, and the tower completed to a point ten feet above the walls by the following month. Terms of payment stipulated that 80 per cent of the work completed each month was to be paid for at the end of that same month, with the remaining 20 per cent to be paid upon final completion of the work "to the satisfaction of the Directors."

Having advised the Directors into this unusual action, Mrs. Eddy wrote to a group of her students:

PLEASANT VIEW, CONCORD, N. H.
MY BELOVED STUDENT:

I have prepared a subscription list for building the Mother Church. The names to be placed thereon I have *carefully selected*. All who sign agree to pay $1000. It is dated Dec. 25, 1893, for my Christmas gift. It reads the same as the slip enclosed. I give this opportunity to as many as I can readily reach of my faithful students to sign, that I may put their names which are attached to the sums severally paid, with my name, and "Science and Health," and my card of thanks, into a box placed in the Corner Stone of our Church. I shall name this special donation as an extra bequest to the Church Building Fund, presented to me for this object, in demonstration of their love for their Teacher, and their devotion to our cause — by my fellow laborers in Christian Science. This box with its sacred contents and associations is to be placed as above named in our monumental Church.

When I receive your name on the slip enclosed I shall send it to the Treasurer, Mr. S. A. Chase, who will paste it on the subscription list. Please send in time for your name and the amount you give, to be memorized as specified. The Treasurer will receipt to you for $1000.

Also for important reasons keep this transaction a sound secret till the time comes for its denouement, the laying of the Corner Stone. Please sign your name twice — one signature is to be pasted on to my subscription list, the other remains on the enclosed slip.

With great love,
MARY BAKER EDDY

Please reply at once.

There were few of the students, probably not more than half a dozen, who possessed one thousand dollars. Except for these few, none could reply with anything but a pledge; but before the spring of 1894 was much more than half over, they had responded with $44,000. This sum, with continuing contributions from other sources, was enough to pay for the walls.

The names of these students were:

Mary M. W. Adams, Julia S. Bartlett, Mr. and Mrs. Edward P. Bates, Mr. and Mrs. Edwin W. Baxter, M. Bettie Bell, Harriet L. Betts, Mr. and Mrs. Ezra M. Buswell, Sarah

J. Clark, Ellen L. Clarke, Janet T. Colman, E. J. Foster
Eddy, Ruth B. Ewing, Alfred Farlow, Dr. and Mrs. Francis
J. Fluno, Caroline W. Frame, Berenice H. Goodall, Eldora
O. Gragg, Judge and Mrs. Septimus J. Hanna, Charles M.
Howe, Emelie B. Hulin, Rose E. Kent, Mr. and Mrs. Ed-
ward A. Kimball, Julia Field King, Hannah Abigail Lar-
minie, Laura Lathrop, Pamelia J. Leonard, Mr. and Mrs.
John F. Linscott, Emily M. Meader, Sue Harper Mims,
Mary W. Munroe, Carol Norton, Caroline D. Noyes, Jose-
phine Curtis Otterson, Mary Hinds Philbrick, Mr. and Mrs.
Silas J. Sawyer, Elizabeth P. Skinner, Augusta E. Stetson,
Mr. and Mrs. John H. Stewart, Ella P. Sweet, Emma A.
Thompson, Emelyn M. Tobey, and Elizabeth Webster.[8]

Unavoidably, the names of Captain and Mrs. Joseph S.
Eastaman were not included among those preserved in the
Corner Stone. It was not until after the Stone was laid that
Eastaman learned of Mrs. Eddy's request. Hurt because his
wife and himself were not included among those whose
names "I have carefully selected," Eastaman went to see
Mrs. Eddy, to learn that she had written him. An investigation by postoffice authorities disclosed that mail was being
stolen from his mail box.

In the July 1894 issue of the *Journal* and under the title
NOTA BENE, Mrs. Eddy made note of the omission:

Among the recent thronging memories of golden
days we note one shadowy form: the absence in the
Corner-stone of the Mother Church, in Boston, of
the names of two beloved students, Captain Joseph
S. Eastaman and Mrs. Mary F. Eastaman, of Boston. I hoped to have treasured their names with

[8] Husband and wife were considered as one.

others of their classmates at my College in that sacred receptacle. But the circumstances which occasioned both my disappointment and theirs, was doubtless a kind providence which reserved their contribution of $1000 to our Church building fund, for the special honor of building its platform and pulpit. For which object it now is to be appropriated, and is most gratefully acknowledged. Also we are pleased to accept this circumstance as serving another good purpose — a type of their solid standing on the platform of Christian Science.

March 1894 came and went, with no work done on the church walls, although daily promises were made by the contractors that they would delay no further. April came, and was more than half gone when the Directors learned, but only after much questioning, of a dispute between the builders and the suppliers concerning the amount of iron needed. It was not until April 24 that the first stone was laid for the walls, and it was not until May 20, one day before the day designated by Mrs. Eddy for the laying of the Corner Stone, that the first iron was delivered.

With only thoughts of the Corner Stone in their minds, the Directors went to the site on the morning of May 21 to learn that the superintendent was absent for the day. They inquired about the laying of the Stone and were told by a foreman it would not be possible without the presence of the superintendent "because he is the only person familiar with the schedule and the building details."

The foreman refused to assume any responsibility but did agree to the request of the Directors for permission to talk with the workmen. Calling the men together, the Directors explained what they wanted done, how they wanted it done, and persuaded the men to arrange in position the long, curved beams without which the Corner Stone could not be put in place — and, then, to place the Stone itself.

Late in the afternoon three Directors [9] took part in a simple ceremony of silent prayer followed by the audible recitation of the Lord's Prayer. The Corner Stone was laid. Sealed within it was a copper box containing a number of articles, wrapped separately in oiled silk:

The Bible, in the finest morocco binding; in similar binding, a copy of the eighty-fourth edition of *Science and Health with Key to the Scriptures* by Mary Baker G. Eddy; other writings by Mrs. Eddy: *Retrospection and Introspection, Unity of Good, No and Yes, Rudimental Divine Science, People's Idea of God, Christian Healing, Historical Sketch of Christian Science Mind-healing, Defense of Christian Science,* five numbers of the *Christian Science Series,* an address, in manuscript, written by Mrs. Eddy for the occasion; the June 1894 issue of the *Christian Science Journal;* April, May, and June 1894, *Christian Science Quarterly Lessons;* three cards containing a list of students who contributed $1000 each to the Church Building Fund; a grateful acknowledgment by Mrs. Eddy; and the names of the Board of Directors, written in hand by Mrs. Eddy.

And in the manuscript that was sealed in the Corner Stone, she sealed her heart, and her hope:

Without pomp or pride, laid away as a sacred secret in the heart of a rock, there to typify the

---

[9] The fourth Director was in Pennsylvania attending to the shipment of the iron beams.

prophecy: "And a man shall be as a hiding place from the wind, and a covert from the tempest . . . as the shadow of a great rock in a weary land." Henceforth to whisper our Master's promise: "And upon this rock I will build my Church; and the gates of hell shall not prevail against it."

To-day, be this hope in each of our hearts — as precious in God's sight as shall be the assembling of His people in this Temple, sweet as the rest that remaineth for the righteous, and fresh as a summer's morn — that from earth's pillows of stone, our visible lives are rising to God. As in the history of a seed, so may our earthly sowing bear fruit, exude the juice of that vine whereof our Father is the husbandman, be poured into the cup of Christ, drunk after the manner of Jesus, and inspire the whole race. . . .

The summer months, and the months of early autumn, made for a taxing period. Iron floor beams, already late in being delivered, were found to be too long . . . the stone was chipped away, so as to make a fit; iron columns for the walls were defective . . . there was a delay of a month before a supplier was found who could furnish columns good enough to pass the inspection of city engineers; masons threatened to strike because they were not paid on time . . . the Directors kept them working by advancing the money for their wages after collecting it from Christian Scientists on the premises; a railroad strike shut off shipments of iron for the roof . . . and the beams did not begin to arrive until September was nearly ended; in October, with building operations far behind schedule, Mrs. Eddy requested Director Joseph Armstrong to devote full time to the work; and, on October 1, the Directors entered into an agreement among themselves — they gave the treasurer entire responsibility for the handling of the money, instructing him not to disclose how much was on hand but only to inform them if what was asked could be afforded.

As November began, there was no roof on the building; there were no windows, no doors — only walls, piles of debris, and wooden floors. The Directors wanted mosaic for the floors and dadoes, but the contractors said two months would be needed to obtain and fit the material, and estimated the church would be ready for occupancy in May 1895.

On the morning of November 6, there was a heavy snowfall. Picking up shovels and brooms, Directors and church members kept the floors clear, and the men working. It was in this period of cold and stormy weather that work was begun on anchoring the iron roof frame into position. It was work that soon stopped, the foreman reporting he could not find more than "two or three men who are willing to work at such height in this kind of weather." The fear was overcome, and a full crew was found that completed the job, so that, as November went into its final week, the floors and the dadoes the contractor said would require two months to complete were ready.

Then . . . the plasterers, when asked to start, insisted they had to have the structure "clear of all other work." "For how long?" the contractor was asked. "At least six weeks. It will take that long for my men to finish what they have to do." The plasterers were prevailed upon to work with the other trades; and were promised extra wages for working Saturday afternoon and night on December 8, so that between the hours of midnight on Saturday and starting time on Monday morning the walls and ceiling would have a chance to harden.

In December, the City stopped the use of Caledonia Street, for the purpose of digging for and laying sewer pipes. With wagons loaded, with materials arriving hourly, day and night, and only one street available for unloading, workmen protested the crowded conditions, and threatened to quit, but finally were persuaded to remain. . . . Adding to the resentment was the denial of the use of a steam hoist to the roofers for the lifting of iron to the tower. Mrs. Edward P. Bates climbed three sets of ladders, located the owner of the derrick, and gained his consent to the use of his apparatus by the roofers for one day. . . . And the general restlessness subsided.

In December, the following contracts were let: December 5 — Decorations, vestry chairs, marble. December 6 — pulpit and furniture for "Mother's Room." December 7 — electric fixtures. December 9 — marble for "Mother's Room." December 12 — stereo-relief work. December 13 — sidewalk. December 14 — bronze torches and brackets. December 18——onyx mantel for "Mother's Room." And, in December, no pews having been delivered although the contract was signed in October, a representative of the Directors went to Michigan.

In Michigan, the representative was told that, in sending his order, the salesman had written the pews would not be needed "before the spring of 1895," which was, he estimated, when the church would be ready.

"The church is almost ready now, and the pews are needed now," the company was told. It solved the problem by putting its entire force to work on the one order, and the pews were in Boston on December 21.

It was nearing midnight on Saturday, December 29. The stained-glass windows, twelve in all, were in place; the platform, the pulpit, the pews, with their hymnals and quarterlies neatly stacked in the racks. . . . Women had scrubbed the floors, and men had cleaned the walls. . . . Outside was a new cement sidewalk. . . . Not long before twelve o'clock the electricians finished the wiring, and all stood watching the lights as they came on by sections — the walls, and then the chandelier . . . Almost at once there were voices of dismay as a short-circuit extinguished the chandelier; but it was quickly fixed, and burning again . . . and it was after twelve o'clock when all the lights but one were turned off, and all left the church but stood on the street, a block away, looking back at the one light, left burning in "Mother's Room." As symbolic of their Leader's teachings, it was their purpose to keep it burning, day and night.

And, in keeping with their Teacher's instructions to the Directors on December 18, to "have the first services in God's Temple, Dec. 30, 1894," [10] the church was ready.

The first services — communion services — were held the following day, December 30; and on this day of communion, Septimus J. Hanna ended his pastorate and began his term as First Reader of the Mother Church.[11]

---

[10] In November, Mrs. Eddy wrote to the Directors advising them to "keep the men at work inside the church every working day, besides your night work until the inside is finished. Finish this church in 1894, even if you have to give up some of your gods such as mosaic floor in the auditorium, or other decorations. . . ."

[11] Hanna succeeded David Easton who, in turn, succeeded Norcross as a pastor of the Boston church. The appointment of Hanna followed a letter to the Clerk of The Mother Church dated March 13, 1894, in which Mrs. Eddy wrote: "The first thing you do that I recommend is this. Give

The day was clear and cold and, in its observance, the choir from the New York church, a choir that was recognized as the best in all Christian Science churches, was invited by Mrs. Eddy to be in attendance. The church, which seated a few more than nine hundred persons, was well filled when Judge Hanna announced the opening hymn and, in delivering the first Lesson-Sermon in The Mother Church, read from the Bible (Mark, 14:12-26) and from *Science and Health* (page 340, paragraphs 2 and 3, and page 348, paragraphs 2 and 3) as follows:

THE BIBLE:

And the first day of unleavened bread, when they killed the passover, his disciples said unto him, Where wilt thou that we go and prepare that thou mayest eat the passover?

And he sendeth forth two of his disciples, and saith unto them, Go ye into the city, and there

---

Mr. Hanna a call for one year to fill your pulpit in Boston. He can carry on the Mag. [magazine] all the same and each month publish one of his own sermons . . . Call a meeting of the Board of Directors and give him a call this week. Do not let the absence of a regular Pastor diminish your audience."

In a postscript, she added: "I want you to have the Com. [Committee] on preparing the S.S. [Sunday School] Quarterly, stop the lessons in the Old Testament and begin at the 18th verse of the 1st chap. of Matt. for the study of the Scriptures. I see your minds need this change to spiritualize thought, greatly need it. Prepare your Quarterly on the same plan that you have adopted, and only change from the O.T. to the New. Also I find the pulpit is making an unwise use of *Science and Health* by reading *too much* from it. The speaker should never select a portion of my book which treats on one topic, especially, then turn and read other portions which include still more topics. This is confusing and they are not able to select more than one to advantage. Therefore, I strictly forbid reading my book *Science and Health* in such a manner, and allow not over *one page* of the book to be read before the sermon . . . Let that *selection illustrate* the sermon."

shall meet you a man bearing a pitcher of water: follow him.

And wheresoever he shall go, say ye to the good-man of the house, The Master saith, Where is the guestchamber, where I shall eat the passover with my disciples?

And he will shew you a large upper room furnished *and* prepared: there make ready for us.

And his disciples went forth, and came into the city, and found as he had said unto them: and they made ready the passover.

And in the evening he cometh with the twelve.

And as they sat and did eat, Jesus said, Verily I say unto you, One of you which eateth with me shall betray me.

And they began to be sorrowful, and to say unto him, *Is* it I? and another *said, Is* it I?

And he answered, and said unto them, *It is* one of the twelve, that dippeth with me in the dish.

The Son of man indeed goeth, as it is written of him: but woe to that man by whom the Son of man is betrayed! good were it for that man if he had never been born.

And as they did eat, Jesus took bread, and blessed, and brake it, and gave to them, and said, Take, eat: this is my body.

And he took the cup, and when he had given thanks, he gave *it* to them: and they all drank of it.

And he said unto them, This is my blood of the new testament, which is shed for many.

Verily I say unto you, I will drink no more of

the fruit of the vine, until that day that I drink
it new in the kingdom of God.

And when they had sung an hymn, they went
out into the Mount of Olives.

Science and Health:

What a contrast between our Lord's Last Supper
and his last spiritual breakfast with his disciples, in
the bright morning hours, at the joyful meeting on
the shore of the Galilean Sea! His gloom had
passed into glory, and his disciples' grief into re-
pentance, hearts chastened and pride rebuked.
Convinced of the fruitlessness of their toil in the
dark, and wakened by their Master's voice, they
changed their methods, turned away from material things, and cast their net on the right side.
Discerning Christ, Truth, anew on the shore of
time, they were enabled to rise somewhat from
mortal sensuousness, or the burial of mind in matter, to newness of Life in Christ.

This spiritual meeting with our Lord, in the
dawn of a new light, is the morning meal which
Christian Scientists commemorate. They bow before Christ, Truth, to receive more of his reappear-
ing, and silently commune with the divine Principle thereof. They celebrate their Lord's victory
over death, his probation in the flesh after death,
his exemplification of human probation, and his
spiritual and final ascension above matter, or the
flesh, when he rose out of material sight.

Our baptism is a purification from all error. Our
church is built on the divine Principle of Christian

Science. We can unite with this church only as we are new born of Spirit, as we reach the Life which is Truth and the Truth which is Life, by bringing forth the fruits of Love — casting out error and healing the sick. Our eucharist is spiritual communion with the one God. Our bread, "which cometh down from Heaven" is Truth. Our cup is the cross, our wine the inspiration of Love — the draught our Master drank, and commended to his followers.

The magnitude of Jesus' work, his material disappearance before their eyes, his reappearance in idea, all enabled the disciples to understand what Jesus had said. Heretofore they had only believed; now they understood. This understanding is what is meant by the Descent of the Holy Ghost — that influx of Divine Science which so illuminated the Pentecostal Day, and is now repeating its ancient history.

His last proof was the highest, the most convincing, the most profitable to his students. The malignity of brutal persecuters, the treason and suicide of his betrayer, were overruled by divine Love, to the glorification of the true idea of God, which they had mocked and tried to slay. The final demonstration of the Truth Jesus taught, and for which he was crucified, opened a new era for the world. They who slew him, wishing to stay his influence, only perpetuated and extended it thereby.

After a solo by a member of the choir, Judge Hanna read the names of the 572 applicants who were admitted to mem-

bership at the December quarterly meeting; and then made
an important announcement:

> The dedication services of the new building of
> The Mother Church, The First Church of Christ,
> Scientist, in Boston, Massachusetts, will be held
> on the first Sunday in January, the sixth, 1895. An
> address from our former pastor, the Rev. Mary
> Baker Eddy, will be read, but she will not be pres-
> ent at these services.
>
> (*Signed*) THE CHRISTIAN SCIENCE BOARD OF DIRECTORS

There were a number of important happenings in this
period. From Concord, on December 19, Mrs. Eddy had
written:

> CHRISTIAN SCIENCE DIRECTORS: —
> My beloved Students, The day is well nigh won.
> You will soon rest on your arms. Thank God you
> have been valiant soldiers — loyal to the heart's
> core. "Who is so great a God as our God?"
> Present no contribution box on Dedication day.
> When you know the amount requisite and have
> received it for finishing the church building —
> close all contributions and give public notice
> thereof.
> Hold your services in the Mother Church Dec.
> 30, 1894, and dedicate this church Jan. 6th. The
> Bible and *Science and Health with Key to the
> Scriptures* shall henceforth be the Pastor of the
> Mother Church. This will tend to spiritualize
> thought. Personal preaching has more or less hu-

man views grafted into it. Whereas the pure Word
contains only the living, health-giving Truth.

With love, mother,

MARY BAKER EDDY

A week before the dedication services, Stephen A. Chase,
treasurer of the Christian Science Board of Directors, announced, "There are ample funds to meet all obligations,
and all contributions should cease after January 6, 1895, as
none can be received which were not subscribed before
that date." [12]

Also, during the week from Concord, there had come to
the Board a new order of Sunday services as established by
Mrs. Eddy:

1. A Hymn.

2. Silent prayer, followed by the audible repetition of the Lord's Prayer, and its spiritual interpretation given on page 322 of *Science and Health,
with Key to the Scriptures.*

3. Hymn.

4. The announcement by one of the Readers
of the Bible Lesson for the day, the subject, golden
text, and footsteps thereof; the reading respon-
sively of the lesson text, followed by the reading of
the expository notes by the readers, who shall be

[12] Christian Scientists were reminded of the incident related in Exodus,
36:5-7:

"And they spake unto Moses, saying, The people bring much more than
enough for the service of the work, which the Lord commanded to make.

"And Moses gave commandment, and they caused it to be proclaimed
throughout the camp, saying, Let neither man nor woman make any more
work for the offering of the sanctuary. So the people were restrained from
bringing.

"For the stuff they had was sufficient for all the work to make it, and
too much."

a man and a woman,[13] one reading the Bible references, and the other the quotations from *Science
and Health, with Key to the Scriptures;* this reading to be done alternately.

5. The collection and an anthem, or solo.

6. A Hymn.

7. The benediction.

From the above it will be seen that the quotations from the Bible and textbook are not to be
written, but read directly from the books.

This change in the services has reference only
to the Mother Church, and is not to be adopted by
branch churches until further notice.

Work remained to be done, and in the week preceding
the dedication services there was no slackening of the effort.
The chimes had arrived, but there was not time for their
installation before Communion Sunday. Early the next
morning the manufacturers asked permission to build scaf-
folding. Rather than have them clutter up the outside of
the edifice, the Directors suggested that the chimes be taken
up an inside stairway to the tower. This was done. The
cushions came, and the pews were covered. Much of the
finishing of the interior remained undone, and a score of
workmen were kept busy through each of the six days. During the week missing parts arrived for the pipe organ.

Snow was falling on Sunday morning. The day was mild,
and as the congregation moved toward the church and the

---

[13] Instead of "a man and a woman," the Readers at the dedication services were Foster Eddy, President of the Church, and Septimus J. Hanna.
Hanna read the quotations from *Science and Health.* Following the dedication services, Eldora O. Gragg occupied the platform with Judge Hanna.

first of five services [14] — this one beginning at nine o'clock — it heard the first ringing of the chimes. They were much in need of tuning, but were bravely playing these hymns: "Shepherd, show me how to go," "The morning light is breaking," "Joy to the world, the Lord is come," "O'er waiting harpstrings of the Mind," "All hail the power of Jesus' name," and "Saw ye my Saviour," [15] the first, the fourth, and the sixth being hymns written by Mrs. Eddy.

Flowers covered the platform, and the third service, beginning at twelve o'clock, was for the children. Two hundred and twenty of them were seated before the older people were admitted to the auditorium. At four-thirty, the final services were over. It was estimated that five thousand, or more, came to worship on this Sunday of dedication — of whom, so the *Boston Globe* estimated, "fully 3000 came from long distances"; and the *New York Sun* thought it was notable that Mrs. Eddy, instead of being present in person, "sent a communication ordaining the Bible and *Science and Health* as the rightful pastor of the church."

The church Mary Baker Eddy foresaw on that evening in Lynn, in 1872, was now inscribed to her sacred purpose.

[14] For full account of services, see Appendix 8.

[15] "Saw ye my Saviour," or the Communion Hymn, was first entitled "Hymn of Science." It was written by Mrs. Eddy when she was living at 8 Broad Street, in Lynn in 1876, and was first published in the *Christian Science Journal*.

CHAPTER FIFTEEN

Pleasant View

IN SPEAKING of the building of The Mother Church, the *Boston Herald* said, "The structure came forth from the hands of the artisans with every stone paid for — with an appeal, not for more money, but for a cessation of the tide of contributions which continued to flow in after the full amount was received." It was Mrs. Eddy's wish that the church be paid for before dedication; and it was this wish that established the custom of not dedicating a Christian Science church until it is free of debt.

In 1889, when the first church organization dissolved, and in 1892, when the twelve First Members of the new Church were chosen, Sunday services were held in Chickering Hall. In the early part of 1894, the owners of the hall gave notice that the building was being converted to business uses, and the lease would not be renewed. Copley Hall, on Clarendon Street, was rented. It had a seating capacity of six hundred and twenty-five, but an adjoining room permitted expansion of the facilities so as to seat one hundred more persons.

It was to this religious group — with the exception of one small outlying edifice, a group without a church — that an invitation was extended to participate in the World's Parliament of Religions at the World's Fair in Chicago, in 1893.

* * *

In issuing the invitations, Charles Carroll Bonney, President of the Parliament, announced that the purpose would be "to contribute to those forces which shall bring about the unity of the race in the worship of God, and the service of man"; and, as indicative of the care she gave to participation by Christian Scientists in the conferences which were scheduled to begin during the latter part of September, Mrs. Eddy, on July 31, 1893, chose nine students "to select the very best, comprehensive quotations to be found in all my works," and to send them to Septimus J. Hanna.

> He [Hanna] will arrange them properly for the presentation of Christian Science at the World's Fair Congress. This is the only presentation of Christian Science that I sanction for their Parliament. My reasons for this are that "What is written, is written." The texts are contained in these works, and I for one would not venture to depart from the fundamental teachings of these books, with all the labor bestowed on them. . . .

In a postscript to her instructions, Mrs. Eddy explained that "the definitions need to be brief, and selected with great care," and each of the nine students was cautioned to "say nothing of this arrangement till the event is over."

In welcoming Mrs. Eddy's followers to the Parliament on September 20, Bonney said:

"I come as general president . . . to salute you and bid you welcome. This great audience filling the Hall of Washington gives me occasion to extend to you with my words of welcome, words of hearty congratulation. When science becomes Christian, then the world indeed advances toward the millennial dawn.

"No more striking manifestation of the interposition of divine providence in human affairs has come in recent years, than that shown in the raising up of the body of people which you represent, known as Christian Scientists. We had come to the state in the world in which science was called infidel, although true science could never look otherwise than up through nature into nature's God. The Christian Scientists were therefore called to declare and emphasize the real harmony between religion and science; and to restore the waning faith of many in the verities of the sacred Scriptures.

". . . To restore a living faith in the efficacy of prayer — the fervent and effectual prayer of the righteous man which availeth much; to teach everywhere the supremacy of spiritual forces; to teach and to emphasize the fact that in the presence of these spiritual forces all other forces are weak and inefficient — that I understand to be your mission.

"That you may so fulfill this mission that not only all Christendom . . . but the whole world and its worshippers of God and servants of man may have cause to rise up and call you blessed, is my sincere and fervent wish. The world assembles here in this great year that its peoples and churches may know each other better. You yourselves, come to make known to the world who you are, what faith you hold, what work you have done, what achievements you have made; and on the other hand to learn from all the others what work they have done, and what faith they hold, in order that, seeing in each other's faces the same spirit of charity, and learning that all are engaged in the same heavenly service, you may take courage in the support of each other. . . ."

* * *

And now, in the forenoon of September 22, on the same platform with Judge Hanna, in another hall, this one called Columbus Hall, were a college professor and four clergymen — including Joseph Cook, whose words of cold acknowledgment of Christian Science in a gathering in Tremont Temple in Boston, on March 16, 1885, had been confined to, "It now becomes my interesting duty to introduce to this audience, Mrs. Eddy."

In contrast, in introducing Judge Hanna now, Bonney extended to Christian Scientists "fraternal greeting, and welcome," — after attributing to them effort which had contributed greatly to "the success of the Parliament."

The title was "Unity and Christian Science" and, in addressing the Parliament, Hanna confined himself to paragraphs from Mrs. Eddy's writings:

> . . . In this revolutionary period the voice of God in behalf of the African slave was still echoing in our land, when this new Christian crusade sounded the keynote of universal freedom, asking a fuller acknowledgement of the rights of man as a Son of God, demanding that the fetters of sin, sickness and death be stricken from the human mind and body, and their freedom should be won, not through human warfare, not with bayonet and blood, but through Divine Science.
>
> God has built a higher platform of human rights, and built it on diviner claims. These claims are not made through code or creed, but in demonstration of "peace on earth and good-will to men." Human codes of scholastic theology, medicine, and hygiene cramp the mind which needs freedom

in Christ, Truth rends asunder these fetters, and man's birthright and sole allegiance to his Maker go on undisturbed in Divine Science.

I saw before me the sick, wearing out years of servitude to an unreal master, in the belief that the body governed them, rather than the Divine Mind. The lame, the deaf, the dumb, the blind, the sick, the sensual, the sinner, I wished to save from the slavery of their own beliefs, and from the educational systems which today hold the children of Israel in bondage. I saw before me the awful conflict, the Red Sea, and the wilderness; but I pressed on, through faith in God, trusting Truth, the strong deliverer, to guide me into the land of Christian Science, where fetters fall, and the rights of man to freedom are fully known and acknowledged. . . .[1]

The *Chicago Tribune* the next day made this comment: "The crowd in the Hall of Columbus yesterday morning was greater than at any time since the Parliament first opened. It was apparently the announcement that the cause of Christian Science would be presented that attracted them"; and, in the *Congregationalist,* there was this salute: ". . . No paper of the day elicited more applause from a part of the audience than one on Christian Science. Here, perhaps it may be said that none of the congresses going on at the same time with the Parliament of Religions, have drawn such immense audiences as that of Christian Science."

One evident result of the Parliament was the acknowl-

[1] For full text, see Appendix 9.

edgment by other religious groups that Christian Science was not a thing of passing moment, but a vital force.

It was the first public acknowledgment by so highly placed an authority as Charles Carroll Bonney that Mrs. Eddy's teachings were "the interposition of divine providence in human affairs"; and that "Christian Scientists were therefore called to . . . restore the waning faith of many in the verities of the sacred Scriptures." Only a few years before or, on May 24, 1889, the *Congregationalist* was saying, "It [Christian Science] is directly opposed to the doctrines of the Bible. . . ."

In November, the *Christian Register* called upon Christian churches generally to display less hostility toward Christian Science, saying: "The number of adherents is probably much smaller than the number of interested inquirers, for there is an immense market for the books and papers published in this interest.[2] Indeed, it is not often that the subject is mentioned in any company without bringing out a more or less sympathetic expression.

"The testimonials to the healing of all manner of sickness and disease among the people are so numerous that enthusiastic disciples do not hesitate to proclaim a new advent of the Christ, or, rather, a return to the methods of Jesus and a vast manifestation of the same power by which he wrought his 'wonderful works.' A movement which has its origin in the new faith of Divine Immanence in Humanity is open to criticism, but it is not to be treated with derision or suspicion.

---

[2] When the Parliament opened, daily requests for the *Christian Science Journal* totaled one hundred; before the meetings closed, the daily demand was for eight hundred copies.

"In its conflict with materialism the Church should not be met with hostility, but should hail as timely allies all who 'lift up holy hands without wrath or doubting' to invoke the Eternal Powers that work for the perfecting of man in the image of the Highest."

Grateful for the better understanding of her work, Mrs. Eddy issued this call in the November *Journal:*

> I HEREBY enjoin upon all Christian Scientists that hereafter they refrain from speaking or writing condemnatory of any Christian denomination, and only promulgate Christian Science through correct statement of the science of Christianity, and by its good works.
>
> This alone is consistent with our attitude and the brotherly place accorded us in the Congress and Parliament of Religions in A.D. 1893.

In March 1894, in an editorial in the *Journal,* Hanna made note of the change in the attitude of other churches toward Christian Science, saying, "The careful sifting process of the authorities of this Parliament . . . should have its effect in removing from public sentiment the erroneous notion that because we are the adherents and advocates of a Christianity which appears to be so at variance with current views and interpretations that it seems new, we are therefore cranks and dangerous propagandists. Would that those who thus misjudge us would come and learn of us what kind of Christianity ours is!"

With recognition by the Parliament of Religions there came a marked increase in membership and, by former students, a marked display of new interest.

In 1894, 1780 new members were admitted to The

Mother Church; also, in 1894 and in numbers, former students were appearing at Sunday services and at the monthly meetings of the Christian Scientist Association of the Metaphysical College. Because they were not returned to positions they once held, they were critical of the First Members.

They revived the worn argument about Christian Science needing no edifice and no organization to express, and protect, the teachings — and made headway with the argument to the detriment of the building operations under way; they sought to re-open the columns of the *Journal* to articles not in accordance with Mrs. Eddy's teachings and, failing, attempted to discourage the renewal of subscriptions to the publication; there were students who did not know how they would be received as applicants for church membership because they had been taught by those who no longer acknowledged Mrs. Eddy as Leader.

The critics sought to discourage these puzzled students from joining the Church; finally, an appeal was made to Mrs. Eddy. She responded in the *Journal,* in February 1894:

> From letters received, I infer, that some of my students seem not to know in what manner they should demean themselves toward the students of those teachers who have turned away from us. This query is abnormal, after "line upon line and precept upon precept" in the Scriptures, and in my books, on this very subject.
>
> In Mark 9th chapter, commencing at the 33d verse, you will find my views on this question. *I have learned* that nothing save love is admissable toward friend and foe. Besides, my own sympathies extend to the above named class of students more

than to any other. If I had the time to talk with all the students of Christian Science, and correspond with them, I would gladly do it, and do my best toward helping them through the straight and narrow path. But I have not moments enough in which to give all the time needed by them, to those of my own flock, and charity must begin at home.

Distinct denominational and social organizations . . . are at present necessary. But all people can love one another, and should, and never envy, never elbow, never slander, never hate, never try to injure, but always to bless their fellow mortals.

In this letter Mrs. Eddy also gave answer to the argument about Christian Science needing no structure, and no organization, to express, and protect, its teachings — just as in this letter, she admonished those who were hesitant about accepting students of teachers no longer loyal. And still, were her words an admonition? Were they not a stimulus? . . . "My own sympathies extend to the above class of students more than to any other."

Previously and in the January issue of the *Journal*, Hanna had struck at dissimulators who were saying there was no need to heed Mrs. Eddy's wishes regarding her Church because only in the first edition of *Science and Health* could be found the way to heal — and, since writing the first edition, Mrs. Eddy had lost her inspiration.

"If *Science and Health* . . . is the help which all who believe in it at all, declare it to be, then what rule of common reason and justice is there which says we may heed or not heed at our pleasure, the requests and wishes of its author? If she is not inspired, *Science and Health* is no more

than any other book, and those who profess to believe it to
be an inspired book with an uninspired author, place themselves in a position at once inconsistent and illogical.

"Those who pretend to believe that she was inspired when
she wrote the textbook, but has since lost her inspiration, are
even more inconsistent. . . ."

Some of the most hostile of the dissimulators had been
given their teaching without charge. In manufacturing the
report that in writing the first edition of *Science and Health,*
Mrs. Eddy had exhausted herself into spiritual bankruptcy,
they gave motive for an excuse to follow her to the door of
her teachings, but not into the house. A scattered few, they
finally departed and set up their own tenets.

Behind their malice was resentment because Mrs. Eddy
had assigned to the First Members the functions previously
performed by the National Christian Scientists Association.
It began to be said that in the exercise of their duties the
First Members were acting in the manner of a Council of
Bishops, when what really was the matter was the proximity
of the First Members. It was a proximity that prevented the
complaining from taking themselves, and their complaints,
to Mrs. Eddy in person.

In proposing to the national Association that it stand
adjourned for a stated period, Mrs. Eddy was disengaging
her teachings from the restriction of organization and bringing them into a framework she intended would serve all
humanity, yet would remain untouched by human hands.
It was a framework she now was building; and it appeared
in 1895. She called it the *Church Manual of the First Church
of Christ, Scientist.*

This woman, seventy-three years old, found her day's work
in preparing the *Church Manual,* refining *Science and*

Health, watching over and directing the building of The
Mother Church — watching over and directing every beat
of the music heard first by her ears, but which now was the
marching song to which thousands were beginning to move.
There still were shadows, of course; but once, from where
she had watched, all was shadow.

One afternoon, after living in Concord for about two
years, Mrs. Eddy paused at a farmhouse while on one of her
daily drives. On Pleasant Street, a mile and a half from
Concord, the farmhouse permitted her to look southward
down a narrow valley and beyond the hills toward Bow —
and toward another farmhouse she could visualize, the farmhouse where she was born.

Making inquiries, she learned it was possible to buy the
property for a reasonable price. Without delay, she did. She
added to the small farm by the purchase of adjoining land,
and set about to make the place attractive with shade trees
and fruit trees, shrubs, low hedges, flowers, sloping lawns,
and old-fashioned gardens. To the dwelling, which was not
large, she added wide verandas, bow windows, a porte-
cochère in front, and, in back, a tower from which, and
from all sides, she could see the horizons of her native state.
She called the place Pleasant View.

This was her retreat, and it was good she had it.

Seventy miles from Boston and in a time of dirt roads, it
discouraged casual callers, yet was close enough to be accessible by train. Planning the gardens, the placement of the
trees, the building of the hedges, and the additions to the
house — all of which she supervised — gave her rest from
the care of a Church and a movement that had leaped the

older boundaries and was spreading over the provinces of Canada and across the ocean into the cities and towns of England and Scotland.

In summer she rose at six o'clock, and in winter at seven. After breakfast, she usually walked in her garden, or along a path under the trees. If the weather was forbidding, from behind the windows of the tower she knew the promise of spring and summer — the soft winds and the perfume of locust and honeysuckle and lilacs and clover — and the carpet of crimson and gold covering the hills in the autumn of the year; the hills, white and strange and beautiful under the snow of winter; the deep, deep blue of the sky. Her love of beauty was abiding; in *Miscellaneous Writings* (page 87) she said that to "label beauty nothing, is ignorantly to caricature God's creation. . . ."

Word of "Pleasant View" soon reached the field, and almost as soon gifts began to flow in, among them being a sum of money for the digging of a little pond for her garden. With the digging finished and water flowing into the excavation from nearby springs, another group of students sent a small boat; and, to give the boat a shelter of its own, Mrs. Eddy built a small boathouse on the edge of the water. It was this gift of a pond that inspired one of her well-known shorter compositions, "Pond and Purpose":

> . . . From my tower window, as I look on this smile of Christian Science, this gift from my students and their students, it will always mirror their love, loyalty and good works. Solomon saith, "As in water face answereth to face, so the heart of man to man."

The waters that run among the valleys, and that you have coaxed in their course to call on me, have served the imagination for centuries. Theology religiously bathes in water, medicine applies it physically, hydrology handles it with so-called science, and metaphysics appropriates it topically as type and shadow. . . .[3]

It was here at Pleasant View that Mrs. Eddy began a strict household management that continued until her passing. Believing that the more the household chores were absorbed into a routine, the greater the freedom for the real work of "improving the moments before they pass into hours,"[4] she held this was a rule for all, at whatever occupation, including meals. The service of God, in its widest meaning, was what she regarded as the real work of herself and her household.

Nor was her household long in learning that when sitting on the veranda of a summer evening, seemingly lost in listening to the first, faint cries of the night birds, she was not idle. Her senses always made everything new; and here at Pleasant View the melody she heard was but a continuation of the same melody that was in her ears on other evenings in Lynn as, sitting among the Red Rocks, she watched the sea hurling its challenges high against the protecting shores.

Writing was her ruling service, and perhaps it was in one of these reflective periods that she received the inspiration for her small book of poetry, *Christ and Christmas*. Written in the latter part of 1893, the small book caused a great deal of discussion, and brought a great deal of criticism in 1894.

[3] For full text of "Pond and Purpose," see *Miscellaneous Writings*, pp. 203–207.
[4] *Miscellaneous Writings*, p. 230.

One of her few illustrated works, it was the illustrations — not the verses — and especially one illustration, "Christian Unity," that brought the harshest comment. In this picture a woman with a scroll in her hand (a scroll marked CHRISTIAN SCIENCE) is shown holding the hand of Jesus. Circling the head of the woman and the head of Jesus are halos of equal size. Soon there were accusations that the artist had used Mrs. Eddy as a model and, in drawing halos of equal size, had given her equality with Jesus.

The accusations were not true, but the discussions assumed such proportions that in the February 1894 issue of the *Christian Science Journal* Mrs. Eddy said, in reply to a minister's question: "The clergymen may not understand that the illustrations in *Christ and Christmas* refer not to my personality, but rather foretell the typical appearing of the womanhood, as well as the manhood of God, our divine Father and Mother"; and, in the same issue, she gave counsel to Christian Scientists.

Intended only to answer immediate criticism, that reply is one of the most notable of her shorter writings. In it she asks Christian Scientists to remember that . . .

> The illustrations were not intended for a golden calf, at which the sick may look and be healed. Christian Scientists should beware of unseen snares, and adhere to the divine Principle and rules for demonstration. They must guard against the deification of finite personality.

In the *Christian Science Journal* she called her composition, "Hear, O Israel"; in *Miscellaneous Writings* (pages 307–310) it appears under the title of "Deification of Personality."

In this composition, after notifying the public that she had stopped the sale of *Christ and Christmas,* although two editions had been printed, Mrs. Eddy cautioned "Whosoever looks to me personally for his health or holiness, mistakes. He that by reason of human love or hatred or any other cause clings to my material personality, greatly errs, stops his own progress, and loses the path to health, happiness, and heaven. The Scriptures and Christian Science reveal 'the way,' and personal revelators will take their proper place in history, but will not be deified."

She agreed that only "a minority of its readers" were ready for *Christ and Christmas,* and commented, "This little messenger has done its work, fulfilled its mission, retired with honor (and mayhap taught me more than it has others), only to reappear in due season. The knowledge that I have gleaned from its fruitage is, that intensely contemplating personality impedes spiritual growth; even as holding in mind the consciousness of disease prevents the recovery of the sick."

In closing, she warned her followers:

> My Christmas poem and its illustrations are not a textbook. Scientists sometimes take things too intensely. Let them soberly adhere to the Bible and Science and Health, which contain all and much more than they have yet learned. We should prohibit ourselves the childish pleasure of studying Truth through the senses, for this is neither the intent of my works nor possible in Science.
>
> Even the teachings of Jesus would be misused by substituting personality for the Christ, or the impersonal form of Truth, amplified in this age by

the discovery of Christian Science. To imperson-
alize scientifically the material sense of existence
— rather than cling to personality — is the lesson
of today.

But, if it was a time of criticism from within, it also was
a time of leavening thought among those who had reviled
her. By adopting it, the Parliament of Religions had approved her use of silent prayer — use which had been condemned from church pulpits, and for which she had been
strongly denounced. By invitation to participate in the
affairs of the Parliament, there was recognition that in her
teachings were pleasant and useful fruits.

Undoubtedly, in those days, Mrs. Eddy thought deeply
of the events of the Parliament, with her mind turning to
a time when all Churches would be one and all would believe — as did Jesus, and as did she, and as said Renan —
"We are one when we love one another."

She disclosed this thought when, in responding to persistent demands, she said in June 1894, in the *Journal:*

I hereby state publicly and *positively,* that
until I advertise through these pages, or send special requests to individuals to the contrary of this
statement, I shall not receive a call from any one,
nor read letters, MSS., etc., which I have not myself
first solicited. I advertise this, after waiting over
two years for sufficient time of my own to arrange
my writing desk, and while having on hand pack-
ages of sermons, with request that I examine them,
other people's correspondence to read, heaps of

MSS., sent for approval, pyramids of letters requiring immediate answers, tired columns of applicants
to call on me, business letters innumerable, etc.

My work for the Mother Church is *done;* and be
it remembered that five years ago I came to Concord, N.H. for the purpose of *retirement.*

If I know myself this is my sole desire — that
all whom I have taught Christian Science, and all
its teachers and students, by whomsoever taught,
yea, that all mankind, shall have one Shepherd,
and He shall gather them into His fold (unto
Himself) Divine Love.

MARY BAKER EDDY

There it is, her turning thought — in the final paragraph:
*If I know myself, this is my sole desire . . . that all man-
kind, shall have one Shepherd, and He shall gather them
into His fold (unto Himself) Divine Love.*

The statement, "My work for the Mother Church is
done," brought hundreds of anxious messages; so many and
so urgent were they, that in the July issue of the *Journal* she
explained her words, and emphasized, again, the need for
the common element of affection:

In your last No. of the *Journal* I said, "My work
for the Mother Church is done." By this I meant
that my approbation of an interest in this Church,
and our other church organizations, are not in the
least abated, but a Sabbath rest was stealing over
me when contemplating what had been accomplished.

The church, more than any other institution, at

present, is the cement of society, and it should be the bulwarks of civil and religious liberty. But the time cometh when the religious element, or Church of Christ, shall exist alone in the affections, and need no organization to express it. Till then this form of godliness seems as requisite to manifest its spirit, as individuality to express Soul and Substance.

In the December 1894 issue of the *Journal* she returned to the subject, this time at some length, and entitled her article "Overflowing Thoughts":

In this receding year of religious Jubilee, 1894, I, as an individual, would cordially invite all persons who have left our fold, together with those who were never in it — all who love God and keep His commandments, to come and unite with the Mother Church in Boston. Coming thus they should be welcomed as of old, greeted as brethern endeavoring to walk with us hand in hand as we journey to the Celestial City.

Also, I would extend a tender invitation to Christian Scientists' students — those who are ready for the table of our Lord. So should we follow Christ's teachings, so bury the dead past, so loving one another, go forth to the full vintage time, exemplifying what we profess. But some of the older members are not quite ready to take this advanced step in the full spirit of that charity which thinketh no evil, and if be not taken thus, it is impractical, unfruitful, Soulless.

. . . As I now understand Christian Science, I would sooner harm myself than another, lest by breaking Christ's command, "Thou shalt love thy neighbor as thyself," I should lose my hope of heaven.

. . . Being often reported as saying what never escaped from my lips when rehearsing facts concerning others who were reporting falsehoods about me, I have been sorry, and wished I were wise enough to guard against that temptation. Oh! may the love that is talked be felt, and so lived that when weighed in the scales of God, we may not be found wanting. Love is consistent, uniform, sympathetic, self-sacrificing, unutterably kind, suffers all inflictions, endures all piercing for your sake, and for the Kingdom of Heaven.[5]

In 1894, instead of hoping, as she did in 1872, that other Churches would permit her to join with them, Mrs. Eddy was hoping other Churches would join with her — "I, as an individual, would cordially invite all who love God and keep His commandments, to come and unite with the Mother Church in Boston."

Believing that a religion reveals its values not on the outside, but *only* from the inside, Mrs. Eddy's writings likewise reveal that she believed the greatest of all values to be love — "May the love that is talked be felt, and so lived that when weighed in the scales of God, we be not found wanting." Her acceptance of this single rule of greatest value was complete: . . . "I would sooner harm myself

[5] "Overflowing Thoughts," revised by Mrs. Eddy into its permanent form, appears in *Miscellaneous Writings*, pp. 311–312.

than another, lest by breaking Christ's command, 'Thou shalt love thy neighbor as thyself,' I should lose my hope of Heaven.''

It was her way of saying God's love is that outpouring of God that belongs to us, and our love is that outlining of us that belongs to God — and we lose, not by failing to take, but by failing to give.

With the writing of the deed of trust, the appointment of the Board of Directors, the selection of First Members, and the preparation of the Tenets and Rules, Mrs. Eddy was projecting her thought of church government into the far years to a time when "though the material superstructure should crumble into dust, the fittest would survive." [6] They were all parts of one plan, her wish being to put her church beyond the reach of schemers, and its government in a state of perpetuity against the hour when she would not be present, in person, to guide it.

The deed of trust contains a number of paragraphs written in anticipation of the hour of her absence:

1. Said grantees shall be known as the "Christian Science Board of Directors" and shall constitute a perpetual body or corporation under and in accordance with section one, Chapter 39 of the Public Statutes of Massachusetts. Whenever a vacancy occurs in said Board the remaining members shall within thirty days fill the same by election; but no one shall be eligible for that office who is not in the opinion of the remaining members of the Board a firm and consistent believer in the doctrines of Christian Science as taught in

[6] *Miscellaneous Writings,* p. 140.

a book entitled "SCIENCE AND HEALTH" by Mary
Baker G. Eddy beginning with the seventy-first
edition thereof. . . .

10. Whenever said Directors shall determine
that it is inexpedient to maintain preaching, reading or speaking in said church in accordance with
the terms of this deed, they are authorized and
required to reconvey forthwith said lot of land
with the building thereon to Mary Baker G. Eddy,
her heirs and assigns forever by a proper deed of
conveyance.

11. The omission or neglect on the part of said
Directors to strictly comply with any of the conditions herein contained shall constitute a breach
thereof, and the title conveyed hereby shall revert
to the grantor Mary Baker G. Eddy, her heirs and
assigns forever, upon her entry upon said land and
taking possession thereof for such breach.

Lawyers have tried to find a weakness in the deed of trust.
Twenty-seven years after its signing, the Trustees challenged
its provisions.[7] Arguing in the Supreme Court of Massachusetts, in 1919, eminent lawyers for the Trustees con-

[7] While it is true that the position of the Directors, as supported by
the Deed of Trust of 1892, was challenged, nevertheless this litigation was
concerned, largely, with another Deed of Trust — Mrs. Eddy's Deed of
Trust of 1898 by which the Trustees for The Christian Science Publishing
Society was established.

During the litigation public attention was focused on this Deed of Trust
of 1898, but the Court's decision — upholding the right of the Directors to
remove Trustees and thus control the management of the Publishing Society — also was based upon the Deed of Trust of 1892, as well as the
Church Manual, and upon Mrs. Eddy's arrangements through which the
powers exercised by the First Members were transferred to The Christian
Science Board of Directors.

tended — unsuccessfully — that the members of the Board of Directors were not church officers and, hence, were not authorized to act under the By-Laws of the Church. Counsel for the Trustees claimed:

". . . May I offer this suggestion, that these gentlemen [the Directors] had been appointed under the name of Directors, although under the Deed of Trust they were thus constituted, and the recognition of them as Trustees under the Deed of Trust does not make them Church officers. I am merely stating our contention. And your Honor will observe that no evidence whatever is offered that the First Members or anybody else ever created an office in the Church of Directors of The First Church of Christ, Scientist, or elected anybody to that office. These gentlemen were appointed under a Deed of Trust, and when we refer to the Christian Science Board of Directors we refer to those under the trust until there has been some other creation by these people."

And claimed again:

"If your Honor please, we desire to call your attention to the fact that here we begin to deal with By-Laws which it is alleged the Directors passed. We have pointed out . . . the Directors were not Church officers at all."

Counsel for the Directors interposed: "Pardon me for interrupting, but haven't we had this argument over and over again?"

Ignoring the interruption, counsel for the Trustees continued: "We therefore object on the ground that the Directors had no authority, not being Church officers, or officers of the Church at all, to pass anything which could be called a By-Law, or accept a Manual. I am not speaking about anything that Mrs. Eddy may have authorized. I am talking about the absolute want of authority of these men who were not even officers of the Church; and on that additional ground we desire to object to this book." [The *Church Manual.*]

Familiar with customary sort of church organization, it was not easy for the attorneys of the Trustees to understand that in establishing the deed of trust as she did, Mrs. Eddy provided fully for the administration of the spiritual and the temporal affairs of her Church.

In stating, "No evidence is offered that the First Members or anybody else ever created an office in the church of Directors of The First Church of Christ, Scientist, or elected anybody to that office," counsel for the Trustees stated a fact. No such evidence could be submitted, because no such election was ever held.

It was not in keeping with Mrs. Eddy's purpose to submit the office of Director to an election by First Members, or by members of the church. To have done so would have opened the office to political maneuvering and consequent danger to the teachings.

As previously said, Mary Baker Eddy *appointed* the Directors, to serve her cause, and, by giving them the privilege of voting among themselves, she made it mandatory that they continue so to serve her cause — even though she was absent in person — by serving the *Manual of The Mother Church, The First Church of Christ, Scientist, in Boston, Massachusetts.*

In deciding in favor of the Board of Directors, the Court merely confirmed Mrs. Eddy's unique way of keeping her Church within the circle of her teachings.

Confirmed, too, the authority of the *Church Manual,* which was another of the extraordinary developments to come out of Pleasant View.

CHAPTER SIXTEEN

"Acknowledged as Law by Law"

To insure her teachings, Mary Baker Eddy had to insure her Church. To protect her Church is the important function of the *Church Manual.*

As with her other writings, the purpose of the *Church Manual* is to lift the individual above an exaggerated belief in the power of matter and into the upward course of Truth; to redeem the automatism of worn phrases with the freedom of Spirit; and to develop man's natural kinship into strong sensitivity with the universal Mind. In Mrs. Eddy's teachings, the church exists for the people, and not the people for the church. Her assurance of this is found in *Miscellany* (pages 251–252) in her words, "Adhere to the teachings of the Bible, Science and Health, and our Manual, and you will obey the law and gospel."

As with *Science and Health,* the *Manual* was not completed quickly. In agreement with the instruction "spiritual ideas unfold as we advance," [1] *Science and Health* and the *Manual* each required many revisions. In the *Manual* are affirmations of the same principles she expressed in her other writings. Mindful of the exaction, "Take heed therefore how ye hear," [2] what she was doing was to require of the individual that he hear with his own ears.

It is this *Church Manual,* unique in religious history, that

[1] *Science and Health,* p. 361.
[2] Luke viii. 18.

was "acknowledged as law by law," that, in 1919, the Trustees sought, unsuccessfully, to refute.

A dozen years, and more, before this court action was begun, Mrs. Eddy prophesied to a member of her household, Clara Shannon, that there would be a time when the *Church Manual* "will be acknowledged as law by law."

From the time of the first organization in 1879, Mrs. Eddy had written the rules of her Church, but with the dedication of The Mother Church, and the rapid increase in its membership, she saw the need for a permanent procedure in church government. She knew the danger in church dissension, and if The Church of Christ, Scientist, in Boston, was to survive, she believed it would have to be protected by rules that would be the "fruit of experience and the result of prayer." [3]

In the early summer of 1895 she appointed Julia Bartlett, Edward P. Bates, Septimus J. Hanna, and William B. Johnson as a committee to make recommendations for the preparation of "a church manual." As for her own effort in putting together the publication, she did as she always did — she turned to within herself.

In *Miscellaneous Writings* (p. 148) she wrote of these preparations:

> The Rules and By-Laws in the Manual of The First Church of Christ, Scientist, Boston, originated not in solemn conclave as in ancient Sanhedrim. They were not arbitrary opinions nor dictatorial demands, such as one person might impose on another. They were impelled by a power not one's own, were written at different dates, and

[3] *Miscellany*, p. 343.

as the occasion required. They sprang from necessity, the logic of events, — from the immediate
demand for them as a help that must be supplied to
maintain the dignity and defense of our Cause;
hence their simple, scientific basis, and detail so
requisite to demonstrate genuine Christian Science, and which will do for the race what absolute
doctrines destined for future generations might not
accomplish.

The first edition of the *Church Manual* was ready in the
autumn of 1895, with announcement of its publication being
made in the October issue of the *Journal*.

Between brown cloth covers, this first edition contains
thirty-nine pages, was printed by the Barta Press, and was
copyrighted by James A. Neal and Thomas A. Hatten. The
contents are under these headings: "Church Officers,"
"Formation of the Church," "Church Tenets," "Church
Rules," "By-Laws," "Instructions to Teachers," "Forms of
Application for Membership," "Deed of Trust," "Finance
Committee," and "Explanatory Note."

Church officers, listed on page four, are as follows:

Rev. Mary Baker Eddy, PASTOR EMERITUS. Ira O. Knapp,
Joseph Armstrong, Stephen A. Chase, and William B. John-
son, CHRISTIAN SCIENCE BOARD OF DIRECTORS; Edward P.
Bates, PRESIDENT; FIRST READER: Septimus J. Hanna;
SECOND READER: Mrs. Eldora O. Gragg; CLERK OF CHURCH:
William B. Johnson; TREASURER: Mrs. Mary F. Eastaman.

Except for two paragraphs — Formation of the Church —
the *Manual* was prepared by Mrs. Eddy. The paragraphs
that were written by the Committee of Four follow:

On the twenty-third day of September, 1892, by the instruction of our beloved Teacher, Rev. Mary Baker Eddy, twelve of her students and church members met and reorganized, under her jurisdiction, the Christian Science Church and named it, *The First Church of Christ, Scientist.* At this meeting twenty other of Mrs. Eddy's students and members of her church were elected members of this church; those with others that have since been elected are to be known as "First Members." The Church Tenets, Rules, and By-Laws as prepared by Mrs. Eddy were adopted.

THE FIRST CHURCH OF CHRIST, SCIENTIST, IN BOSTON, MASS., is designed to be built on the rock, Christ; which includes the understanding and demonstration of Truth, Life, and Love, healing and saving the world from sin, and death. Thus to represent the church universal, and to reflect the church triumphant.

It is apparent that Mrs. Eddy approached the writing of the *Church Manual* with the single purpose of making it a shield that would protect her writings, and establish their use. Written for this single purpose, the *Manual* clothes the Christian Science Board of Directors with their great responsibilities, although, in 1895, most of the responsibilities were vested in the First Members.[4]

---

[4] In 1901, and in heeding a request by Mrs. Eddy, the First Members adopted this By-Law: "The business of The Mother Church hitherto transacted by the First Members shall be done by its Christian Science Board of Directors." In 1903, the First Members became known as Executive Members. From 1901 until 1908, when the titles were abolished, the Executive Members had no church function except as Readers, or as President. Only they were eligible for these duties.

In addition to provisions for holding quarterly meetings, and choosing candidates for church membership, Article II, which consists of four sections, provided that First Members should "attend to the transaction of any church business that may properly come before the meeting."

In SECTION 3, of the same Article, it was required that "if the First Members shall become less than forty in number [the number varied from twelve to one hundred] they shall regain this number, and they shall be persons who have proven themselves, in successive years, strict adherents to the doctrines and practice inculcated in *Science and Health with Key to the Scriptures*. These First Members shall have the same power to act for this Church as the incumbents"; and, to provide against any tampering with this Article and Section, it was stated that "this Rule shall neither be amended nor repealed except by unanimous vote of this Church."

Seven First Members provided "a quorum for the purpose of transacting business for the Church."

The First Members were authorized to expel members; they could place a teacher on probation, or restore him to good standing; they fixed the salaries of the church readers; as Mrs. Eddy made changes, or wrote new By-laws, the First Members adopted them; from 1898 until 1901, and acting together, the First Members and the Directors were authorized to remove Trustees of the Publishing Society.

As for the Directors, the first edition of the *Church Manual* limited their duties to:

Responsibility for conducting services in The Mother Church; election of church officers; selection of Readers and, after approval of the selections by Mrs. Eddy, the task of notifying candidates of their appointments; removal of a

Reader who "is found at any time inadequate or unworthy"; and, with Mrs. Eddy, the choice of the publisher of *Science and Health.* They acted to make sure that "a person who is not suitable . . . to publish the Christian Science textbook, shall in no manner be connected therewith, nor with the house whence it is issued."

Except for the transfer of responsibilities from the First Members to the Directors, Mrs. Eddy made no changes in the basic provisions as first set down in 1895, and as last set down in 1908.

"At different times, and as the occasion required," there were deletions and, of course, additions as well as clarification, but she looked upon the *Church Manual* as she looked upon the church edifice.

Each was "in concession to the period"; and she made it plain that she considered it a concession, by writing: "Will those beloved students, whose growth is taking in the Ten Commandments and scaling the steep ascent of Christ's Sermon on the Mount, accept profound thanks for their swift messages of rejoicing over the twentieth century Manual? Heaps and heaps of praise confront me, and for what? That which I said in my heart would never be needed, — namely laws of limitation for a Christian Scientist. . . ." [5]

In its first edition, as in all editions, the *Church Manual* emphasizes the requirement that the Bible and the writings of Mary Baker Eddy be accepted as the sole source for teaching and for learning Christian Science:

> To become a member of THE FIRST CHURCH OF CHRIST, SCIENTIST, IN BOSTON, MASS., the applicant must be a believer in the doctrines of Christian Science, according to the platform and teaching

[5] *Miscellany*, p. 229.

contained in the Christian Science text-book, *Science and Health with Key to the Scriptures,* by Rev. Mary Baker Eddy. The Bible, and the above-named book, with other works by the same author, must be his only text-books for the self-instruction and practising metaphysical healing. . . .

[Church Rules, Article IV, SECTION I.]

A member of The Mother Church who is professionally teaching or healing, but is disobeying the Church rule, or the C.S.A. by-law pertaining thereto, as published in the *Christian Science Journal* of April, 1895, — shall be dropped from Church membership.

[Church Rules, Article IX, SECTION I.]

The following is the C.S.A. By-Law referred to, as copied from the April number of the *Christian Science Journal,* 1895, pages *a* and 3:

Christian Scientists who are letterly qualified and specially spiritually fitted for teachers can teach annually three classes.[6] Each class must consist of about thirty-three students, carefully selected, and such only as have good past records, and promising proclivities toward Christian Science. The teacher shall hold himself morally obligated to promote the progress of his students, not only during the class term, but after it, and to watch well that they prove sound in sentiment, and practical in Christian Science.

[Article IX, SECTION 2.]

---

[6] Teachers now are limited to one class each year. Each class must contain not more than thirty students.

Teaching Christian Science shall not be a question of money, but of morals and religion, healing and uplifting the race. Teachers shall form Associations, and for the first three years convene as often as once in three months . . . Teachers shall persistently and patiently strive to educate their students in conformity to the unerring wisdom and law of God, and shall enjoin them to habitually study the *Scriptures,* and *Science and Health with Key to the Scriptures.*

[Church Rules, Article IX, SECTION 3.]

If a member of this Church is found trying to practice, or to teach Christian Science contrary to the statement hereof in its textbook *Science and Health with Key to the Scriptures,* it shall be the duty of this Church to admonish that member according to the Church rule, then if said member persists in misteaching and malpractice, his or her name shall be dropped from the Church record.

[Church Rules, Article IX, SECTION 5.]

Having found their worth, Mrs. Eddy used the *Church Manual* to establish them as the permanent pastors of her church.

In SECTION 1 of Article II of the Church By-Laws, she directed:

I, Mary Baker Eddy, ordain the Bible, and SCIENCE AND HEALTH WITH KEY TO THE SCRIPTURES, Pastor over THE MOTHER CHURCH, — THE FIRST CHURCH OF CHRIST SCIENTIST, IN BOSTON, MASS., — so long as the Church is satisfied with this Pastor.

Later, she removed the qualification to make the By-Law read as Article XIV, SECTION I, now reads:

> I, Mary Baker Eddy, ordain the BIBLE, and SCIENCE AND HEALTH WITH KEY TO THE SCRIPTURES, Pastor over The Mother Church, — The First Church of Christ, Scientist, in Boston, Mass., — and they will continue to preach for this Church and the world.
>
> [Article XIV, THE CHRISTIAN SCIENCE
> PASTOR: **Ordination.** SECTION I.]

In addition to the change, she added a second section, **The Lesson-Sermon,** to this By-Law:

> The subject of the Lesson-Sermon in the morning service of The Mother Church, and of the branch Churches of Christ, Scientist, shall be repeated at the other services on Sunday. The correlative Biblical texts in the Lesson-Sermon shall extend from Genesis to Revelation.
>
> [*Church Manual,* page 58.]

In delegating the responsibility of watching over the affairs of The Mother Church to the Board of Directors, Mrs. Eddy specified in the first edition of the *Manual* that it was incumbent upon them when selecting "a male and a female reader, one to read the Bible, and one to read Science and Health with Key to the Scriptures," to make sure they were "intelligible readers and exemplary Christians." It was required that these Readers be Christian Scientists, that they "devote a suitable portion of their time in preparation for reading the Sunday lesson, a lesson on which the prosperity of Christian Science largely depends. They must keep themselves unspotted from the world, uncontaminated with evil, that the mental atmosphere they exhale shall promote health and holiness, even that spiritual *animus* so universally needed."

Readers were forbidden to read "from copies or manuscripts." It was their duty to read from the books, and it was stipulated that when so reading they should announce the full title of the book when beginning to read from it, and also identify, by name, "the author of the text-book."

The required use of Mrs. Eddy's name when quoting from her writings is a sometimes misunderstood event in Christian Science services, and in Christian Science lectures. It came about this way:

As has been told, Mrs. Eddy had many imitators in the early years of her work. Not only did the imitators set up colleges and academies and publications under the banner of Christian Science, but they practised what they called Christian Science healing, and conducted what they called "Christian Science services" in places they called "Christian Science churches." It was the contention of each — and there were many groups contending the same thing — that their teachings were the true teachings.

When, in August 1889, Mrs. Eddy recommended to her Church in Boston that it "lay aside all that is ceremonial, even in appearance in our church [7] . . . read selections from a chapter in the Bible, and if agreeable to pastor and church, a corresponding paragraph from *Science and Health*," she took the first step in distinguishing between her church service and all others. She took the second step in December 1895 when she established the Bible and *Science and Health*

[7] This included baptisms, weddings and funeral services.

with Key to the Scriptures as the two textbooks, and as the *only* preachers in her Church.

In 1892 Mrs. Eddy established the procedure of using her own name to identify all Christian Science services and lectures.

Observing uneasiness among newcomers in the congregation over the identification of *Science and Health* as the textbook of Christian Science, the Reader in a Midwestern church made inquiries and learned that the strangers were recent followers of the teachings of Emma Hopkins. Conversation disclosed there was a lack of acceptance among them that *Science and Health* was such a textbook, and the Reader took the matter to her teacher, Laura E. Sargent.

Mrs. Sargent explained Mrs. Eddy's wishes and the Reader was instructed to say, before opening the book at Sunday services, "I will read from our textbook, *Science and Health,* by Rev. Mary B. G. Eddy, the Discoverer and Founder of Christian Science"; and, in explaining the instructions, Mrs. Sargent "pointed out the error that would separate the book from its author, and told [the student] that these few words of truth spoken in love each Sabbath was a treatment by which we could meet the false claim, and in justice to our beloved Cause, and our Leader, it must be done."

The Reader reported back that "she had followed the instructions, and the noise all ceased, and not one objection was being made." Mrs. Sargent related the incident to Mrs. Eddy, recalled the result and, with Mrs. Eddy's consent, sent out letters suggesting that in accordance with the procedure already established "every pulpit where Christian Science is preached . . . take the same line of action."

But, if "not one objection" was made by the recent followers of Mrs. Hopkins, many objections were made by

Julius Dresser, and others. Determined to destroy Mrs. Eddy's teachings, Julius Dresser and others sought to deny her wish to distinguish her Church from those of her imitators — as once they had sought to deny her authorship of *Science and Health*. Now they accused her of using the pulpit to advertise herself; accused her of destroying the personalities of individual preachers, and of projecting her own; accused her of stealing a position which did not belong to her.

She did not dismantle her plan, or remodel it on another plan. Important to her was not what was being attempted, but what would be the result. Believing she was thinking wrongly unless she was thinking in terms of Christian Science, Mrs. Eddy watched, very carefully, the result of the general letter to the churches.

Not all the churches accepted the suggestion, but enough of them did for the practice of identifying Mrs. Eddy as the "Discoverer and Founder of Christian Science" to be well-tested by the time of the dedication services in The Mother Church on January 6, 1895. The suggestion was found good, but not so protective of the teachings as Mrs. Eddy's requirement that there should be two Readers, "one to read the Bible, and one to read *Science and Health with Key to the Scriptures.* . . . The readers from these books shall commence by announcing their full titles, and the name of the author of the text-book."

In April 1895, this method of identification was made uniform in all Christian Science churches.[8]

[8] On January 25, 1900, the present order of Sunday services in all Christian Science churches was published in the *Sentinel:* "1: Hymn; 2: Reading of a Scriptural Selection; 3: Silent Prayer, followed by the audible repetition of the Lord's Prayer with its spiritual interpretation; 4: Hymn; 5: Announcing necessary notices; 6: Solo; 7: Reading the Explanatory

Mrs. Eddy's great defense against her imitators was in making her book and her name inseparable. By so doing she gave everyone the opportunity to understand that as Jesus, in His teachings, laid the foundation for the fullest possible life, so she, in her teachings, offered nothing in the way of a short-cut. This was why she wrote the *Church Manual* as she did — and made it the law of her Church.

Convinced there were no short-cuts to spiritual understanding, she made no concessions to pretense. In making her *Manual* the law of her Church, and by conferring no powers other than responsibility, she prevented the substitution, or inclusion, at any future time of any ceremony that would distract her followers from the tasks assigned to them.

She made this position additionally secure by stating in the *Church Manual:*

> No new Tenet or By-Law shall be adopted, nor any Tenet or By-Law amended or annulled, without the written consent of Mary Baker Eddy, the author of our textbook, SCIENCE AND HEALTH.
> [Article XXXV, SECTION 3.]

. . . And secured it again by writing to the Christian Science Board of Directors on February 27, 1903:

Note on first leaf of *Quarterly;* 8: Announcing the subject of the Lesson-Sermon, and reading the Golden Text; 9: Reading the Scriptural Selection, entitled 'Responsive Reading,' alternately by the First Reader and the congregation; 10: Reading the Lesson-Sermon. (After the Second Reader reads the Bible references of the first Section of the Lesson, the First Reader makes the following announcement: 'As announced in the explanatory note, I shall now read correlative passages from the Christian Science text-book, SCIENCE AND HEALTH WITH KEY TO THE SCRIPTURES, by Mary Baker Eddy)'; 11: Collection; 12: Hymn; 13: Reading The Scientific Statement of Being, and the correlative SCRIPTURE according to I John iii.1–3; 14: Pronouncing Benediction."

BELOVED STUDENTS: I am not a lawyer, and do not sufficiently comprehend the legal trend of the copy you enclosed to me to suggest any changes therein. Upon one point however I feel competent to advise, namely: Never abandon the By-laws nor the denominational government of the Mother Church. If I am not personally with you, the Word of God, and my instructions in the By-laws have led you hitherto and will remain to guide you safely on, and the teachings of St. Paul are as useful today as when they were first written.

The present and future prosperity of the cause of Christian Science is largely due to the By-laws and government of "The First Church of Christ, Scientist," in Boston. None but myself can know, as I know, the importance of the combined sentiment of this Church remaining steadfast in supporting its present By-laws. Each of these many By-laws has met and mastered or forestalled some contingency, some imminent peril, and will continue to do so. Its By-laws have preserved the sweet unity of this large church, that has perhaps the most members and combined influence of any other church in our country. Many times a single By-law has cost me long nights of prayer and struggle, but it has won the victory over some sin and saved the walls of Zion from being torn down by disloyal students. We have proven that "in unity there is strength."

With love as ever
MARY BAKER G. EDDY

N.B. I request that you put this letter upon our Church records. M. B. E.

In her reference to St. Paul, Mrs. Eddy probably had in mind the apostle's letter to the Corinthians (I Corinthians xii) :

> For as the body is one, and hath many members, and all the members of that one body, being many, are one body: so also *is* Christ. . . .
>
> For the body is not one member, but many.
>
> If the foot shall say, Because I am not the hand, I am not of the body; is it therefore not of the body?
>
> And if the ear shall say, Because I am not the eye, I am not of the body; is it therefore not of the body?
>
> If the whole body *were* an eye, where *were* the hearing? If the whole were hearing, where *were* the smelling? . . .
>
> And if they were all one member, where *were* the body?
>
> But now *are they* many members, yet but one body.
>
> And the eye cannot say unto the hand, I have no need of thee; nor again, the head to the feet, I have no need of you.

"Never abandon the By-laws nor the denominational government of the Mother Church" — here, again, is disavowal of everything that hides the basic teachings.

By establishing the *Church Manual* as law, and the Directors as servants of the *Manual*, Mrs. Eddy charged them — whoever they might be, and whenever they might serve — with the responsibility of being constantly alert to make sure that no pomp and no argument should rise to obscure her teachings, as pomp and argument have risen to obscure the teachings of the Founder of Christianity.

Because the *Manual* is Mrs. Eddy's final instruction in church government, there have been those who have said The Mother Church should be dissolved, or abandoned, because Mrs. Eddy is no longer here for consultation in matters of church administration.

It is clear that she built her Church to continue through all the days of her absence; it is clear she wrote the *Church Manual* to function without her presence.

There was her letter of February 27, 1903, to the Christian Science Board of Directors, in which she anticipated the time of her leave-taking — "If I am not personally with you, the Word of God, and my instructions in the By-Laws, have led you hitherto and will remain to guide you safely"; there is the deed of trust by which she established The Christian Science Board of Directors, and originated The Mother Church. In this document she bound herself and "her heirs, executors and administrators" to the Directors and "their legitimate successors in office forever." In this same deed of trust, there is her reference to the Board of Directors as "a perpetual body or corporation," and evidenced intention that the administrative body of The Mother Church should function perpetually.

In 1898, in another deed of trust — the one by which she organized the Christian Science Publishing Society — there are three different clauses that refer to The Mother Church as being co-existent with this trust, and the trust itself as being "perpetual."

* * *

On July 7, 1905, Mrs. Eddy transferred property at 385 Commonwealth Avenue, Boston, to the keeping of the Christian Science Board of Directors and stipulated that "the First Reader of said Church [The Mother Church] and each successive First Reader thereof forever shall have the use and enjoyment of said real estate free from all charges therefor, each so long as he or she may occupy and perform the duties of that position." The words, "each successive First Reader thereof forever," are clearly intentioned to apply to a Church in perpetuity.

There is the amendment to the By-Laws which was proposed by Mrs. Eddy on December 7, 1906, and which was adopted by the Directors the following day. This amendment is now contained in the latter part of Section 6, of Article XXIII; and it reads:

> . . . The branch churches shall be individual, and not more than two small churches shall consolidate under one church government. If the Pastor Emeritus, Mrs. Eddy, should relinquish her place as the head or Leader of The Mother Church of Christ, Scientist, each branch church shall continue its present form of government in consonance with The Mother Church Manual.

These closing words, "each branch church shall continue its present form of government in consonance with The Mother Church Manual" leads directly into SECTION 7, of Article XXIII, and the "Requirements for Organizing Branch Churches":

> A branch church of The First Church of Christ, Scientist, Boston, Mass., shall not be organized

> with less than sixteen loyal Christian Scientists, four of whom are members of The Mother Church. . . .

This By-Law, with its provision that a branch church "shall not be organized with less than sixteen loyal Christian Scientists, four of whom must be members of The Mother Church," does away with any possibility of separation from The Mother Church, and confirms what the entire *Manual* sustains:

An indivisible Church.

The Mother Church and the branch churches are indivisible. They are one.

There are other provisions, proving Mrs. Eddy's wish that her Church continue until the time when, as she said in *Miscellaneous Writings* (page 145) "the religious element, or Church of Christ, shall exist alone in the affections, and need no organization to express it." But her making the Christian Science Board of Directors her representatives and charging them with the responsibility of transacting the business of The Mother Church does not mean that the Directors can go beyond the *Church Manual* to impose their wishes, or their will, upon members of the Church.

They cannot. They are permitted to act only within the scope of the *Manual,* and its terms are as binding on them as they were binding on Mrs. Eddy, and as they are binding on all who acknowledge themselves as members of any church of The Church of Christ, Scientist.

Writing in the *Christian Science Journal* in April 1922, Adam H. Dickey spoke of knowing "no one who ever expressed such a high regard for the Manual of The Mother Church as our Leader; nor do we know any one who has obeyed it more willingly or more implicitly than did Mrs. Eddy. She has been known to correct some simple thing she herself was doing on finding that it was not in accord with the *Manual of The Mother Church.*"

As the basic law of The Mother Church, the *Manual* contains By-Laws that apply to every phase of Christian Science. Without the *Manual,* there would be no Board of Directors, no Board of Lectureship, no Board of Education, no Committees on Publication, and none of the many departments without which there could be no Christian Science movement as it exists. It is the *Church Manual* that saves, and will continue to save, the movement from disintegration.

Mary Baker Eddy was a wise woman. Knowing her Church would be attacked, she made its government a simple, voluntary, religious organization — with individuals and literature all with responsibilities, and all in place.

She said in the *Christian Science Monitor* on November 25, 1908, that the *Christian Science Journal* has its place as a "record of the divine Science of Truth"; the *Christian Science Sentinel* is on "guard over Truth, Life, and Love"; *Der Herold der Christian Science* is designed to "proclaim the universal activity and availability of Truth"; the *Christian Science Monitor* is charged with spreading "undivided the Science that operates unspent."

Prose Works [9] *other than Science and Health* carries Mrs. Eddy's dedication as being "indispensable to the culture and achievements which constitute the success of a student and

---

[9] This book, *Prose Works*, includes *Miscellaneous Writings, Retrospection and Introspection, Unity of Good, Pulpit and Press, Rudimental Divine Science, No and Yes, Christian Science versus Pantheism, Message to The Mother Church, 1900, Message to The Mother Church, 1901, Message to the Mother Church, 1902, Christian Healing, The People's Idea of God, The First Church of Christ, Scientist, and Miscellany.*

demonstrate the ethics of Christian Science"; in the Preface
to the *Christian Science Hymnal,* the Christian Science
Board of Directors remind their fellow Christian Scientists
that "woven through the structure of this Hymnal, with its
songs of praise and gratitude to God, is the thought contained in the 'Daily Prayer' of Christian Scientists, 'May
Thy Word enrich the affections of all mankind.' (Church
Manual, by Mary Baker Eddy, p. 41.) "

The *Christian Science Quarterly* is the messenger of the
Lesson-Sermon; the Bible is the "guide to eternal Life";
Science and Health with Key to the Scriptures is the textbook; the *Church Manual* is the Constitution of The
Mother Church; the Christian Science Board of Directors
is the administrative body; Trustees, Committees on Publication, teachers, lecturers, editors, Readers, practitioners,
and communicants all are signalmen, each with the individual responsibility of never neglecting "his duty to God,
to his Leader, and to mankind" [10] — and all are in place
when they recognize that Mary Baker Eddy is in her place,
as their Leader.

The *Church Manual* calls for such recognition in Article
XXII, Section I, of the By-Laws:

> In the year eighteen hundred and ninety-five,
> loyal Christian Scientists had given to the author
> of their textbook, the Founder of Christian Sci-
> ence, the individual, endearing term of Mother. At
> first Mrs. Eddy objected to being called thus, but
> afterward consented on the ground that this ap-
> pellative in the Church meant nothing more than a
> tender term such as sister or brother. In the year

[10] *Church Manual,* Article VIII, SECTION 6.

nineteen hundred and three and after, owing to the public misunderstanding of this name, it is the duty of Christian Scientists to drop the word *mother* and to substitute Leader, already used in our periodicals.

It is because it is such a simple form of church government that the *Manual* is a necessity. Without Rules and By-Laws, and obedience to them, The Mother Church soon would disappear. Mrs. Eddy knew this — although at one time, as shown in *Miscellany* (page 229), she believed her followers needed no guidance other than the pilot light within themselves to find their way into "the structure of Truth and Love." [11] Often in her teachings, Mrs. Eddy expresses the belief that man is properly self-governed only when he is governed by God. She considered the *Manual* to be the expression of this self-government.

In an article in the *Christian Science Journal* in April 1922, Adam H. Dickey recalled other words of Mrs. Eddy: [12]

I prayed God day and night to show me how to form my church and how to go on with it. I understand that He did show me, just as much as I understand that He showed me Christian Science, and no human being ever showed me Christian Science. Then I have no right or desire to change what God has directed me to do, and it remains for the church to obey it. . . .

Mrs. Eddy believed she was guided when she declined to organize The First Church of Christ, Scientist, in Boston, under charter from the State.

[11] *Science and Health,* p. 583.
[12] Article entitled "The Mother Church and the Manual."

The Church she visited in her prayers was not one whose dependence was in state charters, but one whose place was determined by God. Out of her prayers came the Church that must always be different from its branches. Unique in its government, it is not local to Boston, but is a Church whose door is open to the world.

As a spiritual concept, it is a Church that has no communion services; [13] it is a Church that is governed not by persons but by Tenets and By-Laws that are final and permanent instructions, a pledge of allegiance to which is required before the applicant can join.

It long was Mary Baker Eddy's conviction that God gives to everyone a place, and requires of the individual that he fill this place. With a voluntary, religious organization to guard, and with everyone in place, she believed her Church impregnable.

That is why she stressed obedience to the *Church Manual;* that is why she taught that when the *Manual* is disobeyed, The Mother Church is in danger.

There is a short essay entitled "Place," which was published in the December 1883 issue of the *Christian Science Journal,* that reflects this view:

> I believe that God has given to everyone a place, and in this harmonious creation there is no void, — nothing left out, nothing lacking, — so we may as well try to breathe without air, or think without mind, as to think we can rotate out of the divine order of being, or take any place other than our own. Others may try to usurp us; they may try to be like us; and they may move earth, and apparently

[13] When the title of Executive Member was abolished in 1908, Mrs. Eddy also abolished communion services in The Mother Church.

heaven, to gain our position; but when God has placed us there, we are there, and naught can move us out of this our rightful inheritance.

If this were understood, many warfares would cease; envy and jealousy be exchanged for the peaceful gleams of joy and gratitude; and mingling with the light of love, would bring to men new health and happiness, — yea Life immortal.

We never see the stars vying for each other's places, nor the sun and the moon at variance; nor have we seen a Paul take a Peter's place, or John the place of our Master, or *vice versa*. Each fills its own, her own, his own place, whether they have knowledge of it or not; and I, for one, would be content in the sweet consciousness that I have a place with Thee, eternal Love; and however grand or great, humble or small, I am of Thy creation; therefore Thine.

As Pastor Emeritus, Mary Baker Eddy still governs The Mother Church — The First Church of Christ, Scientist, in Boston, Massachusetts — through the *Church Manual;* still ordains the Bible and *Science and Health with Key to the Scriptures* as the pastors of her Church; and still requires that they "continue to preach for this Church, and the world."

By this act of writing the *Church Manual,* Mary Baker Eddy disclosed herself. No common person could have done it. No common person would have undertaken such a radical stand. Only persons with a love of mankind build Churches; and only persons with a love of God protect them.

CHAPTER SEVENTEEN

An Unexplained Call

ACCOMPANIED by two members of her household, Mrs. Eddy left Concord on April 1, 1895, arrived in Boston, and went from the railroad station to her church.

It was late afternoon and twilight was gathering as, seeing her church for the first time, she entered the door leading to the center aisle. Deep in meditation, she stood for a moment in the faint dusk filtering through the stained-glass windows before asking that the lights be turned on.

Seventy-four years old, her hair now all white, she walked down the aisle and slowly dropped to her knees on the first step leading to the platform. After a little while, she rose, went up the steps and across the platform to the reader's desk, where, softly, but quite audibly to the two who were waiting in the rear of the auditorium, she spoke the full words of the Ninety-first Psalm: "He that dwelleth in the secret place of the most High shall abide under the shadow of the Almighty. I will say of the Lord, *He is* my refuge and my fortress: my God; in him will I trust. . . ."

As she completed the Psalm, and its promise, "He shall call upon me, and I will answer him: I *will be* with him in trouble; I will deliver him, and honour him. With long life will I satisfy him, and shew him my salvation," she crossed to the other desk, the desk of the Second Reader, and repeated the two verses of the Welsh hymn:

Guide me, O Thou great Jehovah,
Pilgrim through this barren land:
I am Thine, and Thou art mighty,
Hold me with Thy powerful hand.
Bread of heaven! Bread of heaven!
Feed me now and evermore.

Open is the crystal fountain,
Whence the healing waters flow;
And the fiery cloudy pillar
Leads me all my journey through.
Strong Deliverer! Strong Deliverer!
Still Thou art my strength and shield.

She spent the night in Mother's Room in the tower of the church, and left early the following morning, with only a few knowing she had been there.

Nearly two months went by, and it was Sunday. The morning services of May 26 were under way and the congregation was singing when Mrs. Eddy entered the church. The June issue of the *Christian Science Journal* recorded the event, saying, "Her presence was unknown [to most] until her appearance in the aisle of the auditorium on her way to the pulpit. The services had proceeded as usual until they were more than half concluded when she stepped upon the platform. After listening to the organ and a solo . . . she stepped to the desk and without text or note addressed the congregation for upwards of twenty minutes. Her glowing words of kindly greeting, love, admonition and warning, were intently and eagerly listened to by all.[1] At the close of the benediction the audience was requested to remain seated

[1] Extracts from her address are published in *Miscellaneous Writings,* pp. 106–110.

until Mrs. Eddy passed out, as it would have been impracticable to have personally met all the large audience."

In the following January — January 5, 1896, and it was Communion Sunday — Mrs. Eddy again was in the pulpit. This, too, was an unexpected visit. She was introduced by Ebenezer J. Foster Eddy and, as before, she talked without notes. Her message, known as the "Communion Address," is printed in *Miscellaneous Writings* (pp. 120–125).

In part, she said:

> The Biblical record of the great Nazarene, whose character we today commemorate, is scanty; but what is given puts to flight every doubt as to the immortality of his words and works. Though written in a decaying language, his words can never pass away: they are inscribed upon the hearts of men: they are engraved upon eternity's tablets.
>
> Undoubtedly our Master partook of the Jews' feast of the Passover, and drank from their festal wine-cup. This, however, is not the cup to which I call your attention, — even the cup of martyrdom: wherein Spirit and matter, good and evil, seem to grapple, and the human struggles against the divine, up to a point of discovery; namely, the impotence of evil, and the omnipotence of good, as divinely attested. Anciently, the blood of martyrs was believed to be the seed of the Church. Stalled theocracy would make this fatal doctrine just and sovereign, even a divine decree, a law of Love! That the innocent shall suffer for the guilty is inhuman. The prophet declared, "Thou shalt put away the guilt of the innocent blood of Israel."

This is plain: that whatever belittles, befogs, or belies the nature and essence of Deity, is not divine. Who, then, shall father or favor this sentence passed upon innocence? thereby giving the signet of God to the arrest, trial and crucifixion of His beloved Son, the righteous Nazerene, — christened by John the Baptist, the "lamb of God."

Oh! shameless insult to divine royalty, that drew from the great Master this answer to the questions of the rabbinical rabble: "If I tell you, ye will not believe; and if I also ask you, ye will not answer me, or let me go."

Infinitely greater than human pity, is divine Love, — that cannot be unmerciful. . . .

As on the other Sunday, she left, immediately the service was ended, for Concord and Pleasant View.

The two visits brought many letters pleading for more appearances. But having established the Bible and *Science and Health* as "our only preachers," Mrs. Eddy was concerned lest there be reliance in her personality instead of her teachings. In the February issue of the *Journal*, after informing the congregation, "I shall speak in the dear Church at Boston very seldom," she instructed her followers:

The hour has struck for Christian Scientists to do their own work, to appreciate the signs of the times, to demonstrate self knowledge and self government and to demonstrate, as this period demands, over all sin, disease and death. . . .

Her visit on January 5, 1896, was Mrs. Eddy's last appearance in the pulpit of her church.

* * *

There were more than 5500 members of The Mother Church, of whom nearly eight hundred were practitioners located in thirty-seven states and foreign countries. The third annual report of The Mother Church disclosed a cash balance of $7870.72 on October 1, 1895, which was the close of the fiscal year. Expenditures for the year amounted to $10,562.91, and included in the receipts were items such as Sunday collections: $2866.97; Sunday subscriptions: $1647.68; Friday evening collections: $650.05;[2] per capita tax: $5526.31 — the last amount being the result of a yearly contribution of one dollar by each member of The Mother Church.

The largest single collection was received on December 30, 1894. This was the day The Mother Church was opened. The amount was $192.63. (In accordance with Mrs. Eddy's wish, there was no collection on January 6, 1895, the day of dedication.) In the fiscal year ending October 1, 1896, the average Sunday collection was $62.00.

Within another year there were practitioners in Brazil, England, France, Germany, and Scotland, in the four Canadian provinces of Nova Scotia, Quebec, Ontario, and Manitoba, and in all the states of the United States except Arizona, Delaware, Mississippi, and Nevada. Approximately forty-five pages of the *Christian Science Journal* were needed for church announcements and practitioners' cards. There was no uniformity in the space used, nor in the text used. In June 1896, all cards became uniform, with only the name, address, and title being published. There were more than three hundred churches, in the United States

---

[2] In the November (1895) issue of the *Journal,* Mrs. Eddy said, "I especially desire that you collect no monied contributions from the people present on that occasion." The Friday night meetings became the mid-week, Wednesday testimony meetings on June 8, 1898.

and abroad. Under date of October 30, 1895, Canada officially notified The Christian Science Publishing Society that Mrs. Eddy's books were permitted to enter that country free of duty "under the terms of Item No. 515 of the tariff."

Yet, few issues of the *Journal* appeared without containing unwelcome paragraphs telling of the jailing of Christian Scientists for practicing their religion. In most of the cases, the accusers were members of local medical societies — but not always. There were times when Christian bodies sought to put a stop to the growth of another Christian body that was building, so it was said, a new church every week. Also, in the June 1896 issue of the *Journal* there was a paragraph which spoke of trouble of a different nature: "On the 20th day of April, 1895, Mrs. Josephine C. Woodbury was admitted to probationary membership of The First Church of Christ, Scientist, in Boston, for two years. On November 6, 1895, her name was dropped from such membership. On March 24, 1896, she was reinstated. On April 4, 1896, she was finally and forever excommunicated from such probationary membership."

Penitent, apparently, Mrs. Woodbury had appealed to Mrs. Eddy by letter in February 1895, asking forgiveness for the discredit she had brought to Christian Science by her well-publicized claim to motherhood of "the Prince of Peace," the result of "an immaculate conception." On February 27, 1895, Mrs. Eddy acknowledged receipt of the letter, and told Mrs. Woodbury that responsibility for accepting the application for church membership "must rest on the First Members according to the rules of the Church."

Mrs. Eddy closed her letter by saying to Mrs. Woodbury, "May the love that must govern you and the church influence you and your motives, is my fervent wish. But remember, dear student, that malicious hypnotism is no excuse for sin. But God's grace is sufficient to govern our lives and lead us to moral ends."

Unable to wholly persuade the First Members, Mrs. Woodbury made a second appeal to Mrs. Eddy, and was informed on April 8, 1895:

> Now, dear student, try one more year not to tell a single falsehood, or to practice one cheat, or to break the Decalogue, and if you will do this to the best of your ability at the end of that year God will give you a place in our church as sure as you are fit for it. This I know. Don't return evil for evil, and you will have your reward.

Mrs. Woodbury persisted. She went to the Directors, spoke to them of the letter she had received from Mrs. Eddy under date of April 8, 1895, and wrote to her teacher requesting permission to disclose its contents to the Board of Directors and to the First Members.

Mrs. Eddy made prompt reply:

> My Dear Student:
>
> I am willing you should let them read my letter. I forgot to mention this, hence my second line to you. Now mark what I say. This is your last chance, and you will succeed in getting back, and should. But this I warn you, to stop falsifying, and living impurely in thought, in vile schemes, in fraudulent money-getting, etc. . . .[3] I speak plainly even as the need is.

[3] This was in reference to Mrs. Woodbury's practice of threatening her own students with death unless they obeyed her. One disobedient student

I am not ignorant of your sins, and I am trying to have you in the church for protection from temptations, and to effect your full reformation. Remember the M.A.M. [Malicious Animal Magnetism] which you say in your letter causes you to sin, is not idle, but will cause you to repeat them, and so turn you again from the church, unless you pray to God to keep you from falling into the foul snares. . . .

MARY B. EDDY

Instead of requiring that Mrs. Woodbury try for "one year not to tell a single falsehood or to practice one-cheat, or to break the Decalogue" before giving her a place in the church, the First Members voted in favor of "probationary membership . . . for two years."

Mrs. Woodbury, and several of her students, were assigned seats in The Mother Church, and for a number of months were faithful attendants at services. Then, Mrs. Woodbury began complaining because she was not given full membership and, at a Friday evening service, on October 25, voiced these complaints in public and, at the same time, spoke at length in justification of many of the acts which had brought odium to Christian Science. The following Monday, the First Members met and voted to drop her name from probationary membership, and made the action effective on November 6.

---

did drop dead, and Mrs. Woodbury used the incident to further frighten her followers. Also, a man named Fred D. Chamberlain charged her with alienating his wife's affections, and a woman named Evelyn L. Rowe named her as correspondent in a divorce action, claiming that her husband was giving Mrs. Woodbury practically all his earnings for the support of the Prince of Peace.

As soon as the action was taken, Mrs. Woodbury began pleading for reinstatement. She insisted her words were misunderstood. After weeks of explanation and promise, the First Members became persuaded. On March 24, 1896, they renewed her probationary status. In less than two weeks or, on April 4, the First Members were forced to act again.

Instead of keeping her promises, Mrs. Woodbury had forsaken them. This time the First Members excommunicated her, "finally and forever," and forwarded to Mrs. Eddy a documented history of Mrs. Woodbury's indiscretions.[4] After examining the record, Mrs. Eddy wrote to the Clerk of her Church under date of April 29, 1896:

> I have no chance to return this record of crimes
> except via express. God will settle her account and
> I have nothing to do with it. How prosperous our
> cause is, truly we have great cause for rejoicing.
> Oh, that God will save her in His own way.

Again Mrs. Woodbury appealed to Mrs. Eddy and, while endeavoring to persuade her teacher to intercede with the First Members, organized her own church and began conducting services. The location she chose was a hall in the Legion of Honor Building at 200 Huntington Avenue so that those who used Norway Street when leaving The Mother Church — and most did — walked toward Huntington Street, where a large sign advertised Mrs. Woodbury and her "Christian Science services."

[4] At the time the Clerk of the Church sent Mrs. Eddy the history of Mrs. Woodbury's indiscretions, he did not speak of the intention of the First Members to publish their action. It was not until June 11, 1896, when she saw the paragraph in the *Christian Science Journal,* that Mrs. Eddy knew of this additional penalty.

Mrs. Woodbury also wrote a pamphlet. Published in 1897, and entitled "War in Heaven," she declared it to be a collection of experiences in Christian Science. She wrote a series of articles in a publication called *Arene*. In this series she accused Mrs. Eddy of "trafficking in the temple," and with teaching "spiritual conception," and with "perverting and prostituting the science of healing to her own ecclesiastical aggrandizement, and the moral and physical depravity of her dupes . . ."

She published a volume of poems, entitled it *Echoes*, and was given the support of James Henry Wiggin, Mrs. Eddy's proofreader of a few years before.

. . . In Mrs. Woodbury's adherence to unusual ideas [wrote Wiggin] she has encountered something more painful than mere misapprehension — that is, misrepresentation, and what often seems like absolute persecution. . . . It is well, therefore, that this lovely volume should drop from the press "adorned as a bride for her husband," to show the writer's fine nature and lofty ideals.

Praise from Wiggin did not help: Now Mrs. Woodbury and her church attracted fewer and fewer visitors, and less and less attention; and in 1899, seeking to revive an almost spent public interest, she brought suit against Mrs. Eddy. The charge was libel.

In her Communion Sunday message to The Mother Church on June 4, 1899, Mrs. Eddy wrote: "The doom of the Babylonish woman, referred to in Revelation, is being fulfilled. This woman, 'drunken with the blood of the saints, and with the blood of the martyrs of Jesus,' 'drunk with the wine of her fornication,' would enter even the church — the body of Christ, Truth; and, retaining the heart of the harlot and the purpose of the destroying angel, would pour wormwood into the waters. . . ." [5]

Mrs. Woodbury filed suit, saying Mrs. Eddy was accusing her with being "the Babylonish woman." Mrs. Eddy replied, saying the reference was "not of an individual, but of a type."

Mrs. Woodbury was no more successful in this libel suit than she had been in another. When the Boston *Traveler* had told its readers of the divorce action of Evelyn I. Rowe, who charged her husband with spending most of his earnings in supporting "the Prince of Peace," Mrs. Woodbury had sued that newspaper and lost. As for her action against Mrs. Eddy, the Court dismissed the suit after listening to one set of witnesses — the witnesses for Mrs. Woodbury.

Relatively, Mrs. Woodbury's libel suit was unimportant; but it established Edward A. Kimball as one of Mrs. Eddy's most trusted captains.

Suspecting that, as a preliminary to the suit, Mrs. Woodbury might attempt seizure of her assets, Mrs. Eddy sold and transferred all copyrights to her published works to Kimball. The contract was signed on October 9, 1899, with Mrs. Eddy's authorship being protected by a clause in a will made out and signed by Kimball. In assuming ownership, Kimball succeeded Calvin A. Frye, the latter having returned ownership of the copyrights to Mrs. Eddy on October 6, 1899, after holding it since January 12, 1896. [6]

Kimball was the Chicago businessman who was healed through Christian Science of a long illness after haunting

---

[5] *Miscellany,* pp. 125–126.

[6] Kimball owned all copyrights to Mrs. Eddy's writings until May 21, 1906, when he retransferred them to her.

doctors' offices and hospitals in the United States and Europe in search of good health.

A student in Mrs. Eddy's classes at the Massachusetts Metaphysical College in 1888 and 1889, Kimball was in charge of the presentation of Christian Science at the Parliament of Religions in Chicago, in 1893. In 1894, he became First Reader of First Church of Christ, Scientist, in Chicago, and continued in that capacity until 1898. It was while he was serving as First Reader that a new edifice was dedicated. This was in December 1897. The cost was approximately $110,000, all of which was subscribed by about 1300 persons. At the time Kimball was First Reader, the soloist was another who was to become an outstanding advocate in the cause of Christian Science — Bicknell Young.

In 1898, Kimball was invited to Concord, where he attended Mrs. Eddy's last class. He was chosen to read Mrs. Eddy's Address of Welcome to the students who were gathered in Christian Science Hall, in Concord, on November 20, 1898 — a day that, even before it was ended, was a keepsake for all who were there.[7]

[7] Class of 1898: George Wendell Adams, Effie Andrews, Anna B. White Baker, Dr. Alfred E. Baker, Edgar K. Betts, Harriet L. Betts, Julian Blain, Lulu H. Bond, Alice Seward Brown, Ezra M. Buswell, Jessie C. Chamberlain, Henrietta E. Chanfrau, Joseph B. Clark, Judge Joseph R. Clarkson, Lewis B. Coates, E. Rose Cochrane, Marjorie Colles, Emma S. Davis, Rev. Walter Dole, Mary E. Eaton, Emma Gould Easton, the Reverend Henry S. Fiske, Henrietta Foster, Caroline W. Frame, Calvin A. Frye, Camilla Hanna, Judge Septimus J. Hanna, Elizabeth W. Higman, Ormond Higman, Rose E. Kent, Edward A. Kimball, Kate Davidson Kimball, Frances J. King, Daphne S. Knapp, John Carroll Lathrop, Catherine McBean, Margaret S. McDonald, David N. McKee, the Reverend Wm. P. McKenzie, Frances Mack Mann, Joseph Mann, Albert Meehan, Albert Metcalf, Mary C. Metcalf, Frederica L. Miller, William N. Miller, Sue Harper Mims, George H. Moore, James A. Neal, Carol Norton, Edward Everett Norwood, Charles W. Pearson, Annie Louise Robertson, Nemi Robertson, Emma C.

Since the early spring of 1889 when she taught her last class in the Massachusetts Metaphysical College, it had become increasingly doubtful if Mrs. Eddy would teach again. In October 1892, she had said in the *Journal:* "I have seen within the last four months, as never before, the great need that students have of being Christian Scientists in word and deed, in their affections, aims and ambitions. For this cause, I indefinitely postpone my class. In the interest of the student and of our Cause, I do this. . . ."

There was no further public word from her until February 1896, when, in the *Journal,* she wrote: "The dear ones whom I would have great pleasure in instructing know that the door to my teaching was shut when my college closed."

On July 4, 1897, there was a hint that the time of teaching again was not too far away. In addressing 2500 Christian Scientists gathered at Pleasant View, she said:

> . . . Christian Science is not only the acme of Science but the crown of Christianity. It is universal. It appeals to man as man; to the whole and not to a portion; to man physically, as well as spiritually, and to all mankind . . . yea, it is the pearl priceless whereof our Master said, if a man findeth, he goeth and selleth all that he hath and buyeth it. Buyeth it! Note the scope of that saying, even that Christianity is not merely a gift, as St. Paul avers, but is bought with a price, a great price; and what

Shipman, J. Edward Smith, Richard Smith, Rachael T. Speakman, John H. Stuart, Mary Stewart, Daisette D. Stocking, Lida Stocking Stone, Dr. Abraham A. Sulcer, Abigail Dyer Thompson, Emma A. Thompson, the Reverend Irving C. Tomlinson. In addition, two newspaper reporters were present. They were George H. Moses, who was not a Christian Scientist and who later became United States Senator from New Hampshire, and Allan H. Robinson.

man knoweth as did our Master its value, and the price that he paid for it?

Friends, I am not enough the new woman of the period for outdoor speaking, and the incidental platform is not broad enough for me . . .[8]

"I am not enough of the new woman . . . for outdoor speaking . . . and the incidental platform is not broad enough for me."

There were some who heard in these words an intention to teach again; but they read no such meaning into identical telegrams dispatched on November 15, 1898, and promising "a great blessing" if the recipients would be present in Christian Science Hall, in Concord, at four o'clock in the afternoon of November 20, which was the following Sunday. The telegrams were dispatched to students living in places as far away from Concord as Kansas City and Memphis, so the test of their presence was the test of their obedience to a call from their Leader, even though the call gave no inkling of the purpose behind it.

Excepting for one or two, all came, although some did not arrive at the Hall until after four o'clock. The others, still with no knowledge of what was to transpire that afternoon, attended morning services in the Concord Christian Science church; and not until afterwards, when listening to the reading of Mrs. Eddy's message, did they find themselves attaching significance to the Bible text that was read in the morning of that same day:

> After these things the Lord appointed other seventy also, and sent them two and two before his face into every city and place, whither he him-

[8] *Miscellaneous Writings,* pp. 252–253.

self would come. Therefore said he unto them, The harvest truly *is* great; but the labourers *are* few: pray ye therefore the Lord of the harvest, that he would send forth labourers into his harvest. And into whatsoever city ye enter, and they receive you, eat such things as are set before you: And heal the sick that are therein, and say unto them, The kingdom of God is come nigh unto you.[9]

But now the students were not in church, they were in the Hall; and Kimball was reading:

BELOVED CHRISTIAN SCIENTISTS: — Your prompt presence in Concord at my unexplained call, witnesseth your fidelity to Christian Science and your spiritual unity with its Leader. Before informing you of my purpose in sending for you I waited for your arrival, in order to avoid the stir that it might occasion those who wish to share this opportunity, and to whom I would gladly give it at this time, if a larger class were advantageous to the students.

You were invited hither to receive from me one or more lessons on Christian Science, prior to conferring on any or all of you, who are ready for it, the degree of C.S.D. of the Massachusetts Metaphysical College. This opportunity is designed to impart a fresh impulse to our spiritual attainments, the great need whereof I daily discern. And I have waited for the right hour, and to be called of God to contribute my part towards this result. . . .

---

[9] St. Luke, 10.1, 2, 8, 9.

Kimball read the closing paragraph: "What I have to say may not require more than one lesson, this, however, must depend on results; but the lessons will certainly not exceed three in number. No charges will be made for my services." As he finished reading, Mrs. Eddy, escorted by Calvin Frye, came into the Hall.[10]

The next day the Concord newspapers described her quick, light step, her white hair, her skirt of black moire, her waist of white silk, the cape about her shoulders, and the pleasing picture she made as, sitting so straight in a high-backed, red plush chair, she spoke in anticipation of "this opportunity . . . to impart a fresh impulse to our spiritual attainments."

There were two classes, one on Sunday and one on Monday. Mrs. Eddy used the Decalogue and the Sermon on the Mount as the subjects of her teaching, and drew upon the whole Bible in giving emphasis to her words. No stenographic notes were made, but the recollections of many who were present are in the Archives of The Mother Church, and in published writings of these same students. So in agreement are their words that they can be drawn off in sentences, or in paragraphs, and yet brought together so the whole seems the work of one.

Almost without exception they speak of the "tender and happy expression on her face" as their teacher welcomed them on Monday and opened the class by asking each student in turn, "What is God to you?" Nearly all the answers were satisfactory, but the one or two replies that were con-

[10] The wording in the original text is slightly different from that which appears on pp. 243–244 of *Miscellany*. The slight changes for the book form were made by Mrs. Eddy so as to give a permanent character to the announcement.

sidered inadequate received quick correction. The first lesson lasted two hours, and Mrs. Eddy used the latter part of the time to impress upon her students the supreme importance of humility in whatever their effort.

She spoke of an earlier day when some who called for help were healed before she reached them. They were reluctant to believe the healings were the result of her prayers to God, and she became so disturbed over their unwillingness to believe that one day, when a call came, instead of turning to God at once, she made strong protestations to herself that the patient "must not get well until I get there!"

The patient was not well when she arrived. Nor was she able to heal him.

It was an unforgettable lesson. Returning home, she threw herself down and "prayed that I might not be for a moment touched with the thought that I was anything, or did anything, but that this was God's work and I reflected him."

Having established herself in her proper place, and God in His proper place, she had no further difficulty with the case.

On the second day the meeting lasted four hours,[11] during which time the emphasis was on teaching. During these four hours she returned again and again to her basic teaching:

There is one God, and man is His reflection.

In the Archives of The Mother Church are the recollections of George Wendell Adams, and in his writings is this paragraph:

[11] The first class lasted two hours. At its close Mrs. Eddy informed her students there would be but one more meeting — on the following afternoon, at one o'clock.

"She dwelt at length on the point that there could be but one full and complete reflection of one God, and that this must be the basis of all scientific deduction. She indicated that only as her students grasped this fundamental fact that one God could have but one reflection did they have the right basic sense of Christian Science, and there was no other starting point."

During the course of the afternoon Mrs. Eddy was talking about the practice of some who refuse to see evil. She said that those who refuse to have their eyes opened reminded her of the tanner who bored a hole in the door of his shop and put a fox's tail through it, with the bushy part outside.

One stranger passed the shop a number of times, always stopping to ponder the bushy tail, and the small hole that hid the body of the fox.

Finally, the tanner asked the stranger: "Are you a minister?"

"No, I am not that."

"A lawyer?"

"No, I am not that."

"Well, may I ask you what you are?"

"I am a philosopher, and I have been wondering how that fox ever went through that small hole."

This story, recalled as Mrs. Eddy told it, is from the recollections of Mary E. Eaton, who also recalled that as she finished telling the story, Mrs. Eddy commented to the effect that "human beings are always trying to find the reason for something that never happened," and said that in her experience a student who would not, or could not, see evil as something that had to be corrected, was a student who was "unteachable."

On this same afternoon of November 21, Mrs. Eddy gave a class of selected Christian Scientists what they agree was the best instruction they ever received — they tell of how she increased their understanding in healing; of how she proved the daily use of the Sermon on the Mount; brought alive the words of Isaiah, "To the law and to the testimony: if they speak not according to this word, it *is* because *there is* no light in them"; taught them "not to be weary in well doing," no matter how discouraging the task; made them individually aware, with Paul, that when "forgetting those things which are behind, and reaching forth unto those things which are before, I press toward the mark for the prize of the high calling of God in Christ Jesus."

When she finished, the more than threescore of her students crowded about her insisting that she recall her words of Sunday wherein she said, "No charge will be made for my services." She again refused, saying, "I do not want this class to be an affair of money at all."

There were other events. President of The Mother Church and Manager of The Christian Science Publishing Society, Ebenezer J. Foster Eddy was elected First Reader at the annual meeting in October 1895. The honors that had come to him, and the prominence that was his because he was the adopted son of Mary Baker Eddy, made for too great a strain.

Rumors of misconduct began reaching Concord and, despite the efforts of members of the household to prevent it, the rumors reached Mrs. Eddy. She sent for Foster Eddy. He made denials, but the rumors persisted. Among them was one that involved him with a married woman.

He was removed as Reader and, in the hope that different

surroundings would be helpful, he was sent to Philadelphia on a church assignment. He made a poor showing, and his conduct was equally poor. On March 17, 1897, Mrs. Eddy wrote to him. In effect, she told him to do no more work in her name. He refused, and she instructed the First Members to adopt a new By-Law:

> A member of this church who is a student of Rev. Mary Baker Eddy and refuses to leave a place in the field that she knows is for his or her best interest to leave . . . shall be dropped from the roll of membership and he or she be treated by this church as a disloyal student. This by-law can only be amended or annulled by the unanimous vote of every member of this Church.

As a First Member, Foster Eddy argued against adoption of the By-Law and succeeded in persuading the governing body of the Church into appointing a committee to visit Mrs. Eddy, and to make an effort to influence her to withdraw the By-Law. The effort was not successful. Foster Eddy was dropped as a member of The Mother Church. He left Boston, and his name did not appear again in Christian Science affairs for a number of years.

In April 1897, all Christian Science churches were "respectfully requested" by Mrs. Eddy "to have the First Reader read the following at the opening of the Bible lesson on Sunday":

> The Bible, and the Christian Science text-book are our only preachers. We shall now read scriptural texts, and their correlative passages from our text-book — these comprise our sermon.

The canonical writings, together with the word of our text-book corroborating and explaining the Bible texts in their denominational, spiritual import and application to all ages, past, present, and future, constitute a sermon undivorced from truth, uncontaminated or fettered by human hypothesis, and *authorized by Christ.*

The number of our Sunday lessons and the Scriptures they contain follow the International Series.

The present "Explanatory Note," which is a part of the *Christian Science Quarterly,* is different, but not a great deal. The "Explanatory Note" reads:

FRIENDS: The Bible and the Christian Science textbook are our only preachers. We shall now read Scriptural texts, and their correlative passages from our denominational textbook; these comprise our sermon.

The canonical writings, together with the word of our textbook, corroborating and explaining the Bible texts in their spiritual import and application to all ages, past, present, and future, constitute a sermon undivorced from truth, uncontaminated and unfettered by human hypotheses, and divinely authorized.

The afternoon (or evening) service is a repetition of the morning service.[12]

In this period Christian Science churches, including The Mother Church, held one service on Sunday, this being in

[12] Naturally, if there is but one Sunday service, the final paragraph is not read.

the morning. The holding of two Sunday services was being urged in branch churches, and letters of inquiry regarding the nature of such a service, if held, were coming to Mrs. Eddy's desk, at Pleasant View.

On December 10, 1897, she announced that all churches wishing to hold "a second service on Sunday" were free to do so "but the *same* Sunday lesson must be read at both services until April 1898." The qualification, "until April 1898," appears to have been little more than a precautionary formality. The practice of holding two Sabbath day services has continued to be discretionary with individual churches.

In addition to bringing more than one Sunday service, the year of 1898 brought an important change in the conduct of church services. Up to this year, the First Reader read selections from the Bible, and the Second Reader read the explanatory passages from *Science and Health*. In December, the *Christian Science Journal* carried a notice saying that the First Reader should read from *Science and Health*, and the Second Reader should read from the Bible.

It was an eventful year — a very eventful year, this year of 1898.

In January, Mrs. Eddy quieted an attempt to combine the four churches in New York City. Active in the effort was Augusta E. Stetson. Personally ambitious and already a disturber, Mrs. Stetson sought to claim New York as her own.

During the building of The Mother Church she had drawn a severe rebuke when she tried to persuade the acceptance of a gift from her of a statue, in marble, of a woman, and symbolic of Mrs. Eddy, for placement inside, or outside, the church. On that occasion — October 7, 1894 — Mrs. Eddy had instructed Foster Eddy to "stop at once Mrs.

Stetson's getting up the figure in marble. I have written her that she *must not do it. . . .*"

With its four churches, its eighty-four practitioners, its three reading rooms, and its interested thousands, the New York field was an attractive capture. In the January 1898 issue of the *Journal,* Mrs. Eddy did not mention Mrs. Stetson, but reminded her New York followers:

My Beloved Students: According to reports the belief is springing up in your midst, that the several churches in New York City should come together and form one Church! This is a suggestion of error that should be silenced at its inception. You cannot have lost sight of the Rules for branch churches as published in our Church Manual. The Empire City is large, and there should be more than one Church in it.

The Readers of the Church of Christ, Scientist, hold important, responsible offices, and two individuals would meet meagerly the duties of half-a-dozen or more of the present incumbents. I have not had the privilege of knowing two students who are adequate to take charge of three or more churches! The students in New York, and elsewhere, will see it is wise to remain in their own fields of labor and give all possible time and attention to caring for their own fields.[13]

MARY BAKER EDDY

*   *   *

[13] The wording in the original text is slightly different from that which appears on p. 243 of *Miscellany.* The slight changes for the book form were made by Mrs. Eddy so as to give a permanent character to the letter.

In January 1897, Mrs. Eddy had written in the "Preface" of a new book called *Miscellaneous Writings:* "The opportunity has at length offered itself to me to comply with an oft-repeated request: namely, to collect my miscellaneous writings published in the *Christian Science Journal* since 1883, and republish them in book form — accessible as reference, and reliable as landmarks. . . ."

Believing, as she also wrote in the Preface, that *Miscellaneous Writings* [14] was "a graphic guidebook, pointing the path, dating the unseen, and enabling [the reader] to walk the untrodden in the hitherto unexplored fields of Science," Mrs. Eddy had then stopped all teaching of Christian Science for almost exactly a year, beginning with March 14, 1897:

> The Christian Scientists in the United States and Canada are hereby enjoined not to teach Christian Science for one year, commencing on March 14, 1897.
>
> Miscellaneous Writings is calculated to prepare the minds of all true members to understand the Christian Science text-book more correctly than a student can.
>
> The Bible, *Science and Health with Key to the Scriptures,* and my other published works are the only proper instructions for this hour. . . .

[14] As *Miscellaneous Writings* may be said to cover the period between 1883–1896, so does *The First Church of Christ, Scientist, and Miscellany,* cover the years 1897–1910. Clifford P. Smith recalled in *Historical Sketches* that "Mrs. Eddy chose the titles for both of these books, and she chose the entire contents for the first of them. For the second of them, she left a collection of articles which comprises most of its contents. There were reasons for concluding that she did not intend her selections for it to be exclusive. So, when the Trustees under Mrs. Eddy's will published *The First Church of Christ, Scientist, and Miscellany,* they put into this book a few of her published articles which she had not selected for it."

Now, in March 1898, Mrs. Eddy rescinded the order, using the *Journal* to carry this "Notice":

> I hereby notify the field that on March 1st the year expires in which Christian Scientists were requested to abstain from teaching. Today my message to you is that loyal students from the Massachusetts Metaphysical College who have proven themselves good and useful teachers may instruct two classes of not over thirty (30) students during this ensuing year. [Later changed to one class of 30 students yearly.] May our God that is Love teach us this year and every year how to serve Him. May the dear, faithful laborers who are not required to teach this year "wait patiently on the Lord, and He will renew their strength," for that which is to come.

This has been the only period in the history of the Christian Science movement when all teaching was suspended in the United States and Canada.

Also in February 1898, in the *Christian Science Journal,* there was another important announcement. It concerned the organization of a Board of Lectureship, and it was announced in the form of a new Church By-Law:

> This Church shall establish a "Board of Lectureship." This Board shall consist of not less than three members. The candidates for membership shall be subject to the approval of Rev. Mary Baker Eddy. The members of this Board shall be elected annually by the Christian Science Board of Directors.
>
> When the need is apparent, the Christian Sci-

ence Board of Directors of the Mother Church may call on any member of this Board of Lectureship to lecture at such places and at such times as the Cause of Christian Science demands. Also, the branch Churches of Christ, Scientist, through their clerks, may apply to any member of this Lectureship for their aid, and it shall be granted them.

The lecturer's traveling expenses, and the cost of hall shall be paid by the church that employs them, unless the receipts from the lecture are sufficiently remunerative. The lecture-fee shall be left to the discretion of the lecturer.

The present candidates for the "Board of Lectureship" are as follows: Mr. Edward A. Kimball, C. S. B., Rev. George Tomkins, D. D., C. S.; Rev. William P. McKenzie, C. S., Rev. Irving C. Tomlinson, C. S.; Mr. Carol Norton, C. S.

In the *Journal,* in the following month, there was an amendment in the Church Rule. It said: "This Board shall consist of not less than three members, nor more than seven members."

The year of 1898 also brought other lasting news: The teachings had taken hold in England, and in Germany.

CHAPTER EIGHTEEN

Christian Science Abroad

IT WAS TUESDAY, May 26, two days after the celebration of Queen Victoria's birthday in 1885, that *The Times* of London published a letter containing two words new to a British audience. The words, of course, were "Christian Science," and they were contained in a letter from an American correspondent which told of MENTAL HEALING IN BOSTON, U. S. A.

Two columns were used for the printing of the letter, which identified Christian Scientists as being the largest group, and distinguished between them and other mental healers in Boston by saying that Mrs. Eddy, their Leader, taught a specific theology. While agreeing that those who said they had been healed in Christian Science appeared to be truthful, the correspondent was not convinced they had been sick or, if they were, that they had not been given medical help.

In writing about services in Hawthorne Hall, he said: "Hawthorne Hall, where the Christian Scientists worship, is thronged for an hour before the time of service each Sunday. So eager are the people to hear that after the standing room is all taken people crowd around outside the doors, where they catch only an occasional word or two. The service consists of ordinary devotional exercises, preceding a sermon by Mrs. Eddy."

Editorially, *The Times* found the idea of mental healing

"entertaining," was amused by the credulity of Americans, and observed that "Boston still retains a large share of the fresh receptiveness of an earlier age . . . [although] in these latter days the world refuses to be profoundly moved by the birth of a new faith." But even while being "entertained," *The Times,* in its news columns and on its editorial page, was respectful of the "new faith," saying it found Christian Science "hard to classify, since it is at once an art, a science, and a religion."

Probably, the editors of the newspapers would have been interested if they had known that, in America, Mrs. Eddy believed that London, even as Boston, still retained "a large share of the fresh receptiveness of an earlier age."

Nearly twenty years before — in 1868, two years after her own healing — Mrs. Eddy had told a student that she could introduce Christian Science "in England more readily than I can in America." From her letters and from her talks, it is evident that she was anticipating a strong development in the British Isles even before she had a single follower in them.

In 1898 and in 1899, she gave serious thought to going to London for the purpose of teaching one, or more, classes; and in 1899 she wrote a letter in which she said of London that it was "the most important field outside of the United States."

Graves Colles and his wife, Marjorie, of Killiney, near Dublin, Ireland, were the first residents of the British Isles to become Christian Scientists. Visitors to the United States in 1887, they heard about Christian Science and sent to Boston for a copy of *Science and Health.* After reading the book, they went to Boston, sought out Mrs. Eddy, and after several interviews received permission to enter her class of

March 1888, at the Massachusetts Metaphysical College.

Returning to Ireland, Mrs. Colles became the first resident to become a practitioner in the British Isles, the first to be an authorized teacher, and the first person in Ireland to become a member of The Mother Church. The date of her membership was July 1, 1893, and the first appearance of her practitioner's card in the *Christian Science Journal* was in December 1893, although she had been an active practitioner nearly five years. She also was a member of Mrs. Eddy's last class — the class of 1898.

Next among residents of the British Isles to become Christian Scientists were Marcus and E. Blanche Ward. They were living in New York when they became interested in the teachings. Receiving class instruction in New York in 1890, they returned to Belfast in 1891, where Mrs. Ward became a practitioner. Ward died in 1891, and his widow moved to England, to the town of Birkenhead, near Liverpool. Here she distributed Christian Science literature. In 1895, she was in Boston where she had further instruction. Going back to England, she began the practice of Christian Science in Bedford. She was the first practitioner in England to have a card in the *Journal,* the issue being that of September 1895. In the same month, she became a member of The Mother Church.

The first resident of England to be a member of The Mother Church was Catharine Verrall, of Falmer, near Brighton. Miss Verrall's membership was dated July 1, 1893.

About the same time, in Scotland and in Wales, there were others who were becoming interested in the teachings. In Edinburgh, Mrs. Rose Cochrane heard of Christian Science from her mother, who lived in New York and who had been healed of a serious illness by reading *Science and*

Health. In 1893, Mrs. Cochrane came to New York, took class instruction, joined The Mother Church on March 31, 1894, began practicing in Edinburgh, and placed her card in the *Journal* in 1895. She, too, was a member of Mrs. Eddy's last class in 1898.

In Wales, in 1892, Frances Williams, whose father was rector of the Church of England in Llangammarch Wells, received a copy of *Science and Health* from a friend in the United States, began its study, and later went to London, where she received class instruction. Out of consideration for her father's position, she did not begin the practice of Christian Science for a number of years, but she was the first Christian Scientist in Wales.

Marjorie Colles, E. Blanche Ward, Catharine Verrall, Rose Cochrane, Frances Williams — these were the five, the first five active Christian Scientists in the British Isles; and, helping them in their early work of explaining and demonstrating Mrs. Eddy's teachings to the English people were Hannah Larminie, Anna Dodge, Albert C. King, and Julia Field-King.

In 1888, when Mrs. Colles was a student in the Massachusetts Metaphysical College, she met Mrs. Larminie and Miss Dodge who were members of the same class. When the class ended, Mrs. Colles invited Mrs. Larminie to accompany her back to Ireland. Mrs. Eddy gave her consent to Mrs. Larminie's request for a leave of absence from her teaching duties in Chicago, and in the summer and autumn of 1888 Mrs. Larminie was in Dublin where she taught one class, in addition to being a practitioner. At Mrs. Eddy's suggestion, she went from Dublin to London.

In London, Mrs. Larminie found Mrs. Eddy's words being confused with the teachings of those who professed to be

Christian Scientists but who actually were giving instructions in mesmerism. As a result, and as she said to Mrs. Eddy in a letter dated December 14, 1888, her principal work in the British capital was "putting the dividing line between the false and the true, so that people may not be deceived." Mrs. Larminie remained in London until the middle of 1889.

In 1890, with Mrs. Eddy's approval, Anna Dodge went to London from New York, saw the same confusion that concerned Mrs. Larminie, and decided, as she said in a letter published in the October 1890 issue of the *Journal,* to "devote myself to healing, and do no teaching at all for the present — further than to recommend the textbook to all." She explained this decision by saying she thought it necessary to first "let Christian Science do the healing work," believing that when this healing was "seen, and acknowledged . . . [it would] be established for all time."

Correspondence between Boston and London students discloses many healings through the work of Miss Dodge; the same correspondence also shows only a casual interest in Christian Science. At the request of Mrs. Eddy, Mrs. Colles, then living in Monmouthshire, went to London to assist Miss Dodge in organizing the first Christian Science services to be held in England. This was in October or November, 1890. The services were conducted in Miss Dodge's home at 48 Stanhope Gardens. Later, when Miss Dodge moved to 10 Hanover Square, services were held at this address. The services were advertised in the *Christian Science Journal* from February to December, inclusive, in 1890, and were the first church services advertised in the *Journal* from the British Isles.

Miss Dodge returned to New York in the fall of 1891.

After her departure, no public Christian Science services were held in England for nearly four years.

There were occasional visitors from the United States — but not until 1894, when E. Blanche Ward left her home in the country and settled in London, was there a resumption of regular, systematic work. Twice weekly, for more than a year, meetings were held in the drawing room of Mrs. Ward's London home. The drawing room became too small; in February 1896 one of the Portman rooms, at Baker and Dorset Streets, was rented. Mrs. Ward was First Reader, and the post of Second Reader was filled by different students.

At the time the only practitioners advertising in the *Journal* were Mrs. Ward, in London, and Mrs. Cochrane, in Edinburgh. Mrs. Colles and Miss Verrall were practitioners, but were not so advertised. In 1896, in the late winter, Mrs. Colles wrote Mrs. Eddy asking that a teacher be sent to London. Mrs. Eddy sent Julia Field-King, a student in one of her classes in 1888. Mrs. Field-King had been attracted to Christian Science several years previously, after having practiced medicine in Chicago for more than ten years. She arrived in London on April 1, 1896. Arriving there at almost the same time, although not related, was another Christian Science practitioner, Albert G. King.

Interest in the teachings began to grow. As Portman Hall was now becoming crowded, a search began for quarters large enough to serve as church. After a great deal of negotiating for an unexpired sixty-three-year lease on a building that was a synagogue for Portuguese and Spanish Jews, Mrs. Colles bought the lease at a cost of two thousand pounds. An additional twenty-five hundred pounds was needed to adapt the interior of the building to Christian Science services, and a committee was appointed to receive subscriptions.

Money came from Mrs. Eddy (205 pounds), from students of Mrs. Field-King in the United States and Canada (254 pounds, 9 shillings), from the patients of students (85 pounds, 9 shillings), and the balance of nearly two thousand pounds from the small group who acknowledged the teachings, or who were beginning to be interested.

Among those who were active in Christian Science in the British Isles in 1896, or thereabouts, were Lady Abinger, Florence H. Boswell, Richmond I. Cochrane, Lord and Lady Dunmore,[1] Adrienne Eckford, Sarah J. Winslow, and Eleanor Winslow. Among others who were active, and who became teachers, were Hester Grant, Lady Victoria Murray, C. Lilias Ramsay, Violet Spiller (afterwards the Honorable Mrs. Hay), and Mabel S. Thomson.

The church was dedicated on Sunday, November 7, 1897. It was the first Christian Science church in what was then the world's largest city and the first Christian Science church to be dedicated in Europe.

As told in the December 1897 issue of the *Journal,* "The Dedicatory Service was simple, but most appropriate, and was attended by about three hundred people. Music was followed by readings from the Bible and *Science and Health,* and silent prayer. After a well-rendered selection by a quartette of professional singers well-known in London musical circles, and earnest Christian Scientists all, Sir Douglas Galton read a short history of the movement in London from its inception."

Within another twelve years the spread of the teachings was so rapid that, in 1909, there were six churches in Lon-

[1] Afterwards, Earl of Dunmore. He died in 1907.

don, including the new edifice of First Church of Christ, Scientist, the corner stone of which was laid on November 29, 1904. In England, Wales, Scotland, Ireland, and the Channel Islands there were fifty-eight churches, and public auditoriums were not large enough to accommodate the crowds that surged to hear lectures by persons such as Edward A. Kimball and Bicknell Young.

In London, Edinburgh, Liverpool, Belfast, or whatever the city, whenever a Christian Science lecture was announced, special trains carried people across the islands, and boats brought them from the Continent. On April 23, 1907, nearly 8000 persons heard Young in London, and thousands were not able to enter the hall.

On May 21, 1908, Kimball wrote to Mrs. Eddy from Manchester, England:

> BELOVED TEACHER: — I have hesitated to take any of your time, but it seems to me that you will be glad to hear what I can tell you about the status of the Christian Science movement in Great Britain. I had no idea it had taken on such large proportions and was so well known and so largely discussed; moreover, I did not suppose the work was being so favorably presented and maintained by the Christian Scientists as I find to be the case. The characteristic sturdiness and earnestness and stability of the better class of people in these islands serve a very large purpose when these people become Christian Scientists. As a rule they have a high and dignified appreciation of Science itself and of what constitutes legitimate and effec-

tive practice. They have accomplished much over here, and the present situation and activity of our Cause are full of great promise.

The lectures are largely attended — sometimes crowds are unable to gain entrance — and they have received quite as much and as respectful attention from the press as is given them in America. One of the great London religious papers has announced its intention to publish the lecture which I am to give in London tomorrow night, in order that the readers of that paper and the people of that denomination (the Congregational) may have a statement of Christian Science from its advocate rather than from its opponent. The editor has stipulated that I am to speak of certain phases of the subject which he has named, and particularly that I shall tell him "something about Mrs. Eddy."

I think this is the first instance of the kind in our history. No religious paper in America, other than our own, has ever published the full text of a Christian Science lecture. In this case it is opportune, because there is to be a great meeting in June of the Church of England, and at that meeting the delegates are to discuss Christian Science. A Congregational minister said to me, "Mrs. Eddy has presented the only perfectly concatenated religious system in existence. If one accepts the premise, he must accept the conclusion. I am ready to accept the premise, because Christian Science is the only religion that gets God into the world as or through His spiritual idea, instead of as a man."

*   *   *

Mrs. Eddy gave the letter to the *Christian Science Journal* for publication, and made this comment: "Forty years ago I said to a student, 'I can introduce Christian Science in England more readily than I can in America.'"

The interest Kimball wrote about was quite a change from the interest displayed in the first public church services in the British Isles. Forty persons had been in attendance in the Portman room in February 1896.

At almost the same time (it was within a year or so) that Mrs. Colles was introducing Christian Science into the British Isles, Hans Eckert, of Cannstadt, Germany, was in the United States. Able to read and speak English, Eckert took up the study of Christian Science in 1889, had class instruction, joined The Mother Church in 1893, and returned to Germany in 1894. Of evenings in Cannstadt, and in nearby Stuttgart, he read from *Science and Health* and translated it to his friends — until, in 1904, the informal meetings grew into the Christian Science Society of Stuttgart. The first German to become a Christian Scientist, Eckert was not so successful as were others in spreading the teachings.

In that same year (1894), when Eckert returned to Germany, Frau Bertha Günther-Peterson began her studies, in Hannover. The daughter of a physician, and also the wife of one, Frau Günther-Peterson often assisted her father and her husband, and was genuinely interested in healing. She heard of Christian Science through a friend in Minneapolis who had been healed after hope of recovery had been abandoned by the attending doctors. Sending to Boston for a copy of *Science and Health,* Frau Günther-Peterson began studying, and in November 1896 was in New York receiving class instruction. In June 1897 she returned to Hannover, and announced her work by inserting a practitioner's card in the *Journal* in October of the same year.

Her first patient in Hannover was a dressmaker, Fräulein Iserman. Told by her physician that an operation was necessary if she was to be well again, the dressmaker went to see Frau Günther-Peterson. The healing was complete at the end of three weeks, and it attracted so much attention that within a year the practitioner was treating patients from eighteen cities and towns near Hannover. There were more healings, and word of them spread to many parts of Germany.

Meanwhile, in the summer of 1897, a few persons began gathering in Frau Günther-Peterson's home on Sunday mornings to listen while the woman read and translated from the Christian Science textbook. With increased attendance, rooms were rented on another floor in the same apartment building where, in March 1898, fifteen German Christian Scientists organized the first Christian Science church in Germany. They called it that, too: "First Christian Science Church, in Germany." The following year, with only twelve members, but with a Sunday attendance of three to four hundred persons, the name was changed to "First Church of Christ, Scientist, of Hannover."

In 1900, Mrs. Eddy made a gift of one thousand dollars to the building fund of the little church. The site was bought in October 1901, and a year later the building was dedicated.

It was the first Christian Science church built in Germany.

Frau Günther-Peterson was given special recognition in 1899. Because the Normal Class which she had traveled from Hannover to Boston to attend was postponed, she was made a teacher by special permission from Mrs. Eddy. Back in Hannover she began conducting classes and many of her pupils were active in the further development of the movement in Germany, and in Switzerland. Also helping in bringing Christian Science to Germany was Mary Beecher Longyear, of Marquette, Michigan, and Frances Thurber Seal, of New York.

While a visitor in Dresden in the winter of 1896–1897, Mrs. Longyear accepted a number of patients and addressed two or three gatherings. Impressed by the interest in Christian Science, she wrote of the "wonderful awakening in Dresden,[2] and upon returning to New York arranged for the sending of Mrs. Seal, and gave financial support to the effort.

Mrs. Seal's first patient in Dresden was a Russian girl who was studying to be a singer, and who was threatened by tuberculosis. The second healing was the rector of the local Episcopal church. He had been told he was suffering from Bright's disease. In the spring of 1898, after having been in Dresden since December 1897, Mrs. Seal converted one of the two rooms she was renting into a Reading Room. It was the first Christian Science Reading Room in Germany. In January 1899, she became a teacher. In so becoming, she was required to leave Dresden and establish headquarters in Berlin. Here lived Fräulein Johanna Bruno — who, probably, was the first resident of Berlin to become a Christian Scientist.

Before signing a two-year lease on an apartment, Mrs. Seal told the landlord that in addition to living quarters she wanted to use the apartment for the teaching of Christian Science. As he had never heard the words, she tried to explain them to him. Continuing to have difficulty, she told

[2] The *Christian Science Journal,* June 1899.

him she would be teaching Bible lessons. The landlord inquired as to the number of students she expected. She told him she might have as many as twenty-five, but not for two years.

The first Sunday services were held on October 1, 1899, and were attended by eight persons, one of whom was Fräulein Bruno. The next morning Mrs. Seal was asked to help a woman who had been sick for fifteen years.

The sufferer had been a concert singer, and a favorite of the Empress Augusta. When she was first taken ill, physicians said she was suffering from rheumatic gout; and when there was no improvement, the Empress, in addition to assigning her own physician to the case, requested the calling-in of medical men from other countries. Despite the efforts of the doctors, the sick woman grew steadily worse until, at the end of five years, in addition to being bedridden and blind, she was a drug addict, the result of prolonged use of morphine to dull constant pain.

The healing was done under the scrutiny of the court physicians. On New Year's Day, 1900, the woman — Frau Boese — walked down two flights of stairs in her home, rode across the city, and walked up two flights of stairs to Mrs. Seal's apartment.

Not only did the healing attract wide attention, but it brought to the services the wife and the mother-in-law of a German army officer of high rank, attentive listeners. They explained, after several services, that they were spiritualists, and suggested to Mrs. Seal that the services be expanded to include séances. Mrs. Seal refused. The two women persisted, until Mrs. Seal was forced to request that they stop coming to services.

Much offended, the women began holding meetings of

their own in Potsdam. They read from *Science and Health,* used testimonies from the *Christian Science Journal* to persuade their listeners of the effectiveness of Christian Science, and closed the meetings with spirit rappings by a medium.

Using their social positions, the officer's wife and her mother forced full attendance at the meetings, with the result that their efforts were reported to the Emperor. Wilhelm II closed the Potsdam meetings and ordered the arrest of the medium. She was found guilty of fraud, and sent to prison for five years. Nor did Mrs. Seal, and other Christian Scientists, escape the Kaiser's displeasure. Acting under orders, the police began a campaign of harassment.

In Hannover, there was loss in church membership, but not in attendance, the police making it clear that persons who withdrew from the Lutheran Church would encounter difficulties. In Berlin, Mrs. Seal was notified that the Kaiserin Augusta Victoria Saal was no longer available for Christian Science services.[3] This action was taken without warning. In the evening of the same day, it was necessary to post regular attendants along the streets leading to the building to notify people that services had been suspended until further notice. The following day Mrs. Seal's landlord ordered her to vacate her apartment.

"Unless you do," she was told, "your belongings will be set in the street."

She protested to the American embassy, and was advised

[3] Instead of twenty-five students at the end of two years, as predicted, at the end of six months more than one hundred persons had become regular attendants at Sunday services. As a result, it had been necessary to rent the Kaiserin Augusta Victoria Saal. Principal user of that building was an art school under patronage of the Empress. Countess Schoenburg von Cotta was director of the school. Occasionally, she attended services to judge their seemliness before reporting to her patron.

to see a lawyer. The lawyer said she had no choice but to obey the landlord. She was moving her belongings into another building when the police told the new landlord that it would be inadvisable for him to accept her as a tenant. She stored her furniture, and went to live with a friend. The friend was threatened with eviction unless Mrs. Seal left, at once. For weeks, and then for months, Mrs. Seal was on the move, never remaining in one place more than two or three days. She kept in touch with her pupils by calling on them in their homes, and by gathering them into small groups in their homes while she read the Lesson-Sermons.

Finally she heard of a man who owned a home in the city, but who spent nearly all his time in the country. Thinking he might be less susceptible to fear of the police, she went to him, told her story, and asked for permission to rent part of his home. He agreed, but on condition that she restrict her callers to a few persons, and that she hold no services on the property. She agreed, and found another building, the owner of which was an American. He rented her enough space for a Reading Room, and for the holding of church services. He, too, imposed a condition. He required that in the holding of services, there could be no singing, and no music.

After several months of holding services under these conditions, Mrs. Seal heard of a hall that could be rented, with no restrictions.

The neighborhood she visited was poor, being in one of the older sections of Berlin. The building, used as a dancing school, was set back from the street. To reach it, it was necessary to walk under a crumbling archway, and through a yard used for storing carts. But the rent was reasonable, and the owner was not disturbed when she tried to impress upon him that he might have trouble with the police if he rented his property for the holding of Christian Science services. He said he was an Italian citizen, and not subject to the wishes of the German police so long as he obeyed the law.

Eight months had passed since Kaiserin Augusta Victoria Saal had been closed to Christian Science services.

A week, or two, afterwards two policemen appeared at Sunday services in the new location. They presented a list of questions, and demanded answers. Thinking of her landlord's avowal of Italian citizenship, Mrs. Seal went to the American embassy and obtained a letter that identified her as an American citizen. Then, accompanied by Baroness Olva von Beschwitz, a student, she called on the President of the German police.

Although treated with hostility, the two women — one an American, one a German — insisted on an explanation for the continued interference with the practice of Christian Science. The official finally admitted that "in the criminal code of Germany, there is not one line that prevents anyone from worshiping God in his own way," and was immediately reminded by Mrs. Seal that she was not a criminal and, as an American citizen, she expected the German police to live within their own rules.

There was no further interference with Christian Science in Germany for more than forty years — until all Christian Science literature was confiscated, all Christian Science churches were closed, and a great many Christian Scientists were put into concentration camps, by order of Adolf Hitler.

Slowly, and steadily, the movement found its way into Holland, Switzerland, France, Italy, Norway, and Sweden, to South Africa, Johannesburg, and Patchefstroom, to China, to Australia, and to the Philippines. In 1909, there were five churches in Germany, two in Holland, two in Switzerland, one in France, one in Italy, one each in Norway and Sweden, two in the Transvaal, one in Hong Kong, four in Australia, and one in the Philippines. The words "Christian Science Practitioner" were being seen in Belgium, in Russia, in India, and in the Argentine.

There was growing interest in Christian Science in Canada as early as 1880, and Canadian members were in attendance at the Boston and New York meetings in 1886 when the National Christian Scientist Association was organized. In 1895, there was a "large number of members. Toronto and Montreal have strong churches, comparatively, while in many towns and villages single believers or little knots of them are to be found." [4]

Although the Board of Lectureship was not appointed until 1898, lecturing was not a new activity with Mrs. Eddy.

In 1862 she spoke at Colby College, Waterville, Maine, her words being against human slavery in a lecture entitled "The South and the North." Two years later, in Warren, Maine, she denounced spiritualism, and, in *Retrospection and Introspection*, she recalled being invited to "speak before the Lyceum Club, in Westerly, Rhode Island," not long after her healing in 1866; and also recalled how a demonstration of healing in Christian Science "so stirred the doctors and clergy that they had my notice for a second lecture pulled down, and refused me a hearing in their halls and churches."

In these early days of Christian Science, and as she told Irving C. Tomlinson, "in order to interest people, I was forced to adopt many ways and methods. I would lecture to a people and at the conclusion of the address, they would

[4] *Montreal Daily Herald,* February 2, 1895.

seem to grasp little, if anything. One evening, after speaking for a few minutes, I asked all to rise who understood what I was saying, and not one rose to his feet." [5]

Tomlinson also recalled that it was Mrs. Eddy's conviction that "the way to establish the Cause through reason is through writing and preaching, teaching and lecturing. This is temporal. But the way to establish the Cause through revelation is by healing, and this is permanent."

In the Archives of The Mother Church are cards which speak of lectures to be given by Mrs. Eddy soon after she moved from Lynn to Boston.

One such card reads:

> Invitation. Mary B. Glover Eddy, author of "Science and Health," will interest all who may favor her with a call at her rooms with her Parlor Lectures on Practical Metaphysics, and the influence that mind holds over disease and longevity.
>
> How to improve the moral and physical condition of man to eradicate in children hereditary taints, to enlarge the intellect a hundred per cent, to restore and strengthen memory, to cure consumption, rheumatism, deafness, blindness and every ill the race is heir to. Place, College Rooms Columbus Ave. 569 Time, Thursday 3 P.M. Price $0.25.

Of course, Mrs. Eddy, herself, was the first Christian Science lecturer; but, in 1880, or thereabouts, she sent George D. Choate to Portland, Maine, to "teach, heal and lecture." In effect, this was one event that led to the es-

[5] *Twelve Years with Mary Baker Eddy.* Copyright, 1945, The Christian Science Board of Directors, Boston, Massachusetts.

tablishing of the Board of Lectureship. Another was the
effort of early students in their house-to-house work in sell-
ing copies of *Science and Health,* and still another contribution was the work of the Christian Science Dispensaries.

With its founding, in 1892, The Mother Church established a Board of Missionaries "to supply sections that have
no healers or teachers in Christian Science." From 1897
until 1906, the *Church Manual* provided for the electing of
"experienced, competent Christian Scientists for missionary
work," and also stipulated that, as missionaries, they were
to go wherever sent by the Christian Science Board of Directors "to do whatever is needed and required of them —
be it to fill a vacancy, or to spread the gospel of Christian
Science, or to correctly propagate this Science in whatever
locality it is most needed." [6]

Thus, with a Board of Lectureship dating from 1898,
there were both lecturers and missionaries, up to 1906, when
the Board of Missionaries was discontinued. In these years
it was the responsibility of the Directors to prevent conflicts
between missionaries and lecturers in their public duties,
just as beginning in 1908, it became the responsibility of the
Directors to "call on any member of this Board of Lectureship to lecture at such places and at such times as the cause
of Christian Science demands." [7]

There was reluctance within the movement to accept the
Board of Lectureship when it was organized, and in some
cases only Mrs. Eddy's insistent appeals persuaded branch
churches into cooperation. They did not see the need of
lectures, and it was not until several years had passed that

[6] Sixth Edition, *Church Manual,* Article IX, to fifty-third edition, *Church Manual,* Article XXXVI.
[7] SECTION I, Article XXXII, *Church Manual.*

there was a general agreement among the branch churches as to the usefulness of this work.

In establishing the Board of Lectureship, Mrs. Eddy stipulated that she was not to be consulted as to the subjects to be discussed, or how they were to be handled, but she did emphasize the need for wisdom — and she did keep in constant communication with the lecturers, encouraging them or admonishing them, as the circumstances indicated.

She required of them, as she wrote in letters to them, that they "be careful and not berate any religion" — "be charitable toward all men" — "have a cell less in the brain and a fibre more in the heart . . . and it will do much for your lectures and in healing the sick" — "bear testimony to the facts pertaining to the life of the Pastor Emeritus," but speak of her not in praise but "only as a humble servant of our God" and reminded them that the purpose of the Board of Lectureship "is to subserve the interest of mankind, and to cement the bonds of Christian brotherhood, whose every link leads upward in the chain of being. The cardinal points of Christian Science cannot be lost sight of, namely — one God, supreme, infinite, and one Christ Jesus." [8]

Because she perceived lack of proper acknowledgment of the truth they were expressing, there was an occasion when Mrs. Eddy felt impelled to write a similar letter to two lecturers:

> . . . A real Metaphysician knows that Mind is the all and only power and the mental word inaudible more effective as a rule than the audible. Can you shelf this rule and be consistent? Do you heal the sick by physical or audible means?

[8] *Miscellany,* p. 339.

Do you ever think speak act — by reason of matter or mind? Do you declare all this affirmatively in your lectures? Then does right and the demonstration thereof depend on matter or *mind?* If the latter how are you going to act rightly and cause others to do likewise most efficiently? Is it through mind-power and how? Orally or the "still, small voice." I beg you will demonstrate *our God* in Science as the *Principle* that *moves man's actions.* . . . *Think* before you act and your thoughts will govern yours and other men's lives more than your acts can.

The first lecture by a member of the Board of Lectureship was given — appropriately — in Lynn, Massachusetts, on February 14, 1898. The lecturer was Irving C. Tomlinson, and there came to him a letter from Mrs. Eddy in recognition of his being "the first called to lecture on the basis of Lectureship and to one of the most important fields in the vineyard of our God. Well, it is ominous, full of promise. Once that city resounded to my cures. But if there is a hope eternal I feel it. God bless you, prosper the seed you sow. . . ."

On September 28, 1898, Tomlinson also gave the first lecture in The Mother Church. A few weeks before Mrs. Eddy had suggested that, instead of presenting a new lecture with each appearance, the lectures be prepared in the thought of making "one answer for several places. Take the questions uppermost in the public mind and answer them systematically in Science." This suggestion not only permitted lecturers to prepare better lectures, but enabled them to schedule their subjects in better order.

At first, lectures were given on Wednesday evenings and, sometimes, First Readers were permitted to give them. By April 1904, Christian Science organizations had been formed in universities and colleges, and were privileged to call lecturers. In 1908 and 1909, a lecturer visited Hong Kong and Capetown, and at the annual meeting in 1912, it was reported that lectures had been given throughout the world. The first Christian Scientist to complete a lecture tour of the world was Bicknell Young.

In earlier years lecturers were permitted to make as many lectures as they wished. Since 1930, however, all lecturers have been restricted to a certain number of appearances each year. The permitted number approximates three lectures weekly, across a year. Lecturers are allowed to make up their own schedules, and are paid by the church sponsoring the lecture. The fee is the same, no matter what the experience of the lecturer. If sent abroad, or if coming from abroad to the United States, the lecturer's engagements and expenses are arranged so his income remains about the same as though he were in his own land.

In organizing the Board of Lectureship,[9] Mrs. Eddy was aware of the uselessness of attempting to persuade others to believe in Christian Science. She did not then, nor did she ever, ask her listeners to believe one word of her teachings. She sought no favors, and depended upon no appeals to credulity for support of her words. She sought for her teachings only that privilege which was given to others — the privilege to be heard.

She asked only that Christian Science be considered as a

[9] Edward A. Kimball was the first Chairman of the Christian Science Board of Lectureship, and acted in this capacity until his passing in 1909. Also, he was chosen by Mrs. Eddy to teach in the Massachusetts Metaphysical College.

demonstrable science illustrative of the fact that, when properly understood, it is an idea which manifests itself in universal good.

In requiring of lecturers in Christian Science that they "be charitable to all men," she called upon them to publish brotherhood among men — in the knowledge that in all history there is not one instance where love of our fellow men has ever produced evil.

CHAPTER NINETEEN

"And What Singing It Was!"

ONE STORY said Mary Baker Eddy was completely para
lyzed, the other story said she was dying from cancer,
but both said she had thrown away *Science and Health* and
called in the medical men — yet, here she was walking up
two long flights of stairs leading to the stage in Tremont
Temple, in Boston, where, shortly, she would address the
annual meeting of the members of The Mother Church.
The date was June 6, 1899. Lacking forty days, Mrs. Eddy
was seventy-eight years old.

Coming to Boston the previous day, she was met at the
railroad station and driven to 385 Commonwealth Avenue,
the home of the First Reader. She spent the night with Judge
and Mrs. Septimus J. Hanna and, accompanied by them, she
went to Tremont Temple in the early afternoon. To avoid
the thousands who were crowding the entrances, she was
driven to a side door, where it was found that the elevator
was not in running order. Without hesitation, she began
the long climb up the stairs.

When she appeared from the wings, the audience rose
almost as a single person and stood in silence as, with Judge
Hanna as her escort, she walked quickly to her place on the
platform.

There were some who remembered a day fourteen years
before when she had come to this same platform to defend
teachings that now were being heard in India, and China,

and Australia. Unlike that other day, this was an audience that was listening, listening to every word. Wearing a gray satin dress covered with black lace, she was standing before them, saying:

MY BELOVED BRETHREN: — I hope I shall not be found disorderly, but I wish to say briefly that this meeting is a very joyous one to me. Where God is we can meet, and where God is we can never part. There is something suggestive to me in this hour of the latter days of the nineteenth century, fulfilling much of the Divine law and the gospel. The Divine law has said to us, —

"Bring ye all the tithes into the storehouse, that there may be meat in mine house, and prove me now herewith, saith the Lord of hosts, if I will not open you the windows of heaven, and pour you out a blessing, that there shall not be room enough to receive it."

There is with us at this hour this great, great blessing; and may I say with the consciousness of Mind that the fulfilment of divine Love in our lives is the demand of this hour — the special demand. We begin with the Law as just announced, "prove me now herewith . . . if I will not open you the windows of heaven, and pour you out a blessing," and we go to the Gospels, and there we hear, —

"In the world ye shall have tribulation; but be of good cheer, I have overcome the world."

The Christian Scientist knows that spiritual

faith and understanding pass through the waters of Meribah here — bitter waters; but he also knows they embark for infinity and anchor in Omnipotence.

O, may this hour be prolific, and at this time, and in every heart, may there come this benediction: Thou hast no longer to appeal to human strength, to strive with agony, I am thy deliverer. Of His own will begat He us with the Word of Truth. Divine Love has strengthened the hand and encouraged the heart of every member of this large church. O, may these rich blessings continue and be increased! It hath opened the Gate Beautiful to us, where we may see God and live, see good in Good, God All, One, one Mind, and that Divine; love our neighbor as ourselves, bless our enemies. Divine Love will also rebuke and destroy disease, and destroy the belief of life in matter.

It will waken the dreamer: the sinner, dreaming of pleasure in sin; the sick, dreaming of suffering in matter; the slothful, satisfied to sleep and dream. Divine Love is our only physician — never loses a case. It binds up the broken-hearted, heals the poor body, whose whole head is sick and whose whole heart is faint; comforts such as mourn, wipes away the unavailing, tired tear, brings back the wanderer to the Father's house wherein are many mansions, many welcomes, many pardons for the penitent. Ofttimes I think of this in the great light of the present, the might and light of the present fulfillment thereof. So shall all earth's children at last come to acknowledge God, and be one, inhabit

His Holy Hill, the God-crowned summit of Divine Science, the Church militant rise to the Church triumphant, and Zion be glorified.[1]

After the meeting Mrs. Eddy received the Christian Science Board of Directors and other friends in a suite at the Parker House before returning to Concord by train in the late afternoon. The following day the *Boston Globe* reported on her appearance: "She looked as she sat there the ideal of the gentle, kindly old lady, who had led an uneventful life, and who was enjoying the peace and quiet of a conscience-clear old age. The lines on her face were soft, and there was nothing about her in repose to indicate the force of character and genius which she is credited with possessing."

An estimated eight thousand persons, comprising a good 35 per cent of all the Christian Scientists in the world, attended the meeting. In comparison with other religious groups, their numbers were few; but their Leader was one of the most discussed individuals in the world.

In 1899, the *New York Times* was wondering how long people would be "victims of Christian Science"; and, in the same year, in the August and October issues of the *Cosmopolitan Magazine*, Mark Twain, after saying that Mrs. Eddy was "easily the most interesting person on the planet, and in several ways as easily the most extraordinary woman that was ever born upon it," denounced her as a charlatan, a crook, and a woman who regarded herself "a second Christ," or, if not that, a "second Virgin-mother."

Because of his eminence as an author and, also, because

---

[1] The wording in the original text is slightly different from that which appears on pages 131–133 of *Miscellany*. The slight changes were made by Mrs. Eddy so as to give a permanent character to the address.

his was an attack upon Mrs. Eddy, Twain's articles attracted great attention. Impelled to make reply, Mrs. Eddy did so by a letter published in the *New York Herald:*

. . . I stand in relation to this century as a Christian Discoverer, Founder, and Leader. I regard self-deification as blasphemous. . . . I believe in one Christ, teach one Christ, know of but one Christ. I believe in but one incarnation, one Mother Mary. I know that I am not that one, and I have never claimed to be. It suffices me to learn the Science of the Scriptures relative to the subject.

. . . In his article, of which I have seen only extracts, Mark Twain's wit was not wasted in certain directions. Christian Science eschews divine rights in human beings. If the individual governed human consciousness, my statement of Christian Science would be disproved; but to demonstrate Science and its pure monotheism — one God, one Christ, no idolatry, no human propaganda — it is essential to understand the spiritual idea. Jesus taught and proved that what feeds a few feeds all. His life-work subordinated the material to the spiritual, and he left his legacy of truth to mankind. His metaphysics is not the sport of philosophy, religion, or science; rather, it is the pith and finale of them all.

I have not the inspiration nor the aspiration to be a first, or a second Virgin-mother — her duplicate, antecedent, or subsequent. What I am remains to be proved by the good I do. We need much humility, wisdom, and love to perform the functions of foreshadowing and foretasting heaven within us. This glory is molten in the furnace of affliction.[2]

In the *Boston Transcript*, on March 8, 1900, there was an article reprinted from the *Independent*, a New York publication, saying rebellion had broken out in the ranks of Christian Scientists, and that "ten thousand had left the church, and more were leaving every day." In Washington, a publisher whom Mrs. Eddy had befriended, by subscribing to his publication and asking her students to do likewise, was reviling her. Twain's denunciation still was being relished by the denominational and medical press; his words were finding their way into legislative arguments seeking to prohibit the practice of Christian Science, and were being quoted almost as law by prosecutors in demanding jail sentences for practitioners whom they charged with "criminal negligence, or worse" in the treatment of disease.

The criticism was so general that the editor of the *Boston Herald* appealed to Mrs. Eddy for a statement. It came, in one brief paragraph:

To the Editor of the Herald:

I even hope that those who are kind enough to speak well of me may do so honestly, and not too earnestly, and this seldom, until mankind learns more of my meaning and can speak justly of my living.

M. B. G. Eddy

Pleasant View, Concord, N.H., *May 5, 1900*

The violent opposition to Mrs. Eddy's teachings is one of the unhappy aspects in the history of Christian Science. In

[2] For full text see *Miscellany*, pp. 302–303.

1900, according to the annual report as published in the July issue of the *Christian Science Journal,* there were 18,131 members in The Mother Church and, in 416 branch churches, there were 21,040 members. Because of some joint membership, probably the actual total membership did not exceed 25,000.

In a world of millions of people, why did so few disturb so many?

Why should the distinguished Mark Twain so viciously attack Mrs. Eddy and her teachings?

It was not because Christian Scientists quarreled with the beliefs of others. Mrs. Eddy expressly forbade any disparagement of the beliefs of any other sect.

It was not that she required of her followers an unquestioning acceptance of her words, and a blind obedience to her teachings. In her teachings, she often dwelt on the words of Jesus, "And these signs shall follow them that believe; in my name shall they cast out devils; they shall speak with new tongues; They shall take up serpents; and if they drink any deadly thing, it shall not hurt them; they shall lay hands on the sick, and they shall recover." [3]

She required of her followers no unquestioning acceptance, no blind obedience. She required, as she said in her 1901 *Message to The Mother Church,* that they "wait patiently on God; return blessing for cursing; be not overcome of evil, but overcome evil with good; be steadfast, abide and abound in faith, understanding and good works; study the Bible and the textbook of our denomination; obey strictly the laws that be, and follow your Leader only so far as she follows Christ. . . ."

She said, "Jesus' history made a new calendar, which we

[3] Mark, xvi.17, 18.

call the Christian era; but he established no ritualistic worship." [4] She accepted without evasion Paul's estimate of "Jesus Christ, the same yesterday, and to day, and for ever," and the apostle's injunction, "Be not carried about with divers and strange doctrines. For *it is* a good thing that the heart be established with grace." [5]

The God other Christian churches worshiped, she worshiped; the Jesus Christ other Christian churches followed, she followed.

She believed in God and, so believing, thought it not incredible that man, governed by God, should heal the sick.

She believed that Jesus healed according to the law of God.

She believed that the same law which was available to Him, is available to us.

She sought to make the teachings and the practice of Christian Science an exact copy of His words and His works.

But educated to adjust itself to the tragedy of disease, and evil, and all kindred things, the world resented her crusade against sickness, her refusal to allow evil the right of existence, her rejection of the desolate thought that God sends disaster, her teaching that there is no need to be tormented by fear.

Her only recourse against the violence and the hatred for her was the one she took — to wait "until mankind learns more of my meaning and can speak justly of my living." She was content to wait the day when the world would be insistent in its recognition of God.

Mrs. Eddy was too occupied with the affairs of her Church to have the time to quarrel with everyone who wanted to

---

[4] *Science and Health*, p. 20.
[5] Hebrews, xiii.8, 9.

quarrel with her. Her days were carefully managed with the daily routine being slightly changed. She still rose at six o'clock and, except for breakfast at seven, devoted the hours until nine o'clock in meditation and prayer. After nine, her correspondence was brought to her. She worked on it until twelve, writing to The Mother Church, to branch churches, to students, with the mail becoming so heavy after 1900 that five secretaries were needed to answer routine correspondence.

Dinner was served at twelve o'clock and, at one o'clock, she took her daily drive.[6] Returning in one hour, she devoted the remainder of the afternoon to revising *Science and Health*,[7] and making other contributions to the literature of Christian Science. Usually, she completed her day's work before the evening meal at six o'clock, although, when necessary, she worked into the late hours of the night. Often, in the evening, she joined her household around the piano singing hymns, or listening to the phonograph which, then, was new; but she preferred sitting by the window of her upstairs study looking up and beyond the hills to a harmony that continually endures, or across the countryside to the lights of Concord.

Mrs. Eddy had an active interest in the civic affairs of the community. When she moved there in 1889, a single

[6] In earlier years at Pleasant View, Mrs. Eddy took her daily drive at two o'clock, sometimes not returning until four. She purchased two automobiles, one for the use of her household, and one for her own use — a Stanley Steamer; she used it once.

[7] Mrs. Eddy made substantial changes in the edition of *Science and Health* which was published on January 30, 1902. For the first time lines on each page were numbered. The Index was omitted and replacing it was a section entitled "Fruitage," which contained scores of testimonies of healing. Chapters were rearranged into what has become their final form.

horsecar served the transportation needs of the public. The vehicle made hourly trips on Main Street, and cobblestones served as pavement in the few city blocks that made up the business district. In 1899, after a farmer's light wagon and his horse became mired near the entrance to Pleasant View, Mrs. Eddy appealed to the city authorities to improve the condition of the street.

To get the work started, she offered to contribute five thousand dollars, and increased the sum to eight thousand dollars when opposition developed. The opposition increased and Mrs. Eddy was threatened with a lawsuit if she persisted in her efforts to have the street macadamized. She met the challenge of property owners who objected to the expenditure by hiring an engineer to make a detailed study of the requirements. On Tuesday afternoon, September 13, 1899, the city officials held their monthly meeting and, as reported in the *Concord Evening Monitor,* "The Pleasant Street grade controversy was settled, the board established a grade which had [been] agreed upon. . . ." The grade that had been agreed upon was Mrs. Eddy's plan.

On August 8, 1906, the *Boston Herald* reported another civic improvement in Concord: "Through the suggestion of Mrs. Mary Baker Eddy, discoverer and founder of Christian Science, and by vote of the Concord city government tonight, the capital city of the Granite state is to have, in the improvement of State street, one of the finest avenues in New Hampshire. This improvement is the direct result of a request to the city government by Mrs. Eddy, and the generous action of her friends, who have offered to bear half the expense of concreting one of the city's leading and most beautiful thoroughfares."

In June 1898, Mrs. Eddy donated one hundred thousand

dollars for the building of a Christian Science church in Concord and, in February 1899, she suggested to the local society that was holding its meetings in Christian Science Hall — which she had built and given to her Concord followers in October 1897 — that it take needed steps to form itself into a church body. A committee was appointed. By-Laws, very similar to those used by The Mother Church, were drafted, and submitted to Mrs. Eddy.

She returned them, informing the committee that the form of government established for The Mother Church was not appropriate for a branch church. She suggested that they study the By-Laws of different branch churches and draft what was needed in accordance with practices in effect elsewhere, and in keeping with their Leader's desire that "each branch church shall be distinctly democratic in its government, and no individual, and no other church shall interfere with its affairs." [8]

In 1903, Mrs. Eddy wrote to the congregation saying "the Hall looks shabby," and indicated the time was at hand for building a church on the site. Inasmuch as she had attended services, and had given freely to its support, she was invited to write her name at the head of the list of charter members. She declined, explaining it was her wish that the congregation manage its own affairs. When word went out that construction operations were under way, contributions began coming in from all over the United States and Europe, the largest contribution being one of ten thousand dollars given by a group of members of The Mother Church, for use in the purchase of an organ.

Dedicated on July 17, 1904, First Church of Christ, Scientist, of Concord, N.H., was not far from the Congrega-

[8] *Church Manual*, Article XXIII, Section 10.

tional church Mary Baker Eddy attended with her parents
more than seventy years before; and which, as John N.
McCormick wrote in his *History of New Hampshire,* was
"the rallying point of the town, and a great congregation
averaging about a thousand thronged it every Sabbath. They
came from all directions, long distances, and many on
foot."

For the dedication, Mrs. Eddy wrote one of the most
thoughtful of her many thoughtful messages:

> . . . At this period, the greatest man or woman
> on earth stands at the vestibule of Christian Sci-
> ence, struggling to enter into the perfect love of
> God and man. The infinite will not be buried in
> the finite; the true thought escapes from the in-
> ward to the outward, and this is the only right
> activity, that whereby we reach our higher nature.
> Material theories tend to check spiritual attraction
> — the tendency towards God, the infinite and
> eternal — by an opposite attraction towards the
> temporary and finite. Truth, life, and love are the
> only legitimate and eternal demands upon man;
> they are spiritual laws enforcing obedience and
> punishing . . .
>
> . . . It is of less importance that we receive from
> mankind justice, than that we deserve it. Most of us
> willingly accept dead truisms which can be buried
> at will; but a live truth, even though it be a sapling
> within rich soil and with blossoms on its branches,
> frightens people. The trenchant truth that cuts its
> way through iron and sod, most men avoid until
> compelled to glance at it. Then they open their

hearts to it for actual being, health, holiness, and immortality.

. . . Strength is in man, not in muscles; unity and power are not in atom or in dust. A small group of wise thinkers is better than a wilderness of dullards and stronger than the might of empires. Unity is spiritual co-operation, heart to heart, the bond of blessedness such as my beloved Christian Scientists all over the field, and the dear Sunday School children, have demonstrated in gifts to me of about eighty thousand dollars to be applied to building, embellishing, and furnishing our church edifice in Concord, N.H. . . .[9]

During the services a letter from Mrs. Eddy was read to the congregation:

Not having the time to receive all the beloved ones who have so kindly come to the dedication of this church, I must not allow myself the pleasure of receiving any of them. I always try to be just, if not generous; and I cannot show my love for them in social ways without neglecting the sacred demands on my time and attention for labors which I think do them more good.[10]

And while the church in Concord was being built, similar operations were under way in Boston.

When The Mother Church was dedicated on January 6, 1895, it had been expected that its seating capacity of nine hundred would be adequate for a long time. Within a few months people were standing in the back of the auditorium,

[9] *Miscellany*, pp. 159, 160, 162.
[10] *Miscellany*, p. 163.

along the sides, and about the doors, so that beginning with April 26, 1896, it was necessary to hold a morning and an afternoon service on Sunday. The additional service relieved the congestion, but only for a short time. Branch churches were organized in Cambridge, Chelsea, and Roxbury, and from these communities to other suburbs.

Communion services and annual meetings were attended in such numbers that they overflowed The Mother Church, Tremont Temple, Symphony Hall, and the Mechanics Building, so that in her annual *Message to The Mother Church* in 1902, Mrs. Eddy suggested the need for a larger church edifice.

In response, Edward A. Kimball offered a motion to this effect: "Recognizing the necessity for providing an auditorium for The Mother Church that will seat four or five thousand persons, and acting in behalf of ourselves and the Christian Scientists of the world, we agree to contribute any portion of $2,000,000 that may be necessary for this purpose."

The motion was seconded by Judge William G. Ewing, and approved without discussion. In the church treasury was the sum of $33,756.29.

The next day the *Boston Journal* editorialized as follows: "Assembled in the largest church business meeting ever held in Boston — perhaps the largest ever held in the United States — the members of The First Church of Christ, Scientist, Boston, the Mother Church of the denomination, voted yesterday afternoon to raise any part of two million dollars that might be needed to build in this city a church edifice capable of seating between four and five thousand persons. This astonishing motion was passed with unanimity and assurance. It was not even talked over, beyond two brief explanations why the building was needed. Learning that a big church was required, the money to provide it was pledged with a readiness of an ordinary mortal passing out a nickel for carfare."

In April 1903, the *Boston Globe* reported that "the last parcel in the block bounded by Falmouth, Norway, and St. Paul Streets, in the shape of a triangle, has passed to the ownership of the Christian Science church, the deed being taken by Ira O. Knapp, *et al.,* trustees. The purchase of this parcel, which is known as the Hotel Brookline, a four-story brick building also in the shape of a triangle, gives to the above society the ownership of the entire block. . . ."

The work of clearing the land was started in October 1903, and rumors began to be circulated that among the buildings to be demolished was The Mother Church. This was not true, of course, but there was so much speculation regarding the permanence of the original edifice that the *Christian Science Sentinel* in its issue of March 5, 1904, published the following amendment to Section 3 of Article XLI (Section 3, Article XXXIV, in present edition of *Church Manual*) of the Church By-Laws:

THE MOTHER CHURCH BUILDING — SECTION 3. The edifice erected in 1894 for The First Church of Christ, Scientist, in Boston, Mass., shall neither be demolished, nor removed from the site where it was built, without the written consent of the Pastor Emeritus, Mary Baker Eddy.

On June 14, 1904, Stephen A. Chase, treasurer of the building fund, reported that, up to May 31, 1904, there had been received a total of $425,893.66 from Christian Scientists, and from many contributors who were not Christian

Scientists. On hand was a balance of $226,285.73, the difference of $199,607.93 having been used for the purchase of the property, and other requirements.

The cornerstone of the new building was laid at eight o'clock in the morning of Saturday, July 16, 1904. In attendance were The Christian Science Board of Directors, Alfred Farlow, President of The Mother Church; Professor Hermann S. Hering, First Reader; Mrs. Ella E. Williams, Second Reader; Charles Brigham, the architect; and E. Noyes Whitcomb, the builder of the edifice. As in the building of the original structure, the Directors were in charge of the work. The Directors were: Joseph Armstrong, Stephen A. Chase, William B. Johnson, Ira O. Knapp, and Archibald McLellan. Armstrong, Chase, Johnson, and Knapp were the same Directors who built The Mother Church.

In the April 14, 1906, issue of the *Christian Science Sentinel,* there was this announcement:

> The Christian Science Board of Directors takes pleasure in announcing that the extension of The Mother Church will be dedicated on the date of the annual communion, Sunday, June 10, 1906.

On June 9, 1906, there was another announcement in the *Sentinel.* This one was signed by Stephen A. Chase, and accompanying it was an editorial:

> NOTICE TO CONTRIBUTORS TO THE BUILDING FUND
>
> The contributors to the building fund for the extension of The Mother Church, The First Church of Christ Scientist, in Boston, Mass., are hereby notified that sufficient funds have been re-

ceived for the completion of the church building, and the friends are requested to send no more money to this fund.

The editorial stated:

Christian Scientists will read with much joy and thanksgiving the announcement made by Mr. Chase in this issue of the *Sentinel* that sufficient funds have been received by him, as treasurer of the building fund, to pay all bills in connection with the extension of The Mother Church,[11] and to most of them the fact that he has been able to make this announcement coincident with the completion of the building will be deeply significant. Our Leader has said in *Science and Health* (p. 494), "Divine Love always has met and always will meet every human need," and this has been proved true in the experience of many who have contributed to the building fund.

. . . The significance of this building is not to be found in the material structure, but in the lives of those who, under the consecrated leadership of Mrs. Eddy, and following her example, are doing the works which Jesus said should mark the lives of his followers. It stands as the visible symbol of a religion which heals the sick and reforms the sinful as our Master healed and reformed them. It proclaims to the world that Jesus' gospel was for all

[11] Before the edifice was completed there were a number of branch churches in the suburbs of Boston, and it was necessary to hold three Sunday services in The Mother Church — and still the church was not large enough, scores being turned away in the morning, in the afternoon, and in the evening.

time and for all men; that it is as effective to-day as it was when he preached the Word of God to the multitudes of Judea and healed them of their diseases and their sins. It speaks for the successful labors of one divinely guided woman, who has brought to the world the spiritual understanding of the Scriptures, and whose ministry has revealed the one true Science and changed the whole aspect of medicine and theology.

On June 11, 1906, newspapers throughout the United States, Canada, and Europe carried word of the dedication of the extension to The Mother Church. Among the newspapers recognizing the occasion was the *Boston Herald:*

Five thousand people kneeling in silent communion; a stillness profound; and then, rising in unison from the vast congregation, the words of the Lord's Prayer! Such was the closing incident of the dedicatory services of the extension of The Mother Church, The First Church of Christ Scientist, at the corner of Falmouth and Norway Streets, yesterday morning. And such was the scene repeated six times during the day.

It was a sight which no one who saw it will ever be able to forget. Many more gorgeous church pageantries have been seen in this country and in an older civilization; there have been church ceremonies that appealed more to the eye, but the impressiveness of this lay in its very simplicity; its grandeur sprang from the complete unanimity of thought and purpose. There was something emanating from the thousands who worshipped under the dome of the great edifice whose formal opening they had gathered to observe, that appealed to and fired the imagination. A comparatively new religion launching upon a new era, assuming an altogether different status before the world!

Even the sun smiled kindly upon the dedication of the extension to The Mother Church. With a cooling breeze to temper the heat, the thousands who began to congregate about the church as early as half past five in the morning were able to wait patiently for the opening of the doors without suffering the inconvenience of an oppressive day. From that time, until the close of the evening service, Falmouth and Norway Streets held large crowds of people, either coming from a service or awaiting admission to one. As all the services were precisely the same in every respect, nobody attended more than one, so that there were well over thirty thousand people who witnessed the opening. Not only did these include Scientists from all over the world, and nearly all the local Scientists, but many hundreds of other faiths, drawn to the church from curiosity, and from sympathy, too.

. . . Promptly at half past six the numerous doors of the church were thrown open and the public had its first glimpse of the great structure, the cost of which approximates two million dollars, contributed from over the entire world. The first impression was of vastness, then of light and cheerfulness, and when the vanguard of the thousands had been seated, expressions of surprise and of admiration were heard on every hand for the beauty and grace of the architecture. The new home for worship that was opened by the Scientists in Boston yesterday can take a place in the front rank of the world's houses of worship, and it is no wonder that the first sight which the visitors caught of its interior should have impressed them as one of the events of their lives.

First Reader William D. McCrackan, accompanied by Second Reader, Mrs. Laura Carey Conant, and the soloist for the services, Mrs. Hunt, was on the Readers' platform. Stepping to the front of the platform, when the congregation had taken their seats, the First Reader announced simply that they would sing Hymn 161, written by Mrs. Eddy, as the opening of the dedicatory services. And what singing it was! As though trained carefully under one leader, the great body of Scientists joined in the song of praise.

Spontaneous unanimity and repetition in unison were two of the most striking features of the services. When, after five minutes of silent communion at the end of the service, the congregation began to repeat the Lord's Prayer, they began all together, and their voices rose as one in a heartfelt appeal to the creator. . . .

A telegram which had been sent to Mrs. Eddy was read aloud at each of the services; in part, this telegram said:

". . . the Christian Scientists of the world, in tender affection for the cause of human weal, have fulfilled a high resolve and set up this tabernacle, which is to stand as an enduring monument, a sign of your understanding and proof that our Supreme God, through His power and law, is the natural healer of all our diseases and hath ordained the way of salvation of all men from all evil. . . ."

Mrs. Eddy did not attend the services. In a letter dated April 8, 1906, she had written:

Will one and all of my dear correspondents accept this, my answer to their fervid question: Owing to the time consumed in travel, *et cetera*, I cannot be present *in propria persona* at our annual communion and the dedication in June next of The Mother Church of Christ, Scientist. But I shall be with my blessed church "in spirit and in truth."

I have faith in the givers and in the builders of this church edifice, — admiration for and faith in the grandeur and sublimity of this superb superstructure, wherein all vanity of victory disappears and the glory of divinity appears in all its promise.

MARY BAKER EDDY

PLEASANT VIEW, CONCORD, N.H., *April 8, 1906*

At the same time the extension of The Mother Church was being dedicated, Mark Twain was returning to his attack on Mrs. Eddy and Christian Science. This time, instead of two magazine articles, he was extending his effort into a book. The book, entitled *Christian Science*, was published in 1907.

In it, after extensive ridicule, Twain referred to Mrs. Eddy as "the Boston Pope," and predicted that "by-and-by [her successor] will draw his dollar-a-head capitation-tax from three hundred millions of the human race, and the Annex [*Science and Health*] and the rest of his book-shop will fetch, in as much more; and his Metaphysical College, the annual pilgrimage to Mrs. Eddy's tomb, from all over the world — admission, the Christian Science Dollar (payable in advance) — purchases of consecrated glass beads, candles, memorial spoons, aureoled chromo-portraits and bogus autographs of Mrs. Eddy; cash offerings at her shrine — no crutches of cured cripples received, and no imitations of miraculously restored broken legs and necks allowed to be hung up except when of the Holy Metal and proved by fire-assay; cash for miracles worked at the tomb; these money-sources, with a thousand yet to be invented and ambushed upon the devotee, will bring the annual increment well up above a billion. . . ."

Requested by the editor of the *Cosmopolitan Magazine* to reply to Twain's attack, Edward A. Kimball wrote, in part:

Mr. Clemens has written a book through which runs an unbroken thread of purpose to procure the discomfiture of Mrs. Eddy. In this behalf he presents a riot of inconsistency which we may with propriety consider.

In order to gain his point he is obliged to present *Science and Health* as possessing some merit. Then he insists that Mrs.

Eddy never rose to the intellectual altitude that was on a plane of excellence with the book. Then follows the deduction that she did not write it and that her pretense is fraudulent. He thus uses the book for the obliteration of Mrs. Eddy, in apparent disregard of the fact that in another place he has written, "Of all the strange, and frantic, the incomprehensible books which the imagination of man has created, surely this is the prize sample."

He declares that Mrs. Eddy in several ways is the most interesting woman that ever lived and the most extraordinary — that "she launched a world religion which is increasing at the rate of a new church every four days"; that "it is quite within the probabilities that she will be the most imposing figure that has cast its shadow across the globe since the inauguration of our era"; that "she is profoundly wise in some respects," "she is competent," and so forth; and then declares his conviction that she could not have written "the most frantic and incomprehensible book which man has created." And this is the testimony of an expert!

After concluding that the Founder and Leader of this religious movement is a fraud, a cheat, and a tyrant, and that the textbook of this church is an unconscionable lie; that the church organization is venal, its laws outrageous, and its aims degrading, he declares, "I believe that the new religion will conquer half of Christendom in a hundred years," and adds concerning this statement, "I think perhaps it is a compliment to the (human) race."

A doubtful compliment, is it not?

I have been asked to write an answer. . . . I knew I could not do it. I might perhaps be willing to explore and attempt to classify a comet's tail, but to answer the grotesque contradictions of this book is impossible. Bewildered at such a prospect, I feel that Christian Scientists cannot do better than to forgo a war of words and to abide in the confident expectation that Christian Science will continue to justify itself by its fruits and in the knowledge that such justification will stand as a sufficient and imperishable answer forever. . . .

Afterwards, Mark Twain gave his own answer.

In his biography of Twain,[12] Albert Bigelow Paine speaks of a day when, in an exchange of confidences, he mentioned having been greatly benefited by Christian Science treatment. To his surprise, Twain responded:

"Of course, you have been benefited. Christian Science is humanity's boon. Mother Eddy deserves a place in the Trinity as much as any member of it. She has organized and made available a healing principle that for two thousand years has never been employed, except as the merest guesswork. She is the benefactor of the age."

[12] *Mark Twain, a Biography.* Copyright, 1923, Harper & Brothers.

CHAPTER TWENTY

"Gross Deception at Pleasant View"

REPRESENTATIVES of the *New York World* and *McClure's Magazine* visited Concord in September and October 1906, interviewed townspeople, and invaded Pleasant View.

On October 28, 1906, the newspaper began publication of a series of articles [1] in which it was claimed:

1. Mrs. Eddy was senile and decrepit.

2. Mrs. Eddy was cancer-ridden, and was under the constant care of physicians, surgeons, and dentists.

3. Mrs. Eddy was impersonated by a student on daily drives about the streets of Concord.

4. Mrs. Eddy was under the control of "a cabinet" that was looting "treasure estimated at $15,000,000, and an annual income estimated at $1,000,000."

5. "Unscrupulous people are working on the credulity of her [Mrs. Eddy's] many followers to make themselves rich."

6. And, as to Mrs. Eddy's physical appearance, the newspaper said: ". . . Mrs. Eddy looked more dead than alive. She was a skeleton, her hollow cheeks thick with red paint, and the fleshless, hairless bones about the sunken eyes penciled a jet black. The features were thick with powder.

[1] In this same month of October, *McClure's Magazine* began a similar series.

Above them was a big, white wig. Her weakness was pathetic. She reeled as she stood clinging to the table. Her sunken, faded eyes gazed helplessly, almost pleadingly at her visitors . . . to every eye it was clear the unfortunate old woman had been doped. . . ."

Under crashing headlines on Page One, the article met prompt denial. On the same day, Calvin A. Frye issued the following statement:

> PLEASANT VIEW, CONCORD, N.H.
> *October 28, 1906*
>
> The sensational report published in "The New York World" on Sunday, October 28, 1906, to the effect that Mrs. Eddy is physically or mentally incapacitated; that for many months she has not left her room; that she does not drive daily, and that she is impersonated in her carriage by Mrs. Pamelia J. Leonard, or anybody else, is unqualifiedly false.
>
> My position in Mrs. Eddy's household is simply that of a paid employee. She conducts her own affairs, financial and otherwise, today, as she always has, and the statement that Mrs. Eddy is dominated or controlled by any sort of "a cabinet" or combination is positively false — absurdly so to any one who is acquainted with Mrs. Eddy's extraordinary ability as an executive.
>
> Mrs. Eddy, as she herself wrote to the "Boston Herald" on October 19, 1906, is in her usual good health; she is not slowly dying from cancer, nor has she a cancer nor any chronic nor organic nor functional disease. She has never been visited by a

cancer specialist, nor do I nor anybody else provide "old school surgeons and physicians, dentists and the entire range of pharmacopœia" for attendance upon Mrs. Eddy, as is stated in "The World."

Had the reporters for "The World" really desired to learn whether Mrs. Leonard impersonated Mrs. Eddy on Mrs. Eddy's drive, it would have been a very simple matter for these reporters to have called at Pleasant View while Mrs. Eddy was driving and ask for Mrs. Leonard. Had they taken this very ready way of verification they would have had no trouble in seeing Mrs. Leonard and talking with her.

Boston and New York newspapers and press services, including the Associated Press, rushed reporters to Concord where, in a mass interview, they saw Mrs. Eddy and heard her answer three questions they were most anxious to ask:

Q. Are you in perfect bodily health?
A. I am.
Q. Have you any physician besides God?
A. Indeed, I have not! His everlasting arms are about me and support me, and that is enough.
Q. Do you drive daily?
A. Yes.

As a group they saw Mrs. Eddy leave her house unaided, enter her carriage, and wave to them as she drove off. The fifteen or twenty newspapermen and newspaperwomen then inquired if they might inspect the house.

They did so, from top to bottom, even to the extent of examining Mrs. Eddy's wardrobe in what, for some, was a search for medicine and drugs and disinfectants. Completing their inspection, they wrote their impressions.

They found no senility and no decrepitude, no "hollow cheeks thick with red paint," no "faded eyes [gazing] helplessly, almost pleadingly." Contrariwise, nearly all commented on Mrs. Eddy's "alertness," her "clear complexion," and her "unusually expressive eyes, and her abundance of snow-white hair."

They agreed she was thin, but not "a skeleton"; venerable, but not displaying "weakness [which] was pathetic."

Citizens of Concord gave statements to the questioning reporters, all in denial of the charges. These denials, with the impressions of the reporters, were given wide circulation. But having its claims refuted did not trouble the newspaper — nor did it stop publication, by the magazine, of its attack. Continuing their slander, the publications shaped the conspiracy that came into the open on March 2, 1907.

On that day, in wide headlines, the *New York World* announced:

MRS. EDDY'S SON DECLARING HER MENTALLY FEEBLE
BRINGS SUIT TO PROTECT HER AGAINST CHURCH HEADS

Under the headlines, in a story running several columns in length, the *World* said:

. . . The foundations of this action were laid months ago in the public disclosure of gross deception at Pleasant View. . . . At this juncture, public-spirited citizens decided that legal proceedings of the most dignified character were vital and necessary. . . . The selection of a man to direct the legal proceedings of such great importance to those immediately interested, and to society at large, was a great difficulty. . . . The choice fell upon William Eaton Chandler, New Hampshire's distinguished statesman for nearly one-half of a century. . . . [Mr. Glover] welcomes the powerful friends who came to his aid. . . . Influenced by Senator Chandler's letter to take action. . . . It was with the knowledge of these facts that an agent entrusted with the mission of placing before Glover his legal opportunity left New York for Lead City [Lead, South Dakota] on the night of November 22, 1906. This agent brought with him two letters upon which he placed great stress for the successful outcome of his visit to Mary Baker G. Eddy's son. . . .

Continuing, the *World* stated:

. . . Senator Chandler agreed to give to the case the sanction of his standing, and daily since the case became his care his interest in it has deepened and broadened.

As at first, the success of the initial step was due in the greatest part to the suggestion conveyed from Senator Chandler to George W. Glover, so now the augury of success in the courts is that so learned and fearless a statesman and lawyer will conduct the case to his fullest ability.

As facts were evolved in the West, it was clearly shown that the idea of enlisting the services of Senator Chandler was nothing short of an inspiration. Glover was New Hampshire born, and it was thought that, narrowed though his perspective, he must surely know of Senator Chandler as one to command a hearing no matter what the question might be. As eventually proved, Glover did indeed know of Senator Chandler, had been able to follow his career, and watched him as one who added to the fame of his native state.

The "agent entrusted with the mission of placing before Glover his legal opportunity" was a representative of the *World;* and if Glover was "influenced by Senator Chandler's letter to take action," it would appear that Senator Chandler was influenced by the *World* to start the action.

The two letters "upon which he [the agent] placed great stress" follow:

WASHINGTON, D.C. *Nov. 22, 1906.*

MY DEAR MR. GLOVER:

I have consented to act as legal counsel concerning certain questions which arise in connection with Mrs. Mary Baker G. Eddy. They are stated in a letter from me to Mr. Slaght, who will call upon you and can show you my letter to him.

It is important for public and private interests that these questions should be investigated and met and fairly and justly disposed of as questions involving doubts which from large and commendable motives of all good citizens, and especially all relatives of Mrs. Eddy, should help to solve and settle. Therefore, please be sure and give Mr. Slaght a full hearing and possess yourself fully of all the facts which he will be able to give you.

Very respectfully,
(*signed*) WILLIAM E. CHANDLER

WASHINGTON, D.C. *Nov. 22, 1906.*

MY DEAR MR. SLAGHT:

I consent to act as counsel concerning certain questions which arise in connection with Mrs. Mary Baker G. Eddy. It seems clear that there are several doubts about several points.

1. Mrs. Eddy may be detained in the custody of strangers against her will.

2. She may be so nearly worn out in body and mind as a confirmed invalid that she is incapable of deciding any questions whatever, according to any will or pleasure of her own, and necessarily, therefore, incapable of managing her business and property affairs.

3. Being thus restrained or incapable, or without relatives near her, she may be surrounded by designing men who either have already sought or may hereinafter seek to wrongfully possess themselves of her large property, or induce her to make a disposition of it contrary to what would be in her sane and deliberate intentions if she were in perfect possession of her liberty and mental faculties.

These doubts have arisen in connection with investigations recently made. Beyond all question, steps should be taken to solve the doubts, to correct the wrong, if it exists, and to establish the right in every respect.

This new work should be done, if possible, in cooperation with Mrs. Eddy's son, or any other relative who may be impressed with his duties in this regard; and if the relatives do not move, it should be done by such right-minded citizens as are in sympathy with the commendable movement.

Yours truly,

(*signed*) WILLIAM E. CHANDLER

Slaght, the *World* representative, was able to persuade Glover into co-operating with the newspaper's campaign of vilification. On March 1, 1907, a document known as *The Petition of "Next Friends,"* signed by George W. Glover, his daughter Mary B. Glover, and George W. Baker, a nephew of Mrs. Eddy, was filed in court in Concord. On March 11, 1907, Ebenezer J. Foster Eddy and Fred W. Baker, another nephew, added their names to a document which began this way: "The petition of Mary Baker Glover Eddy who sues by her next friends George W. Glover, Mary Baker Glover and George W. Baker *against* Calvin A. Frye, Alfred Farlow, Irving G. Tomlinson, Ira O. Knapp, William B. Johnson, Stephen A. Chase, Joseph Armstrong, Edward A. Kimball, Hermann S. Hering, and Lewis C. Strang . . ."

The *Petition* was in nine sections, briefly as follows:

1. The plaintiffs say that the said Mary Baker G. Eddy is a resident of Concord in said county of Merrimack, that the said George W. Glover and Mary Baker Glover are residents of Lead City in the State of South Dakota, and the said George W. Baker is a resident of Bangor in the State of Maine; and they further say that the defendants Frye,

Tomlinson, Hering and Strang are residents of Concord, New Hampshire, and that the defendants Farlow, Knapp, Johnson, Chase and Armstrong are residents of Boston in the State of Massachusetts, and that the defendant Kimball is a resident of Chicago in the State of Illinois.

2. This section charges that being unable to guard and manage her property, Mrs. Eddy was under the influence, control, "and fraud of others."

3. This section charges Frye and Strang with having custody of Mrs. Eddy, of keeping "her carefully surrounded and secluded . . . so that very few persons are allowed to see her, and no one is allowed to see her except for a few minutes at one time; that the said defendant Frye while thus controlling the said Mary Baker G. Eddy, acts in a multifarious capacity, as secretary, door-keeper, butler, and sometimes as footman in livery, and the said Strang acts as associate secretary and messenger."

4. This section refers to correspondence between Mrs. Eddy and George W. Glover.

5. This section refers to the efforts of the nephew, George W. Baker, to present to Mrs. Eddy a souvenir in the form of a watch.

6. Discusses property owned by Mrs. Eddy in New Hampshire and Massachusetts, the management of which "has been done either in her name by others or by her while unfitted for the transactions thereof."

7. Repetition of section four, and also questions "loyalty of the men and women near" Mrs. Eddy.

8. Certain transactions require "investigation and judicial consideration," among them being:

    a. COPYRIGHTS. Financial returns from (1) *Science and Health,* "of which over 450,000 copies have been sold"; the *Church Manual, Retrospection and Intro-spection, Miscellaneous Writings,* and the periodicals: The *Christian Science Journal,* the *Christian Science Quarterly, Der Herold der Christian Science,* and the *Christian Science Sentinel.*

In petitioning for an accounting of the financial returns from publication sources, it is claimed:

"Various transfers have been made by Mrs. Eddy of her copyrights and various re-transfers made to her, and particularly the following:

"On January 12, 1896, *Science and Health* and nearly all her other works were transferred by her to the defendant, Calvin A. Frye, and on October 6, 1899, he re-transferred them to her. On October 9, 1899, she transferred them to the defendant, Edward A. Kimball, and on May 21, 1906, he re-transferred them to her. In one of her transfers — that of October 8, 1890, to E. J. F. Eddy, a royalty to Mrs. Eddy of $1.00 per volume of *Science and Health* was stipulated."

   b. Massachusetts Metaphysical College. "The receipts of this college from the 3333 practitioners now advertising their power of healing have been over one million dollars; and in addition hundreds of thousands of dollars have been received from persons who have paid the $300.00 but do not now advertise for patients; but the plaintiffs are unable to state the amount nor how much Mrs. Eddy has received, nor how much has been received and retained by the defendants."

   c. The Mother Church. Investigation and judicial consideration of the receipts and expenditures and By-Laws were requested because "the defendants are all members of the Mother Church."

d. "The transactions thus narrated have involved receipts and expenditures amounting to many hundred thousand dollars; probably to several millions of dol·lars; in a large portion of which Mrs. Eddy has had a personal pecuniary interest, both in the receipts and payments taking place in her name and in the name of various organizations mentioned. Her rightful income as owner of all the aforesaid copyrights, as the president of the Metaphysical College of Healing, as the head and Pastor Emeritus of the Mother Church, and as proprietor of all the real estate aforesaid has been of immense value, and has all been controlled or received by the defendants, some or all of them, and yet she has had no complete or sufficient accounting from them therefor.

9. "That in view of the foregoing conditions under which the whole property of the said Mary Baker G. Eddy has been possessed and controlled and her whole business conducted by the defendants without sufficient intelligent expression of any wishes of hers and while she has been incapable of any complete volition concerning her property or business affairs, there is abundant reason to believe the defendants and their private associates have wrongfully converted to their own private uses or otherwise misappropriated, or unlawfully diverted large sums of money and large amounts of property of the said Mary Baker G. Eddy; and the plaintiffs claim that the defendants should now be adjudged to have been trustees thereof and should be compelled to give an account thereof and to make restitution therefor.

"*Wherefore,* the plaintiffs pray:

"1. That defendants be required to disclose and give account of all the business transactions aforesaid and all others relating to the property of said Mary Baker G. Eddy with which they have been connected.

"2. That if they shall be found to have wrongfully received and held or disposed of any of the property of said Mary Baker G. Eddy they be required to restore same to her, or be charged with the value thereof.

"3. That they be enjoined during the pendency of the present suit in equity not to receive money or property of the said Mary Baker G. Eddy; not to pay out any money or part with any property of the said Mary Baker G. Eddy now held by them and not to interfere with or undertake to manage or control any business or property of the said Mary Baker G. Eddy, or to do any act whatever in her name or behalf under any pretext or under any power of attorney whatever; and

"4. That a receiver or receivers be appointed to take possession of all the property of the said Mary Baker G. Eddy now in the hands or under the control of the defendants or otherwise wrongfully withheld from her control by any person or persons and to take charge of and manage all her business affairs; and to make such ultimate disposition of all her estate as this court may hereafter decide to be wise and prudent; and for such further relief as to the court may seem requisite and just.

GEORGE W. GLOVER
MARY B. GLOVER
GEORGE W. BAKER"

Much that was stated in the Petition as being factual was not factual; many things were charged as happening that never happened; legally, it was an unwarranted invasion of Mrs. Eddy's individual rights; morally, it was a vicious attack on the religious beliefs of a group of people who accepted literally what all other Christian denominations accepted professionally — that being, as one journalist pointed out in *Cosmopolitan Magazine:* " 'Verily, verily, I say unto you, He that believeth on me, the works that I do shall he do also; and greater works than these shall he do; because I go unto my Father.' "

This quotation appeared in an article written by Arthur Brisbane.[2] A famous newspaper columnist, Brisbane went to Pleasant View to satisfy himself as to the correctness of the charges being printed in the *New York World* and in *McClure's Magazine.* In his article, Brisbane spoke of Mrs. Eddy's mind as being "perfectly clear," her answers "instantaneous," and described her, and her surroundings:

"Beside a writing desk, in an armchair, sat a white-haired woman, who rose and walked forward, extending her hand in friendly greeting to a stranger. That was Mrs. Eddy, for whom many human beings in this world feel deepest reverence and affection, and concerning whom others have thought it necessary or excusable to write and to say unkind and untruthful things.

"It is quite certain that nobody could see this beautiful and venerable woman and ever speak of her except in terms of affectionate reverence and sympathy. There are hundreds of thousands of Christian Scientists who would make almost any sacrifice for the privilege of looking upon Mrs. Eddy's face. It is impossible now for her to see many, and it is therefore a duty to make at least an attempt to convey an idea of the impression created by her personality.

"Mrs. Eddy is eighty-six years old. Her thick hair, snow-

[2] For complete article, see *What Mrs. Eddy Said to Arthur Brisbane,* copyright by the Christian Science Publishing Society.

white, curls about her forehead and temples. She is of medium height and very slender. She probably weighs less than one hundred pounds. But her figure is straight as she rises and walks forward. The grasp of her thin hand is firm; the hand does not tremble.

"It is hopeless to try to describe a face made beautiful by age, deep thought and many years' exercise of great power. The light blue eyes are strong and concentrated in expression. And the sight, as was soon proved, is that of a woman one-half Mrs. Eddy's age.

"Mrs. Eddy's face is almost entirely free from wrinkles; the skin is very clear; many a young woman would be proud to have it. The forehead is high and full, and the whole expression of the face combines benevolence with great strength of will. Mrs. Eddy has accumulated power in this world. She possesses it, exercises it, and she knows it. But it is a gentle power, and it is possessed by a gentle, diffident and modest woman.

"Women will want to know what Mrs. Eddy wore. The writer regrets that he cannot tell. With some women you see the dress; with Mrs. Eddy you see only the face, the very earnest eyes, and the beautiful quiet expression that only age and thought can give to the human face. . . ."

The Petition, drawn to prove "gross deception at Pleasant View," inevitably had to accuse Mrs. Eddy of incompetency, and the defendants of converting to their own uses and "diverting large sums of money and large amounts of property"; it was also compelled to claim that Mrs. Eddy "has had no complete or sufficient accounting. . . ."

In reply, Fred N. Ladd, treasurer of the Loan and Trust Savings Bank of Concord, who, since March 1898, had made annual audits of Mrs. Eddy's accounts, said in a formal statement:

. . . From the time I began to audit her accounts in March, 1898, to October 8, 1906 (the date of my last audit) I know that all checks and orders on her bank accounts were signed by Mrs. Eddy personally and by no one else.

About the first of 1898 Mr. Frye wanted me to look over his books and accounts to be sure he was correct and wanted me to advise him about keeping his books, both he and Mrs. Eddy telling me that he had never had any experience or knowledge of bookkeeping. Mrs. Eddy told me she did not care anything about having the accounts audited, that she knew Mr. Frye thoroughly and has perfect confidence in him, but that Mr. Frye wanted his accounts audited and, if it was to be done, she would like to have me do it. Mr. Frye also told me that Mrs. Eddy did not care to have the accounts audited but that he wanted it done for his own protection.

Mr. Frye sent or brought the books into the bank some time before March, 1898, and I examined the accounts and vouchers from March, 1898, back to January 1, 1893, and I wrote my certificate on the cash book under date of March 22, 1898, as follows:

"This is to certify that I have examined the cash

book of Mary B. G. Eddy as kept by Calvin A. Frye
from January 1, 1893 to January 1, 1898, and find
that he has accounted for all moneys received and
has proper vouchers for disbursements."

The yearly audits by Ladd from March 1898 to October
8, 1906, and a general audit by Harvey Chase, senior member of the auditing firm of Harvey Chase and Company,
Boston, both revealed a similar regard for Mrs. Eddy's property. It was uncovered by Chase that, in clerical mistakes,
Calvin A. Frye "had made more errors against himself than
against Mrs. Eddy, so that the latter, or her trustees, will
have to pay over a balance of cash to Mr. Frye when the time
for final adjustment of these accounts arrives."

The amount owed Frye was $677.41, and it caused Chase
to observe: "From our entire examination of these books
we have been necessarily convinced that Mr. Frye was an
honest agent for Mrs. Eddy, although mathematically a poor
accountant."

Saying to Ladd that she "had perfect confidence" in Frye
was not a pleasantry with Mrs. Eddy. By transferring to him
on January 12, 1896, the ownership of the copyrights protecting *Science and Health,* as well as copyrights protecting
nearly all her other writings, she gave evidence of this confidence. She displayed similar confidence in Edward A. Kimball.

Had Frye in the years of his control of the copyrights —
the years from 1896 to 1899 — or had Kimball in the years
of his control of the copyrights — the years from 1899 to
1906 — been "unscrupulous," as they were charged with
being, either could have taken possession of the movement.
The teachings were in the writings, and the teachings were

The First Church of Christ, Scientist, in Boston, Massachusetts, and the branch churches all over the world.

What the newspaper, the magazine, the plaintiffs, and the lawyers who brought the suit did not understand, and what Mrs. Eddy did understand, was the total indifference of Frye and Kimball, as well as the other defendants, to material possessions.

By creating a trust fund for herself,[3] as she did on March 6, 1907, Mrs. Eddy also disclosed her confidence in Henry M. Baker, Archibald McLellan, and Josiah E. Fernald. By the execution of this trust fund she surrendered control of all her physical assets to these men. Her purpose in so doing was given in a letter to Judge Robert N. Chamberlin, of the Superior Court in Concord, before whom the suit of the "next friends" first appeared:

PLEASANT VIEW, CONCORD, N.H.
May 16, 1907

HON. JUDGE CHAMBERLIN,
CONCORD, N.H.

RESPECTED SIR:

It is over forty years that I have attended personally to my secular affairs, to my income, invest-

---

[3] On February 25, 1907, Mrs. Eddy created a trust fund for her son, George W. Glover, and his family. It provided him with a lifetime annual income of $1500 and, in the event of his death, instructed the trustees "to pay to his said wife, or for her benefit, such an amount annually during the balance of her life as, in the discretion of my said trustees, may seem reasonable for her comfortable support and maintenance." The trust fund also provided for her son's four children, as well as for Warren S. Shell, who was "the husband of my deceased granddaughter, Evelyn T. Glover."

A number of years previously, Mrs. Eddy built a house for her son, and his family, in Lead City. In addition, she paid the taxes, and maintained the property, besides caring for him and his family in other ways.

For contents of trust fund created for herself, see Appendix 10.

ments, deposits, expenditures, and to my employees. I have personally selected all my investments, except in one or two instances and have paid for the same.

The increasing demand upon my time, labors and thought and yearning for more peace and to have my property and my affairs carefully taken care of for the persons and purposes I have designated by my last will influenced me to select a Board of Trustees to take charge of my property namely Hon. Henry M. Baker, Mr. Archibald McLellan, Mr. Josiah E. Fernald.

I had contemplated doing this before the present proceedings were brought or I knew aught about them and I had consulted lawyer Streeter about the method.

I selected said Trustees because I had implicit confidence in each one of them as to honesty and business capacity.

No person influenced me to make this selection. I find myself able to select the Trustees I need without the help of others. I gave them my property to take care of because I wanted it protected and myself relieved of the burden of doing this.

They have agreed with me to take care of my property and I consider this agreement a great benefit to me already. This suit was brought without my knowledge and is being carried on contrary to my wishes. I feel that it is not for my benefit in any way but for my injury, and I know it was not needed to protect my person or property.

The present proceedings test my trust in divine

Love. My personal reputation is assailed and some of my students and trusted personal friends are cruelly, unjustly and wrongfully accused.

Mr. Calvin A. Frye and other students often ask me to receive persons whom I desire to see but decline to receive solely because I find that I cannot "serve two masters." I cannot be a Christian Scientist except I leave all for Christ.

Trusting that I have not exceeded the bounds of propriety in the statements herein made by me,

I remain most
respectfully
yours,
MARY BAKER G. EDDY

Meanwhile, there had been the usual legal requirements. Frank S. Streeter, of Concord, his associates, Allen Hollis and Edwin G. Eastman, were named as counsel for Mrs. Eddy; Oliver E. Branch, of Manchester, N.H., represented the New Hampshire defendants; and William M. Morse, of Boston, represented the Massachusetts defendants, as well as Kimball. Assisting Chandler for the plaintiffs were Martin and Howe, of Concord, John W. Kelly, of Portsmouth, N.H., Fred W. Peabody, of Boston, and W. C. Harriman, of Nashua, N.H.

Four days after the filing of the Petition, Streeter was interviewed by the Associated Press and, after making a complete denial of all the allegations, expressed the opinion that "the case seems to be an attempt to have the personal rights and privileges of a citizen adjudicated in a way unprecedented in New Hampshire, and if it shall appear that these proceedings have been instituted for purpose other

than the ascertainment and protection of the plaintiff's legal
rights, the method of dealing with such a case will be carefully considered by Mrs. Eddy's counsel before making any
public statements."

Answers were filed by the trustees, Baker, McLellan, and
Fernald, as well as by the other defendants, Frye, Farlow,
Tomlinson, Knapp, Johnson, Chase, Armstrong, Kimball,
Hering, and Strang. They all denied the charges, and on
June 5, 1907, Mrs. Eddy filed a motion requesting an early
trial, and stating:

"1. All the allegations by her alleged 'next friends' set
out in said bill in equity (a) that she is or has been incapable of understanding and protecting her property rights;
(b) that she is surrounded and secluded by any person or
combination of persons who are or have been managing or
controlling her business or any other affairs; and (c) that
such persons have wrongfully converted or misappropriated
any of her property — are untrue.

"2. Her property interests have been and are fully
protected and there is no lawful or just occasion for the
maintenance of these proceedings for any such alleged
purpose.

"3. The trust deed of March 6, 1907, and the appointment of trustees and attorneys thereby were her free and intelligent act, which carried out her own wishes, and the said
trustees and attorneys have thereunder and thereby the full
control and management of her estate, and she desired said
control and management to be continued during the remainder of her earthly life.

"4. These proceedings were not brought in good faith by
said alleged 'next friends' for her personal benefit and are

not now being carried on for that purpose, and the maintenance of these proceedings by alleged 'next friends' is unjust
and injurious to herself, and is unwarrantable interference
with her personal rights under the law of the state and the
established rules of equity and procedure.

"5. She believes and avers that the maintenance of these
proceedings in her name by alleged 'next friends' is an abuse
of the process of the court and is an unwarranted interference with her legal rights, and that she is by law entitled to
speedy relief therefrom.

"6. She believes and avers that, under our Constitution
and laws and the practice in this equity court, she is of right
entitled to an immediate investigation, consideration and
determination by the Chancellor of the following among
other questions: (*a*) Whether her property interests have
been and are now fully protected and whether there is any
lawful or just occasion for the maintenance of these proceedings by said 'next friends' for such alleged purpose;
(*b*) whether the trust deed of March 6, 1907, and the appointment of trustees and attorneys thereby were her free
and intelligent act, which carried out her own wishes; (*c*)
whether these proceedings were brought in good faith by
said alleged 'next friends' for her personal benefit and are
now being carried on for that purpose.

"7. She also believes and avers that she is entitled to have
the prosecution of this case by her alleged 'next friends' suspended until the foregoing questions, together with other
questions arising therefrom, shall have been determined by
the Chancellor, in such manner as will best satisfy his conscience that her representations here made are true; she also
avers that such alleged 'next friends' have no standing in
this court of equity as parties litigant or otherwise to oppose

or prevent such investigation and determination by the Chancellor.

"Wherefore, she prays:

"That this court by its presiding Justice, sitting as Chancellor in equity, may immediately investigate the questions raised by this motion and may consider and determine: (*a*) Whether her property interests have been and are now fully protected; (*b*) whether there is any occasion for having these proceedings maintained on her behalf by 'next friends,' so called; (*c*) whether these proceedings were brought in and are now being maintained by said 'next friends' for her benefit and in good faith; (*d*) to determine all other questions raised by this motion so far as may be necessary for the protection of her rights; (*e*) that the said 'next friends' may be discharged by the Chancellor; (*f*) that the Chancellor may make such other orders as may be necessary or just for the protection of the petitioner and her property; (*g*) that her legal and equitable rights as a citizen of New Hampshire may in all respects so far as these proceedings are concerned be established and determined without further delay; (*h*) that the relations of said alleged 'next friends' to these proceedings may be suspended by order of the Chancellor until the questions hereby raised may be investigated and determined by him."

The vigor of the defense did not impress the editors of the *World*. A letter from the publisher of the Concord *Patriot* to the publisher of the *World,* protesting the New York newspaper's campaign of slander, was not answered.

CHAPTER TWENTY-ONE

A Conspiracy Collapses

O N THE SECOND DAY following the filing, by Mrs. Eddy's attorneys, of the motion requesting an early trial, the case of the "next friends" began to collapse.

The plaintiffs' attorneys became involved in a jangle with Judge Chamberlin over the scope of relevant testimony, and on June 15, George W. Baker asked to have his name stricken from the list of "next friends." Judge Chamberlin, instead of hearing the case, turned it over to the decision of Masters, selected them,[1] and defined the issue: ". . . The Master will hear all pertinent and competent evidence submitted by depositions or orally according to the law and practice in equity in this jurisdiction and determine the fact and report to the court whether on said first day of March, 1907, and for such period of time before that date as to the Master may seem reasonable, Mary Baker G. Eddy was capable of intelligently managing, controlling, and conducting her financial affairs and property interests.

"For the purpose of this hearing the 'next friends' named in the bill may appear by counsel and submit such proofs and competent evidence as they may have or can obtain; and said Mary Baker G. Eddy may appear by counsel and submit such pertinent and competent evidence as she may have or can obtain.

[1] The Masters were Judge Edgar Aldrich, Hosea W. Parker, and Dr. George F. Jelly.

"Having given the parties such reasonable time as may be required to prepare and obtain their evidence, and after reasonable notice, the Master will hear the evidence and the parties at the court house in Concord, New Hampshire, and at such other reasonable places as to the Master may seem proper; and having heard the evidence, the Master will make and file his report with the clerk of the Superior Court for said county of Merrimack, on or before the thirtieth day of September next. . . ."

Failing in his effort to bring Mrs. Eddy into a courtroom and to subject her to cross-examination, Attorney Chandler told the Masters on August 13, the first day of the hearing, (1) that "the plaintiffs were handicapped by lack of funds"; (2) that it was "regretted that the court had disallowed plaintiffs' motion for an allowance from the estate of Mrs. Eddy to meet the cost of the prosecution"; and (3) that "an injustice was done plaintiffs when a jury trial on the competency of Mrs. Eddy was denied," although Chandler admitted "there was no constitutional right upon which plaintiffs could base their demand for a trial by jury."

Various witnesses, such as Richard Kennedy, Daniel Spofford, and other early students of Mrs. Eddy, were called by Chandler in his effort to prove insanity, and as the first day of the hearings neared its close, the lawyer began complaining because he had not been able to talk with Mrs. Eddy, and thus was under a severe handicap. Attorney Streeter sought to solve that problem by informing the Masters: "I saw Mrs. Eddy yesterday and told her about the Masters being here, and I have no doubt, if it is agreeable to you, that the talk could be had tomorrow. And I would ask you to consider making the appointment to get there, say, at two o'clock in the afternoon."

Chandler protested, saying he was insufficiently prepared. The next morning, when court was opened, Chandler proposed that:

1. The first visit to Pleasant View be merely a preliminary visit.

2. He (Chandler) have the right to examine, and be accompanied by George W. Glover and Mary B. Glover to be certain it was Mrs. Eddy he was questioning.

3. There be five examinations.

4. If, as a result of the preliminary examinations, the Masters should decide that Mrs. Eddy could not undergo other examinations, then counsel for the "next friends" be permitted to place her under the observation of persons of their own choosing.

5. If the preliminary examinations disclosed that Mrs. Eddy was unable to be examined further, the Masters should declare the "next friends" had established "*a prima facie* case."

6. Examinations be held at different times; no member of Mrs. Eddy's household be present; no notice be given as to the time of any examination.

Streeter objected to all these proposals, and Judge Aldrich agreed with Streeter, saying: ". . . We are inclined, not arbitrarily, but on equitable and humanitarian lines, to hold this examination entirely in our own hands. It strikes us that the presence of the 'next friends' would be more injurious to the situation than beneficial. . . . I do not understand that the 'next friends' have a constitutional right to be present; I do not understand that counsel have even. This is not a lawsuit in the adversary sense, it is in the nature of an inquisition into the mental condition of Mrs. Eddy to see what her status is with respect to the proceeding that is pending in the state court. We will go at any time counsel agree and will endeavor to have everybody satisfied with the kind of examination that is held."

In a conference participated in by the Masters and the attorneys, it was agreed that Chandler and Streeter would accompany the Masters to Pleasant View. Chandler was told that inasmuch as he had no rights as a questioner, his "lack of preparedness" would not be a handicap because, for the most part, questioning would be done by the Masters. It was agreed that a court stenographer should be present, and that the examination would be held at two o'clock in the afternoon of that same day.

Here are the questions and answers on which the Masters made up their minds:

JUDGE ALDRICH: Mrs. Eddy, the gentlemen here wish to have an interview with you, and we desire to make this call as comfortable as possible for you, and we want you to let us know if we weary you.

MRS. EDDY: I am very glad to see you, and I thank you.

Q.: What is your native town?

A.: Bow, in New Hampshire. My father's farm lies on the banks of the Merrimack. He did much of his haying in Concord, but the house was in Bow.

Q.: How long have you lived in Concord?

A.: At this time, do you mean? About twenty years; between eighteen and twenty since I came here, after my marriage and residence in Boston.

Q.: Well, the gentlemen present want to ask

you some questions, and we all want to make this interview as pleasant for you as possible . . .

A.: Thank you very much.

Q.: And to have regard all the time to your comfort and convenience, and if you feel at all fatigued, we want you to say so at any time.

A.: What?

Q.: If you feel fatigued, we want to have you speak of it and let us know.

A.: Thank you. I can work hours at my work, day and night, without the slightest fatigue when it is in the line of spiritual labor.

Q.: Did you acquire all this property here at the outset, or did you purchase it gradually?

A.: I purchased it at the outset and suggested every construction and arrangement of my grounds throughout, and I still attend to it.

Q.: How many acres have you?

A.: Really, I do not know the number of acres.

Q.: Well, that is something that women do not always carry in their minds.

A.: This little pond (indicating) was made for me by my friends. It is an artificial pond. I have a little boat down there, and the boathouse.

Q. (by DR. JELLY): All this has been done under your direction, has it? The development of this place has all been under your direction, has it?

A.: It has. You can ask my foreman, August Mann. He resides in the cottage.

Q. (by DR. JELLY): We shall be glad to take your word for it, Mrs. Eddy.

Q. (by MR. PARKER) : Do you raise fruit here on the place? I see you have fruit trees.

A.: Yes, sir.

Q.: Oh, you do?

A.: And there were no trees here except pines when I came here. The rest of the trees I have planted, and when I suggested that a large tree be planted they laughed at me, but I said, "Try it and see if it will succeed." Every one of these trees around here (indicating) was planted by myself — that is, not by myself, but at my direction.

Q. (by JUDGE ALDRICH) : I have heard now and then that you have taken an interest in public affairs round about Concord and other places in New Hampshire. What about that? I have heard occasionally that you have given money to the city of Concord, and perhaps to other parts of the state, for highways, and other institutions. What about that?

A.: I have, with great pleasure. When I came here they had no State Fair grounds, and very little pavement. A one-horse car moved once an hour. There was very little being done in Concord then compared with what I anticipated when I came. It seemed to be going out, and I admire the apparent vigor and flourishing condition of this dear city now. I had great desire to build up my native place. . . . Am I talking too much?

Q.: No. We are all interested in what you say.

A.: They asked me in Boston to remain. Jordan & Marsh, White, and other firms requested me not to leave the city, and they said to me, "Have we not helped you to accumulate money since you have been here?" And I replied, "Have I not helped you?" And they said, "Yes, you have, and that is why we want to have you stay." Then I said, "I want to go home and help my native state a little."

Q. (by Dr. Jelly) : And that was how long ago, Mrs. Eddy?

A.: Between eighteen and twenty years.

Q.: Did you go directly to this place then — to this spot?

A.: I did, and there was a hut here, a simple hut. I had it moved off and I made what is here. The house was not built by myself; it was moved from where my cottage is. I built the cottage and moved that house which was then in its place here.

Q. (by Mr. Parker) : Did you come direct from Boston here?

A.: I did.

Q.: To this very place here?

A.: Yes sir. They laughed at me for taking this place, and I said, "You will see, it will be pretty, soon."

Q.: Did you live on State Street here in this town? Didn't you live on State Street at a time?

A.: I did not at this time, but I have resided on State Street.

Q.: When was that, Mrs. Eddy?

A.: It was when I — Well, I should think it was about seventeen years ago.

Q.: How long did you live there, Mrs. Eddy, on State Street?

A.: About two years.

Q.: And from State Street you came here?

A.: Yes.

Q.: Then, when you came from Boston you came and resided on State Street first, didn't you?

A.: I did. I had forgotten that.

Q.: And from State Street you moved here?

A.: Yes sir.

Q. (by JUDGE ALDRICH) : Some one was telling me that you had given to the public streets — the improvement of streets in Concord — is that so?

A.: I have, $10,000 at one time.

Q.: Where was that expended?

A.: It has been expended on this street and on other streets, Main Street and State Street.

Q.: Was it done at the suggestion of anybody, or was it your own idea?

A.: It was mine. They consulted me with regard to it. My students contributed toward it also and left the decision to me. When I built this church here, I put into it one-half of my property. Mr. Whitcomb, the builder, an honest man, told me it cost over $200,000.

Q.: It is a beautiful structure.

A.: I think so.

Q.: Now about your investments; we will touch on those just a little today, not much. About your investments. You have some income, I suppose, now?

A.: Some income, yes.

Q.: My life insurance is coming due pretty soon, and I want to make good use of it. What do you consider good investments?

A.: I do not put it into life insurance. God insures my life.

Q.: I carry a little life insurance and it is coming due, so I am interested, you know. You wouldn't advise my throwing it away, would you? For instance, my life insurance comes due next year.

A.: Yes, I respect that. I respect the life insurance. I think it is very valuable to many, but I have not any need for it.

Q.: It was not really in that sense that I suggested it. I wanted to get your idea as to what would be a good investment.

A.: Yes.

Q.: What did you say?

A.: Shall I tell you my ideas?

Q.: Yes.

A.: Trust in God. God is infinite. Therefore, if we are the image and the likeness of Infinity, we have no beginning and no end, and are His image and likeness; that is my life insurance.

Q.: It is not a question of that at all — at least, my thoughts were not running in that particular direction, but, what would be a sound investment of money that comes from life insurance or anything else?

A.: Well, I should invest it in the hands, at my age, of trustees that I could vouch for and from my own knowledge. And why? Because, when I found my church was gaining over 40,000 members, and the field demanding me all over the world, I could not carry on the letters, make answers to inquiries that were made of me. Then I said, "Which shall I do, carry on this business that belongs to property, or shall I serve God?" And I said — and it came to me from the Bible — "Choose ye this day whom ye will serve. Ye cannot serve God and mammon." Then I chose, and I said, "So help me God," and I launched out, and gave my property — I gave $913,000 to the trusteeship, to others for the benefit of my son — no, not for the benefit of my son, but — $913,000 into the trusteeship for myself. For my son I have $125,000 into trusteeship for himself and for his family.

Q. (by JUDGE ALDRICH) : Where did that idea of putting your property into the hands of trustees originate, with yourself or with someone else?

A.: Utterly with myself. It came to me in an hour in this room, and I think the first one that I named it to was Laura Sargent, and I said to her, "Do not speak of it, but I feel impressed that it is my duty."

Q.: When was that?

A.: That was in February, 1907.

Q.: Last winter, you mean?

A.: I do.

Q.: Now this is all interesting and useful, but still I have not made myself understood. For instance, without regard to your trusteeship now, if you had a hundred thousand dollars to invest to-day, and we will lay aside for the purpose of this question the matter of trusteeship, what kind of investments would you consider sound, municipal bonds, or government bonds, or bank stock, or what?

A.: I prefer government bonds. I have invested largely in government bonds, and I prefer bonds to stocks. I have not entered into stocks.

Q.: Why?

A.: Because I did not think it was safe for me. I did not want the trouble of it, that was all. Perhaps I was mistaken, but that is my business sense of it, and the only time I took the advice of a student and went contrary, I lost ten thousand dollars by it.

Q.: What was that?

A.: That was in an investment that was made in property in the West, where the land, they said, was coming up and going to be a great advancement in value, and I lost it, and I never got caught again. I always selected my own investments.

Q.: How do you select them now?

A.: Now?

Q.: Yes.

A.: I leave them to my trustees.

Q.: Before that?

A.: I will tell you. I have books that give definitely the population of the states, and their money values, and I consult these, and when I see they are large enough in population and valuation to warrant an investment I make it.

Q.: Well, now, upon what philosophy do you base your calculations upon population? Why do you take population as the standard?

A.: Because I think they can sustain their debts and pay them.

Q.: Well, I should think that was pretty sound.
Would you go West for municipal investments, or
would you rather trust yourself in the East, in New
England we will say?

A.: I would rather trust my trustees now. I do
not take those things into consideration.

Q.: Dr. Jelly desires that I should ask you, laying aside for the present the matter of trusteeship,
what would be your idea, whether there was
greater security of investment in Eastern munici-
palities or Western?

A.: The East, I should say.

Q. (by DR. JELLY) : Mrs. Eddy, are you willing
to tell us something about the development of your
special religion? Are you willing to tell us about
how the matter came about, and how it has existed
and developed? It would be interesting to us to
know, if you are willing to tell us, about Christian
Science. Tell us something about the development
of that; are you willing to do it?

A.: I would love to do it.

Q.: Tell us as fully as you please. I think we
would all like to hear about it.

A.: I was an invalid born in belief. I was always
having doctors —

Q.: When you say "born in belief," I perhaps
do not understand what you mean.

A.: I mean born according to human nature,
born not of God, but of the flesh. That is what I
mean. I was an invalid from my birth.

Q.: Can you tell us something about the way in
which you were an invalid, if you can recollect it?

A.: No, I cannot recollect it, only I was considered weak and delicate.

Q.: I asked you to tell us something about the development of Christian Science. Will you go on, if you please?

A.: My father employed M.D.'s of the highest character, and they were estimable men, and they would say — Dr. Renton was one, and he said, and the others said: "Do not doctor your child, she has got too much brains for her body; keep her outdoors, keep her in exercise, and keep her away from school all you can, and do not give her much medicine." Then it was all allopathy, you know.

Q.: Can you tell us how long ago that was, please — about how long? I don't suppose you can tell exactly, but somewhere near.

A.: No. I should say I was eighteen years old, perhaps, and it came to me through Dr. Morrill, he was a homœopath, and I had never heard of it before; it was a new subject in New Hampshire, and father said: "I thought he was a fine fellow, but he must have gone mad to have taken up homœopathy." That was the general idea of things then. When Dr. Morrill came to Concord he healed cases that the other M. D.'s did not, and my father employed him, and I got well under his treatment. Then you asked me to tell my footsteps? I said, I will study homoeopathy. I did. I was delighted with it. I took a case that a doctress considered hopeless, and I cured the case. It was dropsy; the patient looked like a barrel in the bed, and I cured her. I began to think something about what it was that cured, when the highest attenuation —

Q.: What did you say about the highest attenuation?

A.: I began with the highest attenuation in which the drug absolutely disappeared, and I sent that attenuation to Dr. Jackson of Boston and asked him if he could discover the origin of that? It was common table salt.

Q.: Was it Dr. Charles T. Jackson, the chemist?

A.: Yes sir, and he replied to me, "I cannot find a particle of salt in it."

Q.: I knew him personally.

A.: Did you?

Q.: Yes.

A.: Then I said, "I will be safe and see if I am deceived," and went to work on a patient. I gave her a high attenuation of medicine, and she took it and recovered quite rapidly. Then there were symptoms of relapse, and I had been quite interested in homœopathy and thought that by giving too much of this diluted, attenuated medicine there might be a crisis produced and difficulty, so I took away the medicine and gave her a single pellet unmedicated, nothing but a sugar pellet, and she gained just the same. At last I said to her, "Now you need no more medicine; go without it," and she said, "I will." In three days she came to me and said "I feel some of the old symptoms." I repeated my pellet, not one particle of medicine, and she began to gain again.

That was my first discovery of the Science of Mind. That was a falling apple to me — it made plain to me that mind governed the whole question of her recovery. I was always praying to be kept from sin, and I waited and prayed for God to direct me. The next that I encountered were spiritualist who were claiming to be mediums. I went into their seances to find out what they were doing. Shall I go on with this unnecessary detail?

DR. JELLY: I will not trouble you to go into that in any further particulars just now, but Mr. Parker would like to ask you a few questions.

MRS. EDDY: Yes. Shall I continue this subject to show how I entered into the understanding of Christian Science?

DR. JELLY: I will leave that to Mr. Parker.

Q. (by MR. PARKER): I want to talk about everyday affairs. May I?

A.: Yes.

Q.: If we desire on some other occasion to have a talk with you, we will come again.

A.: Thank you.

Q.: Mrs. Eddy, you have not traveled much — you have not gone about the state much, have you?

A.: No, I have not.

Q.: Do you know where I live?

A.: No, I do not.

Q.: I live in Claremont.

A.: In Claremont?

Q.: Yes, over on the Connecticut River. We think it is a very beautiful town.

A.: Yes, it is, I am told.

Q.: In your drives, how far do you drive every day?

A.: I am out anywhere from half an hour to an hour.

Q.: Do you feel refreshed? Why do you go to drive?

A.: Yes, it is a pleasant recreation. It keeps me away from my desk.

Q.: Do you feel refreshed when you come back?

A.: Yes.

Q.: You don't leave your home here; at least you don't go out of town, or out of the city anywhere?

A.: No.

Q.: Would you have sufficient strength, do you think, to take the train for Boston? Could you do that?

A.: I could, but I should not wish to undertake it because I have so much resting upon me here to do.

Q.: I see. How many hours in the day do you work in an intellectual way? How many hours in the day do you keep your mind upon your work?

A.: Well, I rise in the morning early and have few hours during the day when I am not at work, and I have the care of the house as much as I ever did.

Q.: Now, your intellectual work, or your work in connection with your subject. Do you write? Are you writing? Do you write letters nowadays?

A.: I write them or dictate them. Others seldom

write letters for me, save through dictation; then I look them over and see if they are right.

Q.: You look them over yourself?

A.: Yes, I do.

Q.: Is that invariable? Don't you ever let letters go away from you without that?

A.: I do not when they pertain to business of my own.

Q.: Is that so with regard to your property affairs, that you look over the letters before they are sent away?

A.: Yes, unless I know not when they are written.

Q.: My attention is called to your last answer. I asked you if you looked over your letters pertaining to your property matters and you said you did, unless they wrote letters when you didn't know about them.

A.: I am answering you there about my action before I constituted the trusteeship.

Q.: Yes, but I suppose you have more or less business now, don't you, of a financial character?

A.: Yes.

Q.: But the large responsibility you put upon your trustees?

A.: Yes. Mr. Fernald here is the Superintendent of the Old Folks' Home; he is a good man to take care of me, is he not?

Q.: Yes, I know him.

A.: And I know Henry M. Baker, my cousin, and I certainly know Archibald McLellan, and a better man we do not need to have. Now, I am thinking why cannot we have all this in love and unity and good will to man?

Q.: It is. Do you read more or less, Mrs. Eddy?

A.: Indeed I do.

Q.: You do?

A.: Every chance I get, for a rest.

Q.: Are you fond of music?

A.: I used to be exceedingly, and I have an artificial singer in my house. You know what I mean by that. I will have them show it to you in the vestibule. (*Ringing bell for attendant, who responds promptly.*)

MRS. EDDY *to the attendant:* Tell Mr. Frye to come to me.

A. (THE ATTENDANT) : Yes.

MRS. EDDY: It will imitate a voice.

Q.: Were you musical in your younger days?

A.: Yes, I never was taught, but all the other members of the family were, and yet I would compose music.

(*Mr. Frye came in at this point and was introduced to the Board of Masters.*)

MRS. EDDY: Mr. Frye, I want you to show them my artificial singer.

MR. FRYE: Yes. It is a graphophone, gentlemen.

Q. (by JUDGE ALDRICH) : I want to say before going that my mother is still living and she is eighty-seven years of age.

A.: Give my love to her.

Q.: I will.

A.: God bless her. She is not a day older for her eighty-seven years if she is growing in grace.

Q.: Well, she feels pretty happy.

A.: I have no doubt she is. I mean mere decaying when I say "older." She is rising higher. Decay belongs not to matter but to mortal mind. We do not lose our faculties through matter so much as through mind, do we? Now, my thought is, that if we keep our mind fixed on Truth, God, Life and Love, He will advance us in our years to a higher understanding; He will change our hope into faith, our faith into spiritual understanding, our words into works, and our ultimate into the fruition of entering into the Kingdom.

Q.: Well, I will have to say good afternoon.

A.: Pardon my mistakes, if I have made any.

Dr. Jelly: Good afternoon, Mrs. Eddy.

Mrs. Eddy: Excuse my sitting; come and see me again.

Dr. Jelly: We do not want to tire you.

Mrs. Eddy: Thank you.

Mr. Chandler: Good-by, Mrs. Eddy.

Mr. Parker: Good afternoon, Mrs. Eddy. I am very glad to have met you.

Mrs. Eddy: Thank you. (*To the stenographer*) We have kept you very busy. Thank you for your services.

(*After they had listened to the graphophone, a message was brought to Judge Aldrich that Mrs. Eddy wanted to see the Board of Masters again, because she thought there was something she had omitted, and thereupon the Masters returned to her room.*)

Mrs. Eddy: I feel that I did not answer you

fully; that I dropped my subject before I concluded it with regard to the footsteps in Christian Science. Now, allow me to complete that thought. I got to where I told you that I found it was mind instead of the drug that healed . . .

JUDGE ALDRICH: Let me make one remark. There were two reasons why we suggested we would not pursue that branch of the inquiry any further. One was, that we were a little afraid we might weary you, and the other was that in certain quarters it is suggested that this investigation is an attack on your doctrines, and we did not want to have it appear that we were requiring you to make any statements about it.

MRS. EDDY: Not at all. I shall regard it as a great favor if you will condescend to hear me on this.

JUDGE ALDRICH: If you desire it, we are bound to listen to you — if you desire to express yourself about it.

MRS. EDDY: When I came to the point that it was mind that did the healing, then I wanted to know what mind it was. Was it Mind which was in Christ Jesus, or was it the human mind and human will?

This led me to investigate spiritualism, mesmerism and hypnotism, and I failed to find God there; therefore, I returned to God in prayer and said, "Just guide me to that mind which is in Christ," and I took the Bible and opened to the words, "Now, go, write it in a book." I can show you where this Scripture is in the Bible.

I then commenced writing my consciousness of what I had seen, and I found that human will was the cause of disease instead of its cure; that neither hypnotism, mesmerism, nor human concepts did heal; they too were the origin of disease instead of its cure, and that the Divine Mind was the Healer; then I found through the Scripture that "He healed all our diseases." Also the command, Go ye into the field, preach the Gospel, heal the sick, and I felt there was my line of labor, and that God did the healing, and that I could no more heal a person by mortal mind, the mind of mortals, or will-power, than by cutting off his head. I do not know how to use will-power to hurt the sick.

When people began to talk mesmerism, I doubted it; and I said to a facetious student, "Han-over Smith, you go into another room and see if I can sit here and tell lies enough to make you suffer." He went into another room, and I com-menced arguing what they said made folks sick, and I did my best talking it. When he returned to me, I said, "Hanover, do you feel ill?" He replied, "I never felt better in my life than I do now. I feel rested."

A Christian Scientist can no more make a person sick than he can at the same time be a sinner and be a Christian Scientist. He does not knowingly make people suffer or injure them in any way — he has not the power to do it. All the power that Christian Scientists have comes from on High. We have no other power, and no faith in any other power.

I thank you for your kindness and attention, very much.

Returning to the courtroom the next morning, Senator Chandler abandoned the proposition of trying to prove Mrs. Eddy incapable of handling her own money, and with the other attorneys for the "next friends" spent the next three days trying to establish that in Christian Science "the mind is no longer dominated by reason," as Attorney Howe declared, "but reason's place has been taken by an insane belief which persists and abides despite all evidence; and it is to those concrete instances that we address our testimony in this case."

JUDGE ALDRICH: Suppose that a million people believe in such miracles, and perhaps you might say Biblical miracles can be accomplished under divine influence, who has the right, under the constitutional government which protects religious conscience, to say that they are under insane delusions, and such insane delusions as to justify the courts in wresting the management of property from the hands of a large number of people?

MR. HOWE: The number of people who have taken it up and adopted, upon faith, without inquiry as to facts, any particular belief, is no evidence that they are insane, nor is it evidence —

JUDGE ALDRICH: It might not be evidence that would convince you or convince me, but does not the idea of constitutional government recognize the wisdom of not undertaking to deal with such situations?

MR. HOWE: Why, I do not so understand it.

JUDGE ALDRICH: A constitutional government does not condemn large bodies of people on the ground that they are religious insane.

MR. HOWE: I do not understand that the fact that persons please to describe an insane delusion as their religion makes it a religion within the meaning of the word.

After more back-and-forth questioning between the Masters and the attorneys for the "next friends," Judge Aldrich inquired:

Now let me ask another question upon another line for the purpose of testing the position. How many Christian Scientists are there now in the country? You have investigated the subject?

MR. HOWE: I think I read in some of Mrs. Eddy's writings — it is possible that it was in the report of yesterday's interview with her — that there were 40,000.

JUDGE ALDRICH: Connected with the Church. How many are there, Mr. Streeter?

MR. STREETER: It is said by distinguished men that there are from half a million to a million. Mr. Farlow testified so in Boston the other day.

JUDGE ALDRICH: Now, what has been the length of time in which this growth has occurred — something like twenty years?

MR. HOWE: I do not understand, your Honor.

JUDGE ALDRICH: We have had this growth in fifteen or twenty years, I believe.

MR. HOWE: The growth in numbers?

JUDGE ALDRICH: Yes.

MR. HOWE: I am not able to say in regard to that. The figures seem to vary from half a million to a million, and I shall have to rely on my brothers for that.

JUDGE ALDRICH: Suppose in the course of two hundred years the Christian Scientists outnumber all other denominations, and would be more than half the population of this country, and the government should be administered by them, would you hold that it would be a wise administration of government if they passed laws which would declare all the rest as not believing as they do under insane delusions?

MR. HOWE: That condition two hundred years hence, did I understand your Honor?

JUDGE ALDRICH: It is not a probable condition, of course, but is merely to test the question.

MR. HOWE: It may be that the equally improbable condition will then exist, namely, that an insane person cannot be shown to be insane because the insanity is of a religious type. That condition is no less improbable.

MR. PARKER: I wish you would state that again.

MR. HOWE: I understand Judge Aldrich's question to be this: Suppose two hundred years hence the government is in the hands of the Christian Scientists, would it be constitutional for them —

JUDGE ALDRICH: I did not say "constitutional," but would it be a wise administration of the government?

MR. HOWE: A wise?

JUDGE ALDRICH: A wise.

MR. HOWE: I mistook your question entirely, as to whether it would be wise or constitutional.

JUDGE ALDRICH: Take it either way. Of course the constitution would have to be changed.

MR. HOWE: Of course it would be impossible for me to answer the question of the wisdom of it except in this way — I think it is always wise to take care of the property of people who are insane, and the fact that their insanity is of a religious nature should not exclude them from being properly taken care of.

After three days of effort to establish Christian Science as the issue, Chandler addressed the Masters on the morning of August 21:

> May it please the court, it will doubtless be a relief to the Masters to be informed that the counsel for the "next friends" have this day filed with the clerk of the court a motion for the dismissal of the pending suit, and that they hereby withdraw their appearance before the Masters without asking from them any finding upon the questions submitted to them by Judge Chamberlin.
>
> There are many reasons for this action. The principal one arises from a consideration of the unprofitableness of any immediate result of a decision in our favor upon the exact issue as now framed, compared with the burdens and disadvantages to be endured by us, both before and after such a decision.

The suit has been almost wholly altruistic in its nature, and not a single dollar of the large fortune whose existence is disclosed, or which might be enlarged in consequence of this suit, can become at this time the property of the "next friends." There are also reasons sentimental in their character overcoming the strong desire of the "next friends" to prove the facts and vindicate the reasons upon which the suit has been based, which suit, however, is now hereby dismissed.

Scarcely had Chandler concluded when Streeter was on his feet, rejecting the attempt by the opposing counsel to close the court record and shut off the entering of the essential truths of the case:

If your Honors please, in behalf of Mrs. Eddy, my associates, the Attorney General Mr. Eastman, and Allen Hollis, join me in presenting the following motion:

"That the Masters proceed with the hearing, to determine the question submitted, namely, Mrs. Eddy's competency to manage her business affairs. . . ."

Upon this motion I desire to speak briefly, and perhaps, more temperately than the circumstances would justify me in speaking.

If we are allowed to proceed we should show you that on February 12, Mrs. Eddy began to arrange for the entire management of her property during her life, and to make liberal provision for her kindred during that time. I will not go into the details of these matters excepting to say to you if your Honors are not already satisfied we should be able to satisfy you beyond question, not only of Mrs. Eddy's absolute competency to deal with her affairs, but that during the last two weeks of February, the last two weeks before this suit was brought, she was dealing with those questions with sagacity so far as her business matters were concerned, and as a noble Christian woman so far as her next of kin were concerned.

Now, your Honors, neither Mrs. Eddy nor her counsel have the power to prevent her so-called "next friends" from trying to persuade Judge Chamberlin to let them dismiss the bill and get out of court. Neither have we the power to prevent their unconditional surrender in the middle of the hearing before the Masters.

They volunteered to begin this wretched assault upon the person, property, and religious faith of an aged citizen of New Hampshire, and now, six months later, when their charges have utterly collapsed, they run to cover.

This is their legal right, but I speak of the legal rights of Mrs. Eddy.

Let me temperately review the situation. She is an honored citizen of this state, entitled to the protection of its courts. She is the founder and head of a great religious organization, with many hundred thousand devoted followers. On March 1 last, she was living peacefully in her own home, surrounded by faithful friends of her own choice. She was possessed of a large property, acquired almost solely from the sale of her religious writings.

It will sometime appear that, after providing liberally for her own kin, she has devoted much of her
estate to the promotion of the religious views
taught by her. She was a good citizen. She was, and
is, entitled to the protection of the law.

On that day, March 1 last, this suit was instituted by a great newspaper which had hired and
paid eminent counsel to bring it. It was primarily
an attack upon the religious teachings of a great
religious leader. A son and an adopted son incon-
siderately loaned the use of their names as "next
friends" and the agent of this newspaper who visited the son in Lead City, Dakota, November 29,
and the adopted son at Waterbury, Vermont,
March 6, and persuaded them to cooperate, is now
writing in the presence of your Honors at the
reporters' table.

This suit was brought in her name against ten
honest men, alleging, first, that she was incompetent to protect her property, and, second, that these
ten defendants have wrongfully misappropriated
her funds. Not one of these defendants has ever
taken a dollar of her money. They have answered
under oath. The truth of their answers is admitted.
The suit is based on false pretenses. The situation
was unique in legal history. Mrs. Eddy, in the eyes
of the law, was not a defendant, although the proceedings were, in fact, being directed solely against
her. She was not a plaintiff; the suit was brought
against her will.

Her trustees, who held and were managing her
entire estate under a valid deed, prayed for leave

to intervene. Their petition was denied. She personally appealed to the court for protection. She urged that the maintenance of these proceedings by these alleged "next friends" was an abuse of the processes of the court and an unwarranted interference with her constitutional and legal rights, and she was entitled to speedy relief.

She represented that under the Constitution and the laws she was of right entitled to a determination of the questions, first, whether her property interests have been and are now fully protected, and whether there is any lawful or just occasion for the maintenance of these proceedings by said "next friends"; and second, whether the trust deed and the appointment of trustees and attorneys by her was thereby her free and intelligent act and carried her own wishes; and, third, whether the proceedings were brought in good faith for her personal benefit, and as a citizen she prayed for a speedy determination of these and other questions — all without avail.

These so-called "next friends," her assailants, bitterly opposed her petitions and they were denied. They insisted that her competency should be determined by the court, and their requests were granted against her protests.

You were appointed Masters to pass on the question submitted in your commission.

Knowing that upon the evidence there could be but one outcome of this hearing, she did not hesitate to submit to your decision. She has co-operated with you to obtain a full investigation. She has assented to every suggestion made by the Masters to enable them to arrive at a just decision. She has submitted herself to your personal examination in the presence of counsel for the alleged "next friends," and the stenographic report thereof, inaccurate in many respects, has been given to the world. She has been asked to submit herself to the examination of hostile alienists, and, for the purpose of enabling you to reach a just conclusion in your way, she has assented to that. Nothing that your Honors thought would aid in the ascertainment of the truth has been objected to by her or by her counsel.

This trial has been proceeding five days, and with the exception of her own examination before you, the only evidence submitted is a few letters selected out of thousands written by her, and a few fragments of her other writings. Upon the charge that her money has been misappropriated, that her property was not safeguarded, not one word of testimony has been introduced. The charge that she is incompetent has utterly collapsed, and now these altruists who pretended and represented to the court that they brought this suit to her friends, for her protection and in her interests, have made their public confession to the world.

Under these circumstances, we submit that Mrs. Eddy has a legal right to a finding of her competency — to such a finding on the case as it now stands. If you think otherwise, then to a finding upon such evidence as she may produce.

Any other result will bring reproach, in the eyes

of the world, upon the administration of justice here.

I speak, your Honors, not only for Mrs. Eddy, but for every other citizen of this state whose person, property, religious convictions are now endangered. In their name, and in the name of this honorable and honored woman, we respectfully demand that a finding of competency be made by your Honors upon this issue, thrust upon her and submitted to your decision by the court.

Judge Aldrich did not agree. Holding to the technical grounds of the law, he made reply:

. . . We may be wrong in our disposition of your motion, Mr. Streeter, but although this is a friendly suit, as we have said, it in a sense . . . involves the interests of different parties, and when the party who asserts a lack of mental capacity withdraws there is really no controversy left; Mrs. Eddy stands with nothing to answer, as we view it.

If we take the course which I have just suggested, report all the evidence up to the present time, and then report what action has been taken by the "next friends" on your motion, then, in case we are now in error about the effect of this withdrawal, Judge Chamberlin will only have to direct that the trial proceed, and if we are right he will only have to accept the situation as one in which the plaintiffs have the right to dismiss the bill and end the controversy.

If we should go forward, we might do something

unwarrantable, and according to our view we should if we undertook to decide this issue, to go forward in the absence of "next friends" and decide upon the question of Mrs. Eddy's capacity.[2] If we should stop and report what has been done to Judge Chamberlin, there could be no harm done, except such as results from delay.

I think, before these three volumes which have come from the stenographer are formally made a part of the report, the record should be corrected, either by myself or in connection with Mr. Parker and Dr. Jelly, or by counsel. There are necessarily some verbal errors, of course. We do not mean that as any criticism upon anybody. Is there anything further to be said?

On the morning of September 30, 1907, in Superior Court in Concord, Judge Chamberlin heard arguments for the dismissal of the suit, and listened as Chandler sought to file a brief containing objections to the rulings of the Masters. Chamberlin decided against Chandler; and the attorney then argued that "no costs should be allowed against the 'next friends,' but should be paid by the defendants."

[2] At request of Chandler, the Masters appointed and directed Dr. Allan McLane Hamilton and Dr. Edward French, expert alienists, to examine Mrs. Eddy. In his report, Dr. Hamilton found "no visible indication of any motor symptoms of insanity or nervous disease. Her expression was intelligent and in consonance with what she said and did. She was dignified, though cordial, and possessed a certain sense of humor which led her to perpetrate a joke about the so-called 'next friends' to whom she referred as 'nexters.' There was no tremor, no affection of speech — I found nothing the matter with her." Dr. French reported: "I was fully persuaded that there was not the least evidence of mental weakness or incompetency, and I was impressed with her intelligence and business ability. In my opinion she is mentally capable and competent to manage her own affairs of whatever nature."

Judge Chamberlin ruled that the "next friends" could have until October 10, 1907, to file a brief on the question of costs, and that counsel for the trustees must reply by October 15. The hearing scheduled for October 15 was postponed until November 12, 1907, at which time judgment was rendered against the "next friends." They were ordered to pay the costs of the suit.

In an exhaustive study of this suit, under the title of *Mrs. Eddy and the Late Suit in Equity,* Michael Meehan, of the *Concord Patriot,* wrote:

> . . . The New York *Times,* perhaps trying to make amends for having followed the lead of the New York *World* in attacking the founder of Christian Science, and her teachings, interviewed Dr. Allan McLane Hamilton, Chandler's alienist, and quoted him:
>
> "When I met Mrs. Eddy a few weeks ago I had quite a different experience from that reported by many of her interviewers. Remember, I had the experience of the newspaper reporters in my mind and I was thus naturally on the lookout for any evidence of mental weakness in her which they claim to have discovered.
>
> "I found Mrs. Eddy, on the occasion to which I allude, seated in a comfortable armchair in her study, a large back room on the second floor of her house. She was simply attired in a dark dress and light sacque, relieved by a simple ornament, a diamond broach.
>
> "Her white hair was worn in a style made familiar by her pictures. Her face was thin, as was her

body. I was immediately impressed with the
extraordinary intelligence shown in her eyes. In
aged persons the eyes are apt to appear dimmed,
contracted, and lacking in expression. With Mrs.
Eddy, however, they are large, dark, and at times
almost luminous in appearance.

"As she talked to me, or answered my questions,
the play of expression on her features evinced
unusual intelligence, and was in strict keeping
with what she said. Her whole bearing was dignified and reserved, in perfect accord with what one
would expect in a woman of education and refine-
ment."

The historic records, the almost incredible details of
this legal inquisition, are all but unknown, even among
Christian Scientists. They stand, for the record, as they were
documented during that summer of 1907 — and what better
way is there to close this sordid register than to repeat the
words of Attorney Streeter?

"Nothing that your Honors thought would aid in the
ascertainment of the truth has been objected to. . . ."

CHAPTER TWENTY-TWO

The Peace of Her Years

THE NOTICE in the *Christian Science Sentinel* of October 17, 1908, was a simple one:

> We are pleased to announce that with the approval of our Leader, Mrs. Eddy, The Christian Science Publishing Society will shortly publish a daily newspaper to be known as *The Christian Science Monitor*.

Behind that simple announcement were years of thought, and preparation, and prayer.

Preparatory to installing Archibald McLellan as editor of the *Journal* and the *Sentinel* in 1902, Mrs. Eddy wrote a letter in which she said, "Until I start a widespread press, we should have in Boston a born editor." In Mrs. Eddy's view, McLellan was such an editor. He was an easy writer, as well as an experienced executive. In selecting him as successor to Septimus J. Hanna, she was offering the *Journal* and the *Sentinel* as his proving ground.

But, before this, Mrs. Eddy was preparing for the day when "a widespread press" in the form of a daily newspaper would carry the message of Christian Science to the world.

On January 25, 1898, "and for the purpose of more effectually promoting and extending the religion of Christian Science," Mrs. Eddy executed a deed of trust under which she gave to The First Church of Christ, Scientist, in Boston, Massachusetts, the building and real estate occupied by The Christian Science Publishing Society at 95 and 97 Falmouth Street.

In this legal instrument, she also gave to The Mother Church all the publications of the movement, saving only the right to copyright the *Christian Science Journal* in her own name. All the moneys and assets of the publications were to be held in trust by three trustees,[1] whom she charged with managing the business affairs of the Publishing Society, with all profits being turned over to The Mother Church at stipulated intervals.

In Paragraph 10 of this deed of trust, Mrs. Eddy made it clear that the Trustees were subject not only to her wishes but, in the event of her death, to the wishes of The Christian Science Board of Directors. Paragraph 10 of this deed of trust reads:

> Whenever a vacancy shall occupy in said trusteeship for any cause, I reserve the right to fill the same by appointment, if I shall so desire, so long as I may live; but if I do not elect to exercise this right, the remaining trustees shall fill the vacancy. The First Members with the directors of said Church shall have the power to declare vacancies in said trusteeship for such reasons as to them may seem expedient.

In this deed of trust, Mrs. Eddy also provided that "if I do not exercise this reserved option [to withdraw from the trusteeship copyright to the *Journal*] the publication "shall

---

[1] The first Trustees were: Edward P. Bates, James A. Neal, and William P. McKenzie.

remain a part of the trust property forever." Inasmuch as she never exercised this option, the *Christian Science Journal* remains a property of The Mother Church.

In the December [1901] issue of the *Journal,* there was a discussion of the functions of the different publications, in which it was explained:

The periodicals issued regularly, weekly, monthly, and quarterly, are all copyrighted in the name of the Pastor Emeritus of The Mother Church, Reverend Mary Baker G. Eddy. This copyright indicates a reserved privilege, not beneficiary ownership; for the periodicals are managed by trustees for the sole benefit of The Mother Church. The Pastor Emeritus has the privilege of withdrawing the periodicals from such management should they fail to be representative of true Christian Science, and of this guardianship the copyright is token. From the publishing of the periodicals sent out by the Publishing Society, Mrs. Eddy has no pecuniary reward whatever; yet for the welfare of the Cause, she not only contributes to their columns, but on occasions exercises an oversight which demands much time and labor. This cheerful giving of time and thought on her part encourages the responsible workers to a devotion far beyond what their moderate remuneration would demand.

It will be seen that The Christian Science Publishing Society cannot be hospitable to publishing of a general kind, but has to maintain its own clearly defined field of operation. This does not include the publishing of works of fiction, story books, volumes of verse, poems, histories, and so on. Contributions to the columns of the periodicals are always considered; but manuscripts offered for private publication, as well as calendars, bookcovers, wall-maps, books of texts, daily reminders, book-marks, pictures, etc., have to be returned to their senders. . . .

She paused for a moment on the steps at Pleasant View, looked across the hills toward Bow, and then entered the waiting carriage to take her last drive through the streets of Concord. The day was Sunday, January 26, 1908. Snow was everywhere, white and dazzling as the sun shone warmly down from a clear sky. At the railroad station, she walked across the platform and up the steps of the private car attached to the special train that was taking her, and her household, back to Boston.

Word that Mrs. Eddy was leaving had spread quickly about Concord, giving confirmation to the rumors that for days had accompanied each shipment of trunks, and furniture, and boxes from Pleasant View. Now all eyes sought the small figure sitting by a window in the drawing room of the railroad coach. A gray toque trimmed with white and purple ostrich plumes on her head, and about her a sable cloak under which was a gray suit, Mrs. Eddy sat with Laura E. Sargent and Calvin Frye as, inching forward before gathering momentum, the train pulled away from the station.

In Boston, special arrangements by the railroad officials made it possible to route the train directly to the Chestnut Hill station. Here Mrs. Eddy's carriage and coachman and favorite horses, Major and Princess — which had been sent on ahead — were waiting; waiting, too, at her new home, were newspaper reporters.[2] As they crowded about the carriage their questions were lost when one of Mrs. Eddy's helpers, John Salchow, gathered her up in his arms and carried her up the steps and into the house.

The great work of founding her church, writing its *Manual,* establishing its literature, organizing its teachings,

---

[2] Purchased late in 1907, Chestnut Hill, Mrs. Eddy's new home, consisted of a house of twenty-five rooms in a setting of about twelve acres of wooded land. Wild flowers and birds were in profusion on the property, one member of the household reporting more than one hundred varieties of blossoms and ninety species of birds.

appointing its Board of Lectureship, its Committee on Publication, and creating the various institutional activities was largely done. Now her work was of deeper nature — of a nature unseen by the world, and not understood by many, even the most understanding of her students, but explained in a message she sent to her own Association, the Massachusetts Metaphysical College Association, in June 1891:

> MY BELOVED STUDENTS: — You may be looking to see me in my accustomed place with you, but this you must no longer expect. When I retired from the field of labor, it was a departure, socially, publicly, and finally, from the routine of such material modes as society and our societies demand. Rumors are rumors, — nothing more. I am still with you on the field of battle, taking forward marches, broader and higher views, and with the hope that you will follow. . . .
>
> All our thoughts should be given to the absolute demonstration of Christian Science. You can well afford to give me up, since you have in my last revised edition of *Science and Health* your teacher and guide. . . .[3]

Her work now was to lead her followers away from her human personality, and into the path of the spiritual — away from belief in human leadership, and into the promise of Life which, not being born, goes on and on and does not die. These were years of lingering benediction in which she instructed in the way of spiritual progress, saying to all, as she said to her household, "In my childhood, I was taught that religion was a solemn, altogether dolorous affair.

[3] *Miscellaneous Writings*, pp. 135, 136.

Now I know that it should be just the opposite — a religion should beget joy and good cheer."

However, although in her eighty-seventh year, her work of fully establishing the literature of Christian Science was not completed.

The idea of a daily newspaper had been under discussion for years, but it is probable the lurid fakes printed in various publications prior to, and during, the "next friends" suit hastened Mrs. Eddy's decision to introduce her own newspaper. In fact, the idea of a daily newspaper was the principal reason for the removal from Concord to Boston. If there was to be a daily paper, quicker means of communication with her executives were necessary.

In the discussions, first with her household, then with the Directors, and then with the Trustees of the Publishing Society, Mrs. Eddy usually was advised against undertaking such a venture. She was told of the large expense, of the large number of employees that would be needed, of the large additional burden it would place upon her. She shook off all the arguments until the coming of the day at Chestnut Hill when she was compelled to take her stand on the naming of the paper.

She liked the word "Monitor" carried at the masthead of one of Concord's newspapers. She insisted on its use; she also insisted on the inclusion of the words "Christian Science," and the full name, the *Christian Science Monitor*. Without an exception experienced publishers advised against use of the words "Christian Science," saying their use would destroy the value of the paper as a bearer of news. Mrs. Eddy insisted their use would protect the paper. The years have proved her right. Without the words, the character of the newspaper might have survived, but it is doubtful.

Her thoughts on what sort of newspaper the *Christian Science Monitor* should be, as remembered by those who were present, were repeated in the newspaper on September 4, 1934:

> The essential function of a newspaper is to print the news. It is the desire and the determination of the *Monitor* today to record and interpret, in true perspective, all of the world's significant news. The test of all *Monitor* news is whether that news is socially important, whether it is news which we all need to know to be informed and alert citizens. It is the goal of the *Monitor* to give to its readers a newspaper which will be vital, realistic and comprehensive, which will give to the good news, to the encouraging news and to the constructive news the prominence it rightfully deserves. At the same time the *Monitor* ignores nothing essential to a penetrating understanding of all those aggravated social conditions to which readers of the Monitor, particularly, can give healing attention.

This policy came out of the long discussions. There were a good many notions of what the newspaper should be. Some said it should deal only with religion. Some said it should print nothing about religion. Some said it should print only New England news. Some said it should print only world news. Mrs. Eddy listened to all and decided if the *Christian Science Monitor* was to be "a widespread press" it had to be equally interesting in London, in New York, and in Sydney, Australia.

As a part of the effort to satisfy world interest, she required that one article of a religious nature be published daily. The page she selected for the article she called the Home Forum page. The idea for this title had its origin in her wish to appeal to the family circle, and the idea for the page came from a personal scrapbook in which were pasted carefully selected clippings from different publications.

In its announcement of October 17, 1908, the *Christian Science Sentinel* said of the *Monitor* that it was to be "a strictly up-to-date newspaper in which all the news of the day that should be printed will find a place . . . whose service will not be restricted to any one locality, or section, but will cover the daily activities of the entire world." To make sure that the *Monitor,* and all Christian Science publications, should have competent supervision, Mrs. Eddy stipulated that "it shall be the duty of the Directors to see that these periodicals are ably edited and kept abreast of the times." [4]

In the weeks of preparation, letters went out from Archibald McLellan to newspaper people all over the country who were known to be interested in Christian Science, inviting them to send in applications for positions on the staff. The response was immediate. Within a very short time the various departments were fully staffed, and on November 25, 1908, the day before Thanksgiving, the first issue of the *Christian Science Monitor* was on sale in Boston, and in the mails for delivery to subscribers in the United States, Canada, and Europe.

On Page One was an article foretelling a foreign news service that would come to be recognized as one of the finest in the world. The article reviewed conditions in the Balkans, and was introduced as follows: "The *Christian Science Monitor* has arranged to have a comprehensive review of

[4] Article VIII, Section 14, *Church Manual.*

the past and present conditions existing in the Balkan peninsula and a discussion of the future prospects presented to its readers in installments from the pen of a close student of the situation in this near Eastern country."

In its interest in the people of all the world, the *Monitor* reflected Mrs. Eddy's interest.

In 1898, when England was supporting, morally, the United States in the war with Spain, the *London Chronicle* had published a poem entitled "Greetings from England." Mrs. Eddy then responded by calling upon the two nations to "unite your battle-plan"; and followed this behest with the last two lines of her own poem, making the four-line verse read as follows:

Brave Britain, blest America!
Unite your battle-plan;
Victorious, all who live it, —
The love for God and man.[5]

Now in 1908, when England and Germany were disputing each other's claim to mastery of the seas, and Theodore Roosevelt was advocating increased armament, Mrs. Eddy did not hold back. In his message to the Congress on April 14, 1908, Roosevelt had argued: "There is a rank due to the United States among nations which will be withheld, if not absolutely lost, by the reputation of weakness. If we desire to avoid insult, we must be able to repel it; if we desire to secure peace, one of the most powerful instruments in our rising prosperity, it must be known that we are all times ready for war."

[5] *Poems,* p. 10.

Three days before, in April 11, 1908, issue of the *Christian Science Sentinel,* Mrs. Eddy had written:

> For many years I have prayed daily that there be
> no more war, no more barbarous slaughtering of
> our fellow-beings; prayed that all the peoples on
> earth and the islands of the sea have one God, one
> Mind; love God supremely, and love their neigh-
> bor as themselves.
>
> National disagreements can be, and should be,
> arbitrated wisely, fairly; and fully settled.
>
> It is unquestionable, however, that at this hour
> the armament of navies is necessary for the purpose
> of preventing war and preserving peace among na-
> tions.

Mrs. Eddy did not consider peace as hypocrisy, or weakness. She considered peace as the truth, and valor, of life. But
she knew that universal peace begins in the heart of the
individuals, just as she was sure that freedom for all begins
with freedom for one.

Never a pacifist, and never a neutral when her country's
safety was threatened, Mrs. Eddy instructed the Committee
on Publication to distribute copies of the *Sentinel* containing her statement to members of the Congress and Parliament, and other prominent men in the United States and
England.

In a way, the *Sentinel* was the forerunner of the *Monitor.*
Concerned with the attention given by the public prints to
disease and crime, Mrs. Eddy used the *Sentinel* for the distribution of "good news, encouraging news, and construc-
tive news," hoping, as said in the first issue of the publication, that "a brief synopsis of the current events of the

world . . . would keep the busy worker fairly well informed as to the important topics of general interest."

Introduced on September 1, 1898, the *Sentinel* had appeared as the *Christian Science Weekly* until January 26, 1899. Mrs. Eddy, although she had chosen the name of *Weekly,* was never satisfied with it. She believed it lacked definition of the purpose she had in mind, that purpose being a publication that would be "a watcher for the Field." Accordingly and in announcing, in the issue of January 26, 1899, the change in title, it was stated that "our weekly *Sentinel* is to be a watcher for the Field."

Beginning September 1, 1898, and continuing for several years, the first two pages of the publication were given over to brief paragraphs of the news of the world. Events history now remembers were recorded thus:

Sampson and Schley and their men came home in six steel ships, and their coming was the occasion of a most enthusiastic demonstration by the citizens of New York. . . . Aside from the loss of her colonies and the ships destroyed in battle, the war has cost Spain about $374,800,000. . . . Admiral Cervera was given a rousing ovation on his arrival at the Union Station in Boston recently as he passed through on his way to New York. The Spanish officer bowed his acknowledgements with uncovered head. . . . The Barbers' International Union is agitating for shorter hours and the abolishment of the five-cent shop. . . .

Count Cassini, the Russian ambassador, is reported as having recently said, "There has been absolutely no change in Russian sentiment or policy toward the United States, nor does there exist a reason for such a change within my knowledge. Russian policy does not conflict with the interests of the United States in any part of the world, any more in China than in England. Russia seeks only peacable and friendly relations with all other nations." . . . A general revival of business is certain to follow the coming in of peace. If the administration and the politicians, including the members of the Senate and House of Representatives at Washington, will now address themselves to the building up of the country's vast resources with the same energy and in the same non-partisan spirit which characterized their action in relation to the war with Spain, a prosperity will ensue sufficiently general to remove at least some of the oppressions and inequalities now so prevalent. . . .

The pages following the news digest were given over to items of especial interest to Christian Scientists — letters from abroad, news happenings within the movement, texts of lectures, testimonies of healing, instructions from Mrs. Eddy — instructions such as contained in her reply to a correspondent:

> Last evening I was catechized by a Christian Science practitioner because I referred to myself as an immortal idea of the one divine Mind. The practitioner said that my statement was wrong, because I still lived in my flesh. I replied that I did not live in my flesh, that my flesh lived or died according to the beliefs I entertained about it; but that, after coming to the light of Truth, I had found that I lived and moved and had my being in God, and to obey Christ was not to know as real the beliefs of an earthly mortal. Please give me the truth in the *Sentinel,* so that all may know it.

MRS. EDDY'S REPLY

> You are scientifically correct in your statement about yourself. You can never demonstrate spirituality until you declare yourself to be immortal and understand that you are so. Christian Science is absolute; it is neither behind the point of perfec-

tion nor advancing toward it; it is at this point
and must be practised therefrom. Unless you fully
perceive that you are the child of God, hence perfect, you have no Principle to demonstrate and no
rule for its demonstration. . . . In practising
Christian Science you must state its Principle correctly, or you forfeit your ability to demonstrate it.

MARY BAKER EDDY

After the introduction of Christian Science into Germany,
requests for literature printed in German began accumu-
lating in the offices of the Publishing Society, in Boston. As
with every facet of the movement, Mrs. Eddy kept close
watch over the growth of the teachings in Germany. In
1899 — and it was the day before Christmas — Frau Günther-Peterson was in Concord on invitation.

Of the memorable visit, Frau Günther-Peterson recalled
being "ushered into a little parlor to the left of the entrance.
A few minutes later our beloved Leader, then counting
almost seventy-nine years, came downstairs with a light
elastic step and greeted me with warm cordiality as 'dear
child,' both of her outstretched hands taking mine. . . .
Before leaving she took me into her arms, kissed my forehead, and blessed me and my work — saying 'I look upon
the German nation as one of the chief supporters of Christian Science.' "

In 1902, Frances Thurber Seal was in Boston attending
the annual meeting of The Mother Church. Before returning to Berlin, Mrs. Seal decided to visit Concord. While
Mrs. Seal was there, and much to her surprise, Mrs. Eddy
called upon her. "I was indeed overwhelmed," wrote Mrs.
Seal, "for I knew that she had not made a personal visit in

many years. . . . I had not known that she knew aught of conditions in Germany, but she said, 'I know always what my children are doing, and of Truth's progress and triumph.' "

In April 1903, about one year after the dedication of the first Christian Science church in Germany, a periodical printed in their own language was being distributed to Christian Scientists in different parts of Germany. It was called *Der Herold der Christian Science*. Since 1903, and as the need appeared, other *Herolds* in other languages have been added.

One of the most exacting of Mrs. Eddy's duties was completed in 1907. In this year she made extensive, although not the last revisions in *Science and Health with Key to the Scriptures*. In the *Christian Science Sentinel* of September 7, 1907, there was this announcement:

> There is now on sale by the publisher a thoroughly revised edition of SCIENCE AND HEALTH WITH KEY TO THE SCRIPTURES upon which the author has expended much care and labor during the last six months. In making this revision Mrs. Eddy has, for the first time, read her book consecutively from cover to cover, "in order," as she writes in the Preface, "to elucidate her idealism."

The years at Chestnut Hill were good.

Members of the household had bicycles, which they used in exploring the neighborhood; some who were interested in astronomy bought a telescope and installed it in an upper room from where, on clear evenings, it was moved up a short stairs and to the roof; there were wild flowers to classify, birds to identify; there was the daily singing in what was called the Pink Room and, sometimes, a few words from Mrs. Eddy; seated in her rocker in her study, a pad of paper in her lap and a red pencil between her fingers, their Leader used the late morning hours for reading the periodicals, paying particular attention to the editorials, and making notations for the editors; [6] in the early afternoon Mrs. Eddy drove through the boulevards and along the roads bordering the Chestnut Hill Reservoir and, in the evening, seated in a bay window overlooking the drive, she watched, as she had watched in Concord, the deepening shadows of sundown. . . .

By request, callers became fewer as, more and more, Mrs. Eddy withdrew from personal contact, even with the Directors of her church.

But there was one person who was to deny this venerable woman the peace of her years.

Mrs. Augusta E. Stetson — whose proposal to install a marble statue of a woman in The Mother Church at the time of its building had been stopped by Mrs. Eddy — was now planning to elevate First Church of Christ, Scientist, in New York, to the status of a Mother Church. In the *New York American* on November 30, 1908, was an authorized article saying Mrs. Stetson was accepting subscriptions for the building of a church edifice in New York that would rival The Mother Church in Boston, and which, like The Mother Church, would have branches.

---

[6] Mrs. Eddy's last writing for the public prints appeared in *Cosmopolitan Magazine* in November 1907 under the title of "Youth and Young Manhood." See Appendix 11 for facsimile of original manuscript.

The newspaper also quoted its source as saying "Mrs. Eddy is known to be profoundly pleased at this new evidence of growth and prosperity in the faith of which she is Founder. . . ."

Mrs. Stetson was not long in learning that Mrs. Eddy was not "pleased." Under the heading "One Mother Church in Christian Science," the *Sentinel*, in its issue of December 5, carried an editorial signed by Archibald McLellan:

A newspaper of Nov. 30 announces, on information said to have been received from First Church of Christ, Scientist, of New York city, that: "It is proposed to have a church edifice, rivaling in beauty of architecture any other religious structure in America. . . . Mrs. Eddy is known to be profoundly pleased at this new evidence of growth and prosperity in the faith of which she is Founder. . . . It was learned last night that Christian Scientists here have aspired to build another and more splendid edifice, ever since the Boston Christian Scientists erected the $2,000,000 Mother Church."

Concerning these news items, it is to be said that Mrs. Eddy was not "known to be profoundly pleased" with what purports to be the plans of First Church of Christ, Scientist, of New York city, for she learned of this proposed rival to The Mother Church, for the first time, from the daily press.

Three leading facts remain immortal in the history of Christian Science, namely:

1. This Science is already established, and it has the support of all true Christian Scientists throughout the world.

2. Any competition or any rivalry in Christian Science is abnormal, and will expose and explode itself.

3. Any attempt at rivalry or superiority in Christian Science is unchristian; therefore it is unscientific. The great Teacher said: "As ye would that men should do to you, do ye."

Thoughtful Christian Scientists are profoundly grateful to their beloved Leader, Mrs. Eddy, because in her far-seeing wisdom she has ordained The First Church of Christ, Scientist, in Boston, Mass., already famous for originating reforms, as The Mother Church of Christian Science, and all other churches in the denomination as branches of the parent Vine. Says the Church Manual: "In its relation to other Christian Science churches, in its By-laws and self-government, The Mother Church stands alone; it occupies a position that no other church can fill" (ARTICLE XXIII, SECT. 3). It is a fact of general observation that in proportion as branch churches adhere loyally to The Mother Church, and obey implicitly its By-laws, they bear abundant fruit in healing the sick and sinful.

In many of our large cities, when a congregation has outgrown its church building, then other branch churches are organized but each new branch at once becomes an individual church, and has immediate connection with The Mother Church, so that the later organizations are as directly attached to the parent Vine as are any of the earlier branches. The members of each new organization are in no wise connected or affiliated with their former church, except in the bonds of that Christian fellowship which should characterize all true followers of the Master.

The Christian Science movement is in accord with Jesus' words: "The branch cannot bear fruit of itself, except it abide in the vine." Were one branch church to depend upon a neighboring branch for training and support, this action would tend to sever its connection with The Mother Church. The essential condition for fruit-bearing is undivided attachment to the parent Vine. On the other hand, no branch church, however large, is privileged to oversee or supervise another branch. Such action would violate a fundamental rule in Christian Science.

The Church Manual declares: "The branch churches shall be individual" (ARTICLE XXIII, SECT. 6). Thus far the larger churches have resisted the temptation to organize or foster branches of their own, and any failure to adhere strictly to this rule would be a serious departure from the universal practice of the denomination and a flagrant violation of the By-laws of The Mother Church Manual.

The Master said: "I am the vine, ye are the branches: He

that abideth in me, and I in him, the same bringeth forth much fruit: for without me ye can do nothing."

Mrs. Stetson continued to receive subscriptions. On December 7, she was quoted in the *New York Times* as saying she was not planning to establish branch churches, although also saying funds for the new church, to be known as Seventh Church, would be supplied by First Church. In an effort to heal the growing schism, Mrs. Eddy invited Mrs. Stetson to visit her at Chestnut Hill. After returning to New York, Mrs. Stetson acknowledged the visit, and in the same letter told Mrs. Eddy of the abandonment of the plan to build a new church.

During the next several months Mrs. Stetson made numerous protestations of her acceptance of Mrs. Eddy's leadership. It would appear, however, that Mrs. Eddy was not wholly convinced. In the following July (July 12, 1909), Mrs. Eddy wrote to her student: "I have just finished reading your interesting letter. I thank you for acknowledging me as your Leader and I know that every true follower of Christian Science abides by the definite rules which demonstrate the true following of their Leader; therefore, if you are sincere in your protestations, and are doing as you say you are, you will be blessed in your obedience. . . ." [7]

Within two weeks, Mrs. Eddy was writing a sharp warning to Mrs. Stetson:

My Dear Student: — Awake and arise from this temptation produced by animal magnetism upon yourself, allowing your students to deify you and me. Treat yourself for it and get your students to help you rise out of it. It will be your destruc-

[7] *Miscellany*, pp. 357, 358.

tion if you do not do this. Answer this letter immediately.

As ever, lovingly your teacher,

MARY BAKER EDDY

BROOKLINE, MASS.,

July 23, 1909.

The cause of this very sharp warning was the receipt, by
Mrs. Eddy, of a letter from Mrs. Stetson. In her letter, Mrs.
Stetson included a composite letter, written and signed by
twenty-four students — a composite letter so idolatrous that
Mrs. Stetson disclaimed her worthiness to receive it and, in-
stead, inscribed it to her own, as she said, "forever Leader."

In part, this composite letter read:

Dear teacher, your teaching has revealed to me that, to be a
true Christian Scientist, is to so purify my own thought that I
can be subject to the Head of the Body of God, as reflected by
you. Gratitude is expressed only as we become instantaneous
in our response to your mental touch. "God spake, and it was
done."

May a purified life attest the endless gratitude I feel for the
manifestation of the Christ you have given us, while, with
Mary of old I cry, "Rabboni — Teacher."

In grateful acknowledgement of your example and teaching,
we, as members of your body, desire to offer this evidence of
our intelligent loyalty.

Your unselfish life, fast approaching the perfect idea of Love,
is to my hungry sense of Truth, "the bread of heaven and the
water of Life." Eating this bread and drinking this water is to
me eating the body of Christ, and drinking his blood.

And you, our blessed teacher, as the manifestation of Truth.
. . . Our hearts are filled with gratitude and awe as we see in
you Christianity demonstrated.

The voice of the Father-Mother God is ever speaking through
you.

Ever on upward wing, your flight in supernal order has been so far above all touch of the finite, etc., etc.

Your teaching demonstrated by us, your body, constitutes the true furnishing of the "upper room," at this paschal meal, in "the dawn of a new light" (*Science and Health*, p. 35) — the appearing of the masculine and feminine of God's creating, — the spiritual idea, the perfect man.

You are known to us, our beloved teacher, by words which make "our hearts burn within us," and we, your body, quickly and gratefully respond.

We recognize the wealth of inspiration that you have imparted to us from the highest plane of consecration and discernment of Truth, the radiation of the Sun of Righteousness.

Mrs. Stetson made an immediate apology to Mrs. Eddy, but word of other departures from the teachings had come to the attention of the Board of Directors. Among the violations were "practitioners' meetings" [8] held in the church edifice — and for purposes, so it was reported, not far removed from voodooism.

The Board of Directors began an investigation and among those who testified before it were members of the New York church. Mrs. Stetson tried to stop the investigation by appealing directly to Mrs. Eddy. Failing, she began a campaign of vilification against the Directors, with the result that on October 17, 1909, Mrs. Eddy used the *Sentinel* to make a public statement:

[8] At the time practitioners were permitted to have offices anywhere they chose. With Mrs. Stetson's encouragement, a number of them rented offices within First Church. To put a stop to this practice, Mrs. Eddy wrote a new church by-law which was published in the July 31, 1909, issue of the *Christian Science Sentinel*. As SECTION 11 of ARTICLE XXIII of the *Church Manual*, it reads: "Teachers and practitioners of Christian Science shall not have their offices or rooms in the branch churches, in the reading rooms, nor in rooms connected therewith."

I approve the By-laws of The Mother Church, and require the Christian Science Board of Directors to maintain them and sustain them. These Directors do not act contrary to the rules of the Church Manual, neither do they trouble me with their difficulties with individuals in their own church, or with the members of branch churches.

My province as a Leader — as the Discoverer and Founder of Christian Science — is not to interfere in cases of discipline, and I hereby publicly declare that I am not personally involved in the affairs of the church in any other way than through my written and published rules, all of which can be read by the individual who desires to inform himself of the facts.

MARY BAKER EDDY

Mrs. Stetson then turned her words on Virgil O. Strickler, First Reader in the New York church, and her attack was so vicious that the Board of Directors published this open letter:

To Whom It May Concern

As there seems to be an effort to misrepresent the motives of Virgil O. Strickler, First Reader of First Church of Christ, Scientist, New York, in connection with the investigation by the Christian Science Board of Directors of the methods and practices of members of that church, it is proper to state that Mr. Strickler appeared before this Board with great reluctance, and only after he had pleaded with Mrs. Stetson to abandon the practices and teachings which he, with others of her students, saw to be entirely inconsistent with Christian Science. Mr. Strickler hoped that Mrs. Stetson could be induced to see and acknowledge what was manifestly erroneous in her teachings and practices, and to this end he begged the Board to withhold its action, until his efforts along this line had proved unavailing.

Mr. Strickler, as well as all other witnesses who testified before this Board, appeared in response to its summons, and those who frankly disclosed the proceedings in the so-called "practitioners' meetings" were actuated only by the Christian motives of duty and truthfulness.

THE CHRISTIAN SCIENCE BOARD OF DIRECTORS
BOSTON, *Nov. 9, 1909.*

On November 6, a complaint charging Mrs. Stetson with persistent violations of the teachings of Christian Science was filed with the Board of Directors and, on November 15, accompanied by legal counsel, Mrs. Stetson appeared before the Board. Meanwhile, Mrs. Eddy wrote, and mailed, the following letter:

BROOKLINE, MASS., *November 13, 1909.*

TO THE BOARD OF TRUSTEES, FIRST CHURCH OF CHRIST, SCIENTIST,
NEW YORK CITY.

BELOVED BRETHREN: — In consideration of the present momentous question at issue in First Church of Christ, Scientist, New York City, I am constrained to say, if I can settle this church difficulty amicably by a few words, as many students think I can, I herewith cheerfully subscribe these words of love: —

My beloved brethren in First Church of Christ, Scientist, New York City, I advise you with all my soul to support the Directors of The Mother Church, and unite with those in your church who are supporting The Mother Church Directors. Abide in fellowship with and obedience to The Mother Church, and in this way God will bless and prosper you. This I know, for He has proved it to me for forty years in succession.

Lovingly yours,
MARY BAKER EDDY

On November 27, 1909, The Christian Science Board of Directors issued a statement which tells its own story:

A complaint against Mrs. Augusta E. Stetson of New York city was filed with the Board of Directors of The First Church of Christ, Scientist, in Boston, Massachusetts, on Nov. 6, 1909. She was immediately furnished with a copy of it and a copy of the following orders. It was ordered by said Board that the evidence in support of defense of the complaint should be presented in the form of affidavits or documents, except that any evidence given or statement made by the complainant or the accused should be given or made orally and in the presence of the Directors; that the accused should have the right to the assistance of counsel; and that the case should be heard commencing on Nov. 15, 1909 at 9 o'clock A.M.

The hearing commenced at the time and was concluded on Nov. 17, 1909, at 4 o'clock P.M. Mrs. Stetson was present during the trial with her counsel, Hayne Davis. The evidence in support of the complaint consisted of the affidavits of twenty-seven persons, five letters written by Mrs. Stetson to her students, and a composite letter written by some of her students and approved by her. The evidence in defense of the complaint consisted of one affidavit, two letters, and Mrs. Stetson's personal testimony and statements.

After considering the evidence and Mrs. Stetson's statements made to the Directors, it was their unanimous conclusion that the charges made against her had been proved and were true. Mrs. Stetson's name was then dropped from the roll of membership of said church.

The offenses proved against Mrs. Stetson were of two kinds: —

1. Working against the interests of the members of this church who are not her followers and against the interests of this church.

2. Persisting in teachings and practices which are contrary to Christian Science.

On November 22, 1909, and in obedience to the wishes of practically all the congregation, Augusta E. Stetson resigned her membership in First Church of Christ, Scientist, in New York.

Again there was remoteness at Chestnut Hill as Mrs. Eddy continued the struggle of leading her followers into the understanding that the divine law is presently available to humanity; that the divine law alone offers humanity the solution to the problem of evil; that human law alone cannot destroy evil; and that natural law, so called, inflicting evil and death upon humanity, is a deception, a misrepresentation of the divine law which rules the universe.

Endeavoring to clothe all with reality and truth, Mrs. Eddy sought to show that evil can never be destroyed by human authority, and that those who seek, or depend upon, such authority for such purpose are the dictators of mankind.

As light makes the darkness visible, so did Mary Baker Eddy believe that love is the strength that destroys evil — and where there is love of mankind, there is no dictation, and no dictator.

And where there are the Scriptures and her writings, there, too, are her words to her people: "I am still with you, on the field of battle, taking forward marches, broader and higher views, and with the hope that you will follow me. . . ."

CHAPTER TWENTY-THREE

The Things That Bound Them

A WORLD accustomed to drugs found it hard to believe that prayer could heal the sick — and, following the death in London, in 1898, of Harold Frederic,[1] an American novelist, laws were introduced into nearly all the legislatures of the forty-eight states restricting "the practice of healing" to graduates of medical schools.

Frederic's death attracted wide attention in Europe, in Canada, and in the United States. An autopsy developed testimony that prior to his death he had been under treatment by a Christian Science practitioner. London newspapers which, a few years before, were in agreement with *The Times* of London and its observation that "Christian Science is a rather naïve product of a rather naïve people," now denounced the teachings as "a dangerous importation," and demanded the arrest of the practitioner. The practitioner was arrested. The charge was murder.

During the autopsy, and during the trial, British and Canadian newspapers joined with American newspapers in giving close attention to the case; and adding to the clamor was the voice of the *Journal of the American Medical Association.*

[1] In 1884, Frederic became European correspondent of the *New York Times.* He was the author of *In the Valley, The Lawton Girl, The Copperhead, The Damnation of Thereon Ware, Gloria Mundi, The Market Place,* and other books. *The Damnation of Theron Ware,* probably his best-known work, is a study in moral degeneration.

On November 19, 1898, this medical journal stated: "The sacrifice of one valuable life has at last called the attention of the public to the delusions which might perhaps have worked disaster to many more obscure individuals without such effect. . . . So far as known, there has not been a conviction for manslaughter of a Christian Scientist in this country, though occasions for such an event have certainly not been wanting. In so far as the devotees of this delusion actively interfere to prevent the necessary remedial measures and the patient dies in consequence of this, it is hard to see how, with any reasonable interpretation of the law, they can escape its penalties. . . . It will be interesting to follow the proceedings in the Frederic case and to see how British justice deals with the matter; the prominence of the victim and the special issues involved will tend to make it a *cause célèbre*."

And, again, on December 10, 1898: "The case of Harold Frederic is at once maddening and pathetic. All his years the man had lived and fought for the realities, the sanities, and the honesties of life. Finally a cell or a duct in the overworked brain gave way and left him temporarily and partially incapable of distinguishing between the true and the false. . . . Nature, aided by science, would have soon repaired the injury, but at the moment when the clear eyes were darkened and the strong mind was helpless, a miserable creature appeared, stretching out rapacious hands for the sick man's gold. She got it, and Harold Frederic is dead. . . . There is ground for hope, however, that this is not quite the end of the tragic episode. The woman who killed Mr. Frederic has confessed her utter lack of legal qualifications to act as a doctor, and that she accepted fees for treatment. Counsel for the executors warned her, while she was testifying before the coroner's jury, that she was in 'a serious position.' If England has any justice, she will soon be in prison, and stay there for a considerable period."

After the verdict was rendered, *The Journal of the American Medical Association* did not repeat its assertion that "nature, aided by science, would have soon repaired the injury." In the trial it was proved that Frederic was under the care of medical doctors and went in search of a Christian Science practitioner sometime after being told by the medical men that his case was hopeless. The practitioner was acquitted.

But, having begun, the Medical Association found it difficult to stop its attacks on Mrs. Eddy and her teachings.

Through the next several months few issues of its publication were without reference to Christian Science.

July 29, 1899: "The relation between sensual practices and religious delusions among the insane . . . explains the frequent sexual aberration displayed by many fanatic sects. The prophets, John of Leydon, Knipperdaling and the Oneida community — the original 'Christian Scientists' — exhibited these very strongly in their acts. . . ."

August 12, 1899: "The Christian Science fantasy has claimed many dupes and victims. These have generally been those individuals who would be cranks anyhow upon some subject or other."

October 14, 1899: "It is said that Mrs. Eddy has taught over 4,000 students, and that less than 300 of these are loyal to the 'Religious Trust Church,' and further that Mrs. Eddy has guided herself into wealth by the sale of her book."

November 18, 1899: "Knowing nothing of disease, and virtually denying its existence, it should scarcely occasion surprise that the self-styled 'Christian Scientist' should boastfully proclaim his ability to cure the sick and heal the maimed. . . . Steps should be taken to restrain the rabid utterances and irrational practices of such ignorant and irresponsible persons. Liberty is one thing, and license another, and the crime of even suggesting such obviously false doctrines and immoral practices should be prevented by severe punishment. Those who speak thus should know better, or their ignorance is criminal."

December 16, 1899: "During the past week notice was sent to the press of the dedication of a church in New York, erected by the sect at a cost of $500,000. At the dedication it was said a hymn was sung composed by Mrs. Eddy, and later extracts were read from her book, *Science and Health.* The movement seems well organized, and through the energy of the *Medical News* it has been found that back of it all lies an astute lawyer whose advice is sought on doubtful points so that it may be a long time before the strong arm of the law can overcome such a widespread hallucination."

There is little need of retelling stories of men and women being seized, beaten, searched and jailed on complaints sworn to by medical authorities. The violence committed in the name of medicine was a repetition of the violence committed in the name of religion. But, as among the clergy, so among the doctors — there was divided opinion.

In spite of the long, and vicious, persecution of Mrs. Eddy by the editors of the *Journal of the American Medical Association,* there were men such as History Professor Leon C. Prince, of Dickinson College, who, though not agreeing with Mrs. Eddy's teachings, wrote, in a book entitled *The Sense and Nonsense of Christian Science,* which was published in 1911: "Generally speaking, the members of the medical fraternity, when confronted with the attested works of Christian Science, either deny the correctness of the original diagnosis or else deny the cure. The first is a reflection on the competency of their own profession, the second is a blind and utterly indefensible contradiction of the evidence."

Richard C. Cabot, Professor of Medicine at Harvard University, wrote, in the *Twentieth Century Magazine* in January 1912: "That Christian Science has done and is doing a vast amount of good, not only as a religion, but as a health restorer and a protest against the short-sighted naturalism of the doctors, we are firmly convinced. Its affirmations are helpful to thousands."

There were other medical men who turned the attacks back on medicine. John Abernathy, professor of anatomy and surgery, Royal College of Surgeons, said: "There has been a great increase of medical men of late years; but upon my life, diseases have increased in proportion." The celebrated Dutch physician, Professor Hermann Boerhaave, said: "If we weigh the good that has been done to mankind by a handful of true disciples of Aesculapius against the evil brought to the human race by the great number of doctors since the origin of the art of medicine to our own time, we shall doubtless come to think that it would have been better had there never been any doctor in the world." In the United States, Oliver Wendell Holmes added his conviction: "Mankind has been drugged to death, and the world would be better off if the contents of every apothecary shop were emptied into the sea, though the consequences to the fishes would be lamentable."

Few medical men understood that when certain systems of healing are approved over all others, state medicine is already accomplished — and fewer still perceived that atheism is supreme when medicine can decree that where it fails, no one can succeed, even God.

Fortunately, there existed a Constitution, and courts to uphold it.

In every state where medical societies sought to deny to Christian Scientists the right to practice their religion (and the attempt was made in almost every state) the effort failed.

In vetoing, in 1899, an act passed by the legislature for the suppression of Christian Science, the Governor of Colorado said:

The true intent and purpose of the bill is to restrict the profession of medicine . . . and then limit the number of practitioners to suit the judgment of the composite board. People desiring medical or surgical service may employ its licentiates or die without the consolation of the healer. This is but to say that a medical trust is to be established which shall regulate demand and supply by absolute control of the product which forms its basis, the General Assembly furnishing the appliances whereby the trust shall become effectual . . .

The fundamental vice of the bill is that it denies absolutely to the individual the right to select his own physician. This is a right of conscience, and as sacred as that which enables the citizen to worship God as he may desire. It is indeed the same right manifesting itself in a parallel direction.

It is a part of the law of this land, and no civil power is strong enough to deprive the citizen of its exercise. He may indeed select a healer of doubtful reputation or conceded incompetence, but that is his affair just as much as it is his choice of a minister or attorney. His action may prove injurious, possibly fatal, to himself or to some members of his family. It is better so than to delegate to any tribunal the power to say "thou shalt not employ this man" or "thou shalt employ this one." That this bill produces such a result indirectly makes it the more objectionable. It is not the outspoken and aggressive assault upon individual liberty that men should fear, but the indirect or resultant blow that is masked and falls unexpectedly.

This bill, like all kindred forms of paternalism, assumes that the citizen cannot take care of himself. The state must lead him as a little child, lest he fall into trouble unawares. He must be guarded and chided, limited here and licensed there, for his own protection. Such a system, born of the union of church and state, crumbles into ashes in the crucible of experience. It cannot flourish, though disguised in the garments of an alleged public necessity. The privilege of choosing one's own physician is a positive essential to the public health. Yet this bill assumes to thrust the coarse machinery of the criminal law into one of the most sacred relations of human life, to drag the chosen physician, if unlicensed, from the sick-couch to the prison cell, and to substitute for him someone who, however exalted and honorable, may not command the confidence or secure the sympathy of the patient.

. . . It must be remembered that those who believe in and patronize the various arts of healing that are ostracized by this bill form a very large part of every community, nor are they confined to the ignorant and superstitious portions of society. They number in their ranks thousands of the most refined, intelligent, and conscientious people. They recognize in many modern forms of relief to the suffering a religious or spiritual element that appeals to their best and tenderest sympathies. The benefits they claim and the cures they narrate are not imaginary. Shall the government enact by statute that these people shall no longer enjoy their benefits or put them into daily practice? Shall it officially declare these people to be criminally wrong and the three schools (of medicine) legally right? By what authority does it so declare?

A distinguished physician of Massachusetts has recently declared that "the Commonwealth has no right to a medical opinion and should not dare to take sides in a medical controversy." It would be as consistent to take sides in a theological or philosophical discussion. The one would be condemned by all men; the other is equally foreign to the province of government. It may regulate, but cannot prohibit the calling of the citizens; it may prevent the commission of wrong, but cannot deprive the individual of the right to choose his own advisers. . . .

There was a medical man who had reason to be glad that medicine was not able to decree that where it fails no one can succeed — not even God.

The year was 1914. The medical man was E. F. Burton, and his letter, which follows, was addressed to John D. Works, United States Senator from California: [2]

> I am an alumnus of Rush Medical College, Chicago. After graduation I received an appointment, through competitive examination, as interne in Cook County Hospital, of Chicago, one of the largest hospitals in the country, and served an interneship of 18 months, after which I was appointed on the surgical staff of the same hospital, and at the same time an instructor in Rush Medical College. I held these positions until forced by ill health to leave the North. In Arizona I was afterwards appointed acting assistant surgeon of the United States Marine Hospital Service for Arizona. I was a member of the American Medical Association until I left medical for Christian Science work.
>
> About 12 years ago I was advised by Drs. Frank

[2] This letter, written by Dr. Burton at the request of Works, was used by the Senator in January 1915 while speaking in the United States Senate in opposition to a bill providing for a Federal Department of Health and, under it, compulsory medical inspection.

The original statements, signed by witnesses, and other proof relating to the other published cases are on file with The Christian Science Publishing Society.

Billings and John B. Murphy, whose names are widely known, that I must go to Arizona if I would take my one chance for life, as I would soon die with consumption otherwise. For a year prior to this time I had been taking a preparation of opium, which was then considered to be non-habit forming, to subdue the symptoms of consumption. When I went to Arizona I tried to stop the drug, but found that I had a well-founded opium habit, and that when I attempted to break it, which I did several times, the lung trouble became too serious to be borne. Thus the habit increased, as it always does. I had been a moderate drinker, but became less moderate in the use of alcohol, and soon began to use cocaine to alleviate both the effects of the morphine and for throat symptoms. To make a long and miserable story as short as possible, these three things — alcohol, morphine, and cocaine — became my food and drink.

After some time in Arizona I went to Southern California — to Pasadena. Here I sought the aid of a hypnotist to enable me to free myself from these habits, and found this method ineffectual. After this experience the quantity of the three things that I was taking was enormously increased, until toward the end I was taking such quantities of morphine and cocaine as no one has ever recovered from, so far as I know. I became entirely demented and a menace to those about me.

At this point, and when I had been entirely unconscious for 48 hours, my wife was obliged to call for a consultation of physicians, and five of my fel-

low physicians, four of whom had been seeing me
for some time, told her that I could not live three
or four weeks, and that this time must be spent
under the strictest restraint. It was arranged that
I should be sent to the State asylum the following
day if possible. At the urging of a friend whose husband had been benefited by Christian Science,
Mrs. Burton was induced to allow a Christian Science practitioner to call to see me. Again to make a
long story short, he came and spent three hours
with me. I have no memory of his coming or of his
going, but he left me asleep, and I woke on the following morning free from all these habits, normal
in brain and nerves, hungry, energetic, clear-
headed, and happy. I knew the moment that I
awoke that something had happened to me, and
that whatever had done it, I was free from the
awful things that had bound me. But I did not
know what it was that had done it until I was
told.

That was nine years ago the twentieth of April,
this year. From that moment I have never felt the
slightest appetite for an opiate, cocaine, or alcohol
in any form, have never felt any symptoms of lung
trouble, and have been mentally sound and clear.
Nor was there a moment of convalescence. My
bowel condition was normal, whereas these organs
are in such dreadful condition even where a moderate quantity of opium has been habitually taken
that there are weeks of keenest suffering attendant
upon withdrawal of the drug. My nerves were
steady and quiet. I read quietly and with under-

standing, for the greater part of the morning, a book which took a great deal of mental concentration to understand, the like of which I had not been able to do for months. I drove my automobile half the afternoon, also a thing I had not been able to do for some time. I gained 30 pounds in weight the subsequent month, and within 10 days from this memorable morning I undertook and carried to a successful issue the most strenuous piece of work, from both mental and physical standpoints, that I have ever done. A year from the day of this healing I was asked to assist in the surgical work in the Emergency Hospital at San Francisco following the earthquake and fire of 1906, and for three weeks I stood on my feet and operated for about 16 hours a day. This was my last surgery, and coming after a year of study of Christian Science, decided me as to my future course.

I have spent over nine years in constant study of Christian Science, and seven years in its practice. I was most enthusiastic in the practice of surgery and was a Pharisee of the Pharisees as to its virtues. I gave it up only after being most thoroughly convinced that there was something better. I have learned to my entire satisfaction, knowing both sides of the question, that Christian Science is a science, and not only that, but also that it is an advanced step — and a long one — beyond medicine and surgery, and that time will prove this to the whole world. . . .

*　　*　　*

There follow a few of the many thousands of testimonies on file with the Christian Science Publishing Society:

Twenty-one years ago I began the study of Christian Science, not because I desired to adopt its teachings, but because I had made the acquaintance of one of its students and wished to prove to her that it was fallacious. I bought a copy of the textbook, *Science and Health with Key to the Scriptures,* by Mary Baker Eddy, thinking that were I familiar with it I could convince her that it was full of flaws.

. . . Within two weeks the constant study of this little, but mighty book, even though undertaken controversially, distinctly enlightened my consciousness. One of the fetters which fell at once was the wearing of glasses for double astigmatism. This condition, an aggravated one — for even with glasses I could read with but one eye at a time — was permanently healed during that first fortnight, and sometime within a year a decided cast in my right eye, which was congenital and considered incurable, also disappeared, never to return.

Ever since then I have had proof that right thinking confers freedom along all lines. My path has not been flower-strewn. Often it has been rugged, but never, even when trials seemed prolonged, has the hope of victory deserted me; and this hope, based as it is on the assurance that "with God all things are possible," has always resulted in victory.

E. F. S.

. . . After having been treated for six years by medical physicians, five in number, in various parts of the United States for the cure of a disease that developed to be locomotor ataxia and pronounced generally by them, and particularly by two in Milwaukee, to be incurable, I found that I was rapidly advancing to the point of great evidence of incurability, as predicted by these physicians.

During these years I had visited my physician and taken medicine continuously; visited Hot Springs, Ark., as advised by my physician in St. Paul, who was supposed to be a specialist on this particular disease, and did everything possible to regain health, but to no avail.

At this stage of development the study of Christian Science was recommended to me, and while I looked upon it as next to nothing I commenced the study and visited a Christian Science practitioner. At this time I had been away from business for many months, my physical condition compelling me to do so; but after one month's treatment and study of Christian Science I began to see good signs of improvement. In five months' time I returned to my business, and since then, which is five years, I have not lost a day from business on account of this trouble nor visited a physician for treatment.

I attribute my healing positively and absolutely to Christian Science.

When I paid a friendly visit to my good old doctor, whom I dearly esteem, he said, "If Christian Science is doing this for you, it is surely commendable, and I recommend your continuing, as we in medicine have no further hope to offer."

H. H. M.

I have been healed of cancer, and would say to those who are suffering with an incurable disease, you can be healed through Christian Science.

My healing came very slowly, for I was the victim of extreme fear, which seemed aggravated and prolonged by my being constantly reminded of this disease over the radio, in newspapers, and in magazines. However, as the truth of being dawned on my awakened consciousness, the fear lessened, and finally disappeared.

Then, too, there were certain faults of disposition to be eradicated before I was ready to go up higher. Resentment and self-will had to be seen for what they are — lies against God, and His perfect man — and I was forced to make an honest effort to overcome these faults, to love God and my fellow man, and to keep my thought in harmony with the one Mind.

Another phase of mortal mind that delayed my healing was lack of receptivity. I now know that to ask for help from a Christian Science practitioner does not mean that one is receptive, expecting healing. I was indulging in self-pity a great deal of the time, and paying the penalty in suffering and pain, thus closing my thought to Truth and making it difficult for the light to reach me.

It is the waiting, receptive thought which receives the healing. In Revelation it is written,

"Behold, I stand at the door, and knock: if any man hear my voice, and open the door, I will come in to him, and will sup with him, and he with me."

Our beloved Leader says (*Poems,* p. 12) :

> O'er waiting harpstrings of the mind
>   There sweeps a strain,
> Low, sad, and sweet, whose measures bind
>   The power of pain.

Finally, I was willing to undertake the task of evangelizing the human self in God's way. This step brought rapid progress in dominion over the disease, and in a short time I was entirely free.

As I look back over this testing time, I see it as a most joyous one, bringing into my human experience a measure of calmness, confidence, peace, mental poise, and consciousness of my oneness with God, good, that I never dreamed possible. I now know that God "healeth all thy diseases"; I know that Christian Science is the truth which the dear Master, Christ Jesus, taught and demonstrated, and I am comforted with a deeper and more understanding love for our dear Leader, Mary Baker Eddy, and appreciation of the loving practitioner who so calmly and persistently poured the truth into my consciousness in the measure that I could receive it. My gratitude is unbounded.

A. N. H.

As it is considerably over two years since I was healed by a Christian Science treatment of a so-called incurable type of heart disease, it occurred to me a statement from me for publication might, in a small measure, help to pay the deep debt of gratitude I owe to this cause, as my experience would in this way reach, and perhaps influence, some others who may need Christian Science as much as I did.

At the time I took my first treatment, I was practically helpless on account of a serious and aggravated form of the disease above mentioned. I was almost constantly under medical treatment from the time I was stricken until the time I was healed in Christian Science, a period of about six years and a half. When I went to a Christian Science practitioner for treatment, I was like a drowning person that grasps at a straw. I had tried prominent doctors, and "hopelessly incurable" seemed to be the only verdict. They were all good, kind men, who did all they could for me, and I have always been grateful to them for their efforts.

While in this hopeless condition my attention was called to Christian Science by a friend who was not himself a Scientist, and I soon decided to try the treatment. I remember he stated that it could not harm me in any way. When I applied for help I felt so utterly worn out, life seemed so dark and dreary and hopeless. To end it seemed cowardly, however, and so terrible; yet I often wished I had never been born. No words could tell how I suffered. I had not walked any distance for so long that my legs seemed to have lost their former strength; yet under Christian Science treatment I was practically well in less than three weeks, and could walk for miles. In less than six weeks I accepted the position that I had given up over six and a half years before on account of being stricken with this terrible disease. . . .

J. G. P.

I had been a sufferer for many months from that painful and disfiguring ailment, arthritis; my knees were stiff and bent, and I could not walk alone. I was under the care of an osteopath, but in spite of all his treatment I found no relief.

. . . While I was in prayerful meditation, all pain left. I looked down at my feet, wiggled my toes, shuffled my feet about, raised one foot an inch or two from the floor, then the other a little higher, until soon I could raise them both fifteen or twenty inches from the floor.

After a little rest and thanksgiving to God, I got up from the rocker and stood with knees almost straight. I ventured a step forward, then another and another, until, very slowly and awkwardly, I reached the door, turned, and walked back to my rocker. This I did many times, and when my family returned they found a thankful mother able to walk.

This demonstration of God's love and healing was a wonderful experience, and led me to Christian Science.

C. H.

"Give thanks unto the Lord, call upon his name, make known his deeds among the people." (I

Chron. xvi.8) The reading of this verse inspired me to "make known" the many blessings that have come to us through the study of Christian Science, presented to us over twenty years ago.

This truth has brought us "through the valley of the shadow of death." My husband was given but fifteen minutes to live after exhausting the skill of three physicians. A severe case of kidney stones had rendered him unconscious for seven hours. The family had gathered together because of the critical condition. A sister-in-law, who was a Christian Scientist, refused to accept the picture and went off to pray.

Christian Science was something new to me, and when I was asked if I would try it, since all else had failed, I agreed. A practitioner was called, and she asked that I read Isaiah, xli.10–13,[3] which I did and found great comfort and release from fear. In a very short time the patient became conscious and steadily improved, until he was completely healed.

Two sons have had the privilege of attending Sunday School. Both have experienced wonderful healings, including that of scarlet fever, which was very quickly overcome.

[3] Fear thou not; for I *am* with thee: be not dismayed: for I *am* thy God: I will strengthen thee; yea, I will help thee; yea, I will uphold thee with the right hand of my righteousness.

Behold, all they that were incensed against thee shall be ashamed and confounded: they shall be as nothing; and they that strive with thee shall perish.

Thou shalt seek them, and shalt not find them, *even* them that contended with thee: they that war against thee shall be as nothing, and as a thing of nought.

For I the LORD thy God will hold thy right hand, saying unto thee, Fear not; I will help thee.

For the physical healings we are indeed grateful, but the knowledge of our true being which is gained through the study of our textbook is of greater importance. . . .

C. D.

I am the patient referred to in my wife's testimony, and I add my gratitude to hers for this healing .

In the more than twenty years since this first healing, I have received great comfort and help in Christian Science. Finding God to be understandable, loving, ever-present, has been a source of confidence and strength and has carried me through many trials . . .

F. A. D.

Twenty-nine years ago I was sick and discouraged. Doctors of different schools were unable to help me out of what they pronounced the last stages of Bright's disease. A kind, honest physician told my parents that there was nothing known to medical science that could touch my case, adding that one kidney was gone and the other affected; that, in fact, it was the worst case he had ever seen.

For seven months I was under the care of a nurse, day and night, being five months of that time in a helpless condition. . . . The first time I took up *Science and Health with Key to the Scriptures,* by Mary Baker Eddy, it opened at page 113, and I saw these words: "God, Spirit, being all, nothing is matter." With great eagerness I grasped the meaning of the words, and it brought me so much peace and joy that I wanted to know all that the book contained.

The healing was gradual but complete, except one symptom which continued until I detected an erroneous mental picture lurking in thought, causing fear of a return of the disease, which, however, never did return. The symptom mentioned also disappeared; I never knew just when, but it was during a period when I was working to meet and destroy other errors in thought which Truth was uncovering. . . .

D. J. D.

I had been in a collision at an ice rink, but was able to pick myself up without anyone knowing I was hurt; and after a few moments — during which time I nearly lost consciousness because of the severe pain — I was given the strength to proceed to my office to keep an appointment that had previously been made.

My husband, who is not a Christian Scientist, did not notice that there was anything wrong for a few days, until he saw me use only one hand in lifting a heavy scuttle to put coal on the fire. He then insisted on my going to a surgeon for, although the pain and swelling of the arm and wrist had nearly gone, there was still a little left. He was afraid that the wrist would have to be broken and reset, as it had not been set by a surgeon.

After repeated begging on my husband's part I decided, a day or two later, that it would be wise to consent to do as he wished. I knew then there was nothing seriously wrong with my wrist, as I was able to move it and all my fingers. The surgeon told me it had been broken in two places — an exceptionally bad break — but it had set and knit together well. He said, "You have done very well, very well, indeed," and did nothing to the arm. In a fortnight's time after the accident I was shaking hands with my friends and writing letters, and even a week afterward I signed checks.

L. B.

I should like to tell of two healings which stand out prominently. One was of a badly burned face, incurred when I was tending a furnace. By holding steadfastly to the truth as taught in Christian Science, I was freed from pain, and in a few days the burned skin came off, leaving new skin. Moreover, no scar remained.

Recently, I had what is known as a stroke, and my left side became partly paralyzed. Through the work of a consecrated practitioner, I was healed in a few days. The stroke took place on a Tuesday evening and on the following Sunday I was ushering in our branch church. No words can express my gratitude for these healings.

W. K.

The writer has come "face to face" with a case of so-called organic disease, which he is fully convinced was cured in Christian Science.

An article appeared in the *American Medical*

Association Journal, under date of July 27, 1907, which gave a complete statement of the case to which reference is made. By way of explanation it may be said that according to medical opinion blastomycosis is a so-called organic disease, as unsightly as leprosy, and as painful as any form of rheumatic trouble known to suffering mortals. To impress one with the severity of this case, it may be noted that the knife was used some eighty odd times, and that up to the present time there has never been a positive cure of such a case known in the history of medicine.

It may also be of interest to know that the patient suffered from this terrible disease for over two years, and was treated by a number of eminent physicians, and that they agreed upon the diagnosis of the case as given in the medical journal already named.

The writer of this testimony is the husband of the patient, and the facts herein related can be substantiated by any of the medical doctors who attended the case. The article referred to would give the impression that the "out-of-door life" in sunny California had a decided tendency toward the healing of this case, but the facts are that the weather during the patient's stay in California was rainy and disagreeable, which confined her to the house during her entire stay, with the exception of a few hours which were spent upon the porch.

The patient was taken ill the latter part of May, 1904, and was not able to leave her bed except for a short period until taken to California in February, 1906. Upon her arrival in Los Angeles, she was refused admission to all hotels, hospitals and sanitariums, nor was it possible to lease a house after the owner had ascertained the nature of the disease.

At last, as a final resort, it became necessary to purchase a house for her shelter. A remarkable coincidence happened in the purchase of that house. After being turned from door to door, it certainly seemed a miracle to have the owner of the house recommend Christian Science, though she herself was not a Scientist. Like all others who have had to be driven into the acceptance of the truth, my wife scorned the idea of being cured in Christian Science, until she was told point-blank by her Los Angeles physician that her place was at home, where she could "die among her friends."

Then came the resolution to accept the truth, and she did so right there and then. The physician was dismissed in the forenoon and a Christian Science practitioner called in the afternoon. At the time she weighed less than ninety pounds, her normal weight being over one hundred and thirty. The rapidity of her progress under Christian Science treatment was almost phenomenal, and unless substantiated by responsible people would certainly sound mythical, or, to put it stronger, like a downright falsehood.

March 28, 1906, was the last day that the physician called and the first day of the Christian Science practitioner. It may seem past belief, but after the first treatment in Science the patient drank two cups of coffee and ate several doughnuts and a plate of baked beans for her evening meal. She then slept until after seven o'clock the next morning, and without the usual "capsule." Within a month she returned to Chicago, and although able to walk but little, showed rapid daily progress under treatment by a Christian Science practitioner in that city.

In July of the same year she had regained her normal weight, and could walk and stand as much physically as she could prior to her illness. Today she is the same, after having spent the past year in a trip around the world without a sign of the aches and pains which usually accompany such a feat.

It is well worth one's while to take the time to think what Christian Science did in this case. Those who read this article carefully will see that Christian Science actually put life into a human being who had been as it were at death's door for more than a year.

DAVID OLIVER, EVANSTON, ILL.

In *The Journal of the American Medical Association* under date of July 27, 1907, appears an article written by one of the physicians who attended Mrs. Oliver. In this article, the doctor said: "The following case is reported because it is, I believe, the first instance recorded of recovery from generalized blastomycosis." After describing, in detail, the conditions — which included the statement that "the lesions in some instances, as on one of the fingers, destroyed the bone," the doctor gave the names of different physicians who attended, and concluded his article by saying:

"No medicine was taken after March 23, 1906. In August, 1906, the last sore had disappeared. I have seen the patient several times since, and she is apparently, at the date of this writing, July 12, 1907, in perfect health. She writes me under recent date, "I am better now than I have ever been in my whole life, and can endure anything and never have an ache or pain." The diagnosis of blastomycosis was made, not only on the clinical symptoms, including the naked eye appearance of the lesions and the exclusion of other diseases — tuberculosis, syphilis, etc. — but by the microscopic examination of the pus from the wounds with a cultural development of the Blastomyces. The culture experiments were made by Dr. ——. The patient was seen at various time by Dr. ——, ——, and ——. These agreed in the diagnosis of generalized blastomycosis."

When I was about twelve years old my mother discovered that I was growing crooked — until then I had been very straight and erect. I remember that when this information was first communicated to me, the first shadow of disappointment rose upon my horizon, and deep depression came with it. I sought refuge in my room and gave way to a burst of tears, crying for what I hardly knew, only I felt something had gone wrong which I was powerless to control.

Some time after this I went to Philadelphia, where I underwent a careful examination by several physicians. My parents were then informed that I had a curvature of the spine, but might outgrow it in time by wearing a spinal brace and exercising daily. These instructions were heeded, and

I was under the watchful care of one of Philadelphia's eminent physicians.

During these years I wore various kinds of braces, including a leather jacket and a plaster cast. I was obliged to sleep in this cast during a period of six weeks. Yet with all of this I grew into womanhood decidedly deformed and a daily sufferer. There was then no hope for me of ever having a straight back, and this in addition to my suffering was a great trial. I was considered a patient sufferer, as I had been taught to believe that God sent all things; and I tried to be resigned to this trouble, thinking it God's way of disciplining me.

After finishing my school studies there followed a general breakdown in my health, and for some years I went through a siege of suffering. For six weeks I was a surgical patient in the University of Pennsylvania hospital. An operation on the spine was performed, and nervous collapse followed. The years passed, and after I had been married a year and a half, still wearing a spinal brace and continuing to suffer, was it any wonder that I was ready to listen to the "still small voice" of Truth when it spoke to me through the healing of a dear uncle?

This was the first proof of Christian Science brought to my notice, and I was satisfied that it was of God. I found myself an eager listener to all my uncle had to relate, as his healing seemed wonderful to me.

One day while in conversation with him I asked

the question, "Do you think Christian Science could give me a straight back?" His answer, in the words of the Master, " 'With God all things are possible,' " I shall never forget. Hope came to me in that moment, and my only desire was to have Christian Science treatment.

Mrs. Eddy tells us in *Science and Health* (page 1), "Desire is prayer; and no loss can occur from trusting God with our desires." My prayer was answered very soon, as it was my privilege to visit a Christian Science friend. While there I attended my first testimonial meeting, and I shall never forget the bright, happy faces as the different ones testified to the healing power of God. Having gained the consent of my husband, who is a practicing physician, I was not long in seeking a Christian Science practitioner, who faithfully unfolded to me the truth about God, and also man's relation to Him.

In a few days all pain in my back had ceased. I echoed Job's words, "In my flesh shall I see God," as I gradually saw my back assuming its natural outlines, and with no material assistance whatever, as I had removed my brace at the request of the practitioner, after having worn spinal supports for eighteen years. I felt like one taken out of prison to be rid of a rigid steel brace and free from pain. To me the whole truth was transformed! My joy was unbounded. I longed to tell everyone this truth about God. I have been relieved of other ailments and limitations through the study of

Christian Science. Out of weakness I have been made strong.

Nearly five years ago a little son came to us, and he has always been the picture of health and happiness. Christian Science has been invaluable to me in the training of the little child. The study of *Science and Health with Key to the Scriptures* has illumined the Bible to me. I was a daily reader of the Bible before coming into Christian Science, a firm believer in prayer, a member of the Presbyterian church for years, and an active worker in the Sunday school and the Christian Endeavor society; but the joy and fulness of the Christian life came to me through the understanding of this truth, that God is Love, and that He is not the creator of sickness or evil of any kind. My benefits have been so numerous that I feel in giving this testimony "the half has not been told."

E. C. P.

In Isaiah we read: "Behold, the Lord's hand is not shortened, that it cannot save; neither his ear heavy, that it cannot hear." That this is demonstrable fact I have had overwhelming proof.

Sixteen years ago, my second son, then about twelve years old, was examined by an eminent brain specialist in London, England, who pronounced him to be mentally deficient, owing to a supposedly hereditary form of disease, which he diagnosed as epilepsy. As he held out no hope of cure, the boy was placed in an asylum for the feeble-minded, and for eleven years, although he developed physically, there was little change in his mental condition. He could read and write a little, but did not express himself very coherently.

Five years ago I came into Christian Science, and after seeking and finding help for myself, began to work for my boy, he being then twenty-three years of age. I had very little understanding, but my own experience convinced me that this wonderful truth would heal him if I persevered. I knew that God could not create a weak mind, since He is infinite intelligence, and I endeavored to hold this spiritual fact constantly in thought.

There was little change for two years and I often had to meet the suggestion that such a case needed present treatment. I was in America, while my son was in England, and it also seemed more difficult owing to his surroundings, there being nearly five hundred patients in the institution where he was; but Mrs. Eddy tells us that "the transfer of the thoughts of one erring mind to another, Science renders impossible" (*Science and Health,* page 211).

I had not been working on this thought long, before my son was removed to a seaside home in connection with the asylum and kept there permanently. This was done by the authorities without any request. The third year my son's letters showed marked improvement, and I sent him a copy of our text-book, *Science and Health,* telling him to read a little each day. This he did, and after a few months he was able to begin to study the Lesson-

Sermons. Little by little he took greater interest in them, and he then began to improve rapidly.

Step by step he won his freedom, gaining permission to go out and about the small town where the home was situated, and finally enrolled himself as a member of the movement known as General Baden-Powell's Boy Scouts. Very soon he was appointed assistant scout master, taught himself signaling, and became instructor to his corps.

At this point the way opened for me to visit England, and I was enabled to spend some weeks with him. I found him not only normal, but keenly observant, anxious to make up for his lack of education, and full of ambition to take his place in the world. He is now self-supporting, and has gone to South Africa. . . .

I. G.

It is with sincere gratitude for the many blessings which Christian Science has brought to me that I give my testimony.

About thirteen years ago I was attacked with spinal meningitis, from which I did not fully recover. Two years later I was again seized with a similar attack. I was unconscious for seven days, and when I became conscious again my sight was gone. During ten years of total blindness I hardly knew what it was to have a well day. At times I would suffer terribly with my spine, and head.

Eight years after the first attack I was again taken sick with spinal trouble, which left me unable to walk or talk, and my limbs were paralyzed from my waist down. The doctors told me they could not do anything for me, and that I would have to spend the remainder of my days in that condition. At this time I was only able to move about in a wheel-chair, much discouraged and with but little to live for. . . .

Having exhausted all known material means, and being in a hopeless state, Christian Science was brought to me, and after taking treatment for eight months my speech suddenly returned. Six weeks later I arose from my chair and walked. I continued to improve rapidly from then on. After another year's treatment, I awoke one morning . . . to find my sight fully restored. My eyes are strong and my health is perfect since I was healed. . . .

A. E. G.

For years I had been troubled with hay fever. Though I had been all over Europe, to Canada, and to various climates, I had found no relief. Indeed, I had undergone four operations in the hope of removing the cause of the fever, but after the last operation I was worse than before. When someone in the family suggested that I should try Christian Science I refused to have anything to do with it. Yet, at last, when I seemed to have some leisure, I started to read the textbook.

It was what might be termed a surgical healing that came to me through the first reading of *Science and Health,* the healing of an enlarged turbinal that had caused the inability to breathe, especially when lying down. I was also healed of severe hemorrhages . . . I have many other proofs of the protecting power of the truth, including the healing of pneumonia, a felon, and blood poisoning.

J. S. H.

I am so grateful for my healing of asthma that I should like to tell it to everyone suffering from this malady. When every known remedy had failed and I was given no hope by the doctors, except temporary relief, I consented to try Christian Science, still feeling that I was beyond help.

I was struggling for breath and desperate when my husband, a Christian Scientist, urged me to let him call a practitioner. Not being able to speak, I bowed my head in consent. The relief came so quickly that I walked to my bed, lay down and slept peacefully all night. After this I had some attacks at intervals, but was always quickly relieved until a permanent cure was established. I have had no return of these attacks for eighteen years. . . .

K. C. A.

Five years of the World War [World War I] left me a nervous, morose and temperamental wreck. To alleviate these conditions, I had resorted to materia medica and to every form of worldliness, but these gave me no permanent relief. Later, when ill with a tenacious disease, I was led to read my Bible, which I had not done seriously in twenty years, and in a feeble way I asked God to help me.

I little thought anything would come of doing so; but as Mrs. Eddy says on page 13 of *Science and Health,* "If our petitions are sincere, we labor for what we ask; and our Father, who seeth in secret, will reward us openly." Being led to the study of Christian Science was my reward, and for the last twelve years it has been my only guide in my profession, in my home life, and in overcoming every sort of discordant condition.

Christian Science was a constant comforter and healing agent in an acute problem in which unhappiness, injustice, resentment, jealousy, and hatred tried to upset my life. This healing taught me not to return evil for evil, even in my thinking, but to know evil's nothingness. I try to prove my religion practically by better serving, thinking, and loving, thus making practical the Golden Rule. It taught me that God's law of justice is ever operative . . .

One healing came through the *Christian Science Monitor.* I had been slow to subscribe to it . . . but one day I was suddenly seized with acute pain and giddiness. The only Christian Science literature available was my *Monitor,* which had just been delivered. The reading of the religious article in it instantaneously healed me.

When I found myself suddenly faced with no work, radical reliance on God brought me new employment. The fresh duties were, however, quite unlike those in the profession I had previously followed, but the right appreciation of what constitutes intelligence, as understood in Christian Science, quickly enabled me to be successful. Daily prayer to the one Father-Mother God enabled me to rise within a year from a subordinate to a higher position.

I am, however, most grateful to God for the sense of stability Christian Science gives me. It enables me to maintain my poise and to meet others without fear; it gives me a broader but quieter confidence and cheerfulness, instead of an attitude of cynicism. It has transferred my reliance from material means to entire reliance upon God through every conceivable problem.

Words alone cannot express my gratitude for a religion which, if honestly applied, meets every need. One can only join with the multitudes of others in gratitude to God for giving our Leader the inspiration and courage which enabled her to make the healing message of the Christ a practicable, joyful, universal way "for the healing of the nations."

S. P. A. R.

It is with a sincere desire to share my blessings with others that I testify to the healing efficacy of Christian Science. This Science was presented to me by a medical nurse, at a time when I not only was suffering from a so-called infectious disease, but was in great mental darkness, suspected of being a mild form of insanity. Although medical treatment was continued for the infectious disease, Christian Science was my constant companion. It gave me peace and joy that I had never before known.

Six months after taking up my study of this great

truth, I lost all faith in material remedies, relied solely on Mind, and was healed of constipation, from which I had suffered many years. My good physical and mental health I owe entirely to the teachings of Christian Science.

Recently I was able to prove that Mind is complete, and nothing can be added to it. A small growth which seemed to have some sensation appeared on my body. This condition disappeared in a few days through my own understanding of the truth. . . .

W. T. L.

I came into Christian Science for some clearer explanations on spiritual questions rather than for a physical healing. I was a junior in a teachers' college when I realized that someone, somewhere, must be wrong. How could all the theories of physical science which we were being taught possibly be true when they contradicted so emphatically all my former orthodox training?

After sincerely asking God for guidance in this confused state, I was led to write to an aunt of mine, who is a Christian Science practitioner. I still remember her answer. She said that to learn about anything one had to read and study it; so to learn about God and His spiritual idea, man, one needs to do some searching and seeking.

Then she stated Jesus' promises: "Seek, and ye shall find" (Matt. vii.7) , and, "Come unto me, all ye that labour and are heavy laden, and I will give you rest" (Matt. xi.28) ; and the following words from *Science and Health* by Mrs. Eddy (page 454) : "Love inspires, illumines, designates, and leads the way." My aunt had the foresight to add, "God gave you dominion, so you do have the strength and courage to refuse to be tempted with false pleasures and appetites."

These thoughts kept me above many of the false pleasures of college life. The books that helped me in my study of Christian Science were presented to me as a gift from a dear uncle. I have never received a more beneficial gift, for from these books, the Bible, *Science and Health,* and the *Manual of The Mother Church* by Mrs. Eddy, I learned many beautiful clarifying truths, which have resulted in healings. All confusion ceased when I became conscious of this truth. . . .

When my mother and I endeavored to learn the true relationship of God and man, we were strengthened and beautifully protected from a sense of grief at the passing on of my father. The understanding that God, good, is the source of my supply has brought me many blessings.

As a schoolteacher of the elementary grades, I humbly thank God for Christian Science, which has helped me to heed the Master's command, "Cast out first the beam out of thine own eye, and then shalt thou see clearly to pull out the mote that is in thy brother's eye" (Luke vi.42) . Many healings have taken place on the playground and in the classroom, not through direct Christian Science treatment, but because of the general protection afforded me and my work through starting my day with prayer. Our Leader, Mrs. Eddy, states in her *Message to The Mother Church* for 1900 (page 2), "The song of Christian Science is, 'Work — work — work — watch and pray.'"

E. S. G.

A number of years after his healing — in 1891 — in Christian Science, Dr. G. W. Barrett was asked to tell his experience. Before the legislature of Massachusetts was a bill denying to Christian Scientists the full right to practice their religion. Supporters of the bill challenged the truth of the testimony that "all manner of disease had been healed in Christian Science," and demanded evidence of "one healing of *leprosy*."

Dr. Barrett furnished such a statement. It was a statement that was instrumental in defeating the bill. The statement follows:

I was a practising physician for about thirty years. During all this time, however, I was never free from some ailment and continually taking medicine. I thought I could not live without it. It seemed impossible to get rid of biliousness, which, from a mortal standpoint, I had inherited.

I struggled along from year to year, trying every new remedy that promised any relief; growing worse all the time, till finally I was compelled to give up my practice entirely and went to the mountains for a short time, thinking that a change of climate might possibly help me. But all was in vain. I returned to my former home in Kansas City, Mo., worse than when I went away — a physical wreck, suffering from enlargement and softening of the liver, indigestion, ulceration of the bowels in the most aggravated form, heart trouble, and that most dreaded of all diseases, called leprosy, which I had contracted when called to see a patient who was afflicted with it. . . .

Some time afterwards, during my stay in the mountains, I noticed some peculiar-looking spots on my body, so I consulted a specialist on skin diseases and he pronounced it leprosy in its incipient stages. I kept my own counsel, and returned to Kansas City with the expectation of settling up my earthly affairs as soon as possible, for I felt that my days on earth were few.[4] I can see now that it was my fear that fastened the disease upon me.

A few hours after I arrived home, a former patient of mine called to see me and said she had been healed by Christian Science and wanted me to try it. I told her that Christian Science might cure her, but it could not cure me.

I had tried the most powerful medicines known without receiving any benefit, and Christian Science was not half so strong as some of the remedies I had used, so there was no use in wasting precious time with any such foolishness. But she insisted so strongly on my having an interview with the Scientist who had healed her, that I finally said that if it would please her any, I would submit. So finally arrangements were made for her to call the next morning at eleven o'clock. The next morning came

[4] After his healing, Dr. Barrett became a Christian Science practitioner. He was about 90 years old when he died.

and she was on time with the Scientist [5] to whom she introduced me, and then left.

Well do I remember that interview. The first question I asked was:

"Do you pretend to say that Christian Science can cure all kinds of diseases without any medicine whatever?"

Her answer was, "I do, sir; and I am here to demonstrate and prove it to you."

I told her that I had telegraphed to New York for some medicine, but if she wanted to experiment on me while waiting for it she could "sail in"; that I had but once to die, and she could not do any more than kill me, and I would just as soon die as not, for death would be preferable to the condition I was then in.

She gave me a treatment, and talked to me for an hour or more. As she was going to leave, I inquired about my diet — what she would recommend me to eat, etc., as I had not dared to eat any solid food for months.

She laughed, and said, "Just eat anything you like, and all you want of it; it cannot hurt you."

I said to myself, "If you only knew the condition my bowels are in, you would not talk such foolishness as that to me."

Soon after she left, however, the pain began to disappear, and in the course of an hour it was all gone and I began to feel hungry. By the time dinner was ready (just an hour and a half from the time she left) I was as hungry as a bear that had

[5] Mrs. Henrietta E. Graybill, C. S. B., later Mrs. Henrietta E. Bow.

been "holed up" all winter. It seemed as though I could not wait for the dinner hour to come. But I did not dare to say anything, as my family were ignorant of what had been done, and knew that I was opposed to anything of the kind; as I had classed it in with Spiritualism, mesmerism, etc.

When I sat down to the table, I said to myself, "I am going to see if you [the Scientist] can keep this dinner from hurting me." Boiled beef, cabbage, turnips, potatoes, pickles, onions, bread and butter, etc., disappeared as if by magic, and I finished with a quarter of a good-sized pie and a cup of coffee. In fact, I ate until I could eat no more.

I thought if it gets to hurting too bad, I will take a lot of morphine; and if it requires enough to give the undertakers a job, I don't care, I will be one good square meal ahead anyway. But the pain failed to appear, and has never appeared from that day to this. I have been able at all times, to eat anything I desired and all that I wanted of it, without the least inconvenience whatever.

Strange to say, my bowels did not move till the next morning about nine o'clock — perfectly normal, just as though there had never been a thing the matter. Previously, however, at times they would move every few minutes, attended with the most excruciating pain; and when I saw that the signs of leprosy had nearly vanished, words could not express my feeling of joy and gladness. I saw that in healing sickness Christian Science is as far ahead of medicine as the heavens are higher than the earth.

I resolved, then and there, that, if it were possible for me to learn how this wonderful work is done, I was going to know how to go and do likewise.

My healer was to call again that afternoon at two o'clock, but I could not wait, I was so anxious to tell her the good news. I put on my coat and hat and went to her house. She seemed almost as much surprised as I was over the sudden turn in my case and rejoiced with me over the result. I told her that she had proved her faith by her works, and I wanted to know if it was possible for me to learn how it was done.

She assured me I could, if I really wanted to. I told her that was one of the main objects of my visit, and I wanted to know what I should do first. She said to study thoroughly the Bible and *Science and Health with Key to the Scriptures* by Mary Baker G. Eddy. It is all in those two books. She kindly loaned me her *Science and Health* for a few days till I could get one of my own. I shall never forget the first time I opened it and read the first sentence in the preface. It seemed to cover the whole ground. I read it over and over again, and as I went on analyzing every word and every sentence, I felt that at last I had found the "Key to the Scriptures."

I studied day and night, and at the end of three months, I had gone through it once. I gained steadily in health and strength, and increased in weight from one hundred and ten to one hundred and forty pounds. I could stand more cold in my shirt sleeves and slippers than I could before with an overcoat, muffler, arctic overshoes, and the heaviest kind of flannel underwear. The cold, stormy weather did not seem to affect me in the least.

In January, 1892, I went to Cleveland, O., and received class instruction from one of Mrs. Eddy's loyal students, and began at once to prove the superiority of this Science over material methods by the healing of rheumatism, paralysis, tumors of all kinds, stiff joints, cancers, smallpox, indigestion, constipation, chronic diarrhea, hemorrhoids, heart trouble, hernia, deafness, blindness, etc. In fact, every ill that flesh is heir to, has been met and mastered through my little understanding of Truth.

I would like to speak of one case in particular.

A lady, eighty-one years old, had been suffering from the effects of a railroad accident for sixteen years. The left ankle and foot were very badly crushed. The railroad surgeons said the foot must be amputated, or she would die. But she positively refused to submit to such an operation, and prevailed on them to fix it up as best they could. In the course of a few months, she was able to go around the house on crutches, but the bones would not unite firmly, and the entire flesh around the ankle joint became semi-ossified, very much enlarged, and very painful. At the end of four months from the time treatment began, she wrote me that her ankle was perfectly well; she could put on her shoe and button it up for the first time since the accident, and could be on her feet from morning till night.

The Bible that had been laid away for years as a kind of keep sake (and never read) is now a new book to me, full of good things. My whole being has been changed. Everything looks bright and beautiful, which before was filled with doubt and despair. Through the light thrown upon its pages through *Science and Health,* its teachings have become practical instead of theoretical.

I have been able to prove the statement found in Isaiah xl.31. I have never known what fatigue is, since my first treatment, September 25, 1891, and yet I have studied as I never did before, and occasionally performed physical labor without any discord.

Words can never express my deep feeling of heartfelt gratitude for our dear Mother in Israel for the many blessings which have come to me through the understanding of *Science and Health.*

It is truly "The Key to the Scriptures," for it unlocks the storehouse of God and bestows upon us riches that the world knows not of. It shows us the way to Life, not death. *Surely, God is Love, and God is All-in-all.*

CHAPTER TWENTY-FOUR

The Woman the Clergy Derided

H AVING ADOPTED the most powerful force in savage religions — fear of death — into its teachings, the Christian religion began teaching its followers to live in fear, not only of God but of everything else. Here was Mary Baker Eddy's great point of departure from Christian theology as taught for more than fifteen centuries.

She wholly disagreed with any doctrine which taught that death is the victor, and life the victim. Death, she insisted, is no messenger from God. Life is the messenger, else the teachings of Jesus are void of truth: "Yet a little while, and the world seeth me no more; but ye see me; because I live, ye shall live also."

Accepting the Nazarene's words as being true, Mary Baker Eddy found no place for death in what she believed; and she set out to teach people not to be afraid.

She wrote, "Nothing really has Life but God, who is infinite Life; hence all is Life, and death has no dominion." [1] Believing as she did, there was no room in what she taught for anything but the spiritual, no time for genuflection to the material, and no disposition to mix one with the other, Spirit with matter, or matter with Spirit.

But instructed into a belief that fear was salutary, a warning and a precaution against provoking God, the Christian world long worshiped a Deity controlled, in His deci-

[1] *Science and Health*, p. 347.

sions whether to send the supplicant into hell or heaven, by flattery, by cajolery, or by vicarious atonement on the part of selected clerical advisers.

As any examination of its literature will show, God and the devil were the supporting pillars of the Christian church. Heaven and hell were places, heaven somewhere up above, and hell somewhere down below. A personal God was ruler of one; a personal devil was ruler of the other. Eternally these two — God and the devil — struggled for the souls of men.

Mary Baker Eddy would have none of such theology.

To her, God was Supreme, Alone, All — changeless Spirit and endless Love, in whose universe is found only Life. Not death. Life! One who gives vitality to belief, direction to purpose, ideality to existence, sanctity to truth, supremacy to mind, healing to the body.

She discerned God as easy of approach, needing no vestibule to find, and eternally permitting no abduction of what He had created.

Hell was not a place — down below, over this way, or over that way. It was a here-and-now self-inflicted belief in devil, disease, pain, and death — and self-inflicted through submission to a savage superstition that dooms man to cringe in terror before his Maker. She taught the only way to be free of hell was by rejecting a materialistic theory of life, and accepting as truth the words of the Master, "the kingdom of God is within you."

This she took to mean that the Law of God is always present and always available, awaiting recognition and use — and, by its recognition and use, banishing the devils of disease, and pain, and death.

Of her teachings, she wrote in *Science and Health:*

DEVIL. Evil; a lie; error; neither corporeality nor mind; the opposite of Truth; a belief in sin, sickness and death; animal magnetism or hypnotism; the lust of the flesh, which saith: "I am life and intelligence in matter. There is more than one mind, for I am mind — a wicked mind, self-made or created by a tribal god and put into the opposite of mind, termed matter, thence to reproduce a mortal universe, including man, not after the image and likeness of Spirit, but after its own image."

GOD. The great I AM; the all-knowing, all-seeing; all-acting, all-wise, all-loving and eternal; Principle; Mind; Soul; Spirit; Life; Truth; Love; all substance; intelligence.

HEAVEN. Harmony; the reign of Spirit; government by divine Principle; spirituality; bliss; the atmosphere of Soul.

HELL. Mortal belief; error; lust; remorse; hatred; revenge; sin; sickness; death; suffering and self-destruction; self-imposed agony; effects of sin; that which "worketh abomination or maketh a lie."

In refusing to admit any reality to hell and the devil, Christian Science denies the claim that God co-operates with and makes use of evil. In Christian Science, God is infinite good. Being infinite good, He does not, and He cannot, minister to His people by condemning them to disease, death, hell and the devil.

However, it is a religion that recognizes evil as a problem — and gives the solution. The solution is for people to recognize hell and the devil as erroneous belief by seeing them as lies.

In saying there is no life and, hence, no intelligence in matter, Mary Baker Eddy was disputed by physicists of her time. Then, as before, physicists and mathematicians, even so great a mathematician as La Grange, and he was one of the greatest France has produced, told Napoleon that all observable phenomena could be explained through mechanical laws, specifically the Galilean-Newtonian laws, and there was no God.

Even after the turning into the twentieth century, physicists had said the nucleus of the atom was the ultimate in matter. Investigating further, they found ninety-two different kinds of nuclei. Then came cosmic discoveries, and still more discoveries, all bringing further reduction of the atom. Today, physical scientists no longer attempt to explain things through mechanical laws but agree that beyond all that is called nature is a Supreme Intelligence of orderly and unchanging law. Law that denies that life and intelligence are in matter; law that affirms, so great physicists say, that ultimately we all must become spiritual.

There are those, of course, who still contradict this. One of the most notorious of the materialists said — and his disciples affirm — "The materialistic, sensuously perceptible world is the only reality . . . mind is the product of matter . . . world [history] is a picture of how matter moves and how matter thinks." [2]

This materialistic point of view is one that supports itself by persecution, by cruelty, brutality, slavery, torture, and murder. In it morals are already decayed and man is a beast.

[2] Karl Marx.

By declaring belief in materiality as a belief in the devil, and repudiating the claim that God is in league with the father of evil, Mary Baker Eddy brought on herself denunciations that for unrestrained fury have seldom been equaled.

Perhaps all the denunciation was because she was a woman. Perhaps it was because what she was teaching was disturbing. Probably it was both: because she was a woman, and because she believed in a God of love — and, so believing, believed in One who spoke of Truth, and, speaking, spoke with compassion.

In tribal superstition, woman's place is in drudgery, not in council where thought is examined and decisions made. For that matter, and still speaking historically, it has not been long since it was discovered — or, if not discovered, acknowledged that ideas may have birth also in a woman's mind. Especially is this true of spiritual ideas.

God is not a distinguisher of persons. Even scholasticism in its most dogmatic moment concedes that.

When Christian Science appeared, about one hundred and fifty denominations made up what is called Christianity, although it could not have been the purpose of Jesus to have more than one. Nor is specialized knowledge needed to know that in the name of what men have called Christianity, persecutions and atrocities and wars have defaced the pages of history.

With persecution, and atrocity, and war in its wake, and with many explanations of Christianity where once there was one, it can be suspected that scholastic ecclesiasticism, although providing vast literature, is not Christianity.[3] And is it not clear that all their churches, and all their cathedrals,

[3] For a brief history of the early Christian Church, see Appendix 12.

are less than the seashore where He stood? Nevertheless, and in spite of the vast confusion, there are points of general agreement among the different groups.

It is agreed that God is infinite, and exists in Spirit; it is agreed that God created all, and is the sole reason for and basis of the universe; it is agreed that God created life, that God is omniscient and omnipresent, that God is good, that God sent His Son to do His will, that the Son came as the Redeemer; there is agreement about the divinity of the Son; agreement that, while on earth, the Son healed all manner of disease, and restored the dead to life.

Christian Science accepts all these commitments of Christianity, and emphasizes God is Infinite Good.

It is a religion that teaches in healing the sick and raising the dead Jesus was defining His mission in terms of spiritual law — and in the defining of His mission was denying, for all time, that sin, sickness, death, poverty, war, or abnormalities of any kind have standing with God.

God being Spirit, it is a religion which teaches that it is Spirit which is the Christ, and the body which was the corporeal Jesus.

It is a religion which teaches that not Jesus, but the Christ is divine — the Christ which, knowing only God, heals instantaneously. It is a religion which teaches it was this understanding of what is divine that caused Jesus to acknowledge, "I can of my own self do nothing," to acknowledge again, "The Son can do nothing of himself but what he seeth the Father do," and acknowledge again, "The Father that dwelleth within me, he doeth the works."

Accepting as fact that divine law is eternal, is always available, and knows no deviation and no theory of chance, disposes, in Christian Science, of a belief in miracles.

Christian Science agrees with the Unitarian Emerson that "the moment the doctrine of immortality is separately taught, man is already fallen." Divine law does not deal in miracles. It deals only, as Emerson said, "in the thing which is sought."

Having perceived, in her own healing, divine law at work, Mary Baker Eddy took to herself the instructions: "These things shall ye do . . . heal the sick, raise the dead, cleanse the leper, cast out devils." In obedience to that promise she began her search.

Her understanding of the Bible did not require that she accept every word. She knew that in its many revisions and in its many rewritings, with some of the revisions and some of the rewritings being done not by dedicated men, much of the original text was badly mutilated. But, despite the mutilation, and the often uninspired text, she found running through the Scriptures the theme of God as the healer. Verses such as these:

Exodus xxiii.25: ". . . And I will take sickness away from the midst of thee"; Jeremiah xxxiii.6: ". . . And I will cure them, and will reveal unto them the abundance of peace and truth"; Ezekiel xviii.32: "For I have no pleasure in the death of him that dieth, said the Lord God; wherefore turn yourselves, and live ye"; Psalms cvii.20: "He sent his word, and healed them, and delivered them from their destructions"; Luke xx.38: "For he is not a God of the dead, but of the living."

Running through the Bible is another theme. This theme counsels against fear. John xiv.27: "Let not your heart be troubled, neither let it be afraid"; Luke xii.32: "Fear not, little flock, for it is your Father's good pleasure to give you the kingdom"; 1 John iv.18: "Perfect love casteth out fear"; Psalm xci.5, 6, 7, 9, 10, 11: "Thou shalt not be afraid for the terror by night; *nor* for the arrow *that* flieth by day; *Nor* for the pestilence *that* walketh in darkness; *nor* for the destruction *that* wasteth at noon-day; A thousand shall fall at thy side, and ten thousand at thy right hand; *but* it shall not come nigh thee. Because thou hast made the LORD, *which is* my refuge, *even* the most High, thy habitation; There shall no evil befall thee, neither shall any plague come nigh thy dwelling. For he shall give his angels charge over thee, to keep thee in all thy ways."

In *Science and Health,* Mary Baker Eddy defines fear as superstition, and emphasizes "divine love which casteth out fear" (page 180) ; "we should master fear instead of cultivating it" (page 197) ; "nothing but the power of Truth can prevent the fear of error, and prove man's dominion over matter" (page 380) .

In Christian Science love of God is substituted for fear of God; and Christian Scientists are not taught that God is watching every transgression and acting as Lord High Executioner on Judgment Day. They are taught to believe that God is good; that He sees only what is good, that He is the only power — and that all that it is necessary to do to be rid of fear is to take God at His word:

"And God said, Let us make man in our image, after our likeness: and let them have dominion over the fish of the sea, and over the fowl of the air, and over the cattle, and over all the earth, and over every creeping thing that creepeth upon the earth. So God created man in his *own* image, in the image of God created he him. . . ."

"So God created man in his *own* image" — to be rid of fear is to take God at His word, and nothing remains of which one can possibly be afraid.

It is as simple a religion as that; and as difficult.

But simple though it is, and difficult though it may be, it can be said until fear ceases to be taught from all Christian pulpits, there can be no return of Christianity to the guidance of the One who taught no fear.

Naturally, this history of Christian Science does not presume to cover the whole thought and teachings of Christian Science. *Science and Health with Key to the Scriptures* is a book of more than six hundred pages. The teachings are there, in Mary Baker Eddy's own words, and the fundamental of this religion was expressed by Mrs. Eddy when she said, in *Miscellaneous Writings* (p. 25), "That there is but one God, or Life, one cause and one effect, is the *multum in parvo* of Christian Science; and to my understanding it is the heart of Christianity, the religion that Jesus taught and demonstrated."

No one was so constant a student of *Science and Health*, and the Bible, as was Mary Baker Eddy; and it was not uncommon for her to point out various passages in her own book to members of her household as though seeing them for the first time.

By contrast, many of Mrs. Eddy's critics — having read *Science and Health* once or twice, or not at all — maintain they "know all about Christian Science."

Mrs. Eddy never pretended to such knowledge.

Her effort was to find deeper meaning, that she might know, better, the eternal sense of words — words such as

"God is my Life" . . . four words, each a single syllable, but she pondered over their meaning from the day of her healing until the day of her passing.[4] They were the last words she wrote.

It is doubtful if members of any religion study the Bible more closely than do Christian Scientists.

Mrs. Eddy made Bible study an essential part of Christian Science by establishing the Scriptures and the textbook as the only preachers in her church. The Lesson-Sermons, arranged and selected by a specially appointed committee, are made up in their entirety of Bible passages and explanatory text from *Science and Health with Key to the Scriptures,* and apply to subjects regarded by Mrs. Eddy as having been given by God.

Twenty-six in all, the subjects are: God; Sacrament; Life; Truth; Love; Spirit; Soul; Mind; Christ Jesus; Man; Substance; Matter; Reality; Unreality; Are Sin, Disease, and Death Real?; Doctrine of Atonement; Probation after Death; Everlasting Punishment; Adam and Fallen Man; Mortals and Immortals; Soul and Body; Ancient and Modern Necromancy, *alias* Mesmerism and Hypnotism Denounced; God the Only Cause and Creator; God the Preserver of Man; Is the Universe, Including Man, Evolved by Atomic Force?; Christian Science.

The development of these Lesson-Sermons was gradual. In 1888 and 1889 (August 1888 to March 1889) "Bible Lessons," adapted to Christian Science teachings and taken from the International Sunday School Lessons in use in Protestant churches, were published in the *Christian Science Journal.* Inasmuch as they contained, as adapted, few cita-

---

[4] December 3, 1910.

tions from Mrs. Eddy's writings, The Christian Science Publishing Society began publication of the *Christian Science Bible Lessons* in January 1890. The committee appointed by Mrs. Eddy to do this work consisted of Julia S. Bartlett, William B. Johnson, Ira O. Knapp, and the Reverend Lanson P. Norcross.

After being issued in January, February, and March 1890, the publication became a quarterly, and began to be called "the Quarterly," although it was not until later that it was officially designated as the *Christian Science Quarterly (Bible Lessons)*. The contents consisted of introductory comments and expository notes, along with Bible references and, as stated in the announcement, "copious references" to *Science and Health*. For a time the *Quarterly* contained separate lessons for Sunday services, with one Lesson being used in the morning and the other being used in the afternoon, or in the evening. Either was suitable for Sunday School.

It was Mrs. Eddy's desire that Christian Science pulpits teach of God in God's way. The subjects she named covered, as she saw them, the essentials of Christianity, and followed the order she employed in teaching her classes. As stated in Volume I of the *Christian Science Sentinel:*

> As these discourses are made up wholly of passages from the Bible and the Christian Science text-book, they contain nothing of human opinion; they are devoid of man-made theories. They have no guesses at the future, no conjectures regarding the past, and no rudimentary exhortations about the present.
>
> They are free from sensationalism, and they make no effort to please the fancy or foster the pride of mortals.

Paul wrote the Church at Galatia that to which it were well that the Church of Christendom should give earnest heed, "Do I seek to please men? for if I yet pleased men, I should not be the servant of Christ. But I certify you, brethren, that the gospel which was preached of me is not after man. For I neither received it of man, neither was I taught it, but by the revelation of Jesus Christ." Adapted to the present situation, this message reads, Christian Science sermons seek not to please men; for a preacher who seeks to please men is not the servant of Christ. The gospel preached from our pulpits is not after man, neither was it taught of man, but by the revelation of Jesus Christ.

Each Christian Science Lesson-Sermon is preceded by the reading of what is identified as the "Golden Text," which consists of Bible verses. The "Golden Text" is not part of the sermon, nor does it form the text of the sermon. Its purpose is to express the fundamental thought contained in the sermon, and to be a general statement of Truth which the sermon elaborates.

Accepting Truth as infinite, Mrs. Eddy believed that each of the twenty-six subjects could be treated an infinite number of times, with each use bringing practically a new sermon. To illustrate:

Subject: GOD. In Mrs. Eddy's teachings, God includes all of Christian Science, and, hence, such a sermon would cover a wide range of study in a Lesson-Sermon study, such as this: 1. God is the Creator. 2. God is Principle. 3. God is triune, Life, Truth, Love. 4. God is Good. 5. God is omnipotent, omnipresent, omniscient. 6. God is Father. 7. God is Mother. 8. God is Love.

Six months later, when the subject of the Lesson-Sermon again is GOD, the thought of God being the Infinite One would be appropriate, and such a Lesson-Sermon might contain: 1. God is not corporeal, but eternal Love. 2. God is unknown to material sense. 3. God is known to Spiritual Sense. 4. God is revealed by the Scriptures. 5. God is the only Cause and Creator. 6. God is Father and Mother.

And, in another six months, the sermon could speak of God in terms of Principle: 1. God is Principle. 2. As Principle, God is Good. 3. As Principle, God is Love. 4. As Principle, God is the Saviour. 5. As Principle, God was manifested in Christ Jesus. 6. As Principle, God is reflected by man.

Each Lesson-Sermon contains a single theme, divided into three parts — introduction, body, and conclusion. The use of the Bible is threefold.

1. The Bible may state an exact truth, such as "God is Love." The Lesson-Sermon will use extracts from *Science and Health* which treat of God as Love. 2. The Bible may contain a statement such as "Bless the Lord, O my Soul." *Science and Health* explains that, in Bible use, the word "Soul" has two meanings — one meaning applies to God; one meaning refers to the spiritual sense. 3. The Bible may use verses that are symbolic, or figurative, as in Ezekiel xiv. 1–6, where the prophet speaks of "idols" and "the stumblingblock." *Science and Health* discloses that these "idols" and "the stumblingblock" of which the prophet spoke are the false evidences of material sense.

Great stress is laid upon the intelligent reading of the Lesson-Sermon, and what was said in this regard in the *Christian Science Sentinel* of March 16, 1899 has not changed:

> . . . In the work of the Reader there are several things to be considered. The Reader should be correct in his English, and the words correctly pronounced. The Readers should be so familiar with the sermon that the reading from commencement to close will be continuous and smooth. He should know that each scriptural passage has a twofold meaning. It has the outward form and the inward spirit. It has plain statement of fact and its spiritual interpretation. It has its body of Truth and its heart of Love.
>
> His first duty is to become acquainted with the outward. In the case of the Bible texts, the first Reader should familiarize himself with the Bible references and the Second Reader be thoroughly acquainted with those from *Science and Health with Key to the Scriptures*.
>
> In the case of the Bible texts, then, the Reader should study the context, and if an historical incident be referred to he should learn the whole history of the event named. In this study he may be helped by Smith's Bible Dictionary, the Revised Version of the Bible, Rotherham, or other equally high authorities. Having a clear understanding of the outward facts concerning the Bible passages, he should study them in connection with their correlative passages from *Science and Health* to learn their scientific meaning.
>
> Then with prayer and meditation he will behold

their deep inward meaning, and grasp their profound import.

While this study has been going on he has most likely seen the truth which each section of the sermon is intended to set forth. And he sees the intimate bearing which each part has toward the subject as a whole. If not, further study will reveal it.

Often the first sentence from *Science and Health* reference will reveal the import of the section. Often every Bible reference in the section will deal with the phase of the subject to be presented. Again the study of all the passages may be needful to unfold the teaching of that division of the subject.

As every architect, to rightly build a house, first sees its framework, so every interpreter of the Christian Science sermon should know its framework. Understanding this, his interpretation will have strength and character.

As all understand, an important item in the preparation to rightly interpret the sermon is the unity of thought and unity of spirit between the two Readers. . . .

To rightly interpret in Christian Science, the Bible and *Science and Health* are used together; and, to illustrate this joint use, here are certain Scriptural texts with their complementary passages:

THE BIBLE

Luke vi.6–10: And it came to pass also on another sabbath, that he entered into the synagogue,

554 *THE CROSS AND THE CROWN*

and taught; and there was a man whose right hand was withered.

And the scribes and Pharisees watched him, whether he would heal on the sabbath day; that they might find an accusation against him.

But he knew their thoughts, and said to the man which had the withered hand, Rise up, and stand forth in the midst. And he arose and stood forth.

Then said Jesus unto them, I will ask you one thing: Is it lawful on the sabbath day to do good, or do evil? to save life, or to destroy it?

And looking round about them all, he said unto the man, Stretch forth thy hand. And he did so; and his hand was restored whole as the other.

John i.14, 17: And the Word was made flesh, and dwelt among us, (and we beheld his glory, the glory of the Father,) full of grace and truth.

For the law was given by Moses, but grace and truth came by Jesus Christ.

Science and Health

Page 112: From the infinite One in Christian Science comes one Principle and its infinite idea, and with this infinitude come spiritual rules, laws, and their demonstration, which, like the great Giver, are "the same yesterday, and to-day, and forever"; for thus are the divine Principle of healing and the Christ-idea characterized in the epistle to the Hebrews.

Page 316: Christ, Truth, was demonstrated through Jesus to prove the power of Spirit over the flesh — to show that Truth is made manifest by its effects upon the human mind and body, healing sickness and destroying sin.

Page 350: "The Word was made flesh." Divine Truth must be known by its effects on the body as well as on the mind, before the Science of being can be demonstrated.

Page 380: Many years ago the author made a spiritual discovery, the scientific evidence of which has accumulated to prove that divine Mind produces in man health, harmony, and immortality. Gradually this evidence will gather momentum and clearness, until it reaches its culmination of scientific statement and proof.

Page 547: A simple statement of Christian Science, if demonstrated by healing, contains the proof of all here said of Christian Science.

One criticism of Christian Science that has been made many times, and will be made many times again, is to the effect that a religion which has only healing to offer is not much of a religion.

Christian Science literature agrees, but points out that "the one who founded the Christian religion manifested his purpose by healing the sick." That purpose was stated in the command to live "by every word of God." Christian

Science teaches that God's words included healing, and that by healing the sick Jesus was fulfilling the purpose for which He was sent; teaches that healing the sick was a natural — and inevitable — expression of Jesus's fulfillment of His mission among men. Teaching these things, Christian Science requires of its followers that they live "by every word of God."

As testimony to the importance Mrs. Eddy attached to healing, there is a recollection by one of her students: "Someone had sent Mrs. Eddy a collection of twelve or fifteen photographs of the extension to The Mother Church, in order that she might have a clear idea of how the new part fitted into the original building. As I went into her room one afternoon she was looking over these photographs. Presently she asked me to take them and put them away. As I took them from her she remarked that the building was satisfactory and suitable, but she added she would rather hear of one good case of healing than see the most beautiful building in the world."

Mary Baker Eddy did not ask her followers to stop their thinking with her, but instructed them to "study the Bible and the textbook of our denomination; obey strictly the laws that be, and follow your Leader only so far as she follows Christ." [5]

Thus she placed individual responsibility upon them and, over them, no authority but God.

The *Church Manual* confirms that responsibility, and that authority.

Implicit in her writings is the teaching that all life is but one Life and, therefore, whatever is Spiritual is not accountable to anything but Itself.

[5] *Message to The Mother Church,* 1901.

In arranging for the conduct of her Church she protected it from human ambitions that arise in all endeavors, even religion; and fortified it against a ministry of passing opinions.

That is why she wrote the *Church Manual* as she did; that is why, in Christian Science churches, the sermons preached consist of alternate readings from the Scriptures and from the textbook.

It was Mrs. Eddy's conviction that a religion which admitted to any authority but God was a religion that had departed from Him. She did not believe loss was possible when there was trust in God.

By instructing her followers to "study the Bible and the textbook of our denomination," she called upon them to make progress; she required of them, more than she required anything else, progress in the understanding of God and His law.

In Christian Science this is not law that is subject to misinterpretation, referendum, amendment, dilution, abrogation, or majority opinion. It is final and basic law, law that rules forever. It is the duty of Christian Scientists to learn more about its operation, to observe it, and to obey it. It is equally their duty to decide if the Founder and Discoverer of Christian Science was right, or wrong, in her teachings.

That was the task Mary Baker Eddy gave to each of her followers in her *Message to The Mother Church*, 1901: "Follow your Leader only so far as she follows Christ."

These instructions were all part of a design to keep her Church free from ecclesiastical domination.

Established as a denomination that requires of its members individual examination of what is like God, and what is unlike God, it is a denomination that has no need for a hierarchy to decide questions of truth. It is demanded of Christian Scientists that they do not leave custody of such matters to others. Unacceptable in this denomination is scholasticism which decrees, "We shall say, and you shall believe." Unacceptable is mysticism, or answers veiled in mystery.

Acceptable is only that which does not dim the primary declaration: "God created man in His own image."

But ecclesiasticism aside, and scholasticism aside, too, the woman whose teachings the clergy derided has returned and has entered into their pulpits.

Since 1866, pulpits have been getting away from a hell of brimstone and fire; have been using Love and not fear as a synonym for God; more and more they are interpreting the Bible spiritually and searching it for healing; more and more, silent prayer has come into use; more and more, pulpits are lifting their voices in the gladness of life, instead of crying out in lamentation and woe. More and more, they are seeking God as a friend and benefactor instead of fleeing from Him as enemy and executioner.

But even with its great influence, it is scarcely possible — in terms of today's outward scene — that this "new religion will conquer half of Christendom in a hundred years," as Mark Twain predicted half a century ago. So long as there remain those who prefer to turn over spiritual affairs to the custody of others, or find the excitement of pageantry more stimulating than solitude with God, Christendom will remain divided.

In its teachings, Christian Science makes no concessions to display, includes no pomp, and offers, for attention, only that which testifies of itself. But, though a religion as devoid of tinsel as the law it emphasizes, it is a religion that has attracted great numbers of people who choose to be simply witnesses of what it does for those who follow its teachings.

It is not a militant religion.

Its followers are taught, and the teaching is impressed upon them, that as they have the right to believe as they do, so all other groups have equal rights in believing as they believe.

It is a religion that accepts as binding, "This is my commandment, that ye love one another as I have loved you," and thereby prohibits the waylaying of anyone for what he believes. It is aware of the attacks that have been made, and are made, upon it. It answers these attacks not by asking people to believe in its teachings, but to give thought to what the testimony is.

It does not pretend as often has been claimed, that its followers are immune to sickness; it does not pretend that Christian Scientists, as individuals or as a group, are always equal to the teachings. But its adherents insist that such failures in no way disturb the correctness of what is taught — any more than claiming two plus two equals five disturbs the law of mathematics.

They maintain that "scientific government of the body must be attained through the divine Mind"; [6] there are so many testimonials of the healing, in Christian Science, of every kind of disease, all manner of incapacity and poverty, all types of abnormalities — and these healings are offered as testimony for what is believed, and what is declared.

In believing as they believe, and in declaring as they declare, Christian Scientists insist they are but on the thresh-

[6] *Science and Health*, p. 167.

old of the opportunities in their religion — and are accepting, as their Leader accepted, the great promise of man's dominion over his surroundings.

Christian Scientists do not consider it strange that Benjamin Franklin should write as he did, on February 8, 1780, to his friend, Dr. Joseph Priestley: ". . . The rapid progress true science now makes occasions my regretting sometimes that I was born too soon. It is impossible to imagine the height to which may be carried in a thousand years the power of man over matter. . . . All diseases may by sure means be prevented or cured, not excepting even that of old age, and our lives lengthened at pleasure, even beyond the antediluvian standard. Oh, that the moral science were in as fair a way of improvement, that men would cease to be wolves to one another, and that human beings would at length learn what they now improperly call humanity."

Hundreds of thoughtful men before Franklin used different words to say the same thing. It was agreed that someday "sure means [to] prevent or cure all diseases" would be discovered, and such a discovery would come when men had power over matter.

The expressions of Franklin and other thoughtful men are interesting to Christian Scientists not so much because of what these men predicted, as because, being thoughtful men, they recognized the existence of a Science in morals and that there existed a Science in healing — that when understanding came, men would learn about humanity, and know how to heal.

As physical scientists turn to their laboratories for knowledge, so Mary Baker Eddy, a Christian Scientist, turned to God for understanding.

Physical scientists agree that the distinguishing feature

of the physical universe is its orderliness, and point out that
any kind of orderliness destroys any possibility of chance.
That being what the physical scientists say of the physical
universe, Christian Scientists ask if Mary Baker Eddy is to
be heeded in speaking of the spiritual universe as follows:

> The poet's line, "Order is heaven's first law,"
> is so eternally true, so axiomatic, that it has be-
> come a truism; and its wisdom is as obvious in re-
> ligion and scholarship as in astronomy or mathe-
> matics. . . .[7]
>
> Eternal Truth is changing the universe. As mor-
> tals drop off their mental swaddling clothes,
> thought expands into expression. "Let there be
> light," is the perpetual demand of Truth and
> Love, changing chaos into order and discord into
> the music of the spheres. . . .
>
> Mortal man has made a covenant with his eyes
> to belittle Deity with human conceptions. . . .[8]

If Mrs. Eddy was not wrong in speaking of the spiritual
universe as she did, Christian Scientists inquire further:

"Is it too much to believe that the spiritual universe is no
less orderly, nor less subject to chance, than the physical
universe?"

"Is it wrong to believe in God?"

If it is not wrong to believe in God, is it wrong to study
His law which, the Scriptures say, Jesus came to prove?

In Mary Baker Eddy's teachings, Jesus demonstrated this
law, manifested God's eternal order, and established Christ's
eternal victory. In Mary Baker Eddy's teachings, the Christ

[7] *Retrospection and Introspection,* p. 87.
[8] *Science and Health,* p. 255.

is the voice of Christianity — and it is this Christ which counseled against being afraid, which healed the sick, which raised the dead, which spoke of life as eternal, and proclaimed: "Ye shall know the truth, and the truth shall make you free."

It was along toward noon when she saw Him for the first time. He was sitting by the well of Jacob, and as she came to draw water she heard Him say, "Give me to drink."

Astonished that He, a Jew, should ask drink of her, the woman of Samaria reminded Him, "The Jews have no dealings with the Samaritans," but when He talked with her about living water she argued: "Our fathers worshipped in this mountain; and ye say, that in Jerusalem is the place where men should worship."

He answered her, "Woman, believe me, the hour cometh, when ye shall neither in this mountain, nor yet at Jerusalem, worship the Father. . . . But the hour cometh, and now is, when the true worshippers shall worship the Father in spirit and in truth."

There it all is: *"The hour cometh, and now is, when the true worshippers shall worship the Father in spirit and in truth."*

The words are as imperishable as the One who said them. The world does not yet believe, but wherever habitation is, in this vast universe, mankind — when it is tired of its materialism, its superstition, its wars, and its poverty — will return to them.

They are the words of His mission, the rock He put in place on which to build His Church.

APPENDICES

1. "Christ My Refuge," by Mary Baker Eddy[1]

[The first eight verses were published in the *Lynn Reporter* on February 15, 1868; "Christ My Refuge" was first published in the *Christian Science Journal* in the June 2, 1883, issue and was also published in "Christian Science Series" in the issue of January 1, 1890.]

> Over the voice-harp of my soul
>   There sweeps a hand —
> Beyond this mortal, weak control —
>   From some soft band.
>
> Of ministries; a white-winged throng
>   Of thoughts illumined
> By God, and breathed in raptured song
>   With love perfumed.
>
> And in this unveiled presence grew
>   A ladder bright,
> Rising to bear me upward to
>   A world of light.
>
> Not from this earthly home afar,
>   But nearer Thee,
> Father, to shine a loving star
>   O'er crystal sea.
>
> Over the waves of doubt and fear —
>   Time's Galilee —
> Aid me to walk, Christ ever near
>   To strengthen me.

[1] The revised text appears on pp. 253–257, and with music in the *Christian Science Hymnal*, No. 253–257.

And fix my sight on God, the Rock
    Upon my shore
'Gainst which the winds and waves may shock
    O, nevermore.

I am no reed to shake at scorn
    Or hate of man;
I am no medium but Truth's, to warn
    The creedish clan.

'Gainst their oppression and their wrong;
    To crucify
The Christ whose deeds they must prolong,
    To hold Him nigh.

O'er the hushed harpstrings of the mind
    There sweeps a strain —
Low, sad, and sweet, whose measures bind
    The power of pain;

And wake a white-winged angel-throng
    Of thoughts, illumined
By faith, and breathed in raptured song,
    With love perfumed.

Oh, in His unveiled presence grow
    Life's burdens light;
We kiss the cross, and wait to know
    A world more bright.

Not from this earthly scene afar,
    But nearer Thee, —
Father, where Thine own children are,
    And love to be;

Where o'er earth's troubled, angry sea,
   We see Christ walk
And come to us, and tenderly,
   And wisely talk, —

Saying: "Step safely on the Rock
   Upon Life's shore,
'Gainst which the winds and waves can shock,
   Oh, nevermore!

"Thy prayer, some daily good to do
   To Mine, for Me.
An offering pure of love, whereto
   God leadeth thee."

As combined and revised by Mrs. Eddy for hymnal purposes, the title was changed to "Christ My Refuge" and the verses changed to read:

CHRIST MY REFUGE

O'er waiting harpstrings of the mind
   There sweeps a strain,
Low, sad, and sweet, whose measures bind
   The power of pain,

And wake a white-winged angel throng
   Of thoughts, illumed
By faith, and breathed in raptured song,
   With love perfumed.

Then His unveiled, sweet mercies show
   Life's burdens light.
I kiss the cross, and wake to know
   A world more bright.

And o'er earth's troubled, angry sea
   I see Christ walk,
And come to me, and tenderly,
   Divinely talk.

Thus Truth engrounds me on the rock,
   Upon Life's shore,
'Gainst which the winds and waves can shock,
   Oh, nevermore!

From tired joy and grief afar,
   And nearer Thee, —
Father, where Thine own children are,
   I love to be.

My prayer, some daily good to do
   To Thine, for Thee;
An offering pure of Love, whereto
   God leadeth me.

2. Article by Mrs. Eddy in the Lynn *Transcript*, February 3, 1872

To the Public
Moral Science and Mesmerism

Perhaps some of the readers of the *Transcript* may be interested in listening to some of my views of these two very distinct topics — but which will be given only in justice to science, and not as a reply to any libel.

Let us begin, then, briefly referring to the origin of each. Moral Science belongs to God, and is the expression of revelation of love, wisdom, and truth. It reaches the understanding, first, through inspiration, and secondly, by explanation. Those who receive it must obey its requirements if they would understand it; hearing it explained is learning the letter only; obedience to it is the spirit of this higher law that alone enables the learner to give the demonstration of Moral and Physical Science. The idea that expresses moral science, is physical, and we see this idea traced out in one continuous page of nature's bright and glorious character. Every blade of grass, tree and flower, declare, "How manifold are thy works, O Lord! in wisdom hast thou made them all."

The entire creation of God symbolizes nothing else but wisdom, love, and truth. All that He hath made is harmonious, joy-giving and eternal. He also made man in His "image and likeness," and this must be a perfect man, that through the moral science of his creation we may learn the only true physical idea of God. All that is good, God has made, but all that is not good, man has sought out through many inventions. Moral Science enables us to determine good from evil, and to destroy the latter by understanding, first, what is error, and what truth, and secondly, by understanding this great work as Ethan Allen would have claimed the colonies, "in the name of Almighty God."

Moral Science is to put down sin and suffering through the understanding that God created them not, nor made He man to be the servant to his body; and these signs shall follow those who have learned Him aright: — they shall have control over matter and man, over sickness and sin. Jesus demonstrated this moral control over matter and man, but this was not mesmerism, it was God — a moral force reduced to science that gave the right explanation of God by making all things possible to Him, and man able to prove this great truth. All forms of suffering and disease, and even the winds and waves, obeyed the man, Jesus, through his God-being. When casting out disease he said to the woman, "Lo, Satan hath bound thee" — *Not* God. The winds he stilled, turning the currents of earth into harmonious action. But the foul currents of leprosy, and the inflamed action that God created not, our Master destroyed or cast out through Moral Science of God applied to its physical idea, even as the science of music, that reveals one of the sweet harmonies of God, casts out the discord of man's making.

Fearing to think we should follow this example of Jesus is an error of our education, for which theology and physiology are greatly responsible. Jesus gave this example for man's instruction and imitation, saying, "He that believeth on me (*i.e.* who understandeth me), the works that I do shall he do also." To be able to control our bodies by the soul, i.e. through God, is to be able not to let our bodies control us through the senses. Moral Science teaches this soul-control, and just in the proportion to the greater or lesser extent that this truth is understood, will be the success or non-success of its students. If ties of sense weaken, as the stronger and more enduring ties of soul strengthen, what matter? Love is not thus lost, but nearer, far, as we approach God, who is Love. From dust to Deity all is harmonious and eternal that God created. All that is truth and its idea, all that is love and its idea, which is purity, is immortal; but all that is error, and impure, is mortal; but mortality is not imagination, nor to be sneered at; rather is it to be understood so that it may be destroyed, even as Jesus gave the example, by bringing to light immortality. Mortal error (and all error is mortal) must be destroyed by immortal truth, and in no other way can it be destroyed.

So far as I understand it, mesmerism is neither truth nor its idea, i.e. it is neither moral nor physical science, but simply an ism, originating in belief, by which one belief drives away another one, and the last may be even worse than the first. This, therefore, originates with man and not with God. Mesmer was the author of it, and never, to my knowledge, did he claim it was Moral Science; and I, who know no more of the practice of mesmerism than does a kitten, and think much less of it than did the originator, would be loath to steal his thunder, or to attempt to teach what I did not understand. Whereas I do claim to understand the Moral and Physical Science that I teach; and this I add, however, only in justice to the science — that in times past I have demonstrated it is healing the sick, at least sufficiently to test it, and beyond what my students have yet reached, although some of them are healing beyond what other methods are able to do.

I am preparing a work on Moral and Physical Science, that I shall submit to the public as soon as it is completed. This work is laborious, and I have not much opportunity to write, hence the delay in publishing. I withhold my MSS. from all eyes but my students', first, because they are mere outlines of my subject, that requires me to fill up by explanation, and secondly, because I think the mass of minds are not yet prepared to digest this subject.

3. "Principle and Practice" by Mary Baker Eddy[1]

PRINCIPLE AND PRACTICE

The nature and position of mortal mind are the opposite of immortal Mind. The so-called mortal mind is belief and not understanding. Christian Science requires understanding instead of belief; it is based on a fixed eternal and divine Principle, wholly apart from mortal conjecture; and it must be understood, otherwise it cannot be correctly accepted and demonstrated.

The inclination of mortal mind is to receive Christian Science through a belief instead of the understanding, and this inclination prevails like an epidemic on the body; it inflames mortal mind and weakens the intellect, but this so-called mortal mind is wholly ignorant of this fact, and so cherishes its mere faith in Christian Science.

The sick, like drowning men, catch at whatever drifts toward them. The sick are told by a faith-Scientist, "I can heal you, for God is all, and you are well, since God creates neither sin, sickness, nor death." Such statements result in the sick either being healed by their faith in what you tell them — which heals only as a drug would heal, through belief — or in no effect whatever. If the faith healer succeeds in *securing* (kindling) the belief of the patient in his own re-

[1] Article by Mrs. Eddy, written in 1910. Published September 1, 1917, in the *Christian Science Sentinel*. Copyright, by the Trustees Under the Will of Mary Baker Eddy.

covery, the practitioner will have performed a faith-cure which he mistakenly pronounces Christian Science.

In this very manner some students of Christian Science have accepted, through faith, a divine Principle, God, as their saviour, but they have not understood this Principle sufficiently well to fulfill the Scriptural commands, "Go ye into all the world, and preach the gospel." "Heal the sick." It is the healer's understanding of the operation of the divine Principle, and his application thereof, which heals the sick, just as it is one's understanding of the principle of mathematics which enables him to demonstrate its rules.

Christian Science is not a faith-cure, and unless human faith be distinguished from the scientific healing, Christian Science will again be lost from the practice of religion as it was soon after the period of our great Master's scientific teaching and practice. Preaching without practice of the divine Principle of man's being has not, in nineteen hundred years, resulted in demonstrating this Principle. Preaching without the truthful and consistent practice of your statements will destroy the success of Christian Science.

4. Mrs. Eddy's Reply to Bishop Fallows

CHRISTIAN SCIENCE

I have waited for Bishop Fallows to resign his task of misstating my views, in each of your issues. If his design was to call out my fire, I can assure him I hold no masked battery to open upon my enemies, and shall offer no plea or apology for doing good.

Is the above gentleman quite sure that my statement of "God, man, soul, mortal mind, materia medica, science, metaphysics, the Holy Scriptures, etc., has not the slightest connection with the recovery of the sick?" Also, that "hitting upon a novel plan to cause a concentration of one mind upon another, for the well-being of the body, is *all* of metaphysics?" Then he has gained this knowledge through his ignorance of Christian Science. He tried to support his lame logic by this — that "numbers have read my books and gone into the healing business," and some who are healing by mind-cure repudiate the science. Here we ask, Does simply "going into the business" prove or disprove one's fitness to heal? And if one becomes a successful healer merely from reading my books, does it not prove that my statement of Christian Science *has* "connection with the recovery of the sick"? And "out of the mouth of babes thou has perfected praise."

The exorcists of old healed in the name of Christ, and their method might have accorded with Bishop Fallows' views, but not mine. The chief priests of that period said of Jesus' method of healing, that Christian Science would represent, "He casteth out devils by Beelzebub." If my religious system (as he is pleased to term it) exemplifies the teachings and demonstration of our Lord, it should be known by its fruits; and that system or its adherent, that designates this system unchristian, is at fault. Neither by his writings nor by healing, has the aforesaid gentleman furnished the first evidence, on the basis of my scientific statement, that he understands my works, principle or practice. It is a widely acknowledged fact that if he had a correct knowledge of my textbook, he could *prove* my statements true.

I challenge Bishop Fallows to this fair play and Christian consistency, namely: to demonstrate his knowledge of my system by healing the sick, or, failing to do this, and exposing his ignorance of the system that he condemns before understanding, he shall relinquish his vanity as a critic and prove his claim to be a gentleman. As the founder, at this period, of Christian Science, I attest that he utterly fails to comprehend my statement of it. His explanation of one mind transferring its thoughts to another mind, thereby affecting the body, the human giving aid to the divine in its method of healing, is no more correct than to say a man assists the fall of an apple under the law of gravitation. It is virtually a denial of divine power to attribute all healing to mortals, implying it is done, either by mortal mind, or by a drug clad with more power than Deity.

His mental muddle confounding Christian Science with hypnotism, would make it the transference of mortal thought, or the grander secret of concentration! When to comprehend this science in the slightest sense, one must see beyond the rubbish of mortal thought, and be there to demonstrate the science.

To understand my use of the term *"God,"* one must exchange the evidence gained from the material senses, for
spiritual evidence, namely, a true sense of divine power,
the *omnis potens* of Spirit, the scientific sense in which I
employ the term, and should find no fault with it begirt
with additional power.

To learn my meaning of the term *"man,"* one must exchange the sense of man as sinning, sick and dying — that
mortal sense "conceived in sin and brought forth in iniquity" — for the spiritual sense of man, born not of the
flesh, but of Spirit, made after the image and likeness of
God. Then would he improve more rapidly the race, by
transferring God's mind-pictures to mortals, which correct
their poor models, learn in part my definition of man, and
choose according to Christian Science, reason and revelation,
the divine model in thought, which helps to bring out the
true likeness.

To understand my use of the term *"Soul,"* he is to discern
the meaning of this scripture — "the soul that sinneth shall
die," and see that Soul must be sinless to be immortal, the
synonym of Spirit, God. Man but reflects God, and it no
more follows that God, Soul, is in him, than that our earth
contains the sun because it reflects his light.

To perceive the spiritual side and meaning of nature, one
should understand *"metaphysics,"* as Paul expressed metaphysics — "absent from the body and present with the
Lord" — wherein we learn the nothingness of matter, sen-
sualisms, sickness, sin and death, and the great something-
ness of Spirit, through the discipline, purification and sanc-
tification whereby the facts of Spirit are discerned, and the
pure in heart see God. Proportionately as the realities of
Spirit appear, do the so-called pleasures and pains of the

body disappear; to admit the unreality of matter tends to support the great facts of Spirit, eternal Life, Truth, and Love.

To interpret to human thought the divine order of healing and salvation is to discard the paganism of drugs, all idolatries and false gods, since drugging originated in the loss of spiritual power and the mythology of pagan priests. We should adopt the *"Materia Medica"* and theology of the son of the Blessed, for they are one and the same. When the devil was cast out the dumb spake. To master the errors of the flesh with divine truths of Spirit, is the grand verity of Christian healing.

My definition of *"mortal mind,"* is a will opposed to the Divine Mind; all that is sin, sickness and death; the transference of mortal erring thought from one mind to another. Because of the proof that Jesus gave healing the sick, we should not question that it is the will of the Father to save man from sickness as well as sin. Christian Science is not scanned at a glance, summed up a lucky hit at concentration!

One human mind bringing its own supposed forces to concentrate upon another for the accomplishment of any object, is a mistaken kindness, the antipode of science or Christianity; it is a species of animal magnetism capable of all diabolism. The true method of Mind is so to concentrate with the lens of divine science the rays of immortal trust upon mortal error as to destroy it.

On March 15, during my sermon, a sick man was healed. This man had been assisted into the church by two men, a crutch and cane, but he walked out of it erect and strong, with cane and crutch under his arm. I was not acquainted with the gentleman, was not even aware of his presence, he having been helped to a seat before I entered. Other chronic cases of disease of which I was ignorant, were healed while I was preaching. Was that the effect of concentrating my mind upon the sick? Let us obey the divine command, "Render unto Caesar the things which are Caesar's, and to God the things that are God's." [1]

[1] *Mind in Nature,* June 1885.

5. First Church of Christ, Scientist, Oconto, Wisconsin

CHRISTIAN SCIENCE WAS BROUGHT TO OCONTO, WISCONSIN, IN THE FOLLOWING MANNER:

Hugh McDonald, owner of a sawmill at Green Bay, heard a steamboat inspector say that his wife was getting better since having something they called "Christian Science treatment." This was in 1883. At the time McDonald's wife had been ill for more than a year, and physicians had declared her condition beyond healing.

McDonald prevailed upon his wife to visit the Christian Science practitioner in Milwaukee. This was the same practitioner who had healed the inspector's wife and in a short time the sawmill owner's wife discovered she was getting better. Mrs. McDonald then wrote a friend, Mrs. Laura Sargent, who also was in poor health, to join her in Milwaukee. In about a month both women were healed. Each bought a copy of *Science and Health,* and returned to their homes.

Becoming much interested, Mrs. Sargent and her sister asked their mother, who was a Bible student, if she would read Mrs. Eddy's book and advise them if they should continue their studies into Christian Science. They were urged to continue, and a group of students began meeting in the home of Mrs. Lovina Millidge. A Reading Room was opened from 10 A.M., until 9 P.M., and the same parlor was used for Sunday afternoon services.

The fast-growing numbers of adherents made it imperative that they organize and build a church edifice, since there were no halls in Oconto in which to hold meetings. The group organized on June 10, 1886, as "the Christian Science Association of Oconto." They wrote to Mrs. Eddy for permission to build a church. Mrs. Eddy replied, saying they should go right ahead with the building.

The building was erected and finished in October, 1886, at a cost of less than $1000. However, as the members had only appointed trustees to build the church, they did not feel they were sufficiently organized to have the church dedicated. It also was their desire to have a student of Mrs. Eddy's living in Chicago attend the dedication. For these various reasons, the dedicatory service was postponed until February, 1887.

At this early period Mrs. Eddy had not established the uniform Sunday church service, as set forth in the *Church Manual*, and First Church, Oconto, held its services in the following order, which was described by a visiting Christian Scientist in a letter to the *Christian Science Journal* in June, 1887: "The Sunday services were conducted as follows: Silent prayer, followed by the Lord's Prayer; singing; Scripture-reading, conducted by the venerable Edwin Hart; Bible lesson, with explanatory remarks by Mrs. Laura Sargent.

"The Sunday-school services followed, in which a general interest was manifested. Afternoon and evening Bible-readings concluded the services of the day."

Other Christian Science churches in the United States were holding meetings at this time, but none had their own church edifice. Services were held in halls or other public buildings, and usually were conducted in the afternoon.

First Church, Oconto, was the first Christian Science church to conduct services in the morning, as was the custom of churches of other denominations.

Today this church still stands in its original place and is considered one of the historic landmarks of the State of Wisconsin. The outward appearance has changed but little, being of frame construction, buff-colored with cocoa-brown trim. Inside some changes have been made, such as, in 1916, the addition of a basement which houses the furnace.

The basement also includes a Reading Room that is used for a Sunday School room on Sundays. The original carpet is now in use in the Sunday School room. The auditorium seats 100 persons. The comfortable benches are of birch painted mahogany; and, whereas these seats formerly were grouped together in the center of the room, they are now divided on both sides of the auditorium with a wide aisle in the center. The Kimball reed organ continues to send its soft tones through the little church. Modern lighting is accomplished by means of sixteen silver lamps of the old-fashioned oil type, suspended from the ceiling on four silver cables. The cut-glass lightshades, frosted with a grape design, stand on silver rings.

From the church in Oconto came Mrs. Laura E. Sargent, who was known as one of Mrs. Eddy's most intimate companions. The first pastor of The Mother Church was an Oconto Christian Scientist, the Reverend Lanson P. Norcross, formerly a Congregational minister who was benefited by reading *Science and Health*.

This little church was guided and guarded by Mrs. Eddy, and the members did not know until later that they had erected and dedicated the first Church of Christ, Scientist in the world.

6. Building Plans Announced in the *Christian Science Journal*, March 1892

Description of
Church Edifice and Publishing House To Be Erected in Boston, Mass.

In frontispiece of the present issue we present our readers with an excellent perspective in photogravure of the proposed edifice to be erected corner Caledonia and Falmouth Streets, Boston. The detail of well-chosen door, window and roof effects, as well as of the stone wall-trimmings, cannot be done justice in a small design; but combining the photographic with the written description, all are enabled mentally to supply these accessories, and thus gain an exceedingly satisfactory view of the Home that is to be. The accompanying ground plans will also render acceptable aid in following and understanding written details.

Dimensions: Church Edifice, 81 x 60 ft.; Publishing House, 46 ft. front Falmouth St., 30 ft. back line, by 30 ft. deep; First story, both buildings, to finish, 12 ft.

Materials: Underpinning, of granite two feet above grade; walls, brick with stone trimmings. No wood used in interior construction, except for doors and windows.

Aided by the cuts already referred to, we will now proceed upon our tour of inspection.

Entering the church vestibule, at the point of the "flat-iron," we pass on into a hall (17 x 22 ft.) upon the south side of which are two spacious parlors (19 x 20 each) connected by sliding doors. Proceeding to the end of this hall we reach the vestry, or lecture room (29 x 56) which will seat three hundred and twenty persons. Retracing our steps, we find, on north side of the hall, two rooms: one (18 x 35) having direct communication with main workroom of the publishing house proper; the other (11:6 x 24) to be devoted to any purpose for which it may prove adapted. From this side of the church hall, also, is a door opening into the general passageway between church and publishing house.

Now, on facing the street, we note either side the entrance six-foot stairways leading right and left to the audience-room above. Ascending, we find that this auditorium, occupying entire floor room of the building, is admirably seated in the best accepted method of amphitheatre, or horseshoe form, with a capacity of six hundred and fifty sittings. A balcony constructed across the east end, now under contemplation merely, would add one hundred and twenty-five additional sittings.

In passing, it is well to note the peculiar construction of roof and walls, with reference to avoiding the "echo" ever to be guarded against in large halls. The tie-beams forming part of the roof-trusses, finish full size below the ceiling line, supported on brackets and pilasters running to the floor. Thus, soundwaves will be effectually broken, instead of beating against and rebounding from the otherwise flat surface of the walls.

Returning to ground floor and sidewalk, we proceed to front entrance of the Publishing House, on Caledonia Street. We enter a five-foot central hall leading directly through to the back entrance, and containing stairway leading to the second floor. On north side of this hall are two offices; on south side, general workroom containing five hundred and fifty square feet, besides a toilet-room, cellar stairway, sink, etc.

On floor above, we find four rooms having closet in each, also a general toilet-room leading from the hall. All the foregoing descriptions are still subject to modification. Some of the rooms have not yet been definitely assigned, the needs and requirements of prospective occupants, of necessity, having some voice in determining this assignment; but, for the comfort and satisfaction of the "little ones" so heartily and zealously at work, we will say that special thought is directed toward making judicious and acceptable outlay of whatever funds shall be received from them.

Descending to the cellar, we find the general heating apparatus for both buildings; it being not legally allowable, by recent enactment in Massachusetts, to place either boiler or furnace under any public building.

When these prospective buildings are completed — for one cannot now be reared without the other — our present badly cramped Publishing Society will have ample space for all departments of work, except editorial, on the ground floor; which will prove an economic relief from both porter and elevator work. The Editorial Department will doubtless occupy rooms on the second floor, which are in every way adapted to this purpose. To feebly accommodate our publishing business, the Society is now paying heavy annual rental, which ceases on completion of the publishing house proper; thus yielding larger means with which to do good in the dissemination of Truth and Love.

7. Deed of Trust Executed by Mrs. Eddy, September 1, 1892

KNOW ALL MEN BY THESE PRESENTS,

That I Mary Baker G. Eddy of Concord in the County of Merrimack and State of New Hampshire in consideration of one dollar to me paid by Ira O. Knapp of Boston, Massachusetts, William B. Johnson of Boston, Massachusetts, Joseph S. Eastaman of Chelsea, Massachusetts, and Stephen A. Chase of Fall River, Massachusetts, the receipt whereof is hereby acknowledged, and, also in consideration of the trusts and uses hereinafter mentioned and established, do hereby give, bargain, sell, and convey to the said Ira O. Knapp, William B. Johnson, Joseph S. Eastaman, and Stephen A. Chase as trustees as hereinafter provided and to their legitimate successors in office forever, a certain parcel of land situate on Falmouth street in said Boston, bounded and described as follows: Beginning at the junction of Falmouth street and a forty-foot street now called Caledonia street; thence running Southwest on said Falmouth street one hundred and sixteen and eighty-eight hundredths feet; thence Northwest at a right angle to a point where a line drawn at right angles to said forty-foot street at a point thereon one hundred and sixteen and fifty-five hundredths feet Northwest from the point of beginning meets the said boundary at right angles to Falmouth street, sixty-six and seventy-eight hundredths feet; thence at an obtuse angle on said line at right angles to said forty-foot street sixty-seven and thirty-five hundredths feet to said forty-foot street; thence South-easterly on said forty-foot street one hundred and sixteen and fifty-five hundredths feet to the point of beginning; containing seven thousand, eight hundred and twenty-eight square feet more or less, and subject to the agreements and restrictions mentioned in a deed recorded in Suffolk Registry of Deeds Lib. 1719, Fol. 83 so far as the same are now legally operative.

This deed of conveyance is made upon the following express trusts and conditions which the said grantees by accepting this deed agree and covenant for themselves and their successors in office to fully perform and fulfill.

1. Said grantees shall be known as the "Christian Science Board of Directors," and shall constitute a perpetual body or corporation under and in accordance with section one, Chapter 39 of the Public Statutes of Massachusetts.[1] Whenever a vacancy occurs in said Board the remaining members shall within thirty days fill the same by election; but no one shall be eligible to that office who is not in the opinion of the remaining members of the Board a firm and consistent believer in the doctrines of Christian Science as taught in a book entitled "SCIENCE AND HEALTH," by Mary Baker G. Eddy beginning with the seventy-first edition thereof.

2. Said Board shall within five years from the date hereof build or cause to be built upon said lot of land a suitable and convenient church edifice, the cost of which shall not be less than fifty thousand dollars.

---

[1] "The deacons, church wardens, or other similar officers of churches or other religious societies, and the trustees of the Methodist Episcopal churches appointed according to the discipline and usages thereof, shall, if citizens of this commonwealth, be deemed bodies corporate for the purpose of taking and holding in succession all the grants and donations, whether of real or personal estate made either to them and their successors, or to their respective churches, or to the poor of the churches."

3. When said church building is completed said Board shall elect a pastor, reader or speaker to fill the pulpit who shall be a genuine Christian Scientist; they shall maintain public worship in accordance with the doctrines of Christian Science in said church, and for this purpose they are fully empowered to make any and all necessary rules and regulations.

4. Said Board of Directors shall not suffer or allow any building to be erected upon said lot except a church building or edifice, nor shall they allow said church building or any part thereof to be used for any other purpose than for the ordinary and usual uses of a church.

5. Said Board of Directors shall not allow or permit in said church building any preaching or other religious services which shall not be consonant and in strict harmony with the doctrines and practice of Christian Science as taught and explained by Mary Baker G. Eddy in the seventy-first edition of her book entitled "SCIENCE AND HEALTH," which is soon to be issued, and in any subsequent edition thereof.

6. The congregation which shall worship in said church shall be styled "The First Church of Christ, Scientist."

7. Said Directors shall not sell or mortgage the land hereby conveyed; but they shall see that all taxes and legal assessments on said property are promptly paid.

8. Said church building shall not be removed from said lot except for the purpose of rebuilding thereon a more ex-

pensive or a more convenient structure in which said doctrines of Christian Science only shall be preached and practised. If said church building is removed for either of the purposes above set forth, any and all tablets and inscriptions which are or shall be upon said church building at the time of removal shall be removed therefrom and placed upon the walls of the new edifice. If said building is burned, the Directors shall forthwith proceed to rebuild the church.

9. Said Directors shall maintain regular preaching, reading or speaking in said church on each Sabbath, and an omission to have and maintain such preaching, reading or speaking for one year in succession shall be deemed a breach of this condition.

10. Whenever said Directors shall determine that it is inexpedient to maintain preaching, reading or speaking in said church in accordance with the terms of this deed, they are authorized and required to reconvey forthwith said lot of land with the building thereon to Mary Baker G. Eddy, her heirs and assigns forever by a proper deed of conveyance.

11. The omission or neglect on the part of said Directors to strictly comply with any of the conditions herein contained shall constitute a breach thereof, and the title hereby conveyed shall revert to the grantor Mary Baker G. Eddy, her heirs and assigns forever, upon her entry upon said land and taking possession thereof for such breach.

To Have and to Hold the above granted premises with all the privileges and appurtenances thereon belonging to said grantees and their successors in office to the uses and trusts above described forever.

And the said grantor for herself and her heirs, executors and administrators covenants with the said grantees and their successors in office that she is lawfully seized in fee simple of the aforesaid premises, that they are free from all incumbrances not herein mentioned or referred to, that she had good right to sell and convey the same to the said grantees and their successors in office as aforesaid, and that she will and her heirs, executors, and administrators shall warrant and defend the same to the said grantees and their successors in office forever against the lawful claims and demands of all persons.

In witness whereof I, the said Mary Baker G. Eddy have hereto set my hand and seal this 1st day of September, 1892.

MARY BAKER G. EDDY.

Signed, sealed and delivered in presence of

LAURA E. SARGENT.
R. E. WALKER.

September 1st, 1892.

STATE OF NEW HAMPSHIRE }
    MERRIMACK   } *ss.*

Then personally appeared the above named Mary Baker G. Eddy and acknowledged the foregoing instrument to be her free act and deed,

Before me,

R. E. WALKER.
Notary Public.

September 2, 1892

SUFFOLK REGISTRY OF DEEDS, Lib. 2081, Fol. 257.

8. Dedication Services, January 6, 1895

ORDER OF SERVICE

1. ORGAN VOLUNTARY.
2. LAUS DEO . . . . SYDNEY PERCIVAL

Words by Rev. Mary Baker Eddy

Laus Deo, it is done.
Rolled away from loving
    heart
Is a stone, —
Joyous, risen, we depart
    Having one.

Laus Deo — on this Rock
(Heaven-chiselled, squarely
    good)
Stands His Church —
God is Love and understood
    By His flock.

Laus Deo, hear thou it,
Slumber not in God's em-
    brace,
Be awake!
Like this stone be in thy
    place.
Stand, not sit!

Cold, silent, stately stone,
Dirge and song and shout-
    ings low,
In thy heart
Dwell serene, — and sorrow?
    No,
It has none,
Laus Deo! [1]

3. READING.
Selections from the Scriptures, and from the text-book of
Christian Science. SCIENCE AND HEALTH WITH KEY TO THE

[1] As read at the Dedication Services. For changes see *Miscellaneous Writings,* pp. 399–400.

Scriptures; by Rev. Mary Baker Eddy, the Discoverer and Founder of Christian Science:

Revelation xii.10–12. And I heard a loud voice saying in heaven, Now is come salvation, and strength, and the kingdom of our God, and the power of his Christ; for the accuser of our brethren is cast down, which accused them before our God day and night.

> And they overcame him by the blood of the Lamb, and by the word of their testimony; and they loved not their lives unto the death.
>
> Therefore rejoice, *ye* heavens, and ye that dwell in them. Woe to the inhabiters of the earth, and of the sea! for the devil is come down unto you, having great wrath, because he knoweth that he hath but a short time.

Science and Health with Key to the Scriptures, page 560, 3rd paragraph, and page 561, 1st and 2nd paragraphs:

> For victory over a single sin we give thanks, and magnify the Lord of Hosts. Then what shall we say of the mighty conquest over all sin? A louder song, sweeter than has ever before reached High heaven, now rises clearer and nearer to the great heart of Christ; for the accuser is not there, and Love sends forth her primal and everlasting strain. Self-abnegation — by which we lay down all for Truth, or Christ, in our warfare against error — is a rule in Christian Science. This rule clearly interprets God as divine Principle — as Life, represented by the Father; as Truth, represented by the Son; as Love, represented by the Mother. Every

mortal at some period, here or hereafter, must grapple with and overcome the mortal belief in a power opposed to God. . . .

What must the end be? They must eventually expiate their sin through suffering. The sin, which one has made his bosom companion, comes back to him at last with accelerated force; for the devil knoweth his time is short. Here the Scriptures declare that evil is temporal, not eternal. The dragon is at last stung to death by his own malice; but how many periods of self-torture it may take to remove all sin, must depend upon its obduracy.

Revelation xii.13. And when the dragon saw that he was cast unto the earth, he persecuted the woman which brought forth the man *child*.

The march of mind and honest investigation will bring the hour when the people will chain, with fetters of some sort, the growing occultism of this period. The present apathy as to the tendency of certain active yet unseen mental agencies will finally be shocked into another extreme mortal mood — into human indignation; for one extreme follows another.[2]

Revelation xii.15, 16. And the serpent cast out of his mouth water as a flood after the woman, that he might cause her to be carried away of the flood.

And the earth helped the woman, and the earth opened her mouth, and swallowed up the flood which the dragon cast out of his mouth.

[2] *Science and Health with Key to the Scriptures,* 83rd edition.

Science and Health with Key to the Scriptures, page 562, 1st, 2nd and 3rd paragraphs:

Millions of unprejudiced minds — simple seekers for Truth, weary wanderers, athirst in the desert — are waiting and watching for rest and drink. Give them a cup of cold water in Christ's name, and never fear the consequences. What if the old dragon sends forth a new flood, to drown the Christ-idea? He can neither drown your voice with its roar, nor again sink the world into the deep waters of chaos and old night. In this age the earth will help the woman; the spiritual idea will be understood. Those ready for the blessing you impart will give thanks. The waters will be pacified, and Christ will command the wave.

When God heals the sick or the sinful, they should know the great benefit Mind has wrought. They should also know the great delusions of mortal mind, when it makes them sick or sinful. Many are willing to open the eyes of the people to the power of good resident in divine Mind; but they are not as willing to point out the evil in human thought, and expose its hidden mental ways of accomplishing iniquity.

Why this backwardness, since exposure is necessary, to ensure the avoidance of the evil? Because people like you better when you tell them their virtues, than when you tell them their vices. It requires the spirit of our blessed Master to tell a man his faults, and so risk human displeasures for the sake of doing right and benefiting our race.

Who is telling mankind of their foe in ambush?
Is the informer one who sees the foe? If so, listen
and be wise. Escape from evil, and designate those
as unfaithful stewards, who have seen the danger
and yet have given no warning.

Science and Health with Key to the Scriptures, page 563,
1st and 2nd paragraphs:

At all times, and under all circumstances, overcome evil with Good. Know thyself, and God will
supply the wisdom and the occasion for a victory
over evil. Clad in the panoply of Love, human
hatred cannot reach you. The cement of a higher
humanity will unite all interests in the one Divinity.

Through trope and metaphor, the Revelator —
immortal scribe of Spirit, and of a true idealism —
furnishes the mirror in which mortal mind may see
its own image. In significant figures he depicts the
thoughts which he beholds in mortal mind. Thus
he rebukes the conceit of sin, and foreshadows its
doom. With his spiritual strength, he has opened
wide the gates of glory, and illumined the night of
Paganism with the sublime grandeur of Christian
Science, outshining the sorcery of sin, idolatry, and
hypocrisy. He takes away mitre and sceptre. He
enthrones pure and undefiled religion, and lifts
on high only those who have washed their robes
white in obedience and suffering.

Silent prayer, the Lord's Prayer with its spiritual interpretation as it is on page 322 in *Science and Health:*

Our Father which art in heaven,
  Our Father and Mother God, all harmonious,
Hallowed be Thy name.
  Adorable One.
Thy kingdom come.
  Ever-present and omnipotent.
Thy will be done in earth, as it is in heaven.
  Thy supremacy appears as matter disappears.
Give us this day our daily bread;
  Give us grace for today; Thou fillest the fam-
  ished affections;
And forgive us our debts, as we forgive our debtors.
  And Love is reflected in love.
And lead us not into temptation, but deliver us
  from evil;
  And leadest us not into temptation, but freest
  us from sin, disease and death;
For Thine is the kingdom, and the power, and the
  glory, forever.   AMEN.
  For Thou art all Substance, Life, Truth, and
  Love,[3] forever.   *So Be It.[3]*

4. SOLO. "HEAR YE ISRAEL.". . (*Elijah*) . . MENDELSSOHN.

MISS ELSIE LINCOLN

Hear ye, Israel; hear what the Lord speaketh; "Oh, hadst thou heeded my Commandments!" Who hath believed our report; to whom is the arm of the Lord revealed?

Thus saith the Lord, the Redeemer of Israel, and his Holy One, to him oppressed by tyrants; thus saith the Lord: I am He that comforteth; be not afraid, for I am thy God, I will

---

[3] For final spiritual interpretation of the Lord's Prayer, see pages 16–17, *Science and Health with Key to the Scriptures.*

strengthen thee. Say who are thou, that thou are afraid of a
man that shall die; and forgettest the Lord, thy Maker, who
hath stretched forth the heavens, and laid the earth's foundations? Be not afraid, for I, thy God, will strengthen thee."

5. SERMON, WRITTEN FOR THE OCCASION BY THE REV. MARY BAKER EDDY

TEXT: They shall be abundantly satisfied with
the fatness of Thy house; and Thou shalt make
them drink of the river of Thy pleasures.

Psalm 36.8

A new year is a nursling, a babe of time, a prophecy and promise clad in white raiment, kissed —
and encumbered with greetings — redolent with
grief and gratitude.

An old year is time's adult, and 1893 was a distinguished character, notable for good and evil.
Time past and time present, both, may pain us,
but time *improved* is eloquent in God's praise. For
due refreshment garner the memory of 1894; for if
wiser by reason of its large lessons, and records
deeply engraven, great is the value thereof.

Pass on, returnless year!
The path behind thee is with glory crowned;
This spot whereon thou troddest was holy ground;
Pass proudly to thy bier!

Today, being with you in spirit, what need that I
should be present *in propria persona?* Were I
present, methinks I should be much like the Queen
of Sheba, when she saw the house Solomon had
erected. In the expressive language of Holy Writ,
"There was no more spirit in her"; and she said

"Behold, the half was not told me: thy wisdom and prosperity exceedeth the fame which I heard." Both without and within, the spirit of beauty dominates The Mother Church, from its mosaic flooring to the soft shimmer of its starlit dome.

Nevertheless, there is a thought higher and deeper than the edifice. Material light and shade are temporal, not eternal. Turning the attention from sublunary views, however enchanting, think for a moment with me of the house wherewith "they shall be abundantly satisfied" — even the "house not made with hands, eternal in the heavens." With the mind's eye glance at the direful scenes of the war between China and Japan. Imagine yourselves in a poorly barricaded fort, fiercely besieged by the enemy. Would you rush forth single-handed to combat the foe? Nay, would you rather not strengthen your citadel by every means in your power, and remain within the walls for its defense? Likewise should we do as metaphysicians and Christian Scientists. The real house in which "we live, and move, and have our being" is Spirit, God, the eternal harmony of infinite Soul. The enemy we confront would overthrow this sublime fortress, and it behooves us to defend our heritage.

How can we do this Christianly scientific work? By intrenching ourselves in the knowledge that our true temple is no human fabrication, but the superstructure of Truth, reared on the foundation of Love, and pinnacled in Life. Such being its nature, how can our godly temple possibly be demolished, or even disturbed? Can eternity end? Can Life die? Can Truth be uncertain? Can Love be less than boundless? Referring to this temple, our Master said: "Destroy this temple, and in three days I will raise it up." He also said: "The kingdom of God is within you." Know, then, that you possess sovereign power to think and act rightly, and that nothing can dispossess you of this heritage and trespass on Love. If you maintain this position, who or what can cause you to sin or suffer? Our surety is in our confidence that we are indeed dwellers in Truth and Love, man's eternal mansion. Such a heavenly assurance ends all warfare, and bids tumult cease, for the good fight we have waged is over, and divine Love gives us the true sense of victory. "They shall be abundantly satisfied with the fatness of Thy house; and Thou shalt make them drink of the river of Thy pleasures." No longer are we of the church militant, but of the church triumphant; and with Job of old we exclaim "Yet in my flesh shall I see God." The river of His pleasures is a tributary of divine Love, whose living waters have their source in God, and flow into everlasting Life. We drink of this river when all human desires are quenched, satisfied with what is pleasing to the divine Mind.

Perchance some one of you may say, "The evidence of spiritual verity in me is so small that I am afraid. I feel so far from victory over the flesh that to reach out for a present realization of my hope savors of temerity. Because of my own unfitness for such a spiritual animus my strength is naught and my faith fails." O thou "weak and infirm of purpose"! Jesus said, "Be not afraid!"

> What if the little rain should say
> "So small a drop as I
> Can ne'er refresh a drooping earth,
> I'll tarry in the sky."

Is not a man metaphysically and mathematically number one, a unit, and therefore whole number, governed and protected by his divine Principle, God? You have simply to preserve a scientific, positive sense of unity with your divine source, and daily demonstrate this. Then you will find that one is as important a factor as duodecillions in being and doing right, and thus demonstrating deific Principle. A dewdrop reflects the sun. Each of Christ's little ones reflects the infinite One, and therefore is the seer's declaration true, that "one on God's side is a majority."

A single drop of water may help to hide the stars, or crown the tree with blossoms.

Who lives in good, lives also in God — lives in all Life, through all space. His is an individual kingdom, his diadem a crown of crowns. His existence is deathless, forever unfolding its eternal Principle. Wait patiently on illimitable Love, the lord and giver of Life. *Reflect this Life,* and with it cometh the full power of being. "They shall be abundantly satisfied with the fatness of Thy house."

In 1893 the World's Parliament of Religions, held in Chicago, used, in all its public sessions, my form of prayer since 1866; and one of the very clergymen who had publicly proclaimed me "the prayerless Mrs. Eddy," offered his audible adoration in the words I use, besides listening to an address on Christian Science from my pen, read by Judge S. J. Hanna, in that unique assembly.

When the light of one friendship after another passes from earth to heaven, we kindle in place thereof the glow of some deathless reality. Memory, faithful to goodness, holds in her secret chambers those characters of holiest sort, bravest to endure, firmest to suffer, soonest to renounce. Such was the founder of the Concord School of Philosophy — the late A. Bronson Alcott.

After the publication of "Science and Health with Key to the Scriptures," his athletic mind, scholarly and serene, was the first to bedew my hope with a drop of humanity. When the press and pulpit cannonaded this book, he introduced himself to its author by saying, "I have come to comfort you." Then eloquently paraphrasing it, and prophesying its prosperity, his conversation with a beauty all its own reassured me. *That prophecy is fulfilled.*

This book, in 1895, is in its ninety-first edition of one thousand copies. It is in the public libraries of the principal cities, colleges, and universities of America; also the same in Great Britain, France, Germany, Russia, Italy, Greece, Japan, India and China; in the Oxford University and the Victoria Institute, England; in the Academy of Greece and the Vatican at Rome.

This book is the leaven fermenting religion; it is palpably working in the sermons, Sunday Schools, and literature of our and other lands. This spiritual chemicalization is the upheaval produced when Truth is neutralizing error and impurities are passing off. And it will continue till the antithesis of Christianity, engendering the limited forms of a national or tyrannical religion, yields to the church established by the Nazarene Prophet and maintained on the spiritual foundation of Christ's healing.

Good, the Anglo-Saxon term for God, unites Science to Christianity. It presents to the understanding, not matter, but Mind; not the deified drug, but the goodness of God — healing and saving mankind.

The author of "Marriage of the Lamb," who made the mistake of thinking she caught her notions from my book, wrote to me in 1894, "Six months ago your book, Science and Health, was put into my hands. I had not read three pages before I realized I had found that for which I had hungered since girlhood, and was healed instantaneously of an ailment of seven years' standing. I cast from me the false remedy I had vainly used, and turned to the 'great Physician.' I went with my husband, a missionary to China, in 1884. He went out under the auspices of the Methodist Episcopal Church. I feel the truth is leading us to return to Japan."

Another brilliant enunciator, seeker and servant of Truth, the Rev. William R. Alger of Boston, signalled me kindly as my lone bark rose and fell and rode the rough sea. At a *conversazione* in Boston, he said, "You may find in Mrs. Eddy's metaphysical teachings more than is dreamt in your philosophy."

Also that renowned apostle of anti-slavery, Wendell Phillips, the native course of whose mind never swerved from the chariot-paths of justice, speaking of my work, said: "Had I young blood in my veins, I would help that woman."

I love Boston, and especially the laws of the State whereof this city is the capital. Today, as of yore, her laws have befriended progress.

Yet when I recall the past — how the gospel of healing was simultaneously praised and persecuted in Boston — and remember also that God is just, I wonder whether, were our dear Master in our New England metropolis at this hour, he would not weep over it, as he wept over Jerusalem! O ye tears! Not in vain did ye flow. Those sacred drops were but enshrined for future use, and God has now unsealed their receptacle with His outstretched arm. Those crystal globes made morals for mankind. They will rise with joy, and with power to wash away, in floods of forgiveness, every crime, even when mistakenly committed in the name of religion.

An unjust, unmerciful, and oppressive priesthood must perish, for false prophets in the present as in the past stumble onward to their doom; while their tabernacles crumble with dry rot. "God is not mocked," and "the word of the Lord endureth forever."

I have ordained the Bible and the Christian

Science textbook, "Science and Health with Key to
the Scriptures," as pastor of The First Church of
Christ, Scientist, in Boston — so long as this church
is satisfied with this pastor. This is my first ordina-
tion. "They shall be abundantly satisfied with the
fatness of Thy house; and Thou shalt make them
drink of the river of Thy pleasures."

All praise to the press of America's Athens —
and throughout our land the press has spoken out
historically, impartially. Like the winds telling
tales through the leaves of an ancient oak, unfallen,
may our church chimes repeat my thanks to the
press.

Notwithstanding the perplexed condition of our
nation's finances, the want and woe with millions of
dollars unemployed in our money centres, the
Christian Scientists, within fourteen months, responded to the call for this church with $191,012.
Not a mortgage was given nor a loan solicited, and
the donors all touchingly told their privileged joy
at helping to build The Mother Church. There
was no urging, begging, or borrowing; only the
need made known, and forth came the money, or
diamonds, which served to erect this "miracle in
stone."

Even the children vied with their parents to
meet the demand. Little hands, never before devoted to menial services, shoveled snow, and babes
gave kisses to earn a few pence toward this consummation. Some of these lambs my prayers had christened, but Christ will rechristen them with his own
new name. "Out of the mouths of babes and suck-

lings Thou has perfected praise." The resident youthful workers were called "Busy Bees."

Sweet society, precious children, your loving hearts and deft fingers distilled the nectar and painted the finest flowers in the fabric of this history — even its centre-piece — Mother's Room in The First Church of Christ, Scientist, in Boston. The children are destined to witness results which will eclipse Oriental dreams. They belong to the twentieth century. By juvenile aid, into the building fund have come $4,460. Ah children, you are the bulwarks of freedom, the cement of society, the hope of our race!

Brothers of the Christian Science Board of Directors, when your tireless tasks are done — well done — no Delphian lyre could break the full chords of such a rest. May the altar you have built never be shattered in our hearts, but justice, mercy and love kindle perpetually its fires.

It was well that the brother whose appliances warm this house, warmed also our perishless hope, and nerved its grand fulfillment. Woman, true to her instinct, came to the rescue as sunshine from the clouds; so, when man quibbled over an architectural exigency, a woman climbed with feet and hands to the top of the tower, and helped settle the subject.

After the loss of our late lamented pastor, Rev. D. A. Easton, the church services were maintained by excellent sermons from the editor of the *Christian Science Journal* (who, with his better half, is a very whole man) together with the Sunday

School giving this flock "drink from the river of His pleasures." O glorious hope and blessed assurance "it is your Father's good pleasure to give you the kingdom." Christians rejoice in secret, they have a bounty hidden from the world. Self-forgetfulness, purity, and love are treasures untold — constant prayers, prophecies, and anointings. Practice, not profession — goodness, not doctrines — spiritual understanding, not mere belief, gain the ear and right hand of omnipotence, and call down blessings infinite. "Faith without works is dead." The foundation of enlightened faith is Christ's teachings and *practice*. It was our Master's self-immolation, his life-giving love, healing both mind and body, that raised the deadened conscience, paralyzed by inactive faith, to a quickened sense of mortal's necessities — and God's power and purpose to supply them. It was, in the words of the Psalmist, He "who forgiveth all thine iniquities; who healeth all thy diseases."

Rome's fallen fanes and silent Aventine is glory's tomb; her pomp and power lie low in dust. Our land, more favored, had its Pilgrim Fathers. On shores of solitude, at Plymouth Rock, they planted a nation's heart — the rights of conscience, imperishable glory. No dream of avarice or ambition broke their exalted purpose, theirs was the wish to reign in hope's reality — the realm of Love.

Christian Scientists, you have planted your standard on the rock of Christ, the true, the spiritual idea — the chief corner stone in the house of our God. And our Master said: "The stone which the builders rejected, the same is become the head of the corner." If you are less appreciated today than your forefathers, wait — for if you are as devout as they, and more scientific, as progress certainly demands, your plant is immortal. Let us rejoice that chill vicissitudes have not withheld the timely shelter of this house, which descended like day-spring from on high.

Divine presence, breathe Thou Thy blessing on every heart in this house. Speak out, O Soul! This is the newborn of Spirit, this is His redeemed; this His beloved. May the kingdom of God within you — with you alway — reascending, bear you outward, upward, heavenward. May the sweet song of silver-throated singers, making melody more real, and the organ's voice, as the sound of many waters, and the Word spoken in this sacred temple dedicated to the ever-present God — mingle with the joy of angels and rehearse your heart's holy intents. May all whose means, energies, and prayers helped erect The Mother Church find within it home, and *heaven*.[4]

6. "THE LORD IS MY STRENGH AND

SONG" ....HENRY LINCOLN CASE, C. S.

Dedicated to Rev. Mary Baker Eddy

The Lord is my strength and song, and is become my salvation.

I shall not die, but live, and declare the works of the Lord.

I will praise thee, will praise thee; for thou hast heard me, and art become my salvation, and art become my salvation.

[4] *Pulpit and Press,* pp. 1–11, inclusive. Copyright, The Christian Science Publishing Society.

The stone which the builders refused is become the head stone of the corner. The stone which the builders refused is become the head stone of the corner.

This is the Lord's doing. This is the Lord's doing; it is marvellous in our eyes; it is marvellous in our eyes.

This is the day which the Lord hath made. This is the day which the Lord hath made; we will rejoice, we will rejoice, we will rejoice and be glad in it.

Thou art my God, and I will praise thee; thou art my God, I will exalt thee; thou art my God, I will exalt thee.

O give thanks unto the Lord. O give thanks unto the Lord, for He is good; for He is good; for His mercy endureth for ever, for ever.

Words from Psalm CXVIII: Verses 14, 17, 21, 22, 23, 24, 28, 29.

7. READING: "CHRIST MY REFUGE."

O'er waiting harpstrings of the mind
    There sweeps a strain,
Low, sad, and sweet, whose measures bind
    The power of pain,

And wake a white-winged angel throng
    Of thoughts, illumed
By faith, and breathed in raptured song,
    With love perfumed.

Then His unveiled, sweet mercies show
    Life's burdens light.
I kiss the cross, and wake to know
    A world more bright.

And o'er earth's troubled, angry sea
    I see Christ walk,
And come to me, and tenderly,
    Divinely talk.

Thus Truth engrounds me on the Rock,
    Upon Life's shore,
'Gainst which the winds and waves can shock,
    Oh, nevermore!

From tired joy and grief afar,
    And nearer Thee, —
Father, where Thine own children are,
    I love to be.

My prayer, some daily good to do
    To Thine, for Thee;
An offering pure of Love, whereto
    God leadeth me.[5]

        — REV. MARY BAKER EDDY.

8. HYMN 121 CONG. . . .   TUNE, SCIENCE . . . BRACKETT.
Now sweeping down the years untold
    The day of Truth is breaking;
And sweet and fair the leaves unfold,
    Of Love's immortal waking.

For flower and fruitage now are seen,
    Where blight and mildew rested:
The Christ to-day to us, has been
    By word and deed attested.

His living presence we have felt —
    The "word made flesh" among us:
And hearts of stone before him melt —
    His peace is brooding o'er us.

        — LAURA A. NOURSE, C. S. B. Alt. and Abr.

[5] This, one of the best known of Mrs. Eddy's hymns, was not set to music until 1887.

9. BENEDICTION.

Now unto him that is able to keep you from falling, and to present you faultless before the presence of his glory with exceeding joy,

To the only wise God our Saviour, be glory and majesty, dominion and power, both now and ever. Amen.

— JUDE 24, 25.

9. Mrs. Eddy's Address to the World's Parliament of Religions, 1893

Reverend Mary B. G. Eddy, the Discoverer and Founder of Christian Science, was born in the little town of Bow, among the hills of New Hampshire. Her family tree, taking root in illustrious ancestry, spread its branches from London and Edinburgh, Great Britain, to the United States. The family crest and coat of arms bear these mottoes: *Vincere aut mori,* victory or death, and *Tria juncta in uno,* three joined in one. In her work, Science and Health with Key to the Scriptures, the textbook of Christian Science, the author writes:

> In this revolutionary period the voice of God in behalf of the African slave was still echoing in our land, when this new Christian crusade sounded the keynote of universal freedom, asking a fuller acknowledgement of the rights of man as a Son of God, demanding that the fetters of sin, sickness and death be stricken from the human mind and body, and their freedom should be won, not through human warfare, not with bayonet and blood, but through Divine Science.
>
> God has built a higher platform of human rights, and built it on diviner claims. These claims are not made through code or creed, but in demonstration of "peace on earth and good-will to men." Human codes of theology, medicine, and

hygiene cramp the mind, which needs freedom. Christ, Truth, rends asunder these fetters, and man's birthright and sole allegiance to his Maker go on undisturbed in Divine Science.

I saw before me the sick, wearing out years of servitude to an unreal master, in the belief that the body governed them, rather than the Divine Mind. The lame, the deaf, the dumb, the blind, the sick, the sensual, the sinner, I wished to save from the slavery of their own beliefs, and from the educational systems which today hold the children of Israel in bondage. I saw before me the awful conflict, the Red Sea, and the wilderness; but I pressed on, through faith in God, trusting Truth, the strong deliverer, to guide me into the land of Christian Science, where fetters fall, and the rights of man to freedom are fully known and acknowledged.

Christian Science derives its sanction from the Bible; and its divine origin is demonstrated through the holy influence of its Truth in healing sickness and sin. The healing power of Truth must have been far anterior to the period in which Jesus lived. It is as ancient as the Ancient of Days. It lives through all Life, and extends through all space. Science is not the shibboleth of a sect, or the cabalistic insignia of a philosophy. Science is Mind, not matter, and because Science is not human it must be Divine.

In 1867 I commenced reducing this latent power to a system, in a form comprehensible by and adapted to the thought of the age in which we live.

This system enables the devout learner to demonstrate anew in some degree the divine Principle upon which Jesus' healing was based, and the sacred rules for its present presentation and application to the cure of disease.

The Principle of Christian Science is God. Its practice is the power of Truth over error; its rules demonstrate Science. The first rule of this Science is, "Thou shalt have no other gods before Me." The second is like unto it, "Thou shalt love thy neighbor as thyself." To demonstrate these rules on any other than their divine Principle is impossible. Jesus' sermon on the Mount is the essence of the *morale* of this Science. In 1893, for more than a quarter of a century, these rules have been submitted to the broadest practical tests; and everywhere, when honestly applied, under circumstances which made demonstration possible, they have shown that Truth has lost none of its divine and healing efficacy, even though centuries have passed away since Jesus practiced these rules on the hills of Judea and in the valleys of Galilee. Jesus said: "These signs shall follow them that believe: they shall take up serpents; and if they drink any deadly thing, it shall not hurt them. *They* shall lay hands on the sick and they shall recover." This promise is *perpetual*. Had it been given only to his immediate disciples, the scriptural passage would read *you*, not *they*. The purpose of his great life-work extends through time, and touches universal humanity; its Principle is infinite, extending beyond the pale of a single period or a limited following. His miracles illustrate an ever-operative divine Principle, scientific order and continuity. Within one decade this Science has stopped the illicit clamor and advancing trend of "free love;" it has opened dungeon doors to the captives of sin, sickness and death; given impulse to honest inquiry and religious liberty; moderated the appetites and passions of men; reformed thousands of inebriates; healed over one million cases of disease considered hopeless, and advanced the race physically, morally and spiritually.

I learned that all real Being is in the immortal, divine Mind, whereas the five material senses evolve a subjective state of mortal mind, called mortality and matter, thereby shutting out the true sense of immortality and Spirit. Christian Science explains all cause and effect as mental and not physical. It lifts the veil from Soul, and silences the false testimony of sense. It shows the scientific relation of man to God, disentangles the interlaced ambiguities of Being, and sets free the imprisoned mind to master the body.

The first commandment of the Hebrew decalogue unfolds the fact of universal brotherhood; since to have one God is to have one Mind and one Father, and this spiritually and scientifically establishes the brotherhood of man. Also, God being the only Mind, it is found impossible for God's children to have other minds, or to be antagonistic and war one with another. Mind is one, including noumena and phenomena, God and His thoughts. Mind is the center and circumference of all Being, the central sun of its own universe and infinite system of ideas. Therefore Mind is divine and not human. To reduce inflammation, dissolve a tumor, or cure organic disease, I have found Mind more potent than all lower remedies. And why not, since Mind is the source and condition of all existence?

Christian Science solves the problem of the relative rights and privileges of man and woman on their diviner claims. It finds in scriptural Genesis that Eve recorded last is therefore first, she is a degree higher than Adam in the ascending intelligence of God's creation. Woman neither sprang from the dust of which *adamah* was formed, nor from an ovum; she was the first discoverer of human weakness, and the first who acknowledged error to be error. Woman was the mother of Jesus, and the first to perceive a risen Saviour. Woman first apprehended divinely man's spiritual origin; and first relinquishes the belief in material conceptions. It is a woman that discovered and founded the Science of Christianity.

The Revelator had not passed the transitional stage in human experience called death, but he already saw in prophetic vision woman "crowned with twelve stars," types of the twelve tribes of Israel, and the spiritual enlightenment of primal religion.

If brain, blood, bones help constitute a man, when Adam parted with his rib he lost a portion of his manhood. Man is the generic term for God's children, made in his own image and likeness, and because they are thus made, reflected, the male and female of His creating are equipoised in the balances of God. So let it be.

To the sore question "What are the workingmen's rights?" Science answers justice and mercy, wherein the financial, civil, social, moral and religious aspect of all questions reflect the face of the Father. And this question will not rest till both employer and employe are actuated by the spirit of this saying of the meek and mighty Son of God: "Therefore all things whatsoever ye would that men should do to you, do ye even so to them."

The following are the tenets of the Christian Science Churches:

1. As adherents of Truth, we take the Scriptures for our guide to eternal Life.

2. We acknowledge and adore one Supreme God. We acknowledge his Son, and the Holy Ghost, and man in the Divine image and likeness.

3. We acknowledge God's forgiveness of sin, in the destruction of sin and His punishment of "Whatsoever worketh abomination or maketh a lie." We acknowledge the atonement as the efficacy and evidence of Divine Love, of man's unity with God, and of the great merits of the Way-shower.

4. We acknowledge the way of salvation demonstrated by Jesus, as the power of Truth over all error, sin, sickness and death, and the resurrection

of human faith to seize the great possibilities and living energies of the Divine Life.

5. We solemnly promise to strive, watch and pray for that Mind to be in us which was also in Christ Jesus. To love one another, and, up to our highest understanding, to be meek, merciful and just.

10. Deed of Trust Executed by Mrs. Eddy, March 6, 1907

Deed of Trust

MARY BAKER G. EDDY TO HENRY M. BAKER, ARCHIBALD McLELLAN JOSIAH E. FERNALD.

KNOW ALL MEN BY THESE PRESENTS,

That I, Mary Baker G. Eddy of Concord, New Hampshire, in consideration of one dollar to me paid by Henry M. Baker of Bow, New Hampshire, Archibald McLellan of Boston, Massachusetts, and Josiah E. Fernald of Concord, New Hampshire, who are hereby constituted trustees and attorneys in fact for the purposes hereinafter set forth, do hereby grant, convey, assign and transfer unto the said Henry M. Baker, Archibald McLellan, and Josiah E. Fernald, their heirs, successors, and assigns, all my interest of every kind and description in and to any real estate wherever situated; also all my interests of every kind and description in and to any estate, personal or mixed, which I now own or possess, including stocks, bonds, interests in copyrights, contracts, actions and causes of action at law or in equity against any person.

To HAVE AND TO HOLD the above granted and assigned premises, with all the privileges and appurtenances thereto belonging, unto said Henry M. Baker, Archibald McLellan, and Josiah E. Fernald, trustees, to them and their heirs, successors and assigns; *but, in trust, nevertheless,* for the following purposes and upon the following conditions, viz.:

First: To manage, care for, and control all the above granted real estate and interest therein during my earthly life and, at the termination thereof, to dispose of the same in accordance with the provisions of my last will and the codicils thereto; but I hereby reserve for myself the right of occupancy and use of my homestead, "Pleasant View," in Concord, New Hampshire. I hereby also reserve all household furniture, my printed library, and all horses, carriages, tools, and other articles of use or adornment now being or in use in or about my home premises at "Pleasant View." I hereby also reserve the right to occupy and to rent for my own benefit my two houses at 385 and 387 Commonwealth Avenue, Boston, Mass.

Second: I give unto my trustees full power to manage, care for, control, invest, and reinvest all said trust property and the income thereof with all powers necessary or convenient for such purpose, desiring, however, that investments of income and reinvestments of principal shall always be made in bonds or other securities of a conservative character, having regard for the safety of the principal. It is my wish that, in the making of investments, preference shall be given to the state, government, city and municipal bonds; but I leave this to the judgment and discretion of said trustees, relying upon said discretion being conservatively exercised.

Third: Said trustees shall pay to me, from time to time, out of the net income of said trust property, (1) such sums as I may need or desire for the purpose of keeping up the homestead "Pleasant View," and paying the expenses thereof and of my household, in the same general way as heretofore; (2) such sums as I may desire for my own personal expenses and for charitable purposes; and (3) such sums as I may personally desire to use for the advancement of the cause and doctrines of Christian Science as taught by me. Said trustees shall also pay and discharge whatever claims and accounts may be outstanding against me at this date.

Fourth: At the termination of my earthly life, this trust shall terminate, and all the personal estate then held by my said trustees shall pass to the executor of my last will and the codicils thereto, to be disposed of in accordance with the provisions thereof.

Fifth: Said trustees are hereby appointed my attorneys in fact and, as such, are hereby vested with full power and authority for me and in my behalf and in behalf of the trust estate hereby created, either in their own names as trustees or in my name, as they shall decide, to bring, appear in, prosecute, defend, and dispose of, as in their judgment shall seem best for the protection and preservation of the trust estate, any actions, causes of action, suits at law or in equity, whether now pending or hereafter brought with reference to any matter in which I may be personally interested or the trust estate hereby created in any way affected. And I hereby give to my trustees and attorneys in fact full power and authority to employ attorneys-at-law and other agents in such matters and in all other matters pertaining to the trust estate.

Sixth: In case of a vacancy in said board of trustees, caused by death, refusal to act, or resignation of any of them, or for any reason, a new trustee or trustees shall be appointed by me and, in case I fail to act, said new trustee shall be appointed by the chief justice of the Supreme Court of New Hampshire for the time being, preference being given to the nomination of the remaining trustee or trustees.

Seventh: I direct that my trustees shall be liable only for their own acts in the management of this trust and that no trustee shall be answerable for loss or damage which may happen to the trust property without his own willful fault or misfeasance.

Eighth: I desire said trustees and their successors to furnish a surety bond or bonds to the amount of five hundred thousand dollars, and the expense thereof shall be paid from the trust fund.

Ninth: The trustees shall receive a reasonable payment from the trust fund for their personal services as such, and shall also be reimbursed for all expenses incurred by them in the management of the trust estate.

Tenth: The trustees shall render to me personally, semi-annual accounts of the trust property and the income and expense thereof.

IN WITNESS WHEREOF, I have hereunto set my hand and seal this sixth day of March, A.D. 1907.

MARY BAKER G. EDDY [*seal*]

Signed, sealed, and delivered in the
presence of:

FRANK S. STREETER.
FRED N. LADD.

STATE OF NEW HAMPSHIRE, ⎫
    MERRIMACK   ⎬ *ss.*
                    ⎭

On this sixth day of March, personally appeared the above named Mary Baker G. Eddy and acknowledged the foregoing instrument to be her free act and deed.

FRANK S. STREETER,
Notary Public.

Before me:
[*Notarial seal*]   CONCORD, N. H. *March 6, 1907.*

We, Henry M. Baker, Archibald McLellan and Josiah E. Fernald, severally accept the foregoing trust and agree to perform the same according to the conditions and terms thereof; but we severally reserve the right to resign said trust.

HENRY M. BAKER
ARCHIBALD McLELLAN
JOSIAH E. FERNALD
Trustees.

THE BOND

KNOW ALL MEN BY THESE PRESENTS,

That we, Henry M. Baker of Bow, New Hampshire, Archibald McLellan of Boston, Massachusetts, and Josiah E. Fernald of Concord, New Hampshire, as principals, and the United States Fidelity & Guaranty Company of Baltimore, Maryland, as surety, are held and firmly bound to Mary Baker G. Eddy of Concord, New Hampshire, and her executors in the sum of five hundred thousand dollars to be paid to said Mary Baker G. Eddy or her executors, to the payment whereof we bind ourselves and our heirs, firmly by these presents.

Sealed with our seals and dated the eighteenth day of March, A.D., 1907.

THE CONDITION OF THIS OBLIGATION IS, that

WHEREAS, the said Mary Baker G. Eddy, by deed duly executed and delivered on the sixth day of March, 1907, subject to certain reservations therein named, granted, conveyed, assigned and transferred unto the said Henry M. Baker, Archibald McLellan and Josiah E. Fernald, their heirs, successors and assigns, all the grantor's interest of every kind and description in and to any real estate, wherever situated, also all the grantor's interest of every kind and description in and to any estate, personal or mixed, which the grantor then owned or possessed, including stocks, bonds, interest in copyrights, contracts, actions, and causes of action at law or in equity against any person, but in trust, nevertheless, for the purposes and upon the conditions fully set forth in said trust deed; now, if said Henry M. Baker, Archibald McLellan and Josiah E. Fernald, as such trustees, shall not well and truly carry out and perform all the obligations imposed upon them and each of them by and according to the terms, conditions and stipulations set forth in said trust deed, then this obligation shall be void.

HENRY M. BAKER.

ARCHIBALD MCLELLAN.

JOSIAH E. FERNALD.

The United States Fidelity

& Guaranty Co.

by Arthur P. Morrill,

Its Attorney-in-Fact.

Signed, sealed, and delivered in the
   presence of:

FRED N. LADD.

FRANK S. STREETER.

11. "Youth and Young Manhood" by Mrs. Eddy

Facsimile of a manuscript by Mrs. Eddy, which appeared in *Cosmopolitan* magazine, November 1907, with an editorial note saying:

"The *Cosmopolitan* presents this month to its readers a facsimile of an article sent to us by Mrs. Eddy, with the corrections on the manuscript reproduced in her own handwriting. Not only Mrs. Eddy's own devoted followers, but the public generally, will be interested in this communication from the extraordinary woman who, nearly eighty-seven years of age, plays so great a part in the world and leads with such conspicuous success her very great following.

"Mrs. Eddy writes very rarely for any publications outside of the Christian Science periodicals, and our readers will be interested in this presentation of the thought of a mind that has had so much influence on this generation. . . ."

CHRISTIAN SCIENCE SENTINEL

"WHAT I SAY UNTO YOU , I SAY UNTO ALL — WATCH"   JESUS

YOUTH AND YOUNG MANHOOD.

MARY BAKER G. EDDY.

[THE following article by Mrs. Eddy, mention of which was made in the *Sentinel* of Nov. 2, appeared in the *Cosmopolitan* for November with the accompanying editorial note.—EDITOR *Sentinel*.]

EDITOR'S NOTE.—The *Cosmopolitan* presents this month to its readers a facsimile of an article sent to us by Mrs. Eddy, with the corrections on the manuscript reproduced in her own handwriting. Not only Mrs. Eddy's own devoted followers, but the public generally, will be interested in this communication from the extraordinary woman who, nearly eighty-seven years of age, plays so great a part in the world and leads with such conspicuous success her very great following.

Mrs. Eddy writes very rarely for any publications outside of the Christian Science periodicals, and our readers will be interested in this presentation of the thought of a mind that has had so much influence on this generation.

The *Cosmopolitan* gives no editorial indorsement to the teachings of Christian Science, it has no religious opinions or predilections to put before its readers. This manuscript is presented simply as an interesting and remarkable proof of Mrs. Eddy's ability in old age to vindicate in her own person the value of her teachings.

Certainly, Christian Scientists enthusiastic in their belief are fortunate in being able to point to a Leader far beyond the allotted years of man, emerging triumphantly from all attacks upon her, and guiding with remarkable skill, determination, and energy a very great organization that covers practically the civilized world.

Youth and Young Manhood

—-oOo—-

King David, the Hebrew bard sang, "I have been young, and now I am old; yet have I not seen the righteous forsaken, nor his seed begging bread."

I for one accept his wise deduction, his ultimate spirit- *and its reward.* ual sense of thinking, feeling, and acting. This sense of rightness acquired by experience, and wisdom should be early presented to youth and to manhood in order to forewarn and forearm humanity

The ultimatum of life here and hereafter is utterly apart from a material or personal sense of pleasure, pain, joy, sorrow, *The truth of life is* life and death. Life in truth is a scientific knowledge that is portentous; and is won only by the spiritual understanding

of Life as God, good, everpresent good, and therefore life

eternal.

You will agree with me that the material body is mortal,

but Soul is immortal; also that the five personal senses are

perishable, they lapse and relapse, come and go until at length

they are consigned to dust. But say you, "Man awakes from the

dream of death in possession of the five personal senses, does

he not?" Yes, because death ~~xxxxxxxxx~~ alone does not awaken

man in God's image and likeness.   The divine Science of Life

alone gives the true sense of life and of righteousness, and

demonstrates the Principle of life eternal; even the Life that

is Soul apart from the so-called life of matter or the material

senses.

Death alone does/ absolve man from a false material sense
                    not

of life, but goodness, holiness and love do this and so consum-

ate man's being, with the harmony of Heaven; the omnipotence,

omnipresence, and omniscience of Life,—even its all-power,

                            presence
all-~~potency~~, all-science.

Dear reader, right thinking, right feeling and right act-

ing - honesty, purity, unselfishness - in youth tend to success,

intellectuality, and happiness in manhood.   To begin right enables

one to end right, and thus it is that one achieves the Science of

Life, demonstrates health, holiness and immortality.

Mary Baker G. Eddy

12. Brief History of the Early Christian Church

In his *Life of Jesus,* Ernest Renan says of the great Teacher that "all history is incomprehensible without him." And yet, aside from "the scanty and suspicious materials of ecclesiastical history," as Gibbon noted, "very little is known of this Man without whom "all history is incomprehensible."

For centuries scholars and historians have searched without success for the complete story of the Master's life here. Consequently, they have speculated, have argued and have disagreed, but despite the established knowledge that corruption became prevalent in the early Christian Church, even the most skeptical among the scholars and historians have never been able to seriously weaken, or wholly dismiss, the fact that the origin of Jesus's teachings was divine.

Certain it is that at some time the complete life of the Founder of the Christian religion was known; certain it is, too, that His teachings were more extensive than the few hundred words that have come down to us. It could not be otherwise, teaching and healing, as He did, up and down the hills and valleys of Canaan for the three years of His ministry.

It is because there is so little authentic material that it can be assumed that early in the history of the Christian Church much of the material was destroyed, or locked away from sight of the world. But, some things are known; and one of the things that is known is that Christianity in its first hundred years was a greatly different religion from what it became.

In its first hundred years Christianity largely was a group of independent and equal societies governed by presbyters, or bishops, elected from among the membership. While not altogether clear, it is generally accepted that the title of presbyter was in recognition of age, or understanding, while the title of bishop was secondary, and merely confirmed authority to watch over the faith and conduct of the congregation.

As the century neared its close, the title of bishop began to be elevated above that of presbyter, and an episcopal form of government began to emerge. For a time the duties of the bishop were closely confined to the administration of the spiritual affairs of the congregation, to the consecration of ministers, the administration of church funds and the settling of disputes between individual members of the congregation. But the bishop, despite his growing importance, remained the servant of the congregation.

It held him accountable for all his acts, and reposed in him no spiritual authority. Individually, the members of the congregation considered themselves fully equals with the bishop in spiritual affairs.

As Christianity grew — and it grew rapidly — the ambitions of many of the bishops grew with it. By the end of the second century the bishops were meeting together for the purpose of deciding controversy and issuing decrees, so that fairly early in the third century — instead of exhorting their congregations, as did Paul [1] — a hierarchy was issuing com-

[1] See various Epistles in the New Testament.

mands and requiring obedience, not only in spiritual but in temporal affairs.

The Church had grown rich. Bishops were competing with each other in the splendor of their edifices, and their treasures of gold and silver and precious stones. With a zeal for converts that was only equaled by their avarice for authority, they reconciled all the vices of politics, and introduced them into the management of their churches. The spiritual was subordinated to the material, and healing was lost.

Having departed so far from the original teachings, the clergy was forced to invent new forms of worship and to proclaim miracles to prove their improvisings. To make it easier to get converts, and for the converts to call themselves Christians, bishops introduced into Christianity superstitions straight out of paganism and, in so doing, gained for themselves the absolutism accorded pagan priests. By the close of the third century, there were few to protest.

Recognition by Constantine of Christianity in Rome in 313 added to the confusion. The deliberations of the Council of Nicea in 325 over the relationship of Christ to God increased the confusion.

In their hunger for power, the bishops of the Christian church thrived in the corruption that drove the Empire of the Caesars into decay.

What history calls the Dark Ages began, not to be penetrated until the centuries brought Martin Luther, and the Reformation.

Translated and preserved writings of early Christians have been published by The Christian Literature Company. Some of these writings follow:

Justin Martyr, a Gentile, was born in about 100 A.D. in Samaria, near Jacob's well. According to what is known about him, he was well educated, and traveled extensively in search of "the true philosophy." Trying many systems, he found what he thought he wanted in the contemplations of Socrates and Plato, but became convinced — as has been written — that "what Plato was feeling-after he [Justin] found in Jesus of Nazareth."

As did all the other Early Christian Fathers — or, as they are often called, the Ante-Nicene Fathers — Justin wrote about divine healing: "But to the Father of all, who is un-begotten, there is no name given . . . as also the appella-tion 'God' is not a name but an opinion implanted in the nature of men of a thing that can hardly be explained. But 'Jesus,' His name as man and Saviour, has also significance. For He was made man also, as we before said, having been conceived according to the will of God the Father, for the sake of believing men, and for the destruction of the demons. And now you can learn this from what is under your own observation. For numberless demoniacs throughout the whole world, and in your city, many of our Christian men exorcising them in the name of Jesus Christ, who was cruci-fied under Pontius Pilate, have healed and do heal, render-ing helpless and driving the possessing devils out of men, though they could not be cured by all the other exorcists, and those who used incantations and drugs." [2]

Irenaeus, a pupil of Polycarp, bishop of Smyrna, strongly condemned heresies which flourished in his time (120–202 A.D.) : "The more moderate and reasonable among them thou wilt convert and convince, so as to lead them no longer

[2] *Second Apology of Justin.*

to blaspheme their Creator, and Maker and Sustainer . . . but the fierce and terrible, and irrational (among them) thou wilt drive from thee, that thou may no longer have to endure their idle loquaciousness. Moreover, those also will be thus confuted who belong to Simon and Carpocrates, and if there be any others who are said to perform miracles — who do not perform what they do either through the power of God, or in connection with the truth, nor for the well-being of men, but for the sake of destroying and misleading mankind, by means of magical deceptions, and with universal deceit, thus entailing greater harm than good on those who believe them, with respect to the point on which they lead them astray."

Continuing, in *Against the Heresies*, Irenaeus wrote:

> For they can neither confer sight on the blind, nor hearing on the deaf, nor chase away all sorts of demons (none indeed) except those that are sent into others by themselves, if they can ever do as much as this. Nor can they cure the weak, or the lame, or the paralytic, or those who are distressed in any other part of the body, as has often been done in regard to bodily infirmity.
>
> And so far are they from being able to raise the dead, as the Lord raised them, and as the apostles did by means of prayer, and as [has] been frequently done in the brotherhood on account of some necessity — the entire church in that particular locality entreating with much feeling and prayer, the spirit of the dead man has returned, and he has been bestowed in answer to the prayers of the saints — that they do not even believe this

can possibly be done [and hold] that the resurrection from the dead is simply an acquaintance with that truth which they proclaim.

Since, therefore, there exist among them error and misleading influences, and magical illusions are impiously wrought in the sight of men . . . these men are in this way undoubtedly proved to be utter aliens from the divine nature, the beneficence of God, and all spiritual excellence. But they are altogether full of deceit of every kind, apostate inspiration, demonical working, and the phantoms of idolatry, and are in reality the predecessors of that dragon who, by means of a deception of the same kind, will with his tail cause the third part of the stars to fall from their place, and will cast them down to the earth . . . If any one will consider the prophecy referred to, and the practices of these men, he will find that their manner of acting is one and the same with the demons . . .

And the remarks I have made respecting numbers will also apply against all those who misappropriate things belonging to the truth for the support of a system of this kind . . . If, however, they maintain that the Lord, too, performed such works simply in appearance, we shall refer them to the prophetical writings, and prove from these both that all things were thus predicted regarding him, and did take place undoubtedly, and that He is the only Son of God.

Wherefore, also, those who are in truth His disciples, receiving grace from Him, do in His name perform miracles, so as to promote the welfare of other men. For some do certainly and truly drive out devils, so that those who have been cleansed from evil spirits frequently both believe in and join themselves to the Church.

Others have foreknowledge of things to come. They see visions and utter prophetic expressions. Others still, heal the sick by laying their hands upon them, and they are made whole. Yea, moreover, as I have said, the dead even have been raised up, and remained among us for many years. And what shall I say more? It is not possible to name the number of gifts which the Church, throughout the whole world, has received from God, in the name of Jesus Christ. And which she exerts day by day for the benefit of the Gentiles.

Nor does she perform anything by means of angelic invocations, or by incantations, or by any other wicked or curious art; but directing her prayers to the Lord, who made all things, in a pure, sincere, and straightforward spirit, and calling upon the name of our Lord Jesus Christ, she has been accustomed to work miracles for the advantage of mankind, and not to lead them into error.

There is some fragmentary writing by an early Christian named Melito to Antoninus Caesar in about the year 150 A.D.

It is not easy speedily to bring into the right way the man who has a long time previously been held fast by error.

It may, however, be effected, for when a man turns away ever so little from error the mention of truth is acceptable to him. For just as when the cloud breaks ever so little there comes fair weather, even so when a man turns toward God the thick cloud of error which deprived him of vision is quickly withdrawn from before him. For error, like disease and sleep, long holds fast those who come under its influence; but truth uses the word as a goad and smites the slumberers and awakens them, and when they are awake they look at the truth and also understand it; they hear and distinguish that which is from that which is not.

For those men which call iniquity righteousness; now the sin of which I speak is this, when a man abandons that which really exists and serves that which really does not exist, there is that which really exists, and it is called God. He, I say, really exists, and by His power does everything subsist. This being in no sense made, nor did He ever come into being; but He has existed from eternity and will exist for ever and ever.

He changeth not, while everything else changes. No eye can see him, nor thought apprehend him, nor language describe him, and those who love him speak of him thus:

Father and God of Truth, but thou a person of liberal mind and familiar with the truth, if thou wilt properly consider these matters, commune with thine own self, and though they should clothe them in the garb of a woman, remember that thou art a man. Believe in him who is in reality God,

.

and to him lay open thy mind and to him commit thy soul, and then he is able to give thee immortal life forever; for everything is possible to him, and let all other things be esteemed by thee just as they are — images as images, and sculptures as sculptures; and let not that which is only made be put in by thee in the place of him who is not made, but let him, the ever-living God, be constantly present to the mind, for thy mind itself is his likeness; for it, too, is invisible and impalpable, and not to be represented by any form, yet by its will is the whole bodily frame moved.

Know, therefore, that as thou constantly serve him who is immovable, even he who exists forever, this endows with life and knowledge. But when this world was made, and why it passes away, and why the body exists, and why it falls to decay, and why it continues, thou canst not know until thou hast raised thy head from this sleep in which thou hast sunk, and hast opened thine eyes and seen that God is one, the Lord of all, and hast come to serve him with all thy heart, then will he grant thee to know his will, for every one that is severed from the knowledge of the living God is dead and buried (even while in this body) .

Therefore [it is that] thou dost wallow on the ground before demons and shadows, and asketh vain petitions from that which has not anything to give.

Tertullian, one of the greatest of the Early Christian Fathers, was born a pagan. Probably he was educated in

Rome and, also probably, he practiced as a master of civil law, becoming a Christian in 185, or thereabouts, and a presbyter about 190.

In his Apology to the Rulers of the Roman Empire, he declared: "Why, all the authority and power we have over them [the unclean spirits] is from our naming the name of Christ, and recalling to their memory the woes with which God threatens them at the hands of Christ as Judge, and which they expect one day to overtake them. Fearing Christ in God, and God in Christ, they become subject to the servants of God and Christ. So at our touch and breathing, overwhelmed by the thought and realization of those judgment fires, they leave at our command the bodies they have entered, unwilling and distressed, and before your very eyes put to an open shame."

In his Address to Scapula, Tertullian wrote:

> The clerk of one of them who was liable to be thrown upon the ground by an evil spirit was set free from his affliction; as was also the relative of another, and the little boy of a third. How many men of rank (to say nothing of the common people) have been delivered from devils, and healed of diseases! Even Severus himself, the father of Antonine, was graciously mindful of the Christians; for he sought out the Christian Proculus, surnamed Torpacion, the steward of Euhodias, and in gratitude for his having once cured him by anointing, he kept him in his palace till the day of his death.
>
> Antonine, too, brought up as he was on Christian milk, was intimately acquainted with this man. Both women and men of highest rank, whom

Severus knew well to be Christians, not merely were permitted by him to remain uninjured; but he even bore distinguished testimony in their favor, and gave them publicly back to us from the hands of a raging populace.

Marcus Aurelius also in his expedition to Germany, by the prayers of his Christian soldiers offered to God, got rain in that well-known thirst. When indeed have not droughts been put away by our kneelings and by our fastings? At times like these, moreover, the people crying to "the God of gods, the alone Omnipotent" under the name of Jupiter, have borne witness to our God. Then we never deny the deposit placed in our hands; we never pollute the marriage bed; we deal faithfully with our wards; we give aid to the needy; we render to none evil for evil. As for those who falsely pretend to belong to us, and whom we, too, repudiate, let them answer for themselves. In a word, who has complaint to make against us on other grounds?

To what else does the Christian devote himself, save the affairs of his own community, which during all the long period of its existence no one has ever proved guilty of the incest or the cruelty charged against it? It is for freedom from crime so singular, for a probity so great, for righteousness, for purity, for faithfulness, for Truth, for the living God, that we are consigned to the flames; for this is a punishment you are not wont to inflict either on the sacrilegious, or on undoubted public enemies, or on the treason-tainted, of whom you have so many.

In his work, *The Octavius of Minusius Felix,* Tertullian said:

> Since they themselves are the witnesses that they are demons, believe them when they confess the truth of themselves; for when adjured by the only true God, unwillingly the wretched beings shudder in their bodies, and either at once leap forth, or vanish by degrees, as the faith of the sufferer assists or the grace of the healer inspires.

> Thus they fly from Christians when near at hand, whom at a distance they harassed by your means at their assemblies. And thus, introduced into the minds of the ignorant, they secretly sow there a hatred of us by means of fear. For it is natural to hate one whom you fear, and to injure one whom you have feared, if you can.

> Thus they take possession of the minds and obstruct the hearts, that men may begin to hate us before they know us; lest, if known, they should either imitate us, or not be able to condemn us.

Origen, a student of the eminent Clement of Alexandria, who was prominent in the literary and religious world of his time (*c.* 185–254) wrote of the demonstration of the Spirit in his treatise *Against Celsus:*

> Of the Spirit, on account of the prophecies, which are sufficient to produce faith in any one who reads them especially in those things which relate to Christ; and of power, because of the signs and wonders which we must believe have been performed, both on many other grounds, and on this,

that traces of them are still preserved among those who regulate their lives by the precepts of the Gospel. . . .

And there are still preserved among Christians traces of that Holy Spirit which appeared in the form of a dove. They expel evil spirits, and perform many cures, and foresee certain events, according to the will of the Logos. . . .

And the name of Jesus can still remove distractions from the minds of men, and expel demons, and also take away diseases; and produce a marvelous meekness of spirit and complete change of character, and a humanity and goodness, and gentleness in those individuals who do not feign themselves to be Christians for the sake of subsistence or the supply of any mortal wants, but who have honestly accepted the doctrine concerning God and the Christ, and the judgment to come . . .

But after this, Celsus, having a suspicion that the great works performed by Jesus, of which we have named a few out of a great number, would be brought forward to view, affects to grant that those statements may be true which are made regarding His cures, or His resurrection, etc., and adds: "Well, let us believe that they were actually wrought by you."

But then he immediately compares them to the tricks of jugglers, who profess to do more wonderful things, and to the feats performed by those who have been taught by Egyptians, who in the middle of the market place, in return for a few obols, will impart knowledge of their most venerated arts, and will expel demons from men, and dispel diseases, and invoke the souls of heroes, and exhibit expensive banquets, and tables, and dishes, and dainties, having no real existence, and who will put in motion, as if alive, what are not really living animals, but which only have the appearance of life.

And he asks: "Since, then, these persons perform such feats, shall we of necessity conclude that they are sons of God, or must we admit that they are the proceedings of wicked men under the influence of an evil spirit?"

You see that by these expressions he allows, as it were, the existence of magic . . . But, as it helped his purpose, he compares the miracles related of Jesus to the results produced by magic.

There would indeed be a resemblance between them, if Jesus, like the dealers in magical arts, had performed his works only for show; but now there is not a single juggler who, by means of his proceedings, invites his spectators to reform their manners, or trains those to the fear of God who are amazed at what they see, nor who tries to persuade them so to live as men who are justified by God.

And jugglers do none of these things, because they have neither the power nor the will, nor any desire to busy themselves about the reformation of men, inasmuch as their own lives are full of the grossest and most notorious sins. But how should not He, who, by the miracles which He did, induced those who beheld the excellent results to understand the reformation of their characters, manifest Himself not only to his genuine disciples, but also to others, after being more fully instructed in His word and character than by His miracles, as to how they were to direct their lives, [and] might in all their conduct have a constant reference to the good pleasure of the universal God . . .

We, if we deem this a matter of importance, can clearly show a countless multitude of Greeks and Barbarians who acknowledge the existence of Jesus. And some give evidence of their having received through this faith a marvelous power by the cures which they perform, invoking no other name over those who need their help than that of the God of all things, and of Jesus, along with a mention of his history. For by these means we too have seen many persons freed from grievous calamities, and from distractions of mind, and madness, and countless other ills, which could be cured by neither man nor devils.

In *The Clementine Homilies,* written by Clement of Alexandria, there is this paragraph:

For the soul being turned by faith, as it were, into the nature of water, quenches the demon as a spark of fire. The labor, therefore, of everyone is to be solicitous about the putting to flight of his own demon . . . Whence many, not knowing how they are influenced, consent to the evil thoughts suggested by the demons, as if they were the reasoning of their own souls . . . Therefore, the demons who lurk in their souls induce them to think that

it is not a demon that is distressing them, but a
bodily disease, such as some acrid matter, or bile,
or phlegm, or excess of blood, or inflammation of a
membrane, or something else. But even if this were
so, the case would not be altered by its being some
kind of a demon.

There is this fragment from the writings of Dionysius,
believed to have been circulated about 240 A.D.:

There certainly was not a time when God was
not the Father. Neither, indeed, as though he had
not brought forth these things did God afterward
beget the Son, but because the Son has existence
not from himself, but from the Father. Being the
brightness from the eternal light, he himself is also
absolutely eternal. For since light is always in existence, it is manifest that its brightness also exists.
Because light is perceived to exist from the fact
that it shines, and it is impossible that light should
not shine.

Now, this word "I am" expresses the eternal substance, for if he is the reflection of the eternal light
he must also be eternal himself, for if the light subsists forever it is evident that the reflection subsists
forever, and that this light subsists is known only
by its shining. Neither can there be light that does
not give light.

We come, therefore, to our illustrations.

If there is day then there is light; and if there is
no such thing the sun certainly cannot be present.
If, therefore, the sun had been eternal there would
also have been an endless day. Now, however, as it

is not so the day begins when the sun rises and it ends when the sun sets.

But God is eternal light, having neither beginning nor end, and along with Him is the reflection, also without beginning and everlasting. The Father, then, being eternal, the son also is eternal, being the light of light; and if God is the light, Christ is the reflection.

Gregory Thaumaturges, about 250 A.D.:

. . . Where he says: "Be of good cheer, I have overcome the world," and this he said not as holding before us any contest proper only to God, but as showing our own flesh in its capacity to overcome suffering and death and corruption, in order that, as sin entered into the world by flesh and death came to reign by sin over men . . . That sin in the flesh might also be condemned through the self-same flesh in the likeness thereof, and that the overseer of sin, the tempter, might be overcome and death cast down from its sovereignty, and the corruption in the burying of the body be done away, and the first fruits of the resurrection be shown, and the principle of righteousness begin the course in the world through faith, and the Kingdom of Heaven be preached to men, and fellowship established between God and man.

Lactantius — 260–330 — occupied a high place among the Early Christian Fathers because of his grace and his erudition. He was referring to the persecution of the Christians by the Gentiles when he wrote:

They do not therefore rage against us on this account, because their gods are not worshiped by us, but because the truth is on our side, which (as it has been said most truly) produced hatred. What, then, shall we think, but that they are ignorant of what they suffer?

For they act with a blind and unreasonable fury, which we see, but of which they are ignorant. For it is not the men themselves who persecute, for they have no cause of anger against the innocent; but those contaminated and abandoned spirits by whom the truth is both known and hated insinuate themselves into their minds, and goad them in their minds, and goad them in their ignorance to fury.

For these, as long as there is peace among the people of God, flee from the righteous, and fear them; and when they seize the bodies of men, and harass their souls, they are adjured by them, and at the name of the true God are put to flight. . . .

On account of these blows and threats, they always hate holy and just men; and because they are unable of themselves to injure them, they pursue with public hatred those whom they perceive to be grievous to them, and they exercise cruelty with all the violence that they can employ, that they may either weaken their faith by pain, or, if they are unable to effect that, they may take them away altogether from the earth, that there may be none to restrain their wickedness.

INDEX

Index

ABERNATHY, JOHN, 500
Adams, George Wendell, 360
Adams, Joseph, 208; expulsion of, 172–173
Adams, William, 13n.
Adams and Company, publishers, 30
Alcott, A. Bronson, 54, 67, 601; visits Mrs. Eddy, 52, 57
Alcott, Louisa M., 169
Aldrich, Judge Edgar, 437n., 439, 440–458, 458–461, 467–468
Alger, William R., 602–603
Alienists, Mrs. Eddy examined by, 466, 468n., 469–470
Allen, George H., 48
Allopathy, Mrs. Eddy on, 449
American Medical Association, 503; Journal, attacks on Christian Science, 170, 496–499, 516–517, 519–520
American Unitarian Society, 110
Amesbury (Massachusetts), Mrs. Eddy's residence in, 14, 22
Animal magnetism, 57, 188, 223, 488, 578
Anthony, David, 245, 269
Antoninus Caesar, 633–635, 650
Apocalypse, 189
Archives, The Mother Church, 35, 36
Arens, Edward J., 105; Spofford versus Brown case, 56; arrest and indictment, 57–59; expulsion, 69; perpetual injunction, 90–91; Quimby claim, 150

Armstrong, Joseph, 276; publisher, Journal, 235–237; Board Director, 287, 323; "next friends" suit defendant, 422–423, 434
Arnold, Sir Edwin, 134
Arthritis, testimony on cure of, 512
Associated Press, on Mrs. Eddy, 418, on "next friends" suit, 433–434
Association of Christian Scientists, see Christian Scientists' Association of the Massachusetts Metaphysical College

BADEN-POWELL, Sir Robert S., 525
Bagley, Sarah, 14, 22
Bailey, Joshua, 218–220, 235, 237, 238
Baker, Abigail and Mark, Mrs. Eddy's parents, 6n.
Baker, Fred W., "next friends" suit, 422
Baker, George W., "next friends" suit, 422, 426, 437
Baker, Henry M., trustee under 1907 deed of trust, 431–432, 453, 618–623
Bancroft, S. P., 48
Barnett, Lincoln, 46
Barre (Vermont), 198
Barrett, Dr. G. W., quoted, 532
Barrows, C. M., Bread Pills, 159

Barry, George W., 48, 49–51
Barta Press, 323
Bartlett, Julia S., 84, 125, 199, 243*n.*, 261, 265; work on hymnal, 232; *Bible* lessons, 549
Bartol, Cyrus D., 124
Barton (Vermont), 84
Bates, Caroline S., 269
Bates, Edward P., 269, 323
Bates, Mrs. Edward P., 288
Bates, Erastus N., 211
Bay Psalm Book, Stephen Daye Press, 80
"Being, Scientific Statement of," *see* "Scientific Statement of Being"
Bell, Mrs. J. H., 174
Ben Hur (Lew Wallace), 134
Berkeley, George, 96
Berry, Mrs. Mary F., 270
Bible, 218–219; Mrs. Eddy's teachings, study, and interpretations of, 4–5, 8, 15, 18, 27, 31, 42, 95–96, 545, 547, 603; quotations from, 9, 11, 12, 26, 44–45, 545–546, 557; King James Version, 28; use in conjunction with *Science and Health*, 228–229, 233, 294, 347, 553–554; importance in Christian Science of, 548–553
Bible Lessons, 228; Mrs. Eddy's development of, 548–549
Billings, Dr. Frank, 503–504
Bishops, in early church, 628–629
Blastomycosis, testimony on cure of, 517
Blindness, testimony on cure, 525
Board of Directors, *see* Directors, Board of
Body, and soul, 5
Boehme, Jakob, 96
Boerhaave, Hermann, quoted, 500
Bonney, Charles Carroll, 299
Book of Spirit Writings, A, 16
Boston, Massachusetts, students from, 62; early meetings, 66; Mrs. Eddy in, 67, 83, 188; Mrs. Eddy leaves, 198; Mrs. Eddy quoted on, 442–444, 603; Mrs. Eddy's return from Concord to, 474, 476
Boston Christian Scientist, 190, 225
Boston Christian Scientist Association, 174, 177–178
    See also Christian Scientists Association of the Massachusetts Metaphysical College
"Boston Craze and Mrs. Eddy," remarks of L. T. Townsend, 114
Boston Globe, quoted, 396
Boston Herald, quoted, 57, 417–418
Boston Methodist Preachers' meeting, 114
Boston Post, quoted, 139, 141, 142, 144
Boston Transcript, quoted, 398
Boston University, 114
Bow (New Hampshire), birthplace of Mrs. Eddy, 6*n.*, 611; Mrs. Eddy on, 440
Boylston Hotel, 187
Boy Scouts of America, 525
Brackett, Professor Lyman, work on new hymnal, 232
Branch, Oliver E., "next friends" suit, 433
Branch churches, 342; *Church Manual* on, 337–338; *Sentinel* editorial on, 487
Bread Pills (C. M. Barrows), 159
Bright's disease, testimony on cure, 514
Brisbane, Arthur, on Mrs. Eddy, 427–428
Brown, Lucretia, 56
Brown, W. F., and Company, printing of *Science and Health*, 33–34
Browning, Robert, 96
Bruno, Fraülein Johanna, 381
Bubier, S. M., Esq., 3

Buckley, James, 155–156
Buddhism, 136, 137
Building Fund. *See* Church Building Fund
Building lot, Boston, 239, 243–244, 246, 261, 267, 275–276
Burns, Robert, 96
Burton, E. F., 503–506
"Busy Bees," 605
By-laws of Church, 66, 323
    See also Church Manual
Byron, George Noel Gordon, Lord, 96

CABOT, RICHARD C., quoted, 500
Caird, John, quoted, 54–55
California, students in, 110
Calvinism, emphasis on death, 11
Campbell, Mr. and Mrs. J. Allen, 191*n.*
Cancer, testimony on cure, 509
Carlyle, Thomas, 96
Case, Henry Lincoln, 607
Central Music Hall, Chicago, 179
Century, 155
Chamberlin, Judge Robert N., "next friends" suit, 431–433, 437, 461, 463, 467–469
Chandler, William Eaton, "next friends" suit, 419–422, 438–440, 455, 458, 461–462, 468
Chanfrau, Mrs. Henrietta E., 269
Channing, William Ellery, 16
Charlestown (Massachusetts), 62
Charter, provisions of By-Laws, 66
Chase, Harvey and Company, Boston, audit of Frye's books, 430
Chase, Stephen A., 265, 407, 586; Treasurer, 282, 295; Director, 323; "next friends" suit, 422–423, 434
Chestnut Hill, Massachusetts, Mrs. Eddy at, 474, 484–485, 488, 494
Chicago (Illinois), 110, 133, 160, 161

Chicago Christian Scientist, 225
Chicago Christian Scientist Association, 173
Chicago Inter-Ocean, 181
Chicago Times, 180
Chicago Tribune, 181, 302
Chickering Hall, Boston, engaged for Sunday services, 128–129
Children's Quarterly, 220
Choate, Clara E., 104; Mrs. Eddy letter to, 36; expulsion, 105
Choate, George D., 387
Christ and Christmas, 310–313
"Christ My Refuge," 565–568, 608–609
Christian Church, Mrs. Eddy on spiritual basis of, 27, 29; on divisions of, 543; brief history of the early, 627–644
    See also Christianity
Christian Literature Company, writings of early Christians, 629–644
Christian Register, 303
Christian Science, origins, 6, 13, 93; first use of words, 13*n.,* 40; deviators 74, 139, 152, 171, 173, 182–183, 185, 190; importance of demonstration in, 98; growth and development, 104–105, 110, 132–133, 191, 226, 348, 371–376, 379–385, 386, 391; clergy's crusade against, 114, 116, 120–124; relations with other Churches, 194–195; transition into a spiritual organization, 209–215, 225; changes, in service, 229–232, 365; organization of First Church, 262–297; membership, 399; Mrs. Eddy on, 448–451, 456–457; 482–483; legal attack on, 458–461; American Medical Association attacks on 496–499, 500–503; tenets of, 543–548, 557–562, 616–617
"Christian Science," Mrs. Eddy's reply to Bishop Fallows, 575–579

Christian Science (Mark Twain), 413

Christian Science, The Sense and Nonsense of (Leon C. Prince), 499–500

Christian Science Bible Lessons, publication begun, 549
  See also Bible Lessons

Christian Science Board of Directors, *see* Directors, Board of

Christian Science Dispensary Association, 202

Christian Science Hymnal, 232–233, 340, 565*n.*

Christian Science Journal, 104, 105, 116, 339, 548, 581, 605; first issue, 88–89; circulation, 110; Dresser charges, 144–146; ownership, 202, 222, 235, 472–473; editorship, 218, 227, 471; advertising policy, 274; "next friends" suit, 424; on functions of publication, 473; building plans, 583–585

Christian Science literature, 219, 221
  See also Christian Science Publishing Society; General Association for Dispensing Christian Science Literature; Publications

Christian Science Mission and Free Dispensary, 201

Christian Science Monitor, 179–180, 339, 528; establishment and naming of, 471, 476–477; Home Forum page, 478; first issue, 478; news policy, 478–479; and *Sentinel,* 480–481

Christian Science Publishing Society, 137, 219, 336; Committee for Hymnal, 232; deed of trust, 472; function and policy, 473; *Monitor,* 476; German literature, 483; file of testimonies, 507–538; Bible Lessons, 549; building plans for, 583–585

Christian Science Quarterly, 228, 340, 424, 549

Christian Science Reading Rooms, 187, 213

Christian Science rest rooms, 166

Christian Science Sentinel, 19, 339, 484; "next friends" suit, 424; editorship, 471; and the *Monitor,* 478, 480–481; contents, 481–483; on Mrs. Stetson case, 486–488, 490–491; on Lesson-Sermons, 549–550, 552–553; "Youth and Young Manhood" article, 624

Christian Science Weekly, 481

Christian Scientists' Association of the Massachusetts Metaphysical College, 105, 110*n.*, 128, 133; first meeting, 62; expulsions, 69, 73–74; Mrs. Eddy's relations with, 74–75, 135, 182–183; importance of, 104; branches, 133–134; management of *Journal,* 134; rebellion within, 174; 182–185; dissolution, 209–210; membership, 205, 210; on Bible Lessons, 228

Christianity, Mrs. Eddy on, 8, 29; early theology, 9, 27–28, 32, 42–45; change to emphasis on death, 10–11; violence in, 18; materialism, 27–28; scientific, 65

"Christianity or the Understanding of God, etc.," E. J. Arens, 90–91

Church building, plans for, 278–281, 583–585; cornerstone, 281, 284–285; setbacks, 284, 287, 296; first services, 289; Deed of Trust on 587–589

Church Building Fund, 239–240, 243, 248–250, 278; disappearance of Treasurer, 242; letter to contributors, 267, 276–277; subscription list, 281–283; report on contributions, 407–408

Church Manual of The First Church of Christ, Scientist, 36–37, 307,

321–322, 424, 474, 531, 581; first edition, 320, 323; on membership, 326; on teachers, 327–328; on Lesson-Sermon, 329; on duties of officers, 329; on Readers, 329–330; as basic law of The Mother Church, 333–335, 338–341, 342, 487; on branch churches, 337–338; amendment, 407; on Directors, 491; on individual responsibility, 556–557

Church of Christ, Scientist, beginnings, 48; organization, 62, 65–66; first meetings, 63, 66–67, 68; By-Laws and Charter, 66, 69; first communion Sunday, 68; withdrawals, 73–74; requirements for membership and pastors, 194, 196–197; Mrs. Eddy's resignation, 202–203; pastorate, 204; order of service, 206–208; dissolution, 213–214; Deed of Trust, 244–262 *passim;* Boards of Trustees and Directors named, 245–246

See also First Church of Christ, Scientist, in Boston, Massachusetts

Circuit Court of the United States for the First District, 90–91

Clairvoyance, 138

Claremont, New Hampshire, 451

Clark, George, 29–30

Clark, George D. (father), 14, 25

Clark, Sarah J., editor of *Christian Science Journal,* 227

Clarke, Ellen L., 265, 268, 269

Clemens, Samuel L., 92

See also Twain, Mark

Clement of Alexandria, *The Clementine Homilies,* 641–642

Clergymen, attacks on Mrs. Eddy, 113–124

Cleveland (Ohio), 204

Cochrane, Mrs. Rose, 372–373

Coleman, Erwin L., 165

Coles, Abraham, use of words "Christian Science" in verse, 13n.

Colles, Graves, 371

Colles, Marjorie, 372

Collier, George A., 58–59

Colman, Janet T., 265

Colorado, Governor of, veto of act for suppression of Christian Science, 501–503

Communion Sunday, first as a Church, 68

Conant, Mrs. Laura Carey, 411

Concord (Massachusetts), the Eddys and Alcott visit Emerson, 52

Concord (New Hampshire), 483; Mrs. Eddy moves to, 198; degrees presented at, 357–362; church dedicated, 403–404; "next friends" suit, 416–426; Mrs. Eddy on her residence in, 440–444; Mrs. Eddy removes to Boston, 474, 476

Concord Monitor, 476

Concord Patriot, 436, 469

Concord School of Philosophy, 52, 601

Congregationalist, 116, 170, 302, 303

Congress, U.S., *Sentinel* copies sent to, 480

Constantine, 10, 629

Cook, Joseph, 116, 301

Cook County Hospital, Chicago, 503

Corner, Mrs. Abbie H., 170, 175, 183n., 185

Cosmopolitan Magazine, 427; Mark Twain's attack on Mrs. Eddy, 396, 413; "Youth and Young Manhood" by Mrs. Eddy, 624–626

Crafts, Hiram S., first Christian Science practitioner, 14; instructions to, 19–21

Creation, *Science and Health* on, 36, 77, 111, 188

Crosby, Mary H., 165
Cross and the Crown, The, 77–78, 110; symbolical meaning explained, 77–78
Crosse, Mrs. Sarah, dissident, 190
Cushing, Dr. Alvin M., 3

DANIEL (Bible), 96
Dark Ages, 643
Davis, Hayne, counsel for Mrs. Stetson, 493
Day, George B., 172, 179
Day, Jessie, 232
Death, fear of, 10–11, 12, 97; *Science and Health* on, 43; Mrs. Eddy on, 539
Decline and Fall of the Roman Empire (Gibbon), quoted, 9
Dedication Services (The Mother Church), order of Service, 591–610
Deed of Trust, executed by Mrs. Eddy (Sept. 1892), 244–247, 249, 250–262 *passim*, 265, 278, 317–320, 336; *Church Manual* on, 323; text of, 586–591
Deed of Trust, executed by Mrs. Eddy (1907), 471–473; text of, 618–623
"Deification of Personality," *Miscellaneous Writings*, 311
Demonology, 77
Demonstration in Christian Science, 98
Devil, *Science and Health* on, 44; Mrs. Eddy on, 540–541
Dickens, Charles, 96
Dickey, Adam H., 338, 341
Dionysius, quoted on God, 642–643
Directors, Board of, 63, 265, 325–326, 337–338, 472, 476, 478, 485, 490–494, 587–589, 605
Discoverer, Mrs. Eddy as the, 164
Disease, 5, 12, 97; cure of, 9, 13; as error, 47; testimonies on healing, 507–538; Benjamin Franklin on, 560
See also Healing
Divine Love, 87
Divine Mind, 70
Divine Presence, 8
See also God
Doctors, Mrs. Eddy and, 4
Dodge, Anna, 373–374
Dorman, Albert B., 159, 160
Dresser, Julius A., 6, 7, 169, 332; Quimby claim, 138–149; *The True History of Mental Science*, 144
Drummond, Henry, 87, 96
Dudley, J. L., visit to Mrs. Eddy, 57
Dunmore, Earl of, 619
Du Noüy, Le Comte, 102, 103
Dunshee, Mrs. Margaret J., 62, 73
Durant, S. Louise, 73

EAST BOSTON (Massachusetts), residence of Asa Gilbert Eddy, 49
East Cambridge, Massachusetts, 58, 59
East Stoughton (now Avon), Mrs. Eddy at, 14
Eastaman, Joseph S., 187, 243*n.*, 245, 249, 265, 283–284, 586
Eastaman, Mary F., 265, 323
Eastman, Edwin G., 433, 462
Easton, the Reverend D. A., 605
Eckert, Hans, 379
Eddy, Asa Gilbert, 6*n.*, 60; student, 49; marriage to Mary Baker Glover, 50; arrest, 57–59; Publisher, *Science and Health*, 60; founding of Massachusetts Metaphysical College, 70; assistance on *Science and Health*, 76, 79; death, 83; healing of Julia Bartlett by, 125
Eddy, Foster, *see* Foster Eddy
Eddy, Mary Baker, and Her Books, 80
Eddy, Mary Baker, The Life of (Wilbur), 182

Eddy, Mary Baker G., accident and invalidism, 3–7; birth and marriages, 6n.; origins of Christian Science, 8–13, 93; early homes, 14–17; at Lynn, Massachusetts, 14, 22, 32–34; *The Science of Man*, 15; first healing, 17; early hostility toward, 17–18, 31–32, 52–57; method of instructing, 18–19, 86–88; partnership with Kennedy, 22, 24–25; *Lynn Transcript* article on teachings, 23–24, 569–572; prospectus of book (*Science and Health*), 29–30; desire for "church of my own," 30; *Science and Health*, 33–34, 59–60, 77, 80–81, 110, 229, 331–332; first class organized, 35; *Retrospection and Introspection*, 37, 386; Sunday meetings, 48, 62; marriage to Asa Gilbert Eddy, 50; encouragement from Alcott and Emerson, 52–54, 57; trouble with Spofford, 55–56; organization of Church of Christ, Scientist, 62–65; residence in Boston, 67, 83, 188; Metaphysical College, 70, 134; study of copyright laws, 74; withdrawal from Association, 74; declines "patients," 79; *Mary Baker Eddy and Her Books*, 80; *Journal*, 84, 88, 473; personal characteristics, 86; trouble with Arens, 90; declared herself Leader, 93, 341; personal library, 95–96; activity in Chicago, 105; attacks by clergy, 113–116, 120–124; official positions, 134–135; Quimby claim, 139–151; opposition to her leadership, 174–177, 182–188; famous address at Chicago meeting, 178–181; *Miscellaneous Writings*, 180, 367; in New York City, 191–193; moved to Concord, N.H., 198; retirement and resignations, 198, 202, 209–211, 213, 222–224; *First Church of Christ, Scientist, and Miscellany*, 208; dissolves organizations of the Association, College, and Church, 209–211, 213; *Christ and Christmas*, 227, 310–313; misinterpretation of her teachings, 227–228; Deed of Trust (1892), 244–320 *passim*, 586–591; "Ponds and Purpose," 309; Church Manual, 321–343; Pastor Emeritus, 323; use of her name in services, 331–332; *Permanency of The Mother Church and Its Manual*, 341; visits to The Mother Church, 344–347; Woodbury libel suit, 353–354; classes in Concord, N.H., 355; unexplained call for meeting in Concord (degrees conferred), 357–362; lecturing activity, 386–387; addresses to annual meeting of The Mother Church (1899), 393; daily routine of "Pleasant View," 401–402; gift for Concord church, 403; Mark Twain's attack on, 413; *N.Y. World* and *McClure's Magazine* attacks, 416–418; "next friends" suit, 419–436, 437–468, 469–470; Monitor, 471, 476–481; Deed of Trust (1907), 471–473, 618–629; leaves Concord for Boston, 474–476; *Sentinel*, 481–484; at Chestnut Hill, Brookline, 484–485, 494; trouble with Mrs. Stetson, 485–494; American Medical Association attacks, 498–499; references in testimonies, 507–536 *passim*; theology of, 539–548, 556, 560–561; development of Lesson-Sermons, 548–550; "Christ My Refuge," 565–568, 608–609; "Principle and Practice," 573–574; reply to Bishop Fallows, 575–579; on the church in Oconto, Wisconsin, 581; dedication services

(1895), 591–592, 597–607; address to World's Parliament of Religions, 611–617; Arthur Brisbane on, 427–428; "Youth and Young Manhood" (article in Cosmopolitan Magazine), 624–626

Eddy, Mrs., and the Late Suit in Equity, Michael Meehan, 469–470

Edwards, Jonathan, 10–11, 16

Einstein, Universe and Doctor (Lincoln Barnett), 46

Eliot Indian Bible, Stephen Daye Press, 80

Emerson, Ralph Waldo, 16; quoted, 11, 53, 545; Mrs. Eddy and, 52–53

England, 479–480; Christian Science in, 110

Epilepsy, testimony on cure, 523

Error, notes of instruction to Hiram S. Crafts, 20, 21; Melito quoted on, 633–635

Esaias, the prophet, 131

Evans, Dr. W. F., 144; *Esoteric Christianity,* 159

Ewing, Judge William, 406

Exodus, Book of, 545

Ezekiel, Book of, 545

FALLOWS, SAMUEL, attack on Christian Science, 120–123; Mrs. Eddy's reply, 575–579

Farlow, Alfred, "next friends" suit, 422–423, 434, 459

Fear, Mrs. Eddy on, 539–541, 547, 558; Bible counsel against, 545–546

Fernald, Josiah E., "next friends" suit, 431–432, 434; trusteeship, 453, 618, 622–623

Field-King, Julia, 373, 375

Fifty Doses of Mental Medicine (L. M. Merrman), 159

First Church of Christ, Scientist, and Miscellany, The (Mrs. Eddy), 208

First Church of Christ, Scientist, in Boston, The (The Mother Church), 233, 261, 431; order of service, 228–229, 295–296, 363; use of "The" in name, 261n.; organized, 265, 268; Board of Directors, 265–267, 493; "First Members," 266, 324–326, 472; officers and members, 269–270; tenets, 271–272; first service in new structure, 289–290; dedication, 294, 591–610; policies, 294; membership, 304–305, 348, 399; Board of Lectureship, 368–369; Board of Missionaries, 388; Branch Churches, 406, 486–487; Extension of the Mother Church building, 406–408; dedication of Extension, 408, 410–411; Deed of Trust (1892), 472, 586

See also Church of Christ, Scientist; Mother Church, The

First Church of Christ, Scientist, in New York, 485–486, 488, 491–494, 499

First Church of Christ, Scientist, Oconto, Wisconsin, 580–582

First Church of Christ, Scientist, of Concord, N.H., Mrs. Eddy's contribution, 402–403; dedication, 403–404

First Church of Christ, Scientist, of Hannover (Germany), 380

First Members, 266, 324–326, 472

First Methodist Church, Chicago, 178

Footsteps of Truth, *Science and Health* on, 77, 110, 188

Foster, Ebenezer J., teacher of obstetrics in Metaphysical College, 187; Mrs. Eddy's adoption of, 196, 198–199

See also Foster Eddy, Ebenezer J.

Foster Eddy, Ebenezer J., 249, 261, 265, 295n., 346; Mrs. Eddy's adoption of, 187–188, 196, 198–199; offices held, 204, 362; Metaphysical College, 211; dropped from membership, 363; "next friends" suit, 422, 424

Fowler, Stacy, attacks on Mrs. Eddy, 115

Frame, Caroline W., 269

Franklin, Benjamin, on diseases and cures, 560

Frederic, Harold, death in London, 496; furore over, 496–498

Frye, Calvin A., 199, 269, 354, 359, 474; position in Mrs. Eddy's household, 84, 433, 454; *New York World* attack, 417–418; audit of accounts, 429–430; "next friends" suit, 422–424, 430–431, 433–434

GENERAL ASSOCIATION FOR DISPENSING CHRISTIAN SCIENCE LITERATURE, 220–221

Genesis, *Science and Health* on, 189

Germany, 380, 479, 483–484

Gestefeld, Ursula, 159, 171, 232

Gibbon, Edward, quoted, 9, 641

Gifford, Orrin P., 124–125

Glossary, in *Science and Health*, 189

Glover, George W. (Mrs. Eddy's son), "next friends" suit, 419–426, 439; Mrs. Eddy on, 624

Glover, George Washington, Mrs. Eddy's first husband, 6n.

Glover, Mary B. (granddaughter), "next friends" suit, 422, 426, 439

Glover, Mary Baker, 60, 77; first Sunday service, 47–48; marriage to Asa Eddy, 50
    See also Eddy, Mary Baker G.

God, Mrs. Eddy's conception of, 8, 12–13, 28, 63–65, 96–97, 539–544, 546, 550–551, 558, 561, 577; writings of early Christians on, 630–644

Golden Text, 550

Good Templars Hall, Lynn, services at, 48, 61, 107

Goodall, Berenice H., 269

Gordon, A. J., vitriolic attacks on Mrs. Eddy, 116

Gragg, Eldora O., 265, 323

Granite State Water Cure, 6

Graybill, Henrietta E., 534n.

Greene, Eugene H., 245, 269

Greene, Grace A., 269

Gregory Thaumaturges, quoted, 643

Günther-Peterson, Frau Bertha, 380, 483

HALE, EDWARD EVERETT, 124

Hale, Sara Josepha, 13n.

Hall, E. H., work on new hymnal, 232

Hamilton, Dr. Allan McLane, 469–470

Hanna, Judge Septimus J., 237–238, 299, 304, 306, 394, 471; pastorate, 289–290; First Reader, 288, 323; Mrs. Eddy on, 601

Harriman, W. C., 433

Hart, Edwin, 581

Harvard University, 124

Hatten, Thomas A., *Manual* copyrighted by, 323

Hawthorne Hall, 105, 108, 128; Sunday services at, 107–108

Hazzard, Dr. Jean, 153, 155, 156

Healers, training of, 132; discord among, 132–133

Healing, 382, 560; of Mrs. Eddy, 5, 8–10; by early Christians, 9–10, 644–658; by Mrs. Eddy, 17–18, 81–82, 125–128, 130–131, 164–165, 180; *Science and Health* on, 43–44; instruction in, 70, 132; manifestation of Christ-consciousness, 79; legislation on, 496, 500–503, 532; testimonies on, 507–538; Mrs. Eddy on importance of, 555–556

Healing and Teaching, *Science and Health* on, 188

Healing the Sick, *Science and Health* on, 38, 77, 110

"Hear, O Israel" (Mrs. Eddy), 311–312

Heart disease, testimony on cure, 510–511

Heaven, Mrs. Eddy on, 45, 540–541

Hebrew proverbs, sayings of Jesus from, 53

Helberg, C. C., *A Book of Spirit Writings*, 16

Hell, Mrs. Eddy on, 45, 540–541

Hering, Hermann S., "next friends" suit, 422–423, 434

Herold der Christian Science, 339, 424, 484

Hibbens, Anne, 94

Hill, New Hampshire, 6, 7; Granite State Water Cure, 6–7, 139

Historical and Biographical Papers (Clifford P. Smith), 181

Hollis, Allen, "next friends" suit, 433, 462

Holmes, Oliver Wendell, 500

Home Forum Page (*Monitor*), 478

Homiletic Review, 115

Homoeopathy, 163, 449

Hopkins, Emma Curtis, 225, 331; expulsion, 156; schismatic activity, 159, 166

Hour of Unison, 160

Howard, James C., 73, 75

Howe, Attorney, on Christian Science as an "insane belief," 458–461

Hulin, Emilie B., 269

Hymnal, *see Christian Science Hymnal*

Hypnotism, 160, 504, 576

IMPOSITION AND DEMONSTRATION, in *Science and Health*, 38, 60, 77, 111, 188

Instruction, methods of, 18–21, 33, 36; payment for, 34–37; to teachers, 326–328

"International Bible Lessons, Spiritually Interpreted," 166

International Christian Science Association, 166

International Magazine of Christian Science, 159–160, 167, 169

International Sunday School Lessons, 548

"Ipswich Witchcraft Case," 56

Irenaeus, *Against the Heresies*, quoted, 631–633

Isaiah, Book of, 96

JACKSON, DR. CHARLES T., 450

Jairus's daughter, 110

Jacob (Bible), 562

James, Mrs. Lottie, 170

James, William, 67; on Christian Science, 67; mistaken notion of Mrs. Eddy, 67, 68

Jelly, Dr. George F., "Master" in "next friends" suit, 437n., 440–458 *passim*

Jeremiah, Book of, 545

"Jesuitism in Christian Science," 171

Jesus, tenets derived from, 8–12, 53, 63–65, 97, 544, 627; Mrs. Eddy quoted on, 547, 561–562, 578; writings of early Christians on, 630–642 *passim*

Jesus, Life of (Renan), 97

John, Book of St., 96, 545, 554, 629

John of Leydon, 498

Johnson, William B., 183–184, 243, 245–246, 254–255, 265, 267; official positions, 174, 213–214, 323; work on hymnal, 232; "next friends" suit, 422–423, 434; Bible lessons, 549

Journal, see Christian Science Journal

Jude, Book of, 610

Justin Martyr, quoted on divine healing, 630

KANT, IMMANUEL, 95

Keats, John, 96

"Keep to the Scriptures," chapter heading in *Science and Health*, 189

Kelly, John W., "next friends" suit, 433

Kennedy, Richard, 438; student, 22; partnership with Mrs. Eddy, 22, 24, 25

Key to the Scriptures, with a, new words added to title of *Science and Health*, 110

    See also *Science and Health with a Key to the Scriptures*

Kimball, Edward A., 355, 358, 369; healing of, 130–131; Woodbury libel suit, 354; in British Isles, 377–378; answers Mark Twain, 413; "next friends" suit, 422–424, 430–431, 434

King, Albert C., 373

King, Albert G., 375

Knapp, Flavia Stickney, 252, 253, 261, 265

Knapp, Ira Oscar, 243n., 265, 407; explains symbolism of the Cross and the Crown, 77–78; building lot title, 243, 246, 250–261; Director, 323; "next friends" suit, 422–423, 434; Bible lessons, 549; Deed of Trust, 586

Knipperdaling, Bernhard, 498

Knoxville, Tennessee, 23

LACTANTIUS, quoted on persecutions, 643–644

Ladd, Fred N., 429–430, 621, 623

La Grange, Joseph Louis, 542

Lang, Alfred, 267; official positions, 220, 243, 246–247, 249–252, 261

Lang, Susie M., work on new hymnal, 232

Lao-tse, 26

Larminie, Hannah, 174, 373–374

Lathrop, Mrs. Laura, 191

Lead, South Dakota, 420, 464

Leader, Mrs. Eddy declares herself, 93, 216n., 341, 488, 491

Leavitt, Annie V. C., 270

Lectureship, Board of, 386–388, 391, 475; Mrs. Eddy's requirements for lecturers, 389–390

Leonard, Pamelia J., 417, 418

Leprosy, testimony on cure, 532

Lesson-Sermon, 329, 548–553

Letters and Social Aims (Emerson), 11

Life, Science of, 39, 48, 93

Lincoln, Miss Elsie, 596

Locomotor ataxia, testimony on, 508

London, England, Christian Science in, 110, 373–374; death of Harold Frederick, 496

London Chronicle, quoted, 479

Longfellow, Henry Wadsworth, 96

Longyear, Mary Beecher, 381

Lord's Prayer, with spiritual interpretation, 230–231, 595–596

Louisville, Kentucky, Hopkins College of Christian Science, 159

Luke, Book of, 545, 553–554

Luther, Martin, 195, 629

Lynn (Massachusetts), 61; Mrs. Eddy in, 3, 5, 14, 17, 22; Spofford "mental healer" in, 47; services held in, 67

Lynn Christian Church, Mrs. Eddy attends, 25

Lynn Reporter, 3

Lynn Transcript, Mrs. Eddy's statement in, 23–24, 569–572

McClure's Magazine, attack on Mrs. Eddy, 416, 427
McCrackan, William D., First Reader at dedication, 411
MacDonald, Asa T. N., 48
McDonald, Hugh, 580
McKenzie, William P., 369
McLellan, Archibald, trustee, 434, 478, 618, 622–623; Mrs. Eddy on, 431, 432, 453; editorship of *Journal* and *Monitor,* 471; statement on Mrs. Stetson, 486–488
Mammon, God and, 12
Man, Mrs. Eddy's definition, 577
Mann, August, 441
Manual of The Mother Church. See Church Manual of The First Church of Christ, Scientist
Marcus Aurelius, 637
Mark, Book of, 96, 108
Marriage, in Science and Health, 38, 77, 111, 188
Marston, Dr. Luther M., 160, 162
Marx, Karl, quoted, 542*n.*
Mason, Frank E., 163–164, 205; manager of the *Journal,* 187
Massachusetts, Commonwealth of, Eddy-Arens case, 59; Charter for Metaphysical College, 69–70; statutes, 260; legislative attempts to suppress Christian Science, 502, 532
Massachusetts Metaphysical College, 95, 99, 104, 115, 124, 160, 356; beginnings, 69–71; Association formed, 133; Mrs. Eddy and, 134, 194, 475; stricter requirements, 186, 189; classes, 189, 194, 198; questions of organization, 194–198; dissolved, 211; "next friends" suit, 424, 425

See also Christian Scientists' Association of the Massachusetts Metaphysical College
Masters, Board of, *see* "next friends" suit
Materialism, 45–46, 53, 78, 96, 542–543; in Christian Church, 13, 29, 33
Mather, Increase, 94
Matthew, Book of, 19–21, 96
Meader, Mrs. Emily M., 269
Medical authorities, attempts to suppress Christian Science, 496–503
Medical News, 499
Mediums (Spiritualist), 69, 138, 146
Meehan, Michael, *Mrs. Eddy and the Late Suit in Equity,* 469–470
Meionian Hall (Tremont Temple), 174
Melito, to Antoninus Caesar on error, 633–635
Mental Healing, 70
Mental Science, The True History of (Dresser), 144
Merrman, L. M., *Fifty Doses of Mental Medicine,* 159
Mesmerism, 23, 39, 76, 138, 142, 146, 148, 160, 223; in *Science and Health,* 60, 76; Mrs. Eddy on, 457, 569–572
Messenger of Truth, 160
Metaphysics, in *Science and Health,* 60; Samuel Fallows article on, 120–121; Mrs. Eddy's definition, 577
Micah, 96
Millidge, Mrs. Lovina, 580
Milton, John, 96
Milwaukee, Wisconsin, Hopkins College of Christian Science, 159
Mind, Science of, Mrs. Eddy on, 451
Mind Cure and Science of Life (Swartz publication), 161
Mind in Nature, 120–123

Mind reading, 138

Miracles, in early Christian Church, 9, 629, 630–633

Miscellaneous Writings (Mrs. Eddy), 180, 322, 338, 346, 367, 424, 547

Missionaries, Board of, 388

Mohammedans, 136, 137

"Monday Morning Lectureship," 116

Monitor, see Christian Science Monitor

Montesquieu, Baron de la Brède et de, 96

Moore, Hannah, 232

Moral Science, Mrs. Eddy on, 19, 23–24, 569–572; Ralph Waldo Emerson on, 53

Morgan, Mrs. Martha E. S., 270

Morrill, Arthur P., 449, 623

Morse, William M., 433

Mortal mind, definition of, 578

Mother Church, Manual of The. See Church Manual of The First Church of Christ, Scientist

Mother Church, Message to The (1901), 399, 532, 557

Mother Church, The (First Church of Christ, Scientist, in Boston, Massachusetts), 200–201, 212, 213, 556, 582; Archives, 35, 36; "next friends" suit, 424–425; Deed of Trust, 472–473; Mrs. Eddy on New York rivalry of, 485, 492–493; McLellan editorial, "One Mother Church," 486–488; dedication services, 591–610

See also First Church of Christ, Scientist, in Boston, The

Mother Church, The (Joseph Armstrong), 276

Mother's Room, The Mother Church, 289, 605

Mozart, Wolfgang Amadeus, 41

Munroe, Marcellus, 246

Munroe, Mary W., 243n., 265

Murphy, Dr. John B., 504

NAPOLEON BONAPARTE, 542

Nation Christian Scientist Association, formed, 133–134; Chicago meeting, 174, 178–182; Mrs. Eddy and, 202; Cleveland Convention, 203–204; Foster Eddy and, 204; control of *Journal*, 222, 235n., 239; recessed for three years, 235

National School of Christian Science, 169

Natural Science, in *Science and Health*, 38

Neal, James A., 323

New England Conservatory of Music, 165

New Testament, Rotherdam's translation, 218

New York (New York), Christian Science in, 110, 191; National School of Christian Science, 160; Mrs. Eddy's address, 191–193

New York American, article by Mrs. Stetson, 485–486

New Yorld Herald, Mrs. Eddy's reply to Mark Twain, 397

New York Sun, Mrs. Eddy's address in New York, 192

New York Times, Mrs. Eddy's address in New York, 191–192; adverse criticism of Mrs. Eddy, 396; interview with Dr. Hamilton, 469–470; Mrs. Stetson on a new church, 488

New York World, Mrs. Eddy's address in New York, 192–193; attack on Mrs. Eddy, 416–417, 418–422, 427, 464; letter from *Concord Patriot* to, 436; Michael Meehan article, 469

Newhall, Elizabeth M., 48, 51

Newman, Mrs. Anne B., 73, 169

Newton, Isaac, 542

"Next friends" suit, 469–470; petition, 422–426; Mrs. Eddy's answer, 434–436; assigned to Board of Masters, 437–439; Masters' visit to Mrs. Eddy, 440–458; Masters' hearings, 458–461, 461–462, 462–467; dismissal of suit, 467–469; results, 476

Nicea, Council of, 643

Nietzsche, Friedrich Wilhelm, 96

Nixon, William G., work on new hymnal, 232; official positions, 235, 246, 249, 252–256; resignation, 275

Noah's Ark on "Ark edition," Second Edition, Volume II of *Science and Health*, 60

Norcross, Lanson P., 243*n.;* first pastor of The Mother Church, 204–205, 213, 582; Bible Lessons, 549

Norton, Carol, 221, 369

Nourse, Laura A., hymn by, 609

Noyes, Caroline D., 174, 226

Oconto (Wisconsin), Christian Science in, 175*n.,* 580–582

Odd Fellows Hall (Boston), communion service at, 128

Oliver, David, 516–519

Oneida Community, 498

Orcutt, William Dana (University Press), 80

Order of Exercises, for uniformity among Christian Scientists, 229–230

Origen, *Against Celsus,* quoted, 638–641

Otis, Mrs. Ann, 270

Otterson, Mrs. Joseph Curtis, 269

Paine, Albert Bigelow, 415

Palmer House, Chicago, 182

Parliament, England, copies of *Sentinel* sent to, 480

Park Street Congregational Church, 107

Parker, Hosea W., Master in "next friends" suit, 437*n.,* 442–443, 451, 455, 460

Parker, Theodore, Unitarian minister, 16

Patterson, Dr. Daniel, second husband of Mrs. Eddy, 6*n.*

Patterson, Mrs. Mary, 3
See also Eddy, Mary Baker G.

Paul (Bible), quoted, 12, 26, 96, 642

Peabody, Andrew Preston, 124

Peabody, Fred W., 433

Permanency of The Mother Church and Its Manual (Mrs. Eddy), 341

Perry, Baxter E., 244, 253; purchased mortgage for Mrs. Eddy, 243

Perry, George, title of church lot, 243

Personified Unthinkables (Sarah Stanley Grimke), 159

Pettingill, Judge, 170

Phare Pleigh, pseudonym for H. J. Wiggin, 138

Philadelphia, Pennsylvania, Christian Science in, 110

Phillips, Dorr, Mrs. Eddy's first healing, 17

Phillips, Thomas, 17

Phillips, Wendell, quoted, 603

Physicists, Mrs. Eddy on, 542

Physiology, in *Science and Health,* 38, 60, 77, 110, 188

Pilgrim Fathers, 606

Plagiarism, Dr. Eddy on, 76

Platform of Christian Scientists, in *Science and Health,* 77, 111, 188

Plato, 644; Jowett's translation, 96

Pleasant View (Concord, New Hampshire), 356, 416–419; Mrs. Eddy's retirement to, 308–310; Arthur Brisbane at, 427; Masters in "next friends" suit visit, 439–458; Mrs. Eddy leaves, 473–474; Deed of Trust (1907) on, 618–623 *passim*

Plunkett, Mrs. Mary H., 156–157, 159–160, 166–168, 218

"Pond and Purpose" (Mrs. Eddy), 309

Pope, Alexander, 96

Portland, Maine, 6, 139

Practitioners, 177; early, 14; fees, 37; attacks on, 95, 110; uniformity of cards, 348; meetings in church buildings forbidden, 490, 490*n.*; death of Harold Frederic, 496–498; reference in testimonies to, 505, 509, 511, 516, 518–519, 522, 527, 530, 534, 536

Prayer and Atonement, in *Science and Health*, 38, 77, 111, 189

Presbyters, early Christian Church, 628

Priestley, Dr. Joseph, letter from Benjamin Franklin, 560

Prince, Leon C., *The Sense and Nonsense of Christian Science*, 499–500

Prince of Peace, 349, 354

Principle, Mrs. Eddy's emphasis on, 60, 60*n.*, 61, 68, 74, 77

"Principle and Practice," Mrs. Eddy article on, 573–574

Private Meetings, 105

Prose Works other than Science and Health (Mrs. Eddy), 339

Protestants, 28

Psalms, Book of, quoted, 545, 546, 597, 607–608

Public Meetings, 202

Publication, Committee on (The Mother Church), 475, 480

Publication Committee, National Christian Science Association, 202*n.*, 219–220

Publications, functions of, 473

Publishing Committee, *Christian Science Journal*, 237

Pythagoras, 136

QUIMBY, GEORGE A., 146–149; Mrs. Eddy's offer for father's papers, 146

Quimby, Phineas P., 26, 92; "Magnetic healer," 7; Arens's charge on authorship of *Science and Health*, 92; claimed as originator of Christian Science, 139–149

Quimby manuscripts, 146, 147, 149

RAND, AVERY AND COMPANY, Boston, 60

Rawson, Dorcas B., 48, 56, 73

Reader, substituted for pastor, 231, 323; qualifications for, 329–330, 332; *Sentinel* on Lesson-Sermon and, 552–553

Reading Room, Oconto, Wisconsin, 580, 582

Reading rooms, 6
    See also Christian Science Reading Rooms

Reformation, Protestant, 28, 629

"Religious Trust Church," *American Medical Association Journal* on, 498

Renan, Ernest, *Life of Jesus,* quoted, 95, 97, 98, 627

"Reply to a Clergyman" in *Science and Health*, 60–61, 77, 111

"Reply to A Critic," in *Science and Health*, 188–189

Retrospection and Introspection (Mrs. Eddy), 37, 38, 386, 424, 561

Revelation, Book of, quoted, 592, 593

Revised Version (Bible), 552

Rice, Miranda R., 48, 73, 75

Roman Catholicism, emphasis on death, 11

Romans, Paul's epistle to, 12

Rome, 10

Roosevelt, Theodore, 479

Rowe, Evelyn I., 354

Rush Medical College, 503

Ruskin, John, 96

St. Louis Democrat, 123

St. Paul, Minnesota, 159

Salchow, John, 474

Salem, Massachusetts, Supreme Judicial Court, 56; services in, 63, 66

Sargeant, James I, 57–59

Sargent, Mrs. Laura E., 179, 270, 331, 474, 580–582, 590

Schopenhauer, Arthur, 96

Science, God as, 65

Science and Health with Key to The Scriptures, Mary Baker G. Eddy, quoted and referred to, 3–644, *passim;* first edition, 31, 33–34, 38, 40–42, 50–51; Preface, 38–40; chapter headings, 38, 60, 77, 110, 188–189; attacks of press and pulpit, 42; main tenets, 43–47, 541, 546–547; second edition, 50, 59–60; third edition, 74–76, 77, 78–79, 79–81; the Cross and the Crown, 77–78; "Scientific Statement of Being," 78–79; authorship claims, 90–92; sixth edition adds *With a Key to the Scriptures,* 110; complaint of difficulty in understanding, 135–136; twenty-eighth edition, 188–189; use in Sunday services, 206, 229; compared with Bible, 219, 221, 554–555; new editions, 223; use of Mrs. Eddy's name, 331–332; "next friends" suit, 423–424; copyrights transferred, 430; final revisions, 484; use in Lesson-Sermons, 548–549, 551; Readers and, 552–553; Deed of Trust and, 587–588; in dedication services, 591–596, 601–602, 604; quoted at World Parliament of Religions, 611–616

"Science and the Senses" (Mrs. Eddy), 180

Science of Being, in *Science and Health,* 77, 110, 188

Science of Life, 39, 48

Science of Man, The, 15

Science of Mind, 7

Science of Soul, The. See *Science of Man, The*

"Scientific Statement of Being," in *Science and Health,* 78–79

Seal, Frances Thurber, 381, 383–385, 483

Seneca, 96

Shakespeare, William, 77, 96

Shawmut Baptist Church, sermons at, 62

Sinnott, Dr. Edmund, on matter versus spirit, 45–46

Skinner, Mrs. Elizabeth P., 269

Slaght, representative of *New York World,* 421–422

Smith, Clifford P., *Historical and Biographical Papers,* 181

Smith, Hanover P., 164, 269, 457

Smith's Bible Dictionary, 552

Social Hymn and Tune Book, American Unitarian Society, 110

Socrates, 644

Soul, definition of, 577

Soul Control, taught by Moral Science, 24

Spanish-American War, Mrs. Eddy on, 479

Spine, curvature of, testimony on cure, 520

Spinoza, Baruch, 95

Spirit, God as, 12; search for, 27, 32–33; the real and eternal, 52–53, 78

Spirit and Matter, in *Science and Health,* 38

Spiritualism, 16, 117, 138, 160, 451

Spofford, Daniel H., proposer of Sunday services, 47–48; advice to Mrs. Eddy on *Science and Health,* 49–51; struggle for leadership, 55–56; plot against life of, 57–59; witness in "next friends" suit, 438

Stanley, Charles S., 23

Statement of Christian Science, Mrs. Gesterfelt, 171

Steinway Hall, New York City, Mrs. Eddy's address at, 191

Stephen Daye Press, 79

Stetson, Mrs. Augusta E., 269; organization work in New York, 191; aspirations to own *Journal,* 235, 237–238; attempt to create a second Mother Church in New York, 365–366, 485–494

Stevens, Oliver, Esq., 58

Stoughton, Massachusetts, 15

Strang, Lewis C., "next friends" suit, 422–423, 434

Straw, Jane L., 73

Streeter, Frank S., Mrs. Eddy's Concord attorney, 261, 433; Associated Press interview, 433–434; "next friends" suit, 438–440, 459, 462–467, 470; Deed of Trust, 621, 623

Strickler, Virgil O., First Reader, New York, Mrs. Stetson attack on, 491; Board of Directors stand on, 491–492

Stroke, testimony on cure, 516

Stuart, Elizabeth G., 73

Students, Mrs. Eddy's method of instruction, 18–19, 24; difficulties with, 22–23, 50–51, 55–57, 69, 73, 200; more rigid requirements for, 186

Suffolk Registry of Deeds, Massachusetts, 590

Superior Court, Boston, Massachusetts, Arens-Eddy case, 57–58

Superstition, introduced into early Christian Church, 629

Supreme Judicial Court, Salem, Massachusetts, Spofford acquitted, 56

Swampscott, Massachusetts, 3, 14, 143, 148

Swarts, A. J., *Mind-Cure and Science of Life,* 161; joined Plunkett in Boston, 162

Syracuse, New York, 162

TAUNTON (MASSACHUSETTS), 14

Teacher, great, *see* Jesus

Teaching, Mrs. Eddy's method, 18–19, 36, 86–88, 99–100, 103–104; fees, 34–35; suspension, 367–368

Tenets of the Church, 66

Tennyson, Alfred Lord, 96

Tertullian, quoted, 636–638

Thomas, Mrs. Charles, 232

Tilton (New Hampshire), 14

Times, London, quoted on Christian Science, 368–371, 496

"To The Public," third edition *Science and Health,* on plagiarism, 76

Tolstoy, Leo, 96

Tomkins, Rev. George, 369

Tomlinson, Irving C., 7, 369, 386–387; *Twelve Years with Mary Baker Eddy,* 7–8, 81–82; on her teaching, 99–101; Board of Lectureship, 390; "next friends" suit, 422–423, 434

Townsend, Rev. L. T., "Boston Craze and Mrs. Eddy," 114

Tremont Temple, 116; Mrs. Eddy replies to attacks at, 116–120

Trinity, Mrs. Eddy's explanation of, 88

Trust Fund, *see* Deed of Trust

*

Truth, Mrs. Eddy on, 8, 20–21, 62, 93; Preface to *Science and Health*, 38–39; power of, 78

Truth: A Magazine of Christian Science, 159

Truth and Error, Mrs. Eddy on, 61

Truth and Life, in tenets of the Church, 66

Tuttle, George, 22

Twain, Mark (Samuel L. Clemens), denunciation of Mrs. Eddy, 396–398; Christian Science, 413; praise of Mrs. Eddy, 415, 558

Twelve Years with Mary Baker Eddy (Irving C. Tomlinson), 7–8, 81–82

Twentieth Century Magazine, 500

Understanding of God, The, E. J. Arens, 90–91

Unitarians, 16

Unity Publishing Company, 159

Universal life, John Caird on, 55

Universe and Dr. Einstein, The (Lincoln Barnett), 46

University Press, 77, 79, 137

VAIL, DR. W. T., 6, 139

Verrall, Catharine, 372

WARD, MARCUS AND E. BLANCHE, 372, 375

Walker, R. E., 590

Washington, D.C., 82

Watchman, 116

Waterbury (Vermont), 464

Watts, Morrison R., 92

Wayside Hints, in *Science and Health,* 188

Webster, Mrs. Mary, 14

Wentworth, Mrs. Sally, 15

Whiting, Mrs. Abbie, 84

Whittier, John Greenleaf, 80, 96

Wiggin, James Henry, 353

Wilbur, Sibyl, 182

Wilson, John, and Son (University Press), 77, 79, 80

Winslow, Charles, 17

"With A Key to The Scriptures," addition to title of *Science and Health,* 111–112

Woodbury, Josephine C., assistant editor of the *Journal,* 216; excommunicated, 217, 349–352; libel suit against, 353–354

Worcester, Massachusetts, 17, 160

Works, John D., U.S. Senator, California, 503

World's Parliament of Religions, Chicago, Mrs. Eddy invited to participate, 298; enthusiastic reception, 299–300, 302–304; adopted use of silent prayer, 313; Mrs. Eddy quoted on, 600–601; address, 611–617

Worthington, A. Bentley, 168, 169

Wright, Wallace M., controversy with Mrs. Eddy, 23–24

Wyclif, John, use of words *Science and Health,* 34n.

YOUNG, BICKNELL, lecture tour of world, 377, 391

"Youth and Young Manhood" (Mrs. Eddy), *Cosmopolitan Magazine,* 624–626

Zion's Herald, Boston, Townsend challenges Mrs. Eddy, 114, 116